Ambiguous Pleasures

AMBIGUOUS PLEASURES

*Sexuality and Middle Class Self-Perceptions
in Nairobi*

Rachel Spronk

Berghahn Books
NEW YORK • OXFORD

Published in 2012 by
Berghahn Books
www.berghahnbooks.com

© 2012 Rachel Spronk

Library of Congress Cataloging-in-Publication Data
Spronk, Rachel.
Ambiguous pleasures : sexuality and middle class self-perceptions in Nairobi /
Rachel Spronk.
    p. cm.
  Includes bibliographical references and index.
  ISBN 978-0-85745-478-2 (hardback : alk. paper) -- ISBN 978-0-85745-479-9
(ebook)
  1. Yuppies--Sexual behavior--Kenya--Nairobi. 2. Sexology--Kenya--Nairobi. I.
Title.
  HQ18.N27S67 2012
  306.7086220967625--dc23

                                                              2011041085

British Library Cataloguing in Publication Data
A catalogue record for this book is available from the British Library
Printed in the United States on acid-free paper.

ISBN 978-0-85745-478-2 (hardback)
ISBN 978-0-85745-479-9 (ebook)

To Sarah,

and others who could not live to make their dream come true,

and to those who could not live up to their dreams

CONTENTS

ACKNOWLEDGEMENTS

So many people have taken me under their wings, each in their own way, while I was finding my way during the research for, as well as in the writing, of this book. I am indebted to you all.

In Nairobi, and in the other places where they have flown to, I am particularly indebted to those who cannot be mentioned by name: the spirited women and men without whose life stories this book would never have seen the light. Their openness, trust and patience have been vital to this study, as well as personally enriching.

My sincere gratitude goes to Peter Geschiere and Birgit Meyer. Thanks to their dedicated teamwork, as well as their encouragement, trust and intellectual inspiration, this book has been realized. My gratitude for their unfailing support runs deep. I owe my interest in sexuality studies to Han ten Brummelhuis, who taught me the principles of anthropological perspectives on sexuality many years ago. I have found an intellectual home at the Sociology and Anthropology Department of the University of Amsterdam, thanks to the many colleagues who stimulated me before I officially joined them. I want to thank Gerd Baumann, Niko Besnier, Christian Bröer, Sébastien Chauvin, Jan Willem Duijvendak, Alex Edmonds, Sjaak van der Geest, Trudie Gerrits, Anita Hardon, Gert Hekma, Giselinde Kuipers, Annemarie Mol, Annelies Moors, Mattijs van de Port, and Oskar Verkaaik.

The Amsterdam School for Social Science Research (now Amsterdam Institute for Social Science Research) not only generously financed the research on which this book is based, but also provided an academic home and sheltering work environment during my graduate years. The conversations around the coffee machine and debates during seminars haven been of tremendous value throughout the years when this book was written. The bureau has always been ready with a solution to my questions, thanks to Linda Atjak, Teun Bijvoet, Anneke Dammers, Annelies Dijkstra, Miriam May, José Komen and Hans Sonneveld. Moreover, the writing of this book would not have been possible without the support, intellectual input and friendship of my sisters and brothers in arms of the

ASSR anthropology club: Ze d'Abreu, Jose Carlos Aguiar, Irfan Ahmad, Miriyam Aouragh, Eveline Buchheim, Francio Guadeloupe, Lotte Hoek, Nghiem Lien Huong, John Kinsman, Anouk de Koning, Shifra Kisch, Eileen Moyer, Nienke Muurling, Martijn Oosterbaan, Matthijs Pelkmans, Esther Peperkamp, Yatun Sastramidjaja and Marleen de Witte. Thanks to Erik Bähre, Christian Bröer, Sjoukje Botman, Trudie Gerrits, Eelke Heemskerk, Silke Heumann, Ferdinand de Jong, Barak Kalir, Abdoulaye Kane, Reinhilde König, Baz Lecocq, Marcel Maussen, Courtney Lake, Marie Rosenkrantz Lindegaard, Marina de Regt, Inês de Sousa, Getnet Tadele, Sonja van Wichelen and Mara Yerkes for making the ASSR a pleasant work place. Thanks too to the VOC members Marieke Bloembergen, Alex Edmonds, Jeroen de Kloet, Tonny Krijnen, Giselinde Kuipers, Natalie Scholtz, Jan Teurlings, Olav Velthuis and Sikko Visscher for the inspirational conversations, whether intellectual or not.

In 1997, I was warmly welcomed by Professor Bahemuka and Professor Nzioka at the University of Nairobi. When I returned for the research for this book in 2001 and 2004, I could not imagine a better intellectual and collegial springboard for my study. I am very grateful for their help and commitment, as well as to Professor Gakuru, Dr Machera, Dr Mbatia, Dr Owiti and the bureau at the Department of Sociology for making me feel at home at another university, and for their critical remarks and important suggestions regarding my research.

Crisscrossing the years through which I have been working on the book, as friends or colleagues and as sources of inspiration, have been Anouka van Eerdewijk, Julia Hornberger, Marloes Janson, Jeroen de Kloet, Graeme Reid and Marleen Renders, as well as Stefan Dudink, Frances Gouda, Jan Jansen, Anke van der Kwaak, Lorraine Nencel, Christine Obbo, Robert Ros, Bonno Thoden van Velzen, Ineke van de Wetering, and Karin Willemse. I hope to enjoy for many more years the expertise of *Etnofoor* editors Yolanda van Ede, Erella Grassiani, Rivke Jaffe, Martijn Oosterbaan, Thijl Sunier and Marleen de Witte. Thanks to Mindy Standford and Robert Berold for making my text into a readable book, and to Mirjam van Heugten for the help with the very last logistical matters of the manuscript.

If anything kept me going, it is the group of family and friends whose interest in the study and support of the project never failed. My parents Neeltje and Cees have taught my sisters and me to approach the world with curiosity, a quality that is the fundament on which the book rests. Their support and love has been, is, and will always be, an important guide in my life and work. My dear sisters Esther and Janneke always knew, and know, how to uplift me with their sisterly love and humour. My dearest friends Akke, Christel and Wilma never got tired of listening to my endless reminiscences and their ability to bring a new perspective to my work has been revitalizing. Thanks too to my brother-in-arms, Matthijs, for helping to avoid complacency as we both became part of academia. And many thanks too to my friends Christian, Pascal, Lotte, Shifra and Ze for the talks, laughs and support in the Netherlands, and to Doris, Gertrude, Japhet, Joyce, the Kamadi family, Ken, Leah, Norah, Orutwa, Robinson, Terry and Kamata in Nairobi for the *nyama choma* and for making us feel at home.

Victor, for you there are no words to express my gratefulness for your love, intellectual discussions, support, patience, help with the computer and text, and humour. In the course of writing this book our two sons, Julian and Tobias, were born. I hope we will enjoy numerous adventures together, in Africa and elsewhere.

INTRODUCTION

This is Nairobi! If there is a miracle in the idea of life it is this: that we are able to exist for a time, in defiance of chaos. ... Phrases swell, becoming bigger than their context and speak to us as *truth*.... For us, life is about having a fluid disposition. Nairobi is a shot of whisky.

Binyavanga Wainaina[1]

Patrick and I met at a party of a friend in 2001; he was aged 28. We were leaning over the balcony staring into the Nairobi night, while the sounds of the party made up the background noise. He asked what had brought me to Nairobi and we engaged in a discussion about the lifestyles of his generation. A generation marked by a spirited approach to life, 'hip and ambitious'. A generation he also characterized as 'dangerously nearing "westernization"'. He got somewhat agitated and started fulminating about the dominance of 'the West'. Somewhere along the discussion we started talking about female circumcision and then he got very upset. 'Female circumcision', he said, was 'part of our African culture. You do not know how important it is for women themselves; they are not forced to do it in my community [the Abagusii ethnic group]. While they want to be circumcised, it is criminalized by outsiders, Westerners. Where I come from, the place is infested with NGOs trying to estrange the women. You guys should not interfere with these issues that are not of your business.' I kept quiet so as not to anger him further.

At the time I met Patrick I was living in Nairobi for a year to study the lifestyles of young professionals like him, aged between 20 and 30. My aim was to study their search for a new sexual morality by focussing on their love and sexual lives – both ideas and practices – to find out how sexuality was embedded in social relations and meanings, and, therefore, how sexuality was related to processes of social transformation. When Patrick agreed to participate in the research two months after our first meeting, we discussed the matter of female circumcision again, after I had had an interview with a circumcised woman from the Gusii community. The woman, aged 36, explained how she ran off one day to join the group of girls on their way to be circumcised, against the will of her parents. She was very proud of the fact that she was 'a true woman'.

Patrick listened without interrupting and after I had finished he looked at me for a long time. 'Terrible,' he said, 'I cannot approve of this. And she will circumcise her daughter as well? It's useless, it has no necessity.' I asked him why he had defended female circumcision the first time we met. He answered: 'Because you're a foreigner [looked at me for a while]. You might have been one of those to come to tell us how we should live. I don't need that. You know, I cannot marry a circumcised woman, because I want an equal sexual relationship. I want us both to enjoy sex. Female circumcision is no option for me, it's barbaric. How can I have a fulfilling sexual experience while my girlfriend cannot? I don't think I can have sex with a woman who is cut, I would feel like I exploit her, because it would be for my own satisfaction only.'

Hip and ambitious in Nairobi

Why, when discussing the lifestyles of young professionals, did Patrick and I come to talk about female circumcision – two topics that seem hardly related – within a few minutes? Why did Patrick express a different opinion about female circumcision when we discussed it in relation to sexual intimacy? This study sets out to answer these questions, and many like them. It is organized around two themes: how sexuality and issues of cultural belonging or identification are interrelated in the lives of young professionals in Nairobi; and how these young people experience these issues personally. Although the opening vignette of the book introduces the topic of female circumcision, it will not be widely discussed. For one, female circumcision is not practiced by the majority of the Kenyan population and even less by the families of this particular group. The topic of circumcision though, serves as a typical example of the way sexuality is moralized and politicized in Kenya. In this book I examine how the seemingly most intimate details of private experience are structured by larger social relations. Sexuality is a public as well as a personal affair, involving communal concerns and individual desires and – as we learn from Patrick's account – sex can be the cause of ideological debate as much as a source of pleasure. Moreover, sexuality is crucial in the development of contemporary notions of selfhood among young adults like Patrick. In this study I explore the meanings of public understandings and personal experiences of sexuality and their intricate interface, the ambiguity of sexual practices and relationships, as well as debates about 'African' heritage in relation to notions of personhood. The question is: how to understand the interconnections between sexuality, culture and personhood? When one looks at the existing literature on sexuality in Africa and at the body of knowledge concerning gender and sexuality in general, two observations stand out.

The first is that sex in Africa tends to be studied from a public health perspective. The global AIDS epidemic exposed the deficiency of our knowledge about the complexity and variety of sexual behaviour. As a result, there has been an impressive increase in research activities aimed at responding to this discrepancy. The AIDS epidemic in Africa has resulted in an avalanche of epidemiological studies on sexuality since the 1980s, most of them characterized by the quantification of sex into behavioural frequencies and attitudinal scores. Such research has severe limitations, because, while it shows patterns, it does not explain the human motivations that underlie them. In other words, sex becomes de-eroticized to an act devoid of meaning. As I will show in Chapter I, these studies tend to look only at the social problems of sexuality, and, in their compulsion to link research to policy, generate simplistic stereotypes of 'African sexuality'. As a result, knowledge and analysis of sexuality in Africa is at best partial, and a more differentiated conceptual framework is urgently needed.

The development of the field of gender and sexuality studies is in many ways related to the dominance of medical approaches to gender and/or sexuality. The interdisciplinary approach to the study of how gender and sexuality are socially constructed is the springboard of this work. Secondly, this study calls attention to the fact that this approach tends to pay less attention to the experiential and sensorial aspects of sexuality. The negligence of the embodied experience of sexuality is largely due to the epistemological position of the current paradigm. The study of the social construction of sexuality postulates the discursive analysis of sexuality, in other words, how discourse defines the realities of sexuality before it is experienced by individuals. I will therefore argue for the need to go beyond a constructivist approach, as I explore how a phenomenologically inflected approach complements discursive analysis.

Combining existing but often separate approaches, I propose three foci for sexuality as a field of study: the personal, intersubjective and social dimensions of sex. Sex is a vehicle for powerful feelings that are experienced very subjectively, in other words, sex is personal. Sex is an intimate exchange between people (which varies in intensity and meaning); so sex implies intersubjectivity. Sexuality is also a particularly sensitive conductor of cultural influences and, hence, of social and political divisions; sexuality is also socially defined. Such a study requires a special method. To understand the practices, attitudes and experiences of young Kenyans in a rapidly changing world, I designed a research methodology that used progressively more personal ways of interviewing, which included sharing daily activities with a limited group of informants. This methodology allowed me to distinguish and analyse the personal, social and intersubjective aspects of their sexuality, and to incorporate pleasure, emotion and affection.

Patrick's account is not unique. A small group of female and male young professionals in Nairobi, such as information and communication technology (ICT) professionals, accountants, and junior nongovernmental organization (NGO) staff, share many of his experiences and concerns. These young professionals represent an emerging social group that is not clearly defined, but nonetheless still recognizable. Their attitudes articulate a spirited approach to life and their lives highlight the diversity and energy of the cultural melting pot that Nyairo describes in her analysis on popular culture (2005: 11). These women and men see themselves as explorers of a 'modern' or 'sophisticated' lifestyle in Nairobi. Important aspects of their lifestyle are reflected in having a 'fast life' and in the ideal of a 'modern marriage' at some point in the future. Since they delay marriage because of their careers and living conditions, they tend to have temporary sexual relations. These relationships are possible because sex involving the use of contraceptives does not lead to reproduction. As will become clear, sexuality as a realm of exploration, pleasure and agency is related in particular ways to their lives as young professionals. Strengthened by their independent financial position, they form a social group of women and men who implicitly and explicitly critique conventional gender roles. One consequence is that people tend to accuse them of being 'westernized' and 'un-African'. This accusation cuts deep, as they consider themselves to be very conscious of their cultural identity. It will become clear how they take pride in taking a particular trans-ethnic position in a country that is troubled by ethnic division. Hence, this study is not representative of the Nairobian or Kenyan population as a whole; it is a case study of a group that sees itself as being in the vanguard, and which I use to work out the social complexities of sexuality in the context of modernity.

Patrick was working with an ICT company as a programmer. In the evenings he studied Business Administration at the USIU (United States International University), a private university. When we met he was single, but after some time he met Nsiza with whom he maintained a 'committed' relationship. Patrick was a tall, attractive man, self-assured and composed, who held strong views on certain topics which he did not withhold. He came from a humble background: his father was a primary school teacher and his mother was a secretary at a public university. His parents had migrated in the 1970s to Nairobi, where Patrick and his two sisters were born. Although they were 'proud' members of the Gusii ethnic group, his parents had not 'passed on much culture' to their children. Patrick remembers that when they visited their relatives in the rural areas during school holidays, their grandmother made them wear red slippers in order to 'avoid dangers'. 'What these dangers were… actually I don't know… It must have been something with bad spirits because of jealous neighbours, you know, but my parents never gave much attention [to such things].' He assumed that his mother was circumcised, a topic he could not inquire about out of respect for his mother. His parents chose not to circumcise his sisters. He believed that his female relatives 'up-country' were 'likely' to be circumcised. He had never intimately known a woman his age who was circumcised, and he believed that his generation was beyond that.

Where, then, did his fierce defence of female circumcision during our first meeting come from? How should we read such a response? According to Patrick it was a response to my presence as a foreigner, a Westerner. However, there was more to it. As he indicated in our first meeting, and as became clear during our interviews, his defensive attitude was related to anxieties arising from the issue of 'westernization' (commonly used to mean the adopting of Western attitudes and ways of life) and 'being African'. He framed female circumcision not as a Gusii custom but as part of 'African culture'. As such, he was defending a custom he actually objected to. This contradiction was related, on the one hand, to the importance of proclaiming cultural authenticity in the light of what he contemptuously called 'westernization'. On the other hand, according to his own norms he could not be considered 'authentic' himself. When, years before, his grandfather had scorned him for being a foreigner to his own culture, as Patrick could not speak the family's vernacular, he experienced a deep sense of humiliation. 'He [the grandfather] is right, I am an embarrassment to him.' Not being able to speak a local language implied that he was bereft of a cultural familiarity. He, and many like him, used the notion of 'African culture' to represent a cultural knowing as essential to cultural belonging. The term 'African' is used by many young professionals in a reified manner to essentialize cultural particularity, hence elevating it to an 'African' universal.[2]

There are groups in Kenya, such as the Mungiki, an extremist religious group calling for the reintroduction of 'traditional African religion', that advocate the restitution of female circumcision as a means to halt the advancing 'westernization' of Kenyan society.[3] This stance by the Mungiki shows how anxieties about cultural heritage and about the sense of belonging in a fast changing world are projected onto matters of sexuality. Such groups place the body and its pleasures at the centre of efforts to criticize the present and glorify the past. As a 'modern' man, however, Patrick could not agree to female circumcision despite his call for 'Africanness'. He could not marry a circumcised woman, as there would be a physical inequality between them that would undermine their relationship. To him, mutual sexual pleasure was essential, something he related to the notion of 'modern relationships'. Sexuality was thus a mode for identifying himself as a contemporary person. Such an 'articulation of identity', where sexuality becomes central to self-perceptions (Weeks 2003: 4), is characteristic of an emerging generation in middle class Nairobi society.

Patrick used to say he was 'rather philosophical' about relationships, and that he had thought a lot about them. Despite his respect for his parents, he wanted a different, more egalitarian, kind of relationship: 'True love exists between equals and not when one looks up to the other', he used to say. When he had to apply his philosophy to his incipient relationship with Nzisa, theory and practice did not always correspond. In the beginning he was insecure, as Nsiza maintained an elusive attitude when having sex that made him feel apprehensive: 'All these magazines you women read are full of stories about what love is and how men should behave, am I doing something wrong then?' Her attitude and his response created some reservation between them, while he was looking for 'something deeper' – a 'love relationship'. Sex was essentially 'good' because it was enjoyable and because it made him 'feel man'. However, there was a strand of anxiety. As he wanted something 'deeper' he had to 'expose' himself emotionally and he wondered, in our interviews, whether he was not 'letting go too much'. Since, generally speaking, men in Nairobi are expected to be initiators and achievers in sexual encounters, he risked losing control by aspiring to another approach to a sexual relationship. With time, the sex life of Nsiza and Patrick improved as they became more 'involved emotionally'.

To understand the role of sexuality of young professionals in Nairobi in the process of self-identification, it is necessary to elaborate on their historical and contemporary environment. This is an important approach if one intends to study the dynamics of an African setting. Young professionals are an unusual group to research in African studies, but they are particularly interesting because – as I shall argue – they embody postcolonial transformations regarding culture, gender and sexuality. According to Ogola, urban youth in Kenya 'seem to be moving the centre' of social relations (2006). Furthermore, they seem to be more occupied with issues of Africanness than other groups in Kenyan society, which suggests that they experience modernity as particularly problematic. In the debates about modernity, questions of identity are brought to the fore (cf. Geschiere et al. 2008) and consequently questions of sexuality become politicized (Janson and Spronk 2005; Oldfield et al. 2009; Posel 2005; Reid 2003).

Conceiving sexuality

To understand Patrick's ambivalent motivations and behaviour, and those of others like him, we need to place his experience in context. Sex is a medium for a variety of feelings, emotions and needs; people have sex for fun, to fulfil a desire for intimacy, for a physical thrill, to procreate, to exert power, to humiliate and much more. Sexuality is also fundamental to a community because the social organization of sexuality, through rituals such as marriage or circumcision, is based on conventional gender and sex roles. How to study the interconnection between the personal and social aspects of sexuality?

As I shall argue in Chapter I, sexuality is often introduced as a self-evident concept that hardly needs any definition in scholarly debates such as on AIDS or reproduction (Spronk 2007). There is a tendency to re-search sex as a social and/or health problem, resulting in a limited body of knowledge on sexuality in Africa. Moreover, sexuality is often conflated with gender, neglecting sexual behaviour and experience. This instrumental use of the term sexuality indicates a failure to take into account issues of desire, pleasure and intimacy, and how these relate to self-perceptions. It is important, therefore, to distinguish sex and sexuality, two terms with multiple meanings that should already alert us to the complexity of the subject. The term 'sex' can refer to an act (erotic practices) and to a category (female or male sex), to a practice and to a gender, to having sex and to identifying as 'woman' or 'man'. The word 'sexuality' (an abstract noun referring to the quality of 'being sexual') developed its modern meanings in the second half of the nineteenth century (Weeks 2003: 4). It came to mean the personalized sexual feelings that distinguished one person from another, as in 'my sexuality'. Sexuality is also used as a concept to depict a larger configuration of various aspects of social life, including ideologies and practices of kinship, gender relations and reproduction. In relation to this, sexuality also refers to the social arena where power relations, symbolic meanings of gender, and hence moral discourses in relation to sexual behaviour, are played out. Lastly, sexuality is about sexual desire, what Tuzin calls the 'appetite for sexual pleasure' (1995: 256), which relates to experience itself and which is not directly related to sexual conduct. This summary of the range of meanings should indicate the necessity to be precise as to what is being studied with regard to sexuality.

In this study sexuality is employed as a relational concept (Salo and Gqola 2006). A person's sexuality develops in interaction with social axes such as gender, age or religion, which give meaning to particular notions of sexuality. Take the example of Patrick feeling uneasy with Nsiza's aloof attitude. Here, Nsiza's aloofness could indicate a personal disposition, but could also stem from a social pattern: in Nairobi, female sexuality is often equated with reproduction, and femininity often associated with motherhood and wifehood. This ideology can affect the sexual experience of women such as Nsiza if they are not married or not intending to become pregnant. Moreover, a newly engaged couple will be inclined to sound out each other carefully. Partly driven by personal curiosity and partly informed by social sense, two people constitute an intimate realm of possibilities or of compliance. As will become clear in this study, people's sexual behaviour is created by forms of affection, emotion and agency; by different networks of sociability; by the place occupied by reproduction and family; by the potential for validation or censorship that the social world exerts over persons; and, critically for this study, by the way in which the person reproduces certain discursive meanings while at other times challenging them. To study this topic requires bridging discursive analysis and empirical investigation by analysing how discourses with regard to self are generated in context, and how sexuality is constitutive to how people 'feel' a sense of self and become oriented in the world.

In Chapters II and III, I set out a discursive analysis of sexuality. I elaborate how political and economic transformations have influenced social organizations of sexuality and how these transformations have reorganized the contexts and texts in which people understand sexuality (Laqueur 1992; Ross and Rapp 1997). The social transformations that occurred in the twentieth century have generated changes in marriage patterns, morality, the way in which women and men relate both practically and symbolically, gender construction, and more. As a result, people's orientation in the world changed and continues to change. Young professionals' lifestyles testify to a 'process of social fragmentation deeply affecting familial structures, especially in the metropoles, resulting and giving rise to changes in patterns of cohabitation and sexuality' (Mbembe 2008: 110). Relations between women and men are being redefined, and the lifestyle choices and aspirations of young professionals point to 'an emerging levelling process of existing differences in the status of women and young men' (ibid: 100). In short, social transformation generates new modes of being. These processes are paralleled by changing or contested perspectives on sexuality, and therefore I will also analyse how sexuality is being understood and represented, in other words, how it is 'put into discourse' (Foucault 1990 [1976]). To organize sexuality accurately, 'proper' and 'improper' sex have to be defined and distinguished by recognized authorities, such as elders, the medical profession, religious authorities, or role models featured in the media. I will show how this societal questioning and classification frames the knowledge about sexuality, which people then experience as defining their bodily possibilities and pleasures.

Foucault showed how discourses prescribe different subject positions, or modes of being. The 'self' is to a certain extent an effect of particular knowledge generated by dominant discourses. In Victorian times, for example, different ways of being a woman related to different perceptions of sexuality, such as that of the 'wife' (for whom sex was a marital duty) or the 'hysteric woman' (who was incapable of having sex). Foucault pointed out how particular knowledge (for example about women) creates a certain 'truth' (about women's sexuality) and it highlights how people internalize certain perceptions of being (a 'wife' or a 'hysteric' woman). He concluded that the discourse on sexuality has been crucial to the development of the 'self': that one becomes the subject of one's sexuality; with a 'self' at the centre; with a rich and conflictual inner world. This self-understanding is shaped by dress, body language, lifestyle, etc. These processes of subjectivation direct the analysis of sexuality to the influences of societal forces and transformations, and as such, to how persons are subjected to social conditions and knowledge about sexuality, as well as constructed as subjects themselves.

Such an approach identifies the social context in which the self is studied as an object of domination, which can be deconstructed in order to show how sexuality is framed at a particular time and place. According to Van de Port, anthropologists have excelled in deconstructing realities, as they have 'discerned discourses, texts, scripts and performances, invented traditions, simulacrums, staged authenticities and imagined communities'. Now they should also 'include an account of the continuous human effort that goes into manufacturing and maintaining a sense of "authentic grounding"' (2005: 7). Similarly, Moore argues that theories of the subject and agency remain inadequate because agency is considered primarily in terms of antagonism to normative structures (2007). Indeed, there is a growing literature by anthropologists studying how culture structures sexuality; however, they do not always study how people actually experience sex. In other words, the sensorial aspects of sexuality are often neglected. Moore broadens the analysis of sexuality by theorizing the role that fantasy, desire and unconscious investments play in the process of subjectivation. Whereas she develops a theoretical framework that takes the imaginary, and consequently the unconscious, as its starting point, I start with the sensorial.

Therefore, complementing the constructionist approach, which emphasizes the self as an effect of subjectivation, I include an analysis of the self by including the experiential, or the 'subjectiveness' of sex. In recent years, the anthropology of the body has gained new impetus (Lock and Farquhar 2007). Embodiment has become an important analytical tool for looking at human participation in a cultural world. There are roughly two perspectives: the semiotic–textual view of the body as representation, and the phenomenological view of the body as being-in-the-world (Csordas 1993). The first perspective is dominant in the anthropology of sexuality, as it provides a good starting point for the critical study of power relations and of representation. I am concerned with the second here.

According to Csordas, 'embodiment as a paradigm or methodological orientation requires that the body be understood as the existential ground of culture; the body's role is to transform ideas into things; it realizes existence and is its actuality' (1993: 135). In other words, the body mediates culture in order to make it real. This approach is in contrast to seeing bodies as objects that come into being as the result of social processes or structures (such as colonialism, globalization or media influences). The body is not a barrel that can be filled with social meanings, but, instead, the body is needed to bring those meanings into the world. This logic of embodiment is that people exist through their acts, affects, emotions and speech, and that embodiment is the moment of giving meaning, of signifying (cf. Merleau-Ponty 1958).

The body, then, is the productive starting point for an analysis of culture and self. The self, then, is an indeterminate process of engaging or becoming oriented in the world; it appears through the interaction (embodiment) between bodily experience, cultural milieu or world, and habitus. This notion of the self, by foregrounding bodily experiences, directs us to self-perception, to self-esteem, to a sense of belonging to a group or society, to how a person identifies herself or himself as 'woman' or 'man', as it indicates the experiential dimension of personhood. Inspired by this approach, I use the notion of a person's 'sense of self' – self-perception. The meaning of subjectivity I employ, therefore, is not (merely) the description of the 'lived experience' of individuals (Zigon 2009). Instead, I wish to bring out the dialectic between cultural milieu and personal experience that constitutes subjectivity. Using embodiment as an analytical tool to elaborate on the process of how people constitute and define their personhood has helped me to grasp the experience of sex and sexuality in relation to people's place in society. It has also directed my focus to the way in which a gendered sense of self affects sexual desire and pleasure, as well as to how sex is constitutive of a gendered sense of self.

By focussing on people's sexual conduct, I analyse how sexual intimacy becomes a matter of the self, of the sexual subject, in a symbolic interaction with another subject (Jamieson 1998: 1). Rather than asking the question 'what is self?', my aim is to document how people create or maintain a sense of self and a sense of belonging, and how this is connected to sexual experience. The experiential dimension of sex is often experienced as 'natural', while it is also associated with other modes of being (as a woman, a man, a young professional, a Kenyan). In this study, I thus propose to study sexuality as a prism through which to analyse how social developments have generated new notions of self(-perceptions), in other words, new subjectivities or new ways of being and knowing.

Interfaces of pleasure and anxiety

Nairobi is what one can call a 'worlding' city (Simone 2001; see also Simone 2005), reflecting the practice of the global homogenization of urban space in Africa. In African urban studies, many scholars focus mainly on the poor, while this study explores the relatively wealthy urbanites. Nairobi is the regional headquarters of international banks, nongovernmental organizations and transnational corporations, and is a major centre for accounting, legal and informational services. The cityscape is dominated by office developments, shopping malls and hotels. White collar employment is expanding, as are residential areas for the middle class and wealthy elite. These developments are taking place alongside the emergence of the media and entertainment centres. At the same time, these formal and modern manifestations coexist with the informal ways of living and working that are characteristic of the lower classes of the Nairobi populace. According to Simone, more and more Africans living in cities are left without coherent traditional local and national structures because of their material deconstruction. As a result, a certain 'worlding' has been enforced on them so that they see themselves operating as urban citizens who are seeking out the global world in their local context.

And indeed, young professionals see themselves as operating in a subculture that is part of a global world. Thus Nairobi is a site reflecting the effects of a 'stylization of consumption' (Mbembe 2004: 400). The lifestyles of young professionals are a celebration of the cosmopolitan possibilities that have been ushered in by the processes of globalization, which Appadurai terms a 'new cosmopolitanism' (1996) that unites the cultural, financial and political flows within and between non-Western and Western societies. Young professionals are cosmopolitans, not because of a cultural orientation to the West, but because of the convergence of global and local 'cultural compliance' (Ferguson 1999) that they embody. Cosmopolitanism is not simply an expression of class or social status because cosmopolitan styles can be found at every socio-economic level; so that professionals who are not born and raised in Nairobi can differ remarkably from the Nairobian professionals I spoke to. Nyairo describes how popular culture in Nairobi is the realm *par excellence* for the appreciation of a multitude of identities, or modes of being, based on a mix of local and global qualities (Nyairo 2005; Nyairo and Ogude 2005).[4]

The label 'young professionals' applies to a relatively small social group of young adults that is not part of the larger impoverished population or the smaller political-economic elite. These young adults come from backgrounds ranging from lower to upper middle class, though these differences tend to level out once they enter their professional fields.[5] Their parents occupy typical lower middle class positions such as teachers, lower ranking managers, or civil servants, while they mainly seek careers in the private sector. These young professionals are born in Nairobi, unlike their parents who migrated to Nairobi later in life after independence in 1963. As such, this group is not the first generation to be born and raised in the city, but the increase in their numbers is fairly recent. What is most remarkable is that a significant number of these young professionals, like Patrick for example, do not speak a local language, since their parents spoke to them in English or in Kiswahili (the lingua franca of East Africa) from childhood onwards. Among themselves they speak English, Kiswahili and *Sheng* – the slang of their youth subculture, made up of different ethnic languages, Kiswahili and English.[6] They actively date people from different ethnic groups. The basis of their social life is trans-ethnic, and so are their neighbourhoods, churches and professional lives. However, within their families, they are less vocal about their trans-ethnic attitudes, since the older generations tend to be more mono-ethnically oriented.

The majority of young professionals are unmarried, preferring to delay marriage until they are around 30. This leads to prolonged dating and the maintenance of 'casual relationships'. Dating, in fact, is an important element of their lifestyles. They are financially independent from their parents due to their relatively stable jobs. This translates into choices such as living on their own, with or without friends or with like-minded relatives, instead of staying at their parents' home. A trendy lifestyle marks the lives of these young professionals. Fashionable dressing, going out and progressive attitudes are important markers of their contemporary personality. To 'have a life' is a credo for many people and these markers serve to distinguish them as 'sophisticated' or 'modern'. These young professionals, especially the women, are engaged in a process of 'aesthetization' that is constitutive of detraditionalization of gender and its transformations regarding conventional gender constructions (Adkins 2002). I interpret young professionals' lifestyles not merely as expression, but as realizing and maintaining subjective realities. I use lifestyle, inspired by Ferguson's 'cultural style' (1999), as a descriptive notion to elaborate on their dress, bodily disposition, consumption patterns – style as self-presentation – as well as an analytic term to point to their lives as signifying practice.

Through my research I came to understand that young professionals see themselves as explorers of a 'sophisticated' lifestyle. They are proud to be icons of a global subculture that focusses on fashion, music and dating, while at the same time they are wary about it. Their desire to act out a 'modern' lifestyle often coincides with certain Western modes, such as designer labels or music. But because they feel that these products originate from a 'Western' source, they feel compelled to reject them. Burke analyses a similar deep ambivalence towards consumerism in Zimbabwe (Burke 1996; see also Miller 1992).[7] In both Zimbabwe and Nairobi, certain consumer items are closely associated with privilege and come to represent social mobility. However, there are also strong negative associations with 'Western' style consumption patterns because of their 'non-African' character, engendering anxieties about the 'erosion of tradition', which exist alongside the desire for the 'modern'.

Young professionals react defensively to accusations of 'westernization' directed against them. But these accusations also get to the heart of the matter they are struggling with, which is that they embody a range of new possibilities, but that the cost of this privilege is cultural change. The phrase 'westernization' needs closer attention though. It implies that culture is a stationary set of practices and ideas and it conceals that cultures in Kenya have a long history of hybrid change. The expression, therefore, points towards a deep ambivalence towards capitalism, in terms of the opportunities and of the ruptures it generates. Young professionals react against 'westernization', equating it with imperialism. As a result, young professionals reify Africanness and see the West as significantly different; something Western is non-African and thus non-authentic. The point is that being a group of socially mobile young professionals cuts across existing patterns of ethnicity and class. As a result, many call themselves 'African' rather than describing themselves, to a certain extent, as belonging to an ethnic group such as Kamba, Luyha or Meru. These contradicting perceptions and emotions give rise to feelings of anxiety about their cultural identity and such contradictions are typical of what some young professionals called 'being modern the African way'. They desire to be, and in fact are, modern, perceiving themselves as having progressive attitudes. As such they follow up on other groups who perceived themselves to be modern in the Kenyan past like the schoolgirls in the 1960s described by Thomas (2006). However, their modern aspirations sometimes conflict with common sense regarding culture, ethnicity, politics and sexuality, as this study will explore.

In Nairobi, sexuality is a fiercely debated topic in public debate, as sexual pleasure often seems to be in conflict with social conventions. As Patrick's account shows, there is often a tension between practices and ideologies, between personal experiences and public opinion. Exactly how these interfaces connect is explored in some detail in this study. Almost all the people I spoke to viewed sex as a source of physical pleasure, of emotional fulfilment and crucial to self-perception. Enjoying sex is explained as a moment of bliss; of pure physical sensation; of ultimate closeness. It makes women 'feel sexy' and therefore 'feel woman', while for men it means the confirmation of 'being man' and a 'good lover' when they can sexually satisfy a woman. These understandings of sexuality are discursively constructed and thus embodied, and experienced as 'natural'. To have a fulfilling sexual relationship, whether a 'casual' or a 'committed' one, is perceived as a positive ambition. A 'committed' relationship is seen as the ultimate achievement of 'love', as both emotional and physical satisfaction are seen as fundamental to a couple's happiness. All the people I spoke to have this kind of love in mind as the purpose of a relationship. However, as will become clear in the following chapters, this is not always feasible, because often sex is also a source of uncertainty and suspicion, and a battleground for power. Sexual encounters can thus be ambiguous.

In Nairobi sex is both celebrated as the source of life and a source of pleasure. Sexual intercourse is seen as necessary for physical and mental health, especially for the union between women and men, for the fulfilment of their roles as gendered persons as well as members of descent groups. At the same time sex is condemned as the source of many evils, such as social disintegration, AIDS and cultural loss.[8] Much of the way in which sexuality is discussed in public debate is related to the extent of anxiety invoked by the debates concerning (the loss of) cultural heritage. Since the advent of AIDS, public reactions have focussed the discussion about AIDS on sexuality. AIDS is associated with decadent lifestyles, prostitution, the breakdown of social control and moral codes, and other social vices. These discourses, dominated by important public figures such as religious leaders, politicians and journalists, present the negligence of 'African morals' (hence 'African culture') as the origin of AIDS and of the social disintegration from which Kenya is 'suffering'. AIDS is generally perceived as being a disease born of wrongdoing or transgression (Spronk 1999). The cosmopolitan interest in lifestyle matters demonstrated by young professionals is at odds with these sentiments.

Patrick's account shows how intersections between sexuality and the debates concerning cultural heritage can cause feelings of anxiety. These feelings were shared by many young adults like him and are typical of this particular social group. Sex, which is central to self-expression, is somehow associated with 'being modern', while at the same time it feels 'natural'. In their self-expression, their notions of self are 'African', 'non-Western', 'nontraditional'. Hence they are caught up in the ensuing discussion over belonging. According to Sahlins, cultural structures are reproduced through the actions of intentional subjects who do not necessarily 'use existing categories in prescribed ways' (Sahlins 1985: 145). As such, ideologies provide the terms of debate for members of society, and categories may be contested, but they belong to the same social structure. Young professionals cannot escape using the categories 'African' and 'Western', or 'traditional' and 'modern' because they are directly caught up in the current debates which polarize 'African' on the one hand against 'Western' and 'modern' on the other (cf. Geschiere et al. 2008). As we shall see, in their lives young professionals actually inflate the categories of 'African', 'Western', 'modern' and 'traditional'.

The focus in this book is on the intersections between sexuality and debates concerning cultural heritage and the anxiety they provoke. These ambiguities of pleasure contribute to other worries that people have about sexuality, in Kenya as elsewhere, because of social and cultural expectations as to what is considered (proper) sex. Sex is almost always imbued with some degree of uncertainty or unease. Feelings of shame, fear of losing the partner, fear of disappointing, fear about violation of trust, anxiety about failure to enjoy sex or have an orgasm, and fear of arousing suspicion: all these experiences serve to highlight the precarious and complex nature of a sexual encounter. I will show that pleasurable and anxiety-evoking aspects of sex are not mutually exclusive. Certainly, the troubled aspects of sex need our attention, but rather than only studying sex as something which is problematic, as has become common, this needs to be put properly into context.[9]

Young professionals as a group embody the processes of social transformation; in other words, they are creations of postcolonial Kenya. Yet, they also choose to explore new boundaries. Their lifestyles involve a process of reflection on self-perception with regard to gender (being 'woman' and 'man'); issues of belonging (being 'African'); and questions of relationships ('casual' or 'committed' relationships). I will show how young professionals make moral distinctions about sexual relations while incorporating and advocating changes. My aim is not to position them as an emancipation movement but instead to explore how they 'remoralize' normative gender and social organizations of sexuality. Instead of interpreting their agency in a strictly positive manner, Butler's notion of the 'paradox of subjectivation' (1997) is helpful. It implies a reconceptualization of power as a set of relations that do not simply dominate the subject, but also form the conditions of being dominated and its possibilities to modify domination. Agency, then, is not simply a synonym for resistance to relations of domination, but a capacity for action that specific relations of subordination create and enable. Such an approach is important for understanding young professionals in Nairobi, who are in constant interaction with normative discourses on femininity and masculinity, in that they both comply with and challenge common sense. Their narratives are structured by accounts of love and desire, where sex is related to notions of contemporary womanhood and manhood. In this way, sexual pleasure becomes an identity badge for an emergent generation at the dawn of the twenty-first century. Nevertheless, there is always a flipside. When probing the personal narratives, pleasure and feelings of anxiety emerge as two sides of the same coin. The resulting tension in personal lives, sometimes vocalized on a group level, centres around concerns about feelings of belonging.

Structure of the book

This study analyses sexuality as a prism through which to explore both how it is constituted socially (in relation to postcolonial transformation processes) and how it is experienced personally. By focussing on public debates on the one hand (preoccupied with redefining sexuality into the realm of cultural identity), and personal sexual relationships on the other, I explore how sexuality has gained a new meaning in modern lifestyles and how sex has become central to self-expression. Young professionals embody postcolonial transformations, and in their ensuing lifestyles constructions of sexuality, gender and culture come to shift, engendering new modes of being oriented in the world.

Therefore, following the first chapter on the study of sexuality in Africa, this study continues with an analysis of the processes of subjectivation characteristic of postcolonial Kenya. Chapter II addresses the effects of social change on gender and sexuality, as well as the historical background of the families of young professionals. The second half of Chapter II concentrates on young professionals as a group, although closer investigation shows that, of course, young professionals are not a homogenous group. Chapter III seeks to provide a better understanding of the volatile moral discussions of the early twenty-first century which, I argue, bespoke wider concerns about the shape and direction of Kenyan society. These discussions reveal recent processes of subjectivation.

Chapters IV and V address women and men's subjective experiences via selected biographical narratives. My aim is to look in depth at the trajectories of individual women and men and at emerging trends in their sexual lives, in order to analyse how sexuality is embodied and experienced. Chapter IV focusses on women's lives by analysing how they engage in different life paths as they get older. Chapter V focusses on men's lives and on the different choices they make in similar situations. Women and men's sense of self is linked to notions of gender in relation to perceptions of sexual desire as 'natural'. I show how perceptions of sexual pleasure become central to love and sexual relationships and, hence, how sexuality becomes central to self-expression. How people individually deal with the volatile discourses is also addressed in these chapters.

Besides sexuality, romantic love has also become central to self-expression. Young professionals' love lives and sexual lives are characterized by the important role of the media and Chapter VI takes as a point of departure how current processes of subjectivation and identification interact. The focus here is on the representation of romantic love in the media in relation to imaginations of romantic love among young professionals. I show how, in the media, issues of love, sexuality and cultural identity are engaged with and recreated in the representations of being young, urban and modern. Finally, in the concluding chapter, I reflect on the constructionist approach to studying gender and sexuality, and upon the limits to this approach that I came upon when translating young professionals' experiences into academic language.

The process of reorganizing sexuality is characteristic of young professionals as a social group in Nairobi. I explore how for young adults, sex is personal (central to self-expression), intersubjective (shared in relationships), and social (how it relates to social structures). In other words, sexuality offers a strategic vantage point to study the interface between Nairobi society and the personal experiences of young adults in the context of modernity.

Notes

1. *Discovering home* by Binyavanga Wainaina (2003: 8, 10, 38–39).
2. In this study I use the term African (without quotes) when it is used in a geo-political rather than essentialist sense and the term 'African' (in quotes) when people imply an innate sense of 'Africanness' in terms of a shared history, 'race' or 'culture'.
3. In Kenya, there are so-called 'traditionalists', a small minority of the population advocating a more profound 'return' to 'African morals', for example, by calling for the reinstitution of female circumcision, ritual oaths, ancestor worship, and polygamy. The most visible group is the Mungiki religious movement which is aligned mainly with the cultural ideology and practice of the Kikuyu ethnic group.
4. Nyairo analyses the birth of Kenyan hip hop, citing Hardstone's '*Uhiki*' hit, as an example of how new identities are forged by 'editing' older cultural practices. The song is based on the lyrics of a traditional Gĩkũyũ folksong and on a remix of Marvin Gaye's award winning hit 'Sexual healing'. See Nyairo 2005 for an interesting analysis.
5. The political-economical ruling elite of Kenya are people with family capital, who do not have to work themselves up via education and jobs as these young professionals need to.
6. *Sheng* has not replaced local languages. Instead, it is a 'fusing of tongues' that is testament to postcolonial Kenya: '[it] attests to the multiple and fluid identities that are increasingly defining postcolonial, particularly urban, Kenya' (Nyairo and Ogude 2005: 239).
7. Young professionals' preoccupation with 'sophistication' reflects Miller's argument about consumerism in the context of modernity in Trinidad. He suggests that the experience of rupture underpins the assertion of particular forms of self-identification through a preoccupation with style amongst black diaspora populations (Miller 1992).
8. HIV and AIDS are acronyms, i.e. Human Immuno-deficiency Virus and Acquired Immuno Deficiency Syndrome. In this study 'AIDS' refers to the syndrome and opportunistic diseases that people with AIDS suffer from, as well as to the discourses relating to the complex configuration of the social, political and medical processes and realities of the infection and the disease.

9.   There are certain moments, feelings, or desires associated with sex that people called 'a dark urge', 'something ferocious', or 'when you want to revenge the world it expresses itself in sex' (Njeri, aged 26) or 'sex can be so instinctual' (Joram, aged 23). When asked, they could not describe exactly what this was. Despite people's attempts to give sex meaning, there is a realm of sexual desire that is beyond social science research, a realm of sex that is difficult to objectify. Medical discourse defines this 'murky' (Paglia 1991: 13) realm of sex by describing the biological functions, while psychoanalytical theory explains it by childhood traumas. It is beyond the scope of this study to discuss these perspectives with regard to young professionals' experience. I acknowledge that there is an elusive part of sexuality that is difficult to objectify both for people themselves and for researchers.

This realization brings up the question of what kind of information, or truth, a researcher on sexuality is seeking. It is erroneous to think that there is a core of sexuality we can capture, a deep-seated mechanism that will bring us to the heart of sex. When discussing the intimate aspects of our lives in my study in Nairobi, a crucial aspect of what people were trying to elucidate evaporated the moment they tried to express it. Language, in particular academic language, is too restricted if we want to include the sensuality and eroticism of sex, and we are often limited to using metaphors to transfer meaning from ineffable experiences (Fernandez 1991). People's exclamations of sex as 'bliss', 'gut feeling' or 'release' shows how erotics is an interesting area of study because it escapes our categories. Roland Barthes' notion of *jouissance* points at exactly this, *le petit mort*, or orgasm, often described as a momentary loss of self, a particular, ultimate pleasure that is common knowledge, yet singular in its experience. Similarly, Maurice Merleau-Ponty pointed out that the scholar's problem is that there is no 'tactile representation of sexual activity' (1958 [1945]). I believe we need to acknowledge our limitations as social scientists, in that we are unable to grasp a particular essence of sexuality. Nevertheless, sex(uality) is important to people's being and knowing and remains therefore an important subject for research, as Malinowski still reminds us.

CHAPTER I

THE STUDY OF SEXUALITY

This study takes up the challenge set by Malinowksi: to analyse erotic encounters as a 'fundamental factor in the scientific analysis of society' (1982 [1929]: I) – in this case, of Nairobi society. I aim to analyse the intertwined discourses on cultural heritage, gender relations and sexuality, the varying directions that young professionals take in their intimate lives, and how these crossing points play out in their personal experiences. Before doing so, however, it is necessary to reflect on the development of research on sexuality in Kenya, and Africa, as this provides the departure point for this study.

Sexuality research in Kenya

The study of sexuality in Kenya shows several interesting shifts in scholarship. The first phase of study took a cultural and socio-economic perspective as a point of departure and analysed institutions of sexuality from the late nineteenth century to the middle of the twentieth century.[1] These studies provide systematic descriptions of initiation, marriage, birth and rites of passage and explore how these cultural institutions relate to the cosmology of a group. From the 1960s onwards, attention shifted to an examination of the transformations of these institutions.[2] These studies typically describe cultural phenomena, such as the status, roles and powers conferred on men by patriarchal ideologies, elaborating on the division of labour according to gender, reproduction and descent. Sexuality is described as an indispensable aspect of a people's culture, with an emphasis on the social organization of sexuality. Usually, a chapter in a monograph of a specific ethnic group is confined to sexuality, such as for example 'Sex life among young people', a chapter in Kenyatta's *Facing Mount Kenya* (1938). It offers an interesting account of the institution of *ngweko* (fondling): girls and boys were permitted to meet and enjoy 'lovemaking' without full sexual intercourse by placing the penis between the thighs of the girl. Kenyatta depicted such practices from an ideal, almost nostalgic, perspective. He detailed the moral rules and obligations pertaining to young people, which he described as being strictly enforced.[3] What he left out, however, was information about trespasses or conflicts, which would have elaborated on people's actual behaviour.

During the second half of the twentieth century, a few anthropological studies emerged in which sexuality was incorporated as a key theme. These studies covered subjects such as prostitution or its various forms, virginity, and female circumcision or same-sex sexuality.[4] Apart from these studies, research on sexuality in Kenya is limited by the fact that sexual desire and practices are not studied as a distinct and separate theme. Instead, sexuality is studied as a sub-theme of other topics such as circumcision, reproduction, gender, and later, AIDS.

From the 1960s onwards, research on sexuality was conducted as a sub-theme primarily from a medical or health perspective. Three fields of sexuality-related research can be distinguished for this period. From the early 1960s onwards, family planning programmes studied sexual behaviour in relation to fertility. The primary interest was in analysing the frequency of the coital act, the use and choice of contraceptives, and to a limited extent spousal decision-making with regard to family size and contraception. This research was largely quantitative in nature and conducted mainly within the fields of demography, population and fertility studies. Even today, these studies play a central role in the production of knowledge about sexuality. From the 1970s, adolescents became a particular focus of study. And from the 1980s onwards, as part of the new focus of interest on public health, the emerging framework of reproductive and sexual health gained popularity. But apart from these demography, population and fertility studies, sexuality has remained a minor research topic. However, from the mid-1980s, the AIDS epidemic changed the climate for sexuality research dramatically. The need to determine levels of AIDS awareness led to the examination of patterns of sexual behaviour and the exploration of 'risk behaviour' or 'transactional sex' among subgroups of the population such as sex workers, migrants, adolescents, etc. Recently, studies have also looked at sex among discordant couples and the sex lives of infected people.

The impact of AIDS has forced the topic of sexuality onto the broader academic agenda, because sexual practices have become a potential cause of large-scale suffering for individuals, families and communities. This has resulted in a body of scholarship dealing with different social issues in relation to AIDS. Currently, research on sexuality in Kenya tends to be linked to epidemiological, demographic and development studies that are part of AIDS research: essentially, sexual behaviour is studied in relation to HIV infection. For example, the issue of *Culture, Health and Sexuality*, entitled 'Recent Research on Sexuality in East Africa' and consisting of six articles, dealt only with sex and sexuality as they related to HIV/AIDS (Birungi et al. 2009). Most of this literature typically deals with assessing knowledge, behaviour and attitudes regarding sex(uality), HIV and AIDS, violent and/ or risky sex, or the age of sexual début of adolescents, the frequency of sexual contacts, and condom use. These quantitative studies have been useful for detecting trends in behaviour in large samples of people or in regions.[5]

Together with the quantitative studies, qualitative studies were conducted to interpret these trends in sexual behaviour.[6] These interpretative studies have provided much insight into different experiences, practices and justifications of sexual behaviour. However, the literature tends to present only a certain kind of knowledge about sexuality, since sexuality is only studied as a public health problem in a context where the urgency of the AIDS crisis underpins much research. Any approach which views sexuality primarily as a societal problem only highlights certain aspects of sexuality while ignoring others, such as the difference between sexual behaviour and sexual identity, love and intimacy, the desire for affection, or the aspect of pleasure.

Leaving to one side the frequently acknowledged fact that research on sexuality remains limited because sex is a sensitive subject, and hence difficult to study, little of this work has led to the development of an adequate research epistemology for studying sexuality in Kenya, or, for that matter, Africa as a whole. In fact, the terms sex and sexuality are often used interchangeably in sexuality-related research. These patterns reveal a flawed way of thinking about sexuality and AIDS.[7] Although the scope of sexuality studies has broadened over recent years and much innovative work is now being done, I believe it is necessary to highlight certain trends that continue to impede the understanding of sexuality. The epidemiological or health approaches in the context of AIDS have framed knowledge about sexuality in African societies in a particular way.

Health approaches to sexuality

With epidemiological, demographic and development studies – in short, health studies – the quantification of sex into behavioural frequencies and attitudinal scores has characterized much of the research on sexual behaviour in Africa since the 1980s. While it is important to map patterns of HIV infection among a population, within a region or between regions, there is a need to further interpret this data. Epidemiological studies show patterns but do not explain the causes of these patterns, that is, they cannot explain the motivations of particular groups of people according to their social characteristics such as gender, religion, age, socio-economic situation, etc. Nevertheless, there is a tendency to treat epidemiological data as the end result. In many quantitative studies sex is reduced to an act done either before, during or outside marriage. Further, the term 'sexuality' can indicate a range of topics such as reproduction, circumcision, gender, HIV infection and condom use. This instrumental use of the term sexuality indicates a failure to understand different practices and mentalities. Moreover, the methodology of surveys or questionnaires is not always unproblematic with regard to obtaining valid data (see for a discussion Abramson et al. 1995; Hewett et al. 2003). Lastly, the large-scale approach of epidemiological work necessitates a certain amount of generalization and the creation of categories that might not always reflect social realities, such as the category 'prostitute' (Pheterson 1990).

Among the first to study sexuality in relation to AIDS were John Caldwell, Pat Caldwell and Pat Quiggin (1989a, 1989b). They studied sexuality in relation to AIDS in Nigeria, and Africa in general, from an epidemiological perspective from the late 1980s until the turn of the century. Their attempt to study sexuality in greater depth is commendable, although their analyses are debatable.[8] Their work serves as an example of the dominant trend of sexuality research in Africa. Moreover, their work has been cited many times and has become a standard point of reference. In short, they have produced an 'African sexuality thesis', which is used in highly generalized ways to explain higher numbers of HIV infections throughout the continent. They argue that compared to the 'Eurasian' system, chastity in the 'African' context is little valued; that there is no 'evidence' supporting high levels of female pleasure; that the conjugal bond is 'emotionally weak'; and that sex 'many times' is a commercial interaction. They also state that in conjunction with 'the evidence that [historically] Africans neither placed aspects of sexual behaviour at the centre of their moral and social systems nor sanctified chastity', African sexuality can be characterized as, 'above all, permissive' (Caldwell et al. 1989b). Despite their own caution (see note 5, p.78), it is disheartening to see such huge generalizations being made for a continent as vast as Africa, based only on a few case studies in one particular country and by means of surveys. This type of gross generalization caricatures and devalues complex and diverse emotions and practices. By writing about 'African' sexuality in relation to 'Caucasian' sexuality, they emphasize differences, rather than possible similarities, such as the relation between poverty or class and sexuality (Parker 2001) or people's inclination to intimacy (cf. Jankowiak 2008). Their work reveals a narrow interpretation of female sexual pleasure, as well as an ethnocentric and ahistorical analysis of notions regarding morality, sexual behaviour, female sexuality and chastity (for further discussion, see Ahlberg 1994; Heald 1995; Le Blanc et al. 1991).[9]

This work serves as an evocative example of a larger trend in sexuality research in African societies. Its overall perspective presents us with three stereotypes that still impede much research. The first stereotype is the construction of a single entity called 'Africa' that does not leave much space for the many variations and diversities that exist on the African continent. The next is that of promiscuous 'African men' who have extensive sexual networks and behave irresponsibly. The third stereotype is the construction of the category 'African woman', which depicts 'African women' as 'disempowered' to the point that they 'often' have sex for material gain. Related to this latter notion is the idea of a 'lack' of female sexual pleasure in 'the African sexual system'. What is lacking in work that relies on these stereotypes is a sound theorizing of sexuality and a coherent reflection on research epistemology.

When we look at the assets and limitations of epidemiological approaches to sexuality, an interesting contradiction arises. In order to show patterns of behaviour in a population, surveys focus on individual knowledge, attitudes, behaviour and practices. The failure to take into account the causes of these individual factors highlights an inability to consider the social dimensions of sexuality. In response, scholars have been looking at incorporating social aspects of sex in order to explain particular HIV patterns. Thornton, for example, criticizes the standard statistical medical-epidemiological approach of AIDS and sexuality research in Africa and proposes going beyond the individual by focussing on what he calls sexual networks (2008). He rightly points out that statistical aggregates of individual behaviour do not explain why HIV does not progress like most other viral and bacterial epidemics. Instead, Thornton suggests focussing on the issue of the formation of sexual networks, defined as the links between people by way of having sex with more than one steady lifetime partner (serial or simultaneous). However, his important contribution – including wider aspects of how individual shape their lives – has resulted in individual personal motivations and experiences, once again, being overlooked. In order to understand the abstracted tables, figures and mappings, we also need to study people's personal and intimate considerations.

I certainly do not want to deny the problems of AIDS and the disadvantaged position of certain groups of women (and men) in Africa as a whole. However, taking into account that AIDS studies are conducted from a particular perspective (which see sex as the problem behind HIV infection), it is important to realize that research on sexuality from this perspective has emphasized only some aspects of sexual relationships, and that sexuality is often studied in relation to other topics. These themes have become the primary source of information on sexuality, which means that sexuality tends to be studied in instrumental terms. This results in a subtle process where the definition of women's sexuality in African societies is not just complex but fundamentally flawed (Spronk 2005a); and that of men's sexuality as not just complex but fundamentally coercive (Spronk 2005b). There is virtually no literature on pleasure, the relationship between affection and sex, eroticism, conjugal intimacy, or female pleasure. The difference between this presentation of African sexuality and the literature on Western societies is remarkable. Studies dealing with, for example, erotic pleasure or the meaning of intimacy are almost nonexistent for Africa. However, this is changing, albeit on a small scale (Biaya 2000; Spronk 2011).

Ideally, epidemiological and interpretative studies should complement each other. That this is not often the case is problematic, yet characteristic. Crossing disciplinary boundaries, as Besnier points out, is an arduous but important endeavour. An important step is the 'appreciation of how scholars in other disciplines couch research questions, what kind of presuppositions underlie these questions, and what counts as evidence as they go about trying to answer them' (1995: 559). My critical reflections about trends in the development/health research on sexuality should not be interpreted as dismissing the discipline. On the contrary; more effective ways to cooperate need to be explored, such as successful interdisciplinary projects. An interesting approach to the study of sexual patterns where quantitative and qualitative methods are combined is the Relationship History Calendar (Luke et al. 2011). However, there is a tendency to take HIV infection patterns as the end result, thereby excluding or minimalizing the interpretation of contextual factors. This is also due to the fact that research in Africa tends to be monopolized by development-related work that is policy driven and hence dependent on political trends and rapid-assessment approaches. Development projects around the world aimed at promoting population management, disease prevention, and maternal and child health, intentionally and unintentionally shape ideas about what constitutes 'normal' sexual practices and, as a result, generate very particular knowledge about sexuality (Adams and Pigg 2005).

The reasons behind these tendencies can be found in what Jansen has called the 'guises of ethnocentrism' in development discourse. The belief in and the creation of a systematic difference between the West and the South is one of these major guises. There is also a preference for abstractions over actual social relations, while the South is further perceived as consisting of static and unchanging cultures (Jansen 1989). 'Africa' is portrayed as a 'paradigm of difference' (Mudimbe 1994). Much of the Western/white discourse on black sexuality still has its roots in the 'psychological need for projection of "Otherness"' (Vaughan 1991: 19).

Sexuality research in the context of AIDS in Africa

When in 2001/2 I explained to Western AIDS or development professionals that in my research I was studying sexuality in the context of modernity in Nairobi, people often responded by saying things like 'ah yes, condom use is such a problem in these cultures', or 'right, AIDS is really killing them off here isn't it?' Such remarks reveal two premises. Firstly, that research on sexuality in an African society is often automatically related to AIDS and is not viewed as a possible topic of study in its own right. Secondly, it reveals the widespread assumption that the problem of AIDS – that is, the high HIV infection rates due to sex – stems from the peculiarities of 'African' culture. Sometimes people were more explicit and named the problem of 'African' cultures. For example, an epidemiologist who was invited to speak about 'AIDS in Africa' at the Free University in Amsterdam in 2003 explained that 'African men like to sow their seeds' and thus have multi-partnered sex as 'part of their culture'. Similarly, in 2001 the nongovernmental organization VSO (Voluntary Service Oversees) had the following slogan on a poster which depicted unspecified black people in the background: 'They believe AIDS originates from witchcraft. We know better. Come and work at VSO to give them a better future.' These are two random examples of situations one encounters in the context of development work, which point at the necessity for continuous efforts to reflect upon and integrate ethics in the development and research agenda (Nyambedha 2008).[10]

How exactly are studies of sexuality framed by the AIDS paradigm? According to Packard and Epstein (1991), the development of medical research on AIDS in Africa resembles earlier efforts to understand the epidemiology of tuberculosis and syphilis in Africa. In all three cases, early research focussed on the question of why these diseases exhibited different epidemiological patterns in Africa to those exhibited in the West. Early explanations of these differences focussed on the peculiarities of 'African' behaviour, while largely excluding the wide range of contextual factors. Packard and Epstein analysed how these initial perceptions shaped the subsequent development of AIDS research, encouraging a premature narrowing of research questions. As early as 1991, the authors warned that, as has happened in the research on tuberculosis and syphilis, this early narrowing down might generate inadequate and inappropriate responses to the AIDS

epidemic and limit our understanding of the disease. However, their warning appeared to do little to reconfigure the general scope of AIDS research,
probably because of the pressure to act immediately on the imminent crisis. But how did these presumptions originate in the first place?

According to Patton (1992), colonial constructions of black sexuality
were revived in the attempt to explain the heterosexual character of AIDS.
The idea of 'Africans' as being sexually promiscuous by nature became
a discursive reality once again.[11] In other words, scientific knowledge is
not objective or free from the influence of history and hierarchical social
relations. The knowledge gained through research on AIDS and sexuality
in Africa is far from complete (Arnfred 2004; Heald 2003; Undie and
Benaya 2006; see Vaughan 1991 for a general discussion on constructions
of race and sexuality in biomedical discourse in Africa).

In her insightful book on the politics of AIDS research in Kenya, Booth
(2004) shows how these premises affect research. She analyses in detail
how one of the most famous AIDS research projects in Africa was organized, ideologically and practically, and what kind of knowledge on HIV
infections, women and men, and sexuality was generated. She highlights
what was not asked, what was not thought about, or what was discarded
as irrelevant and excluded from the research results. For example, a description of the socio-economic status of the deprived and unattached
men, on whom the research focussed, was initially included in the research
design. Later, however, this information was ignored when the behaviour
of these men was explained.[12] Instead, the concept of 'African men' as a
self-evident category of sexual agents was used to explain their behaviour.
Such ways of thinking about culture figure prominently among Westerners and, ironically, also among Nairobians when discussing people with
AIDS outside their own social group (Spronk 1999). In fact, what we
may call the AIDS paradigm and the construction of African sexuality are
enshrined in the development/health discourse, whose institutions are the
main donors for sex research to date.[13] The perception that geographical
difference and promiscuity are central to the problem of AIDS in Africa 'lies at the heart of the scheme that the World Health Organization
[WHO] developed between 1986 and 1988 and that continues to organize international scientific and developmental thinking about the crisis'
(Booth 2004: 50).

From the 1980s onwards, such misconceptions have been seriously
challenged by scholars working with computer models to understand HIV
patterns, as well as by medical sociologists working in Africa, such as Max-
ine Ankrah. Nevertheless, the idea that Africans engaging in promiscuous,
multiple-partnered sex during their life course is the explanation for HIV
infection remains pervasive (see chapter 3 of Epstein 2008, for a stunning

account of how scientific research and knowledge production can be severely limited by stereotypes and lack of epistemological reflexivity). During the first decade of the twenty-first century, the concept of 'concurrent sexual partnerships', which means the engagement in two or more sexual relationships at the same time, has become the dominant mode of understanding sexuality in Africa. According to its proponents, despite the fact that concurrent relationships are often equated with multiple-partnered relationships, these computer models show that, ironically, people in Europe and the US engage in sexual relations with more partners compared with people in Africa. The difference is that the former engage in serial monogamy, multiple partners successively, and that the latter are more likely to engage with fewer partners but two, and sometimes more, partners at the same time. These concurrent relationships are particular prone to HIV transmission because of HIV's highly infectious period during the first three months after infection (see Epstein 2008; Thornton 2008). However, there is a huge controversy concerning the validity of the concept, especially regarding its methodological accurateness. The main problem is the lack of detailed estimates on prevalence and characteristic; as a result it is difficult to distinguish between concurrency and serial monogamy and, moreover, there is a tendency to overestimate concurrency levels (Lurie and Rosenthal 2010; Sawers and Stillwaggon 2010). The controversy shows, once again, that there is no shortcut to researching the complexity of sexual relations. Moreover, the idea that some form of risky behaviour peculiar to Africa, rather than, for example, economic or biological factors, is responsible for the spread of HIV, continues to guide research on sexuality and HIV/AIDS in Africa (Sawers and Stillwaggon 2010).

A related misconception has plagued much AIDS research. 'Culture', of course, has been held responsible where 'cultural practices', such as 'wife inheritance' in western Kenya, were seen as contributing to HIV infection. The over-representation of the practice of wife inheritance in the literature of the early 1990s is remarkable, since in fact it occurs in only a few of the many ethnic groups in Kenya, and within these groups it is practiced by a minority (Nyanzi et al. 2008). But because of the attention it received from Western researchers, it came to be seen as a typical 'Kenyan' practice responsible for the high rates of HIV infection, hence misrepresenting the nature of the epidemic. The same is true of the 'sugar daddy' stereotype (Luke 2005). Another effect of the 'AIDS paradigm' is the defensive reaction from people from Africa against such discriminating attitudes, as we have seen from Patrick's account. The political correctness of development workers and scholars and the defensive attitudes of people from Africa (who, ironically, all invoke 'culture'), have sometimes resulted in a stalemate, where the subject is avoided altogether.[14]

The current development/health discourse has thus framed sexuality research in African societies to a large extent. The representation of women's and men's sexuality in medical discourses on AIDS in Africa demonstrates fixed certain assumptions about people's social and presumed exclusively heterosexual identity (Epprecht 2008), their risk status and their responsibility in AIDS prevention (Hunter 2010; Silberschmidt 2001), and their sexual lives. As a result, AIDS campaigns have missed the point by focussing solely on the incidence of particular attitudes and practices, instead of studying the various reasons why people engage in sex. When one reads the literature on Western societies, it becomes clear that people engage in sex for many reasons. To name a few: the pursuit of pleasure; a desire for intimacy; an expression of love and/or affection; erotic expression, definition of a gendered sense of self; procreation; domination; money; or any combination of these reasons. From the eight reasons listed here, only the last four are described in the literature on sexuality in Africa and only recently is the component of pleasure being taken up. We can conclude that for Africa, sexuality has long been understood in terms which do not allow for personal and erotic specification.

I have discussed major trends in the research on sexuality and its impressive expansion. After more than three decades of AIDS intervention, this is a good moment to reflect on research, policy and implementation, as many new initiatives testify. This is not to say that there have not been studies that challenge these trends through different approaches. Within the social sciences a growing literature is looking at sexual conduct in its social context, and many proposals within the development/health discourse are reflecting on more inclusive approaches to sexuality (such as providing 'sexual counselling' within AIDS projects, or including notions of 'sexual pleasure' in project outlines). The establishment of the Africa Regional Sexuality Resource Centre (ARSRC) in 2003 is a great initiative, aimed at giving visibility, depth and legitimacy to the field of sexuality. In short, there are two major challenges to research about sexuality in Africa. Instead of focussing on frequency of sex in the context of HIV infection, the focus should be readjusted to the sexual act in relation to intimacy, eroticism, psycho-social aspects, socio-economic status, etc. Second, a more adequate research epistemology is urgently needed; without adequate theoretical grounding and methodological sophistication, research will remain flawed. The challenge therefore is to reformulate sexuality research, taking into account how, on one hand, society organizes experience and structures desire and motivation, and how, on the other hand, livelihoods or lifestyles frame people's sexual behaviour. To understand how this interaction takes place requires not only the mapping of explicit gendered power relations; it also requires the exploration of people's motivations, justifications, and agency. This study is therefore positioned within current debates in the social sciences about the social and cultural analysis of sexuality.

The dynamics of sexuality: the focus of this study

Despite Bronislaw Malinowski's call '[T]hat which means supreme happiness to the individual ["the erotic phase"] must be made a fundamental factor in the scientific treatment of human society' (Malinowski 1982 [1929]: 6), it is interesting to note that the study of sexuality has a tendency to ignore the erotic pleasures of sexuality, in favour of studying gender, identity, kinship, or reproduction. In this part I would like to address the question why anthropologists tend to ignore, in the words of E.E. Evans-Pritchard, 'the flesh and blood' in their writings on sexuality (1974: 9).

Anthropology and sexuality

As Andrew and Harriet Lyons point out in their book on the history of anthropology and sexuality, it is curious that sexuality has rarely been, and is still hardly a dominant theme in ethnographic research despite strong interest in the topic on the part of some of anthropology's founding practitioners and their descendents (2004: 2). In the 1920s and 1930s, anthropological studies emphasized the cultural variability of sexuality. Malinowski's work on the Trobriand Islands and Mead's work on Samoa showed that the sexual lives of primitive societies were quite variable and both scholars used these social facts as a mirror for their own societies to highlight the cultural nature of marital sexuality (Malinowski 1982 [1929]) and adolescent sexuality (Mead 1950). Malinowski provided an interesting research programme into sexuality as one of the key sites of social life whereby to study culture. Unfortunately, his legacy lay dormant until much later. It is generally understood that during the Great Depression and the two decades following the Second World War there was a relative silence among anthropologists concerning sex (Lyons and Lyons 2004; Tuzin 1995). The structural-functionalist orientation introduced an approach which looked at sexuality in relation to social structures. Moreover, the topic was decentralized in the sense that sex and gender were reconceptualized by the more disembodied terms of marriage, family and social structure. E.E. Evans-Pritchard's work on Zande homosexual and heterosexual eroticism in the 1920s was not published until 1974, and he suggested that his generation of anthropologists may have 'lost the flesh and blood' in their writings about African societies (1974: 9).

In the post-war years the influence of Levi-Strauss redirected anthropology's attention towards rituals and cosmology. The study of sexuality came to be limited to sexual symbolism, that is, how symbols of sex and the body referred to plants, colours, and social groups. In the 1950s and 1960s a differentiation between British and US anthropology took place. The theoretical direction in anthropology in Britain had for some time ruled out any consideration of individual motivation and bodily processes, whereas US anthropology was more open to such considerations. Nevertheless, it was notable that even the neo-Freudian culture and personality movement in the United States produced few ethnographic descriptions of adult sexual behaviour. The culture and personality studies approach focussed on the daily practices of socialization, hence on the social institutions of sexuality such as initiation rituals, marriage, etc. (Benedict 1934).

Since the 1960s, sexuality has reemerged as a focus in anthropological theorizing because of pioneering work on sexuality through feminist and gay and lesbian studies. So far, the study of sexuality had been the domain of sexology and other biomedical disciplines, apart from the above mentioned studies, whereas the new approaches are generally recognized as studying the social construction of sexuality. Feminist efforts focussed on a critical review of theories which used reproduction to link gender and sexuality, thereby explaining the inevitability and naturalness of women's subordination (see Vance 1991: 876). This theoretical reexamination separated sexuality and gender into two different concepts. A second impetus arose from issues that emerged through the examination of male homosexuality in nineteenth-century Europe and North America. The emerging gay and lesbian scholarship distinguished homosexual behaviour and homosexual identity and found the latter to be a recent historical development (Katz 1976; Weeks 1977). As such, this body of work introduced the concept of the relation between sexuality and identity. These two approaches – studying the politics of sexuality regarding gender and identity – have since remained the dominant themes in sexuality studies.

According to Carole Vance, anthropology 'rediscovered sexuality' as a result of these new approaches and in conjunction with a more general reflexive turn in the social sciences (1991). Vance distinguishes between the 'cultural influence models' as the dominant approach to sexuality and the 'social construction approach' that replaced the former:

> the cultural influence model recognizes variations in the occurrence of sexual behaviour and in cultural attitudes which encourage or restrict behaviour, but not in the meaning of the behaviour itself … .anthropologists working within this framework

accept without question the existence of universal categories like heterosexual and homosexual, male and female sexuality, and sex drive. … A social construction approach to sexuality examines the range of behaviour, ideology, and subjective meaning among and within human groups, and views the body, its functions, and sensations as potentials (and limits) which are incorporated and mediated by culture. (p. 879)

Whereas the majority of the studies before the 1960s focussed on non-Western societies, the introspective wave introduced by feminism in the 1960s also opened Western societies as possible objects for the anthropological study of sexuality.

Since the 1980s, AIDS has radically changed the field yet again. The advent of AIDS encouraged the resurgence of biomedical approaches to sexuality through the repeated association of sexuality and disease, which had been for a long time the legitimate reason for the scientific study of sexuality (Oosterhuis 2001). The limitations of biomedical knowledge on sexuality soon became enough clear, and a new field for sexuality research arose, this time from a social science perspective. Therefore, a social constructionist approach to sexuality – which is complementary to epidemiological studies – has become commonplace in health/development studies in the global South. Whereas sexuality studies in the global West have created a niche in mainstream anthropology, most work on sexuality in the global South is conducted within the health framework, studying sex as a sub-theme to reproduction, gender, HIV/AIDS, domestic violence and condom use.

It can be concluded that the majority of sexuality studies in anthropology are carried out from a constructionist approach where the focus is on theorizing difference and agency (within normative systems), cross-cultural difference, criticizing the foregrounding of identity, the relation between gender and sexuality, and how meanings and desires are influenced by culture. Within the constructionist approach, there are two main methodologies by which to study sexuality (Alsop et al. 2002). One is the materialist account, which looks at structural features and patterns to understand what it means to be 'gendered' and how that influences sexuality. A critique of this approach is that less attention is paid to the subjective aspect of gender and sexuality because it focusses rather on the politics of sexuality. The second is the discursive account, which pays attention to the construction of meaning and significance in language and representation. Studying sexuality from a discursive perspective involves focussing on the way in which subjectivity is engendered. Both approaches are concerned with how identity comes into being and both rely on the idea of the sexual subject as culturally dependent and historically specific. Accordingly, they need to begin their analyses with an examination of the social context and describe how, through processes of subjectivation, the social context or discourse creates subject positions. As a result, sex and sexuality are studied as the result of external factors, and sex and sexuality are the direct objects. The body, also, becomes studied as an object that is constituted through discourse; as an object to be studied in relation to culture (Shilling 2003). However, such an approach cannot explain sexuality as an embodied sensation, because the analysis ends with sex and the body as the results of processes of subjectivation. In fact, it is here that we encounter the limits of a constructionist approach to sex, sexuality and gender, because of its lack of interest in and inability to study bodily experiences and how these experiences are constitutive to being.

In conclusion, anthropologists working on sexuality have favoured, and continue to favour, the cognitive qualities over the sensory experience in their attempts to study culture. In order to bring together the personal experiences and the social context of sexuality, theorists of sexuality have approached the topic by analysing how the social context constructs and informs people's subjectivities. According to Donald Tuzin, this is the result of the 'grooves of mind-body dualism scored deeply into Western consciousness' that continues to be axiomatic for anthropology (1995: 258). It is also the consequence of working within a constructionist paradigm.

The social construction of sexuality, and its limits

The constructionist field of study has been criticized with regard to its methodology (for a general discussion, see Hacking 2001) and for its assumption that sexuality, like any other topic, can be socially deconstructed without taking into account its physiological characteristics. A chasm has arisen between the 'hard' sciences and the social sciences. Scholars studying sexuality from a biological perspective see the 'social construction' of sexuality as speculative, while the diehards among the social constructionists reject any biological explanations. As a result, there is virtually no cooperation between the different disciplines (for an interesting exception, see Abrahamson and Pinkerton 1995). According to Tuzin, we can overcome this chasm by focussing on the 'excluded middle', which is the experience of having sex, of desiring – in short, the subjective experience of sex:

> We need to focus on the experiential domain emergent from the blending of psychobiological proclivities and cultural meanings acquired through social learning. Sexual behaviour displays with exceptional clarity the synergism of cultural and biological effects, thereby challenging us to enter conceptually into the domain of the 'excluded middle', which is experience itself.... One such mechanism, clearly,

is the phylogenetically based capacity and appetite for sexual *pleasure* [...]. To be sure, as an inducement to coitus, genital pleasure is an essential lubricant in the evolutionary engine of humans.... None would deny, either, that sexual pleasure is a profoundly organic phenomenon, the experienced manifestation of an astonishingly intricate organic combination of physiological events.... Millions of people through the ages have eagerly risked life, limb, property, freedom, tranquillity, family, reputation, happiness, have even accepted such sure and eternal damnation, all for the attainment, not of offspring, but of sexual pleasure. The bio-evolutionary character of sexual pleasure cannot be disputed; but, for humans, the quest for this experience is also governed by a battery of normative and idiosyncratic controls no less intricate and subtle than those of organic origin. (Tuzin 1995: 259)

This study takes Tuzin's argument as a starting point: the biological base of sexuality is always experienced culturally, through a translation into culture. In my view, the constructionist approach to the study of sexuality begins where the biological approach ends: how do social contexts frame desire, behaviour and identity in addition to the 'natural' element of sexuality – the bodily dispositions we recognize as lust, desire or pleasure caused by hormones? People have sex, in general, for pleasure, but what is experienced as pleasurable differs according to person, social group and region. In other words, the 'bare biological facts of sexuality do not speak for themselves: they must be expressed socially' (Ross and Rapp 1997: 153). The seemingly most intimate details of private experience are actually structured by larger social relations. Sexuality studied from a social science perspective, then, reveals the cultural conventions about what erotic excitement and/or satisfaction are, and how these perceptions also shape the physical sensations themselves. Sex is, in short, as much about nature as about culture, as much about individuals as about society. However, there is a tendency in the constructionist approach to study sex as discursive practice, that is, how language defines reality before it is experienced by individuals. Yet, sex is mainly experienced as 'natural' and personal. Discursive analysis tends to overlook this dimension of sexuality because of its epistemological position. As I will elaborate below, this study analyses how sex feels personal, private, and above all natural, and how those feelings always incorporate the rules, definitions, symbols and meanings of the worlds in which they are construed. It thus follows a constructionist approach, while incorporating the experiential element of sexuality. In short, an anthropology of sexuality should include an analysis of gender, sex and erotic pleasures.

Gender is an important analytical tool in studying sexuality. Gender is an essential part of how people understand themselves, and it refers to social understandings and representations of being wo/man. Moreover, gender operates as a social variable, structuring the pathways of people and giving rise to hegemonic normative gender constructions. The relationship between notions of gender and sex is far more complex than biomedical discourse presumes (which is normally that one's gender identity corresponds with one's sex). There is an increase in studies on Africa that show how sexual identities do not necessarily coincide with the sexual practices thought to be part and parcel of these identities.[15] In feminist scholarship, there are two main approaches to understanding the relationship between sexuality and gender. One is the materialist feminist account, which looks at structural features and patterns to understand what it means to be 'gendered'. This approach focusses on the politics of sexuality when, for example, studying restrictions on abortion and birth control, sexual harassment, rape, prostitution and domestic abuse. The second is the discursive approach that pays attention to the construction of meaning and significance in language and representation. Studying sexuality from a discursive perspective focusses on the way in which subjectivity is engendered. According to Butler (1990, 1993) there is no authentic gender; gender is a performance and this performance constitutes the real. She suggests that enacted differences emerge not simply as an effect of structure (or genitals), but as a form of self-fashioning. I agree with this in respect of how gender 'works' and informs. However, Butler does not pursue her analysis on an empirical level – how people 'feel' a gendered sense of self – which is the approach of this study. In fact, it is here that we encounter the limits of a constructionist approach, in its lack of interest in and inability to study bodily experiences. The focal point in this study is to investigate how notions of femininity and masculinity inform people's sense of self, and how this relates to the experience of sexual desire.

As I set out in the introduction, in this study I aim to bridge discursive analysis and empirical investigation. I do this by analysing how discourses with regard to self are generated in context, and I analyse how sexuality is part of how people 'feel' a sense of self. So far, anthropologists have tended to study how culture structures sexuality; however, they do not always study how people experience sex. Therefore, complementing the constructionist approach, which emphasizes the self as an effect of subjectivation, I include an analysis of the self by including the experiential, or the 'subjectiveness' of sex.

Sex as embodied experience

Thomas Csordas's interest in the realizing capacities of bodily experience (1990) has resulted in a plea for a 'paradigm of embodiment'. His concern is in recognizing the body for what it is in experiential terms; embodied selves inhabit a behavioural environment which is much broader than any singular event. The body is the 'existential ground of culture'; it is the productive starting point for an analysis of culture and self (1990: 5). In other words, the body mediates social processes and provides meaning to them. As such, this approach draws attention to the self as an embodied and contextual process, highlighting the 'essentially intersubjective and social nature of bodily experience' (1994: 14). This brings us to the study of the embodied experience of sexuality.

The fact that young adult women and men in my study referred to their corporeal experiences in a variety of ways cannot be written off by pointing out that sex is first and foremost a sensual experience. The way in which Pamela (aged 22 in 2001) describes how the sensation of being touched by her boyfriend Emmanuel 'made her feel like a woman' for the first time is indicative (Chapter IV). It stimulated her to explore this part of herself, her womanhood, and as a woman rather than a teenage girl she began to see herself as entering a new phase of her life, namely, as a young adult woman. With adulthood comes the search for independence, the importance of a career and the need to be recognized as a hip and ambitious Nairobian. Discovering desire was not only a pleasurable experience; the corporeal experience of being a woman enacted and constituted her sense of self. Wambui's (aged 29 in 2001) explanation that '[I]t was as if an undiscovered part of myself was explored' is telling. For both Pamela and Wambui, their sensuous experience realized their being. As I shall show, whereas women need to appropriate sensuality as indexical to their self, for men sex is constitutive for manhood; being a man is dependent on having sexual intercourse. Any shifts in the meaning of gender, as explained by the men, are therefore experienced and realized through the body. Many men told me that they want to be 'different' from their father; when they were encouraged to be more explicit, they said that they were looking for a distinctive intimate relationship and hoped to be another kind of man, a 'modern' man. Such a notion of being a 'modern' man refers to cultural meanings that implicate men's corporeal experiences in their self-perceptions.

Sex is meaningful in two ways. It is by and large a corporeal and sensory experience, but is also an act loaded with social significance. The point is to uncover the dialectic between them, and the analytical tool of embodiment as put forward by Csordas helps to connect these two dimensions: the social significance of sex is realized through the body, thereby creating a particular sense of being-in-the-world as well as making social meanings real. The manner in which the concept of embodiment elucidates the process of how people understand and define their personhood has helped me to grasp the experience of sex in relation to the place of young professionals in society. Young professionals' explanations about the importance of sex relate to the way in which sex is an intense corporeal experience, which augments a gendered sense of being woman or man. These meanings of gender are related to particular notions of being young, urban, modern and African, which, in turn, reflect the outcomes that social transformations have had on gender, sexuality and culture in Kenya.

Studying sexuality as an embodied practice directed me to the subjectiveness of sex; to how the self is realized through sex. Analysing young professionals' sexual acts as embodied practices demonstrates how sex is a sensory experience and how the experience of sex is informed by social meanings concerning gender, cultural identity and class, hence how the practice of sex mediates and constitutes cultural categories of self (modern) and other (traditional) in Nairobi. It thus highlights how the body mediates culture and how it imbues sexuality with meaning. Moreover, it directs our attention to the erotic experiences of sexuality.

Inspired by Csordas's inclusive notion of self as an indeterminate process of engaging or becoming oriented in the world, I employ the notion of people's sense of self. This notion of the self, studied through bodily experiences, relates to self-esteem, to a sense of belonging to a group or society, to how a person identifies herself or himself as 'woman' or 'man'; and it indicates the experiential dimension. By focussing on people's sexual conduct, I analyse how sexual intimacy becomes a matter of the self, of the sexual subject, in a symbolic interaction with another subject (Jamieson 1998: 1). I am not only interested in what people do, with whom and how many times, but also how they make sense of it by focussing on their experience of sex. The sensorial dimension of sex is often experienced as 'natural', but it is also associated with other modes of being female, male, a yuppy or a Kenyan. I thus propose to study sexuality as a prism through which to analyse how social developments have generated new notions of self-perceptions. To do so, a historical approach is imperative.

Historicizing sexuality

The ambiguities experienced by young professionals, such as those exemplified by Patrick and mentioned in the introduction, are thus part and parcel of contemporary life in Nairobi. Societal transformations cause 'shifting relations, including the symbolism of sex and gender' (Ross and Rapp 1997: 162), consequently undermining patriarchal ideologies of the social organization of sexuality. Yet, these changes have also opened up new spaces for the experience of sexuality and for the formation of relationships; thus a new terrain of sexuality has been opened up.

In the literature on sexuality in Western societies, the historicization of sexuality is an important element in understanding the transformations in the organization of sexuality, as well as the reactions to this. Sexuality in the twentieth century is characterized by a process that has been described as 'the transformation of intimacy' (cf. Giddens 1992). The severing of sexuality from reproduction (facilitated by birth control methods), the democratization of family life and the growth of 'expert systems' (for example the psychological advice-giving system, the authority it confers, and the fact that people put trust in it) have changed the foundations of intimate and marital relations. Unsettled by such social transformations, the practical and symbolic relations between women and men have shifted. For example, in various capitalist oriented societies, female professionals undermine the ideals of domestic motherhood and of husbands as breadwinners. Social transformations thus challenge various forms of female subordination and male domination. Moreover, the social organization and regulation of sexual beliefs and morals by religion, family, and/ or state, are undermined. In Chapter IV, I provide a historical sketch of colonial and postcolonial Kenya in order to understand similar processes. This is important, as sexuality studies on African societies do not usually historicize their subject, apart from studies on same-sex relations (Epprecht 2008).

During my research, many young professionals explained their lifestyle choices in relation to, and sometimes in opposition to, the lives of their parents. Whereas previously conjugal love was framed by normative common sense, religious tradition and jurisprudence and traditional customary law, their definitions of love diverged from these institutionalizations. They mentioned two fundamental differences between their own and their parents' generation. Whereas for their parents conjugal love entailed a lifelong commitment not only to a spouse but to an entire family, a defining feature of contemporary love is that intimacy is sought as a means to self-realization. Second, whereas their parents identified themselves through family relationships and ethnicity, younger generations take a different direction. As the authority of conventional ways of living is increasingly undermined, lifestyle choices – the choices people make between competing practices of everyday living – become the very core of how they identify themselves. Young professionals are inclined to enter relationships that centre on the pursuit of hip lifestyles. Other factors which distinguish their generation from the older generation are the general tendency towards the 'democratization' of relations (the waning of the moral authority of older men) and the focus on the nuclear family as opposed to the extended family. The emergence of a youth culture progressively legitimizes intimacy with the other sex as an intrinsic feature of socialization into adulthood. The autonomy of couples has grown with the increase in college attendance by young women and men, and has continued as jobs provide financial, and hence social, independence.

As a result, sexuality, in the sense of one's own sexuality, also becomes a way to identify oneself, as the relationship between gender and sexuality becomes more personalized by the weakening of the institutional organizations of sexuality. Sexuality, then, comes to function as a 'malleable feature of self, a prime connecting point between body, self-identity and social norms' (Giddens 1992: 15). These new spaces are explored by young professionals, consciously and unconsciously. In their biographical narratives, presented in this study, intimacy is a defining aspect of their sexuality. Companionship, egalitarianism and mutual sexual pleasure have come to characterize their relationships. Similarly, Smith (2001) shows how young women and men in Nigeria increasingly insist on choosing their own marriage partners and how ideas of love are reshaping their perceptions of relationships and marriage (see also Bochrow 2005; Larkin 1997). Historicizing sexuality is crucial to understanding contemporary phenomena, such as the cosmopolitan young professionals in Nairobi.

Methodological aspects of sexuality research

During my research I was often asked by colleagues and other professionals how I was going to 'make them talk', how I imagined that men would confide in me, how I would cope with the inevitable situation when a person would expect 'more' (meaning an erotic encounter), and other remarks that questioned the possibility of conducting research into African people's intimate lives. The so-called great taboo is not insurmountable. Sexuality research should not be viewed lightly as talking about people's intimate lives can be intrusive. On the other hand, I do not believe that it is any less intrusive to ask people about their financial situation. Conducting research on sexuality caused uneasiness as well as curiosity among both colleagues and non-scholars, which demonstrates that in this field in particular, it is vital to clearly define the position of the researcher vis-à-vis the participants and the research process (Abramson 1992; Kulick 1997).

Before setting out on the journey of how to research sex and sexuality, I would like to mention that I believe we need to acknowledge our limitations as social scientists. Our data mainly consists of people's reports on their sexual desires, conduct and experiences. This is not only due to the particularly ephemeral nature of sex (see Introduction, note 9) but also because of the limitations of ethnographic research on sexual practices. Ralph Bolton initiated a debate concerning the quality of sex research where a researcher does not seriously participate and observe (1992). Bolton's argument rests upon the premise that definitions of sex in general and of sexual practices in particular are mediated both by culture and by individual respondents' particular understandings, making questionnaires and other modes of verbal reporting suspect. Consequently, the physical facts of sex are considered as factual and potentially knowable through participant observation. However, Paul Abramson contends that participant observation is not immune to the distorting effect of lies, partial truths and misunderstandings that cloud our knowledge about our own sexual practices and those of others. His solution is intensive ethnographic triangulation – the use of multiple sources of information and longitudinal follow-up (1992, see also chapter nine in Lyons and Lyons 2004) – with which I agree. Despite these challenges, sex(uality) is important to people's being and knowing and therefore continues to be an important research matter, as Malinowski reminds us.

In February 2001 I set out to study sex and sexuality in Nairobi for a period of one year. I had devised a research strategy that enabled me to place personal narratives within the social context of Nairobi. It involved a way of understanding interviews as 'text in context' (Willemse 2007), paying particular attention to non-verbal gestures, silences, omissions and different ways of telling the same story over time and in different circumstances. In this way I assembled biographical narratives, which meant maintaining a self-reflexive questioning of myself as the researcher.

Researching sex and sexuality: research places and practices

The research started with people – teenagers at that time – who had participated in my MA research carried out in 1997/8 on AIDS and sexuality.[16] Through them and their friends, other people became involved. In March 2001 I wrote a 'letter to the editor' of the popular *Saturday Magazine*, the pull-out section of the *Daily Nation*, saying how much I appreciated their work and explaining my own interests. I mentioned that I would like to meet with young professionals for interviews on contemporary life in Nairobi. I received forty-two answers. I then met with thirty-seven of the people who had responded for a cup of coffee. For various reasons it turned out that a few did not want to continue any further, so I ended up pursuing the research with twenty-six of them. I explained during the first meeting that my aim was to study love and sexual relations and that, as such, I would like to follow them in their daily lives. Additional participants, known to the original participants, later joined in.

The interviews consisted of one-on-one discussions between each participant and myself. I was affiliated with the University of Nairobi where I had a small office on the campus and at first I tried to meet with people there, but that did not work. Working from the office was problematic perhaps because it gave me too much of the status of a scholar, or perhaps because it was too official; whatever the reason, it was difficult to get beyond a short awkward dialogue. Therefore I relocated the meetings to public spaces like coffee bars. Meeting at a small table in a crowded bar created the intimacy that was needed for an engaged discussion. From then on I met with people in downtown Nairobi, in the gardens of bars a short way outside the city centre, at their home, and sometimes at my home. Many people saw the process as a joint undertaking, and would sometimes phone me to make an appointment because they had 'news', to give me articles they had kept for me, or to introduce me to friends who could be informative about a particular topic.

The research was carried out in English, which is the first or second language of these young professionals and also my second language. The majority of interviews were not taped, but were recorded in writing immediately after the meeting. I started by dutifully taping the first few meetings but found the technology too disruptive. People were very conscious of the tape recorder and it made them hold back. I began to memorize the meetings so that I could write them up immediately afterwards. This method turned out better than I initially thought possible. I developed a way of recollecting the discussions by memorizing key words that came up during the meeting. I was able to effectively remember the sequence of a discussion; and I found that if certain issues were especially important I could remember them in great detail. This obviously entails a 'subjective' selection by the researcher and therefore I always consulted with the interviewees afterwards to check that I had represented our discussions properly. In some cases I did go on to tape interviews if people were comfortable with it; meeting at my home proved to be a good setting for doing this. When some participants realized that the research entailed interviews with other people, they would ask what these others had told me. Several people asked me to organize a group discussion, and in December 2001 several people had lunch at my house followed by a group discussion. I teased them beforehand by saying that they had to play open cards, as I would know whether what they said was plausible. It turned out to be a success; if I had not left in February we would have met again.

The study involved twenty-four women and twenty-five men; they can be divided into two groups of research participants. The first group consists of people with whom a rapport was established to such an extent that I was confident I could build on and interpret what they told me. With the second group, I was not quite sure how to interpret their accounts, or I felt I did not have enough understanding of them to be confident of drawing conclusions. However, the data from this second group complements the other data. The research was conducted from February 2001 to February 2002. In January and February 2004 I presented the twelve biographical vignettes from my manuscript to each participant individually, so that they could comment on the accuracy and give their consent for me to use the material. I also met with the other participants to discuss how I used their narratives. With six women and five men I continued to discuss the first drafts of the chapters by e-mail. They all reacted differently, from being 'curious what I had made out of them', to the more indifferent 'it's okay, I trust you to write an honest book'; but everybody who read their portraits and chapters responded positively. Sometimes I had to change details, but none of them asked me to make major changes. The women all read the accounts meticulously, while only a few men did so; the majority of men were not inclined to read and responded by saying they trusted me to do my job well. For example, Tom (aged 28 in 2004) explained that he did 'not want to be confronted with facts he was trying to forget'. All the participants asked me to publish the book to sell it in Nairobi because 'this is stuff that we can no longer ignore – we, the young, but also them, the older generation' (Laura, aged 23).

Researching sex and sexuality: collection and validity of data

In this study, I make use of biographical narratives. These are personal narratives of women and men, which give an insight into their ideas, behaviour and justification regarding love and sex, complemented by information gained through my direct observation of them. Research on sexual relations and experiences of sex has a practical limitation as the data is based on reports, and opportunities for participant observation are limited. How, then, to collect valid information? First, whatever people communicate about their sexual lives is information, even though they leave out certain topics, emphasize others, or boast about yet others. As Plummer has stated, people's narratives 'do not in fact take us towards the Sexual Truth: towards a full, absolute, real grasping of our essential, inner sexual nature. ... [Instead], *sexual stories can be seen as issues to be investigated in their own right*' (1995: 5, emphasis in original). The various kinds of information given by a participant need to be interpreted against the background of their daily practices and overall life. There is a high chance of receiving answers that interviewees consider to be socially desirable or acceptable, especially during the first meetings when the interviewee and the researcher do not yet know each other so well. Socially desirable answers are not necessarily problematic if the information is not taken to be a final statement, the end result of the study; in fact, it is the first step in the research process of gathering data.

Secondly, it is essential to create a 'rapport'. Instead of focussing on sexuality immediately, it is fruitful to approach the topic via other related topics, in order to create the necessary trust to allow the interviewee to speak openly. The young professionals were first asked about a number of issues before we arrived at the topic of sexuality. First came general intro- ductory discussions: about family background, reflections on childhood, puberty and adulthood, career and lifestyle, and religion. These first sets of interviews took on average three to five meetings. When I felt there was enough rapport, the focus of the interviews shifted to relationships and the meaning of marriage, sexual relationships and practices, abstinence and the meaning of sex, sexual pleasure and worries about sex and sexual- ity. This second set of interviews took five to ten meetings. These inter- views mostly took place over a period of four to nine months, and with a few individuals up to eleven months, in 2001/2002. The interviews were supplemented by participant observation of the people at their homes, with their families, in their social lives with friends, on social occasions like weddings and funerals and, most importantly, in the context of Nai- robi nightlife. The information on sexual behaviour gathered through this methodology is only based on reports, as the participant observation has to stop, so to speak, at the bedroom door.

Thirdly, it was important to develop ways of substantiating the consis- tencies and inconsistencies in the narratives and, eventually, of bringing each person's set of interviews together to build an overall picture. For example, it was important to remember the names of the different part- ners that people dated in order to track the accounts of each particular relationship or experience. Another approach to substantiating the narra- tives was to study the correlation between the narratives that people gave and their actual behaviour. This is where the importance of participant observation can be seen. For example, Laura (aged 23) always gave the impression that she had a deferential attitude towards men, talking about how she learned to 'respect' men regardless of their behaviour. However, seeing her at work and in bars, I got a very different impression. This ap- parent contradiction was a useful starting point for us to begin discussing her attitude towards men.

The nature of this research can be called 'dialogical', which is a require- ment in collecting valid data. The ethnographic interview, in the spirit of Bakthin (1981), has become more dialogic than monologic: anthro- pological knowledge may be seen as something produced in interaction, instead of being 'extracted' from people. The importance of a dialogical approach lies in the space it creates for the presence of sensitivities, shame, doubts and reflection. It is common to find that being engaged in a research process can confront participants with issues that they have not previously translated into language, and that the dialogues may lead to further reflection. In this study, the interviews became a sounding board for the people involved. Many of the participants, after some time, asked my opinion. For example, when I asked Tom (aged 26) why a certain date had 'dogged' (cheated on) him, he responded: 'I dunno, tell me, you are the expert on my life by now'. It was a joke, of course, but he was serious as well, because he was wondering why he had been unable up to that point to have a lasting relationship. He had previously hinted that he wanted to know my opinion about him, but had not done so openly. After this interview he would jokingly call me 'psych' and called our meetings 'consultations'. With women, the atmosphere was more open to engaging in reflective discussions as 'women amongst each other'.

An unmarried with partner, non-Kenyan, white female young professional

> The ethnographer, like the artist, is engaged in a special kind of vision quest through which a specific interpretation of the human condition, an entire sensibility, is forged. Our medium, our canvas, is 'the field', a place both proximate and intimate (because we have lived some part of our lives there) as well as forever distant and unknowable 'other' (because our own destinies lie elsewhere). In the act of 'writing culture', what emerges is always a highly subjective, partial and fragmentary – but also deeply felt and personal – record of human lives based on eyewitness and testimony. The act of witnessing is what lends our work its moral character. So-called participant observation has a way of drawing the ethnographer into spaces of human life … which draws others [by reading] there as well, making them party to the act of witnessing. (Scheper-Hughes 1992: VII)

For generations, ethnographers pretended there was no ethnographer in the field, behaving as if they were invisible. In so doing, the ethnographer did not have to examine critically the subjective bases of the questions s/he asked (and the ones s/he failed to ask), the kinds of data s/he collected and the theories s/he developed. At the end of the 1970s and early 1980s, a new generation of ethnographers emerged, who problematized the idea of objective research in relation to the formation of data and knowledge, by critically reflecting on their own role in the research process (Clifford and Marcus 1986). They maintained that qualitative research cannot easily be disassociated from the researcher, as the personality, status and background of the researcher has an effect on the communication with the people involved; and also that the style and interest of the researcher shapes the interpretation of the information flow. My being a female, unmarried, non-Kenyan, white young professional fashioned the course of this research in particular ways.

First of all, I believe that the way I presented my research was of importance in being accepted among such a critical group of young adults, who are somewhat sceptical about the scores of foreign researchers sweeping over Kenya. It annoyed them that Westerners came to Kenya to study 'African problems', thereby continuing the cycle of imagining and representing Africa as problematic or hopeless. When I introduced myself as 'intending to write a book on contemporary life in Nairobi, focussing on relationships', or as 'wanting to write a book about your lives, your perspectives about your generation', they appreciated the fact that I did not wish to focus on a 'problem like AIDS'. It was a more positive approach, which softened their sceptical attitude.

Secondly, being a woman turned out to be positive since it enabled me to talk to both women and men. It was easier as a woman to approach other women and to become personally involved with them. It would have been difficult for them to share intimate experiences with a male researcher. However, it took a longer time on average for the women to speak about their private sexuality than it did for the men. I found that men rarely discussed intimate issues with anyone, but they said they trusted me. The majority of men claimed to have told me about things that they had never shared with others. It was 'not done' to share such sensitive information, and when opening up to close friends they addressed concrete problems, rather than feelings and thoughts, which is what I was interested in. There was one man with whom I continued to conduct the research despite the difficulties he seemed to experience about my being a younger woman. He had taken it upon himself to tell me about 'life in Kenya' in an authoritative manner and refused to answer my questions about his personal life. Piece by piece I gathered his biography together, sometimes via his friends. I never lost the impression that he found it difficult to speak to me because of my gender and Western background; nonetheless, he never abandoned the research.

Third, my situation – being under 30, unmarried, but living with my partner – represented exactly the position of my research group. If Victor and I had been married, we would have belonged to a different category of young adults and that might have caused a barrier. Like them, we had not yet become 'serious' about life by taking on the full responsibilities of marriage, starting a family and 'slowing down'. We were also seen as free to participate in the nightlife. My relationship with Victor also worked out positively for my research work as it provided me with the status of being engaged. Throughout the course of the research, Victor supported my work and his public role as my partner. I included Victor in the research by mentioning him in my tales. Many people also met him. In this way I made sure it was obvious that we had a 'committed' relationship, as a way of preventing interest in me as a lover. Victor met them as my 'friends'. He participated to an extent in the research by attending weddings, parties and other occasions with me, as well as the Sunday lunches when we had our group discussions. At times he would distance himself, especially when he knew that women were watching him and me to see how we acted as a couple. I was clear about the fact that I would not become emotionally involved with any of the participants beyond the level of friendship and I made it clear that I was engaged in a research process. I would, for example, joke every now and then by exclaiming that the 'researcher reports on herself!' I suspect that some of the men were erotically curious about this '*mzungu*' ('white') woman at the beginning of the research, but they gave up any ideas of an intimate relationship once the details about the research became clear.

Being a non-Kenyan was probably one of my most useful attributes for the purposes of the research. Not being a Kenyan meant that they assumed I would not judge them according to Kenyan morals and ideologies. Moreover, being Dutch worked out even better, as they had an image of the Netherlands as one of the most liberal societies with regard to non-marital sexuality and other morally disputed pleasures such as drugs. Being non-Kenyan and Dutch gave me the aura of being liberal, not easily shocked and possibly a little defiant with regard to moral expectations.

Being white, however, did prove to be a liability every now and then. As I explained above, my interviewees had an ambiguous attitude towards Western societies, and with my white skin I came to represent 'the West'. With a few of the people who answered my letter in the *Saturday Magazine*, I got into such a polemical debate that we could not resolve it; I tried to tone down the political by searching for a more personal exchange about our lives, but it was to no avail, and we had to cease working together. With those I got to know better and for whom I represented 'the West' only every now and then, it did not disturb our relationship. The racial divide was an issue, especially with those with whom I had not established an easy rapport. Discussing sensitive racial and 'westernization' matters became part of the research, exactly because it moved beyond an anonymous context.

Being a young professional myself worked out very positively, as we could identify with each other in age and social category – we were 'yuppies'. Moreover, the idea of researcher and participants being alike contributed in a positive way to their idea of a global subculture, composed of certain lifestyles and of a group of people with a higher level of education. At the appropriate moment I also let them know about my previous relationship with a Kenyan man. This always triggered a new and more engaging stage in our relationship. Women reacted – almost invariably – as it was another example of solidarity, besides being a fellow woman: 'Oh, so I don't have to tell you about our men'. Men were more intrigued and were fascinated by the idea of a mixed couple: 'Ah, so you know [about Kenyan men]'. It also provided a way of overcoming some of the sensitivities about our different backgrounds.

In order to be able to construct arguments about this group of young professionals, I looked for consistency across the sample and coherence of my analysis, despite the differences among people. The way in which I found participants (the snowball effect and letter to the editor) had the effect of making this sample more homogenous, but then this homogeneity is a significant factor in this study. Furthermore, this study cannot always grasp 'what people [are] doing but what they believe or claim should be done' and what they believe they have done (Lévi-Strauss 1969 [1949]: 144). I tried to determine why it was meaningful for some things to be said and for others not to be said. I can only put together this knowledge on the basis of people's self-perceptions, inner struggles, anxieties, pleasures, and the dreams and hopes they provided about themselves. My interpretative authority is paradoxical: it evolves from attentive listening in the hope that sharing such knowledge will grant young professionals greater autonomy, while I exercise my authority in order to increase or restore the authority of the young professionals in interpreting themselves. According to Lyons and Lyons (2004), however, the fact that 'dialogic' and participatory anthropological fieldwork may be considered as 'conscription' – in that it reaffirms existing hierarchies – is an inevitable ethnographic and theoretical feature. Such is the nature of ethnographic research.

Notes

1. See for example Evans-Pritchard 1950; Forde 1954; Kenyatta 1938; Leakey 1977; Mair 1953.
2. See for example LeVine and LeVine 1966; Mair 1969: Molnos 1973; Nyamwaya and Parkin 1987; Paulme 1963.
3. Kenyatta was writing in the context of the European ideal of adolescent chastity. His conclusion that Kikuyu premarital sexual practices allowed adequate release and healthy pleasure tells us more about the moral debates of the time than about people's experiences.
4. An example is White's famous book on prostitution in colonial Nairobi about how women got by in a city where they were not allowed to live and work (1990a). Shaw wrote about

the Kikuyu ethnic group in the context of colonialism, with a considerable part dedicated to female sexuality such as virginity and clitoridectomy (1995). A remarkable book has been written by Steeves about the recurrent theme of adolescent secondary school rape by boys, focussing on the media representation of a gang rape of over seventy girls where nineteen girls died (1997). Besides books, there have been various articles addressing sexuality, such as Nelson (1987) about urban women's sexual lives in poor areas and how (occasional) sex for sale was considered, or Amory (1998) about men who have sex with men on the Swahili coast.

5. See the documentation by WHO, UNAIDS, and other nongovernmental organizations; see also journals like *AIDS, AIDS CARE, AIDS and Behaviour, Population and Development Review* and *Social Science and Medicine*, among others. Far more knowledge is being generated by different nongovernmental organizations but this is, unfortunately, not always published, with the exception of interesting studies conducted by the Guttmacher Institute, the Population Council Kenya, and others.

6. See for example Maticka-Tyndale et al. 2005; Ojwang and Maggwa 1991; Prazak 2001 on adolescents; Bauni and Jarabi 2000; Nzioka 1996 on condom use; and Kielmann 1997 on prostitution.

7. Among others, see Arnfred 2004; Booth 2004; Huygens et al. 1996; Packard and Epstein 1991; Patton 1992; Salo and Gqola 2006; Schoepf 1991; Seidel 1993; Silberschmidt 2001; Spronk 2005a, 2005b; Stillwaggon 2003.

8. They started their undertaking with a thorough review of a diverse range of older ethnographic literature about different African societies. More importantly, their first paper engaged with debates on the stereotyping, racializing or condemning of 'African' or 'black sexuality' (Caldwell et al. 1989a). They observed how certain presumptions, despite being well-intentioned attempts to reduce perceived racialism, are pervasive and subtle. However, they then go on to write about 'sexuality in Africa' as a self-evident concept (Caldwell et al. 1989a, 1989b, 1991a, 1991b, 1992, 1995, 1997; Caldwell 2000).

9. Their historical analysis relies on the writings of others that may have been coloured by a special paradigm, such as structural functionalism with its problems of being unable to take social transformation into account. Their initial attempt can be interpreted as a call for more ethnographic research on contemporary sexualities in diverse (culturally as well as economically) contexts. Caldwell et al. have not followed up on their 'African sexuality thesis' and continue to study sexual behaviour from mainly an epidemiological point of view.

10. Westerners know how to speak and write in ways that are politically correct in the light of colonial legacies and contemporary poverty related explanations regarding sexuality. Nevertheless, a paternalistic attitude is present, often unconsciously but sometimes intentionally.

11. Cindy Patton analyses the process of how AIDS became defined as a health threat, which she calls 'the invention of African AIDS'. This process was generated by medical and social scientists, journalists and editors, politicians and bureaucrats in the United States and European countries. The 'African paradigm' was based on three assumptions. First, there was the assumption that one could speak of 'Africa' as a single entity. There was no room to acknowledge the emerging evidence that infection levels varied greatly among continental and national regions, and among cities and different groups of people. Second, there was the idea that Africans could not diagnose AIDS correctly; for example, African physicians' warnings that the first test kits could not distinguish between HIV and malaria infection were dismissed. For years, Western researchers accepted the inflated statistics. The third assumption was related to colonial constructions of 'dark' Africa as the source of un-civilization and vice, usually taking the form of terrible diseases. AIDS became synonymous with natural disaster, un-development and cultural peculiarities. Several scholars have pointed out how such constructions were easily revived in the attempt to explain the

heterosexual AIDS pandemic (Gilman 1988; Sabatier 1988; Watney 1990, among others).

12. For example, trends in HIV infection or multi-partnered sexual relations detected in large surveys are of interest in framing new questions, such as 'why do certain men engage in multi-partnered sex and what is the difference between them and men who don't?' It could be argued that in a complex psychological way, feelings of failure are compensated for by having sex (Campbell 2003). Such a conceptualization of sexuality – as an essential aspect of one's social identity, shaped by both social and cultural factors – has recently begun to emerge in research on African societies.

13. The integration of the AIDS paradigm into the development/health discourse happened thanks to a widely cited article circulated by the WHO (World Health Organization) in the late 1980s (see Booth 2004: 50). The article was written by Piot (now the head of the joint UN Programme on AIDS); Mann (the first director of the WHO's Global Programme on AIDS); and Plummer (the director of the AIDS/STD project in Nairobi), three influential people in the administration of AIDS organizations. See Booth 2004 for an interesting analysis.

14. As I experienced during a panel at the 'Sexuality Beyond Boundaries' International Conference in 1997 in Amsterdam, in 2003 during the 'Sex and Secrecy' International Conference in Johannesburg, and through personal communication with Kenyan and other scholars from Africa. The miscommunication and irritation often arose from Westerners reproducing racial stereotypes and Africans reacting defensively to the slightest hint of racial stereotyping.

15. For example, certain married men in Dakar identify themselves as heterosexual because their masculine sexual identity is related to their social identity as fathers and husbands. They also engage in receptive anal intercourse with other men, generally considered effeminate, hence discursively non-masculine (Niang et al. 2003). See Morgan and Wieringa (2005) about women's narratives and same sex relationships in different African societies. See Murray and Roscoe (1998) for a similar discussion about men.

16. From October 1997 until August 1998 I conducted research for my MA about discourses on AIDS and sexuality among middle class adolescents (Spronk 1999).

CHAPTER II

YOUNG PROFESSIONALS: EMBLEMS OF SOCIAL TRANSFORMATION

The word [transformation] consists of two parts: the prefix 'trans', which is the Latin for across, the other side...; and 'form', which means to give structure to, to create, to bring forth. In its deepest structure, then, the word 'transformation' means to start creating where you are going.

Antjie Krog[1]

This chapter addresses how changes in sexuality provide a link between young professionals and Kenya's social transformations. I elaborate on this by providing a brief history of the social organization of sexuality from colonial times to the beginning of the twenty-first century. Placing young professionals in the context of social change in the twentieth century demonstrates how this group in part embodies the results of changes in gender, sexuality and culture. The lives of the group of young professionals reflect a continuum of transformation that began with their grandparents and parents. Each of these three generations has in its time been modern, in the sense that it has chosen, to different extents, a different approach to life from the one that was commonly expected (cf. Thomas 2006). These processes and their effects on gender relations reveal the reconfiguration of sexuality in Kenya that is marked by both continuity and rupture.

This chapter analyses these transformation processes by focussing, in the first part, on how societal processes have affected gender relations and sexuality and, in the second part, on how young professionals, as a group, embody these social transformations. I will provide a brief sketch, highlighting trends within the various historical processes without going into detail about region or ethnic group. Kenya's cultural diversity and the different responses to historical processes will not be examined, as the aim is to explore how processes make and transform lifeworlds. Because of the naively ahistorical trend in the study of sexuality in Africa – sex is either seen as particularly embedded in 'traditions', or anthropologists become lost in what Geschiere derisively calls 'Anthropology-land' (1999b) – I give a brief history of sexuality in order to understand the emergent lives of young professionals. In the second part of this chapter, I further describe the lifestyles of young professionals. One of the most striking effects of social transformation in the context of colonialism and postcolonialism is the contentious issue of cultural heritage. It will become clear that young professionals are implicated in a complex process consisting of accommodation, appropriation and resistance to both local and non-local ways of life, and this includes balancing sexuality (as central to self-expression) with matters concerning cultural heritage.

Young professionals are breaking down old boundaries while exploring new ones. They cause a shift in existing social hierarchies – between elders and youth, women and men – which are experienced as the fundaments of community and culture by the moral authorities, hence the volatile reactions of the wider society. These reactions can be understood as a response to the Nairobian society 'in flux': 'people's awareness of being involved in open ended global flows seems to trigger a search for fixed orientation points and action frames, as well as determined efforts to affirm old and construct new boundaries' (Geschiere and Meyer 1998: 602). Therefore, young professionals, more than other groups, make visible how Kenyan society has changed over the last century.

Sexuality and societal transformations

Gender and sexuality in colonial times

Nairobi was founded by and for settlers in 1899. Unlike other capitals in settler societies, Nairobi had no industrial base, as the wealth of Kenya lay in its agricultural sector. A system of 'hut tax' was introduced to coerce the much needed black Kenyan labour to work for cash on the settler farms and for the colonial infrastructure. The migrant labour system prohibited women from following their husbands to the urban centres, so the 'native' areas in Nairobi became occupied by single men. The institutionalization of official racial segregation was completed with the creation of Pangani, a neighbourhood in Nairobi with barracks for single 'African' men only. Through a system of identity cards, black Kenyan labourers were allowed to enter and travel in Nairobi. In short, while Nairobi was being organized along lines of racial difference, the colony as a whole was becoming segregated by gender.

Colonial administrators in the service of the imperial power had a number of different reasons for keeping women out of the city. To maintain an economy based on low-paid migrant labour, they needed women to reproduce the labour force at little or no cost to employers or the state, and this could most easily be done by keeping women in rural areas. Furthermore, the low male wages were in fact subsidized by rural women who did much of the work in subsistence agriculture. Another 'imperial interest' in keeping women out of Nairobi was related to cooperative agreements between the colonial administration and some rural chiefs, after many of the latter had been removed from the best agricultural land. These rural rulers agreed to send their sons to work for the British, and in return the British had to help them to maintain their wives and daughters at home. If the elders lost control over young women's labour, sexuality and progeny, they lost their ability to use the promise of marriage and the importance of children and inheritance to pull young men back home.[2] Nevertheless, women started to move to Nairobi as early as 1900, thus manipulating the colonial system to their own advantage (Bujra 1975; Presley 1992; White 1990a).

From the beginning of the twentieth century, male labour migration took place from the reserves and later from villages of origin as well. More and more men were forced to migrate, both in order to pay hut tax and to make a living, as more and more people lost their land. The massive male labour migration was needed to provide labour on the settler farms, to establish the colonial infrastructure, which entailed, for example, road construction and erosion control measures, and also to maintain the colonial capital Nairobi. For example, by 1928, '40% of adult males were absent from some Central Province districts', while between 1940 and 1950, 'military recruitment and wage labour removed most able-bodied men' (Robertson 1997: 85, 110). The effect of male labour migration and other colonial policies was that '[T]he exploitative burden of colonialism in Kenya fell heavily on women, who, in addition to an increased agricultural workload at home, did much of the forced labour on roads and farms, while their authority structures were either ignored or disrespected by British administrators and missionaries' (Robertson 1997: 246; see also House-Midamba 1990; Lonsdale 1986: 183; Stichter 1987).

In the following quotation, an elderly lady recounted the situation as follows:

After Nguiri [a battle between British and local residents in Embu], when we were defeated by the Europeans, the men left and we had to do men's work. We had to do all the clearing and heavy digging before the rains, watch over the livestock in the fields. We also had to repair the broken fences around the kraals and homestead. Life became very difficult. Wambugi wa Njanja, born circa 1880. (Nyaggah 2003: 1)

Practically speaking, women thus took over 'male work' like clearing land before planting season, digging roads and clearing forests as demanded by the colonial administration, because men were absent for the larger part of the year.[3] This meant a shift in the gendered division of labour because women had to assume many male roles. In short, though the patriarchal ideology prescribed that men should be the heads of the household, men became breadwinners, providers who were absent for the larger part of the year, and certainly not active heads of the household and integrated members of the daily practices of the household. This change caused a major shift in conjugal relationships. Since detailed biographies or analyses about these changes are not available, I can only speculate on what the effects on relations between wives and husbands were. The following account tells a tale that is likely to be indicative:

> I was barely 15, but I was encouraged to migrate to Nairobi by my friends and relatives who told me they could help me get a job in the city. The salary of between fifty and hundred shillings sounded good. Once in town, I landed to [*sic*] my first job in a warehouse where I worked for nearly a year. In the next few years, I moved from job to job. After working for five years I married my long-time girlfriend from my village. At that time, I hoped to be able to raise a family from my income, educate my children beyond primary school, buy a farm back in Kiambu and lead a happy old age under my children's care. However, my troubles started almost immediately after the birth of my first child, Muthoni, when I lost my job and could not find another one. I started a business brewing and selling traditional beer. But I had no experience in business and I lost all my money. At this time, my problems weighed heavily on me and I started drinking. We had to depend on my wife's vegetable business to keep the family running. I started drinking *chang'aa* [illegal distilled liquor], I was alone in Nairobi and my marriage dissolved. Kamau [man, no age cited]. (Nyaggah 2003: 16)

Kamau's narrative acquires more weight when read against the background of White's book on women migrating to and settling in Nairobi despite the pass laws against women. As White points out, the unequal ratio of men to women, the inability of men to bring a wife to the city, the absence of other cash generating activities for women, and the division of labour by gender all created a situation where single men would look for women to do their domestic work in the towns. This meant that selling sex, often packaged with other 'domestic' services, was a relatively common occupation among these early urban women. The absence of men from their nuclear family was likely to cause estrangement between wife and husband, exacerbated by the fact that many men were having unofficial relationships in the city. Similarly, husbands also lost sight of their wives' lives and it is quite possible women had lovers as well.[4] When women took over male roles, it is probable that male power lost its hegemony, which men therefore needed to re-establish every time they went home, perhaps by force. Eventually, men's hegemony was also eroded on a symbolical level:

> Although men had the requisite agricultural skills to do plantation work, both the loss of control over their daily activities and the knowledge that their critical tasks at home were not being accomplished made this forced labour a burden. In addition, they experienced the dynamics of a racially stratified society for the first time, in which a circumcised man was not given the respect he was due in his culture. (Nyaggah 2003: 11)

Now, in the absence of their husbands, wives were also obliged to settle disputes and redistribute resources (on South Africa, see Moody 2001). This meant a further change in the structure of authority.

As well as male migration, the migration of both women and men to the white settler farms also occurred. According to Nyaggah, the change in gender roles on settler farms was more immediate and drastic. Men were more directly challenged by changes in gender patterns, since they now had to work alongside women in the farmlands, which had formerly been an exclusively male preserve. The customary gendered division of labour disintegrated further and women gained more space for negotiation. Furthermore, women's negotiating power was enhanced by the fact that nuclear families had become the common pattern on the plantations. The absence of the lineage kinship members, who monitored family decisions and who were a constraining factor, gave women more space (Nyaggah 2003: 12). All in all, it seems safe to conclude that these transformations in gender roles and their effects on marital relations caused a volatile situation which gave rise to conflict between wives and husbands. '[S]ocio-economic change left men with a patriarchal ideology bereft of its legitimizing activities' (Silberschmidt 2001: 657). It is probable that conjugal relationships deteriorated in this context. 'The decision-making authority for men was no longer based on his dominant role as the main source of family support. Women negotiated for greater input into the decision making since they were also working in the fields with men and earning remittances' (Nyaggah 2003: 11; see also Cornwall 2003). Furthermore, women's increasing role in trade since early 1900 (Mutongi 2007; Robertson 1997) also contributed to the transformation in gender roles.[5]

In essence, when the practical relations between women and men changed, the symbolic relations between the genders transformed as well. 'Wifehood' and 'husbandhood' had changed in practical terms over the years as wives and husbands had taken on different roles. In symbolic terms, a range of adjustments of the basic notions of femininity and masculinity became unavoidable. Exactly how these adjustments occurred requires more in-depth research. It is likely that, for example, the duties of wifehood were extended from typical household ones to include business activities to supplement the family's income. As a result, women's self-perceptions about womanhood became oriented beyond the household. By conducting business, joining missions to pursue education, or enrolling in plantation work (Kanogo 2005), women functioned outside the extended family oriented household and became more independent. I do not mean that this was a process of emancipation, but more that it was a logical outcome in the context of change.

The Christianization process in Kenya also affected the cultural organization of sexuality to a large extent (Ahlberg 1994; Mutongi 2007). Protestant missionaries, in particular, condemned certain customs, which they presumed were evil and had to be eradicated. There was a specific ban on initiation rites, especially female circumcision (Thomas 2003).[6] Missionaries were also preoccupied with maternal and child health, polygamy or premarital sexual practices without sexual intercourse – like *ngweko* among the Kikuyu – with the aim of eradicating 'repugnant' practices or 'improving health'. In general, Christianization focussed on domesticity in an attempt to exert control and induce change, thereby defining race and class hierarchies and drawing sexual boundaries (Thomas 2003: 18).[7] According to Beidelman, the impact of missionaries on the beliefs and practices of Kenyans was more far reaching than the influence of colonial administration and business (Beidelman 1982). Similarly, Comaroff and Comaroff (1992: 258) speak of an 'ideological onslaught' to describe how missionaries in Africa, as self-styled bearers of European civilization, aimed to reconstruct the everyday social and moral worlds of Africans. The aim of the missionaries to change overall beliefs and practices was based on particular patriarchal notions of gender and family life. These Western notions, which defined men as providers and women as domestic wives, disrupted previous gender roles (which were more complementary regarding the provisions for the household or which prescribed women more public roles); they were 'essentialist, binary constructs of gender and generation dominant in the modern west [that] are by no means universal' (Comaroff and Comaroff 1992: 78). The spread of Christianity, together with capitalist processes, has led to a conceptual and moral redefinition of gender roles, sexuality and relationships between women and men.

The patriarchal gender and racial ideology of missionaries and colonial administrators particularly affected women through its focus on men (House-Midamba 1990; Mutongi 2007). The education opportunities provided by missions excluded women, in the same way as women were excluded from participating in cash crop production. The negotiation or

enforcing of colonial rule, the installation of male chiefs – even though female chiefs existed – and the installation of customary law have all excluded
women to a large extent. Colonialists were not always aware of women
councils and women were not considered when regulations were enforced
that affected what had been their domain, such as female circumcision and
reproduction. Thomas's analysis of the 'politics of the womb' brilliantly
shows how, through concerns about race and sexuality, reproduction became a crucial site of state intervention and popular debate and how Western gender ideology was introduced in colonial Kenya (Thomas 2003).

In a study of the Yoruba in Nigeria, Oyěwùmí (1997) goes so far as
to say that patriarchal notions of gender as we encounter them today in
Nigeria, and possibly elsewhere, are a product of colonial intervention.
She explores how the categorization of female and male into gender is
a relatively new phenomenon, as Yoruba society was based on age and
class hierarchies where both women and men held leadership roles. It is
beyond the scope of this study to explore this interesting hypothesis (see
also Sudarkasa 2005); it suffices to note that women were excluded from
the newly created colonial public sphere, on which the postcolonial nation
state was built. The newly independent state was built on certain legacies of male dominance, which were sometimes 'new' and at other times
a continuation of existing patterns, and which led to the 'wifization of
citizenship' of women (1997: 127). What I label patriarchal ideology and
gender roles therefore has its roots in historical entanglements. Oyěwùmí
rightly points out that perhaps the most lasting effect of relegating women
to a subordinate position may be its psychological effect on both women
and men and how this has come to inform their gendered sense of self
(Oyěwùmí 1997: 134). As I did not study this retrospectively, I focus on
this aspect of gender among present-day young professionals.

The 'falling apart' (Achebe 1996 [1958]) of the communal organizations and the subsequent decline of the power of the extended family was
a gradual process and one which varied according to region, ethnic group
and individual families. For example, the fertile lands of central Kenya
and the Rift Valley were more implicated in the processes described above
than other regions (see for example Moore 1996). These processes of
transformation, in turn, opened up new possibilities and new forms of
consciousness. The following account is an example of how change provides opportunities and gives rise to further changes:

> My childhood was spent in Murang'a, helping my parents work in their small five-
> acre plot of land where all the family sustenance was derived, and learning the value of
> hard work for survival. I knew about Nairobi because my father often travelled back
> and forth to Nairobi to sell potatoes. This was his way of earning the poll tax which

we had to pay the colonial government… Many of my friends had married and were raising families. I had not found someone I loved and my parents did not believe in arranged marriages, so I had not married. It was during this time that my older brother and I decided to go to Nairobi and try to trade there, instead of selling bananas wholesale we would sell them retail … I built my vegetable business next to this thriving restaurant in Kariakor. Ms. Wamwega [no age cited]. (Nyaggah 2003: 15)

Ms. Wamwega's success shows that societal transformations also implied the creation of opportunities, in this case for women. Moreover, it shows how social change was not only affected by colonial interventions, but by larger configurations of changes in ideas and/or individual decisions, such as the fact that her parents 'did not believe in arranged marriages'. Anthropologists now see colonialism as a process of struggle and negotiation rather than strictly one of progress or exploitation (Pels and Salemink 1999) or as a matrix of action (Bayart 2000: 234). This view allows one to see colonial societies as 'eclectic communities deeply divided by political frictions, class antagonism or competing cultural claims' and it places 'issues of gender and race or identity and status on center stage' (Gouda and Clancy-Smith 1998: 3). For example, colonial laws emphasizing individual subjectivity also created new possibilities for individuals who wanted to escape from the gerontocratic structures. Women used the colonial law to get divorced (House-Midamba 1990; Kanogo 2005). Similarly, because of the declining hegemony of the lineage (in correspondence with the declining hegemony of the indigenous moral system), couples that left their regional homes could live together in Nairobi without being sanctioned. Pamela's grandparents were such 'runaways' who later reconciled with their relatives. This brief overview may serve to highlight how processes of change during colonial and postcolonial times have affected intimate life in Kenya.

Gender and sexuality in postcolonial times

The parents of young professionals are commonly referred to as the 'Uhuru generation', the ones who took over from the British and worked to build the postcolonial nation state.[8] They were the ones who maintained a vision of a modernizing Kenyan society. The post-independence narratives on progress and, later, the global discourse on development in Africa, have sustained the idea of modernity as a linear process bringing forth a certain degree of global uniformity with regard to a functioning nation state. That this did not come about has become self-evident. In view of this fact, Ferguson describes how Zambian copper belt workers understood global modernity as characterized not by 'a simple, Eurocentric uniformity but by coexisting and complex socio-cultural alternatives', before scholars came to the same conclusions (1999: 252). For these workers, as for the majority of Kenyans, modernity was 'a shattering, compulsory socio-economic event' (ibid: 253). In reality, modernity is simply the result of capitalist transformation processes that for many have led to an intensification of the struggle for a living. A historical ethnography of modernity criticizes the unilineal and Eurocentric concept of modernization in the social sciences (cf. Geschiere et al. 2008).

The history of postcolonial Kenya is characterized by a process of steady urbanization and migration that separated families for shorter or longer periods of time.[9] At the dawn of independence, the peasant economy supplied more labour than the wage economy could absorb and this has been the case ever since. This unfavourable situation has further affected gender roles. Silberschmidt's work on impoverished rural men shows how processes of male labour migration affect male gender roles, ideologies and men's self-perceptions (2001). The negative spiral of landlessness, unemployment and endemic poverty affects men's feelings of self-worth, as they perceive themselves failing as husbands and fathers, and in general as falling short of being adequate men. This situation also tends to create conflicts between wives and husbands. Some men estrange themselves from their families by engaging in multi-partnered sexual relationships in order to compensate for their negative self-perception.

At the same time, women continue to search for independent work, like the women described by White (1990) and Kanogo (2005). Robertson's book on the history of the Nairobi bean trade documents the crucial roles played by women in feeding Nairobi throughout the twentieth century. Shifting marriage patterns, such as the rise of premarital pregnancy and divorce, made the bean trade more attractive for women, especially after the Second World War (Robertson 1997). Nelson (1987) describes a similar group of Kenyan women – the petty traders and small shopkeepers in Mathare Valley in Nairobi – and describes how commercialized sexual relations relate to normative ideas about sexuality. Both authors analyse how these women have largely come to identify themselves through their work, which implies a weakening in their identification with kinship groups or region. However, these studies do not discuss the mothers and fathers of the young professionals in this study, as these parents were in general white-collar workers and not labourers. There is a lack of literature about these middle classes, whose lives generally do not match the lives of poorer people.

One study does cover the parents of contemporary young professionals.[10] In 1979 Sharon Stichter conducted a large-scale study among urban middle classes. These women and men were employed in commerce, services and government, and among them male white-collar workers predominated. According to Stichter, the gender roles remained much the same as before, although she does not indicate exactly what the previous situation was (Stichter 1987).[11] Possibly constrained by the feminist paradigm of that time – which understood the position of women in terms of victimization – and by the lack of more ethnographic studies based on women's experiences, Stichter's analysis remains speculative about the extent to which there was or was not a change in gender roles. I wonder, instead, whether the fact that the majority of the couples had two incomes suggests that women's control over their own financial recourses made it possible for them to maintain leverage and autonomy in marriage (see note 11). According to the few mothers of the young professionals I spoke with, there was a significant change, compared with their own mothers, in terms of autonomy, lifestyle and an egalitarian conjugal bond. They also said that they believed that their daughters and sons would engage in different (marital) relationships that they called 'more progressive'.

An interesting contradiction arises in the literature on modern marriage in Africa. On one hand, it is assumed that urbanization, education and professionalization result in more egalitarian relationships between men and women (cf. Cornwall 2005). It is also assumed that economic independence for women, together with more leeway will allow for more personal approaches to partner choice, companionship and sexual satisfaction, in contrast to a sole focus on reproduction, ethnic compatibility, and customary jurisprudence. Given these assumptions, it is surprising to find studies showing that marriages have not in fact become more egalitarian (Vincent and McEwen 2006). Hollos concludes that in Nigeria, female small traders who engage in polygamous marriages have more autonomy than their more educated counterparts (1991). Other studies contest the assumption that urbanized and better-educated couples are more likely to set up nuclear family structures. For example, Ohadike contends that urban middle class households are obliged to bear the burden of supporting relatives (1981). Hollos suggests, however, that the youngest couples whose level of education and income are identical may be the exception to the contradiction mentioned above.

Transformation in gender (roles) is, of course, a highly complex process and it occurs within individuals, within groups and within institutions and tends to take place at a slow rate. Looking at the transformations described above, a characteristic pattern is that the grandfathers of the people in this study were among the first labourers migrating to Nairobi and settler farms, while their wives stayed at the homestead. I met a few grandmothers and grandfathers who described their lives as such. Their

children – the second generation, and the parents of the young professionals – grew up with an 'absentee father' as it is called in Nairobi, while the
mother managed the household. The first generation, as it appears from
Kamau's account, were eager to educate at least a few of their children.
They sent children to mission schools in the rural areas. These children,
the second generation, were among the first group to receive an education, which allowed them to work in the administration of the newly
independent nation state. They migrated to Nairobi to work as civil servants, teachers, managers of emerging companies and so on. With this
generation, the pattern of the nuclear family was strengthened as they became more and more focussed on their life in the city. Nevertheless, they
maintained a bond with their rural 'homes', educating some relatives and
giving a helping hand. Often the men built their own house in the family
compound as custom required. Furthermore, they often bought land in
their rural 'homes' that they leased to landless families. Their children, the
third generation and the focus of this study, are the young professionals
who are the first generation to be born and raised in Nairobi.

Among both the second and the third generation, 'absent fathers' were
common due to migration and separation. Almost every young professional I spoke with has lived for a shorter (a few months) or longer (a few
years) period of time without their father and sometimes without their
mother. Parents working in the government sector were subjected to unexpected transfers. When the mother was transferred, often a female relative came to live with the family. With almost half of the people I spoke
with, the parents had lived apart, from a few months up to several years
or permanently, because of work or because of marital problems. When
Grace (aged 28), who was of Luo ethnic origin, explained to me how her
family history was marked by the absence of fathers and brothers in her
grandmother's, mother's and her own generation, I realized the effects
that the labour and migration system had had on different members of the
family and on the family as a whole. She reported that:

> Romantic love was hard to hold on to in those days, I mean, my parents hardly
> lived together, my father was transferred for his work throughout Kenya [as a sec-
> ondary school teacher] and my mother had her job in Nairobi. How do you expect
> them to be romantic, like we want these days? Also, my grandmother tells me how
> our grandfather used to come home only for two weeks for Christmas, because he
> was working in Mombasa for Whites.

According to Grace, although strong emotional bonds are a feature of
Luo ethnic family relations, the bond between wife and husband could
hardly be maintained in an affectionate way. Instead this bond became a

pragmatic relationship based on what is commonly called 'responsibility', i.e. taking care of the family.[12] From the way in which her mother compared herself to her grandmother and in which Grace compares herself to her mother; it becomes clear that every generation throughout the twentieth century lived a life that was novel and/or progressive at that time. It can be concluded that women and men's gendered identities and roles, domestic arrangements and symbolic relations changed over time and in relation to larger historical developments.

Social transformation and moral anxiety

The wider processes of transformation described above resulted in an emerging middle class lifestyle in Nairobi. Change – as well as rupture – also implies possibilities. The possibility of new formations created by economic and political change frequently works through the force of imagination as a 'staging ground for action and not only escape' (Appadurai 1996: 7). These imaginations, which create the possibility of alternative life worlds, labour prospects or moral economies, are in turn stimulated by the processes of transformation. The current generation of young urban professionals grew up in the context of a trajectory of modernity that cannot be understood as proceeding from traditional to modern times, in the way Africa is popularly depicted, but as a modernity that is relational to particular historical processes where the meaning of 'modern' and 'traditional' constantly change (cf. Berman 1998). Modernity is being formed by global, intersecting imaginations and materialities, and in connection to the way it is appropriated in particular ways. For example, during an evening at Pamela's grandmother's place in Central Province, we were flipping through the family album. Pamela was shocked to see pictures of her mother and aunts in mini-skirts above the knee in the 1970s, something that was unthinkable in 2001. Later Pamela asked her mother about it and her mother told stories about the heydays of soul and dance in Nairobi. She told me afterwards that she had never realized that her parents had been youthful too. A narrative of modernity reveals that different generations are exploring different meanings and patterns of sexuality and gender, resulting in different notions of love and sexual relations. At the same time, however, these processes of transformation do not go unchallenged.

The effect of these social transformations on sexuality is distinctive, due to the moral significance of sexuality. Certain oral traditions describe the social order as having emerged from the taming of reproduction and sexual chaos (Thomas 2003: 14). Myths speak of a distant time when women and men related to each other more freely and incest and divorce were rampant. This state of affairs was corrected through the introduction of bride wealth and female circumcision, through making men into the head of the household and through strengthening marriage as an exchange between families. These stories of the past make a connection between social turmoil on one side and unruly women and aberrant sexual acts on the other; moreover, they suggest that people 'have long associated social harmony and success with a patriarchal order that can effectively manage sexuality and reproduction' (Thomas 2003: 15). Whether these myths should be seen as relatively recent responses or as older legends is an interesting point for further exploration. The point is that these stories and sentiments existed in the past as well as today. Sexuality is perceived in every society as essential to the social and moral order. Sexual relations are seen as crucial to social cohesion, as they help to structure the gender and sexual identities of individuals and thus to maintain societal patterns of gender difference. Sexual relations are an integral part of the normative and practical order of everyday life and they give meaning to gender roles. These notions of gender and sexuality create a 'deep-seated mechanism central to the construction of normative subjectivity and thus of social cohesion' (Crimp 2002: 301). This social organization of sexuality is experienced as being fundamental to a society or community. Therefore, transformations which affect this organization often invoke a moral response because changes in sexuality bring about changes in the larger moral system. Sex, '[as a strong emotion] is thought to be difficult to control, and its course unpredictable' (Beidelman 1986). In consequence, sex can be a potential threat to the social order.

In Kenya, since society is based on gerontocratic power structures, conflicts between (older) men and women and between generations are unavoidable. According to Prazak, writing on rural Kenya, 'this century has brought about many changes, particularly in intergenerational and intergender relationships ... the norms governing sexual behaviour are one arena within which the struggle between the new and the old, the appropriate and the inappropriate, is being negotiated' (2001). This moral order is guarded by the authority of gerontocratic power structures, which are mainly controlled by older men in power positions, such as in the government, in religious institutions and in kinship organizations. These men have been and are still vocal social actors in the public sphere, sometimes accompanied by older women. The discrepancy between changes in gender and sexuality on one hand, and the continuation of patriarchal ideologies on the other hand invokes strong moral reactions mainly amongst these vocal social actors.

Different groups of men, such as religious leaders, opinion makers in the media and government authorities, have expressed their concerns about women who have become 'visible' through the transformations of the last decades. The lives of these 'wayward' women typically disrupt 'the web of social relations that define and depend on them as daughters, sisters, wives, mothers and lovers. Often these women directly or indirectly challenge normative expectations of "respectability"; they are no longer the "good" wives or daughters they are supposed to be' (Hodgson and McCurdy 2001: 6). Women migrating to Nairobi (Booth 2004: 24; Stichter 1987; White 1990a), the female Nairobi bean traders (Robertson 1997: 94-99), otherwise outstanding women (Kanogo 2005) and single or divorced women (Oriang' 2001) became the focus of moral anxieties. Robertson shows that the decades before independence marked the height of Kenyan men's concerns over the social mobility of women traders, usually considered as 'insubordination' and 'immorality' (1997: 95). After independence these anxieties took the form of state harassment (Robertson 1997: 272). Recently, women who differ 'visibly' from normative ideas about womanhood, in terms of their employment, dress or conjugal relations, remain a focus of male anxiety (Janson and Spronk 2005).

Men are not immune from such moral reactions. Gerontocratic power structures imply a hierarchy of men, and hegemonic masculinity is threatened by men, as well as women, who differ from the norm. Younger men are told to maintain certain definitions of masculinity that they do not believe are realizable anymore. The practical and legitimizing foundations of the patriarchal ideology have disintegrated – for example, it is difficult for a man to continue being the provider when increasing numbers of women also have salaries – but the ideology lives on, affecting young men's sense of masculinity. However, the tacit approval of double standards when it comes to morality often precludes public condemnation of men when they deviate from normative expectations, such as when they conduct multi-partnered relationships. Although some agents of patriarchy, such as Christian leaders, also focus their moral anxiety on men, women's 'immorality' generally causes more anxiety.

Ongoing articles, letters to the editor and radio programmes often concentrate on the acute social issue of a 'generation that shuns marriage' and articulate a fear of chaos and discontent about changing social and power structures (see, for example, Kweyu 2001). In the postcolonial era, a shift has occurred from 'arranged marriages' organized by the family to 'love marriages'. Changes in the criteria for, and process of, partner selection also reflect the transformations in the social organization of African societies. Individual choice in the selection of marriage partners and the emergence of conjugality as an important dimension of marriage have been, and still are, associated with the breakdown of collective kinship oriented systems of production and reproduction (Gluckman 1955; Mair 1969). This means that women and men had to, and still have to, adjust how they had learned to identify themselves and others as 'women', 'men', 'wives', 'husbands', and also to rethink what was regarded as proper and improper in the context of social transformation (Appadurai 1996: 44). The lives of young professionals thus reflect a continuum of change in Kenya.

The young and ambitious in Nairobi

So far, I have provided an exploration of a political economy of sexuality (cf. Lancaster and Leonardo 1997) in Kenya. Socio-economic processes frame the social organization of sexuality, which influences people's sexual experiences. A political economical analysis offers explanations for changing patterns of sexual behaviour, but cannot help us understand people's experiences thereof. To understand how in the subculture of the young professionals in Nairobi an alternative morality is created, we also need to study people's motivations, from their point of view.

Criticizing essentialist ideas of unchanging rural 'Africans' who are unable to adapt to urban situations, Ferguson uses the term 'cultural style' to account for the urban culture of the Zambian Copperbelt. Instead of seeing style as a secondary manifestation of a person's individuality, or using it to refer to a prior identity which style then expresses, he employs style as 'a signifying practice' that indicates 'socially significant positions and allegiances': '[I]t is not simply a matter of choosing a style to fit the occasion, for the availability of such choices depends on internalized capabilities of performative competence and ease that must be achieved, not adopted' (Ferguson 1999: 96). He criticizes the idea that culture is the ideational content of expressive behaviour, and advocates moving away from this quest to locate the 'real' underlying identities and orientations. This approach helps us to understand the lives of young professionals in various ways. First, cultivating a viable style requires investment: in the figurative sense of investment – in appreciating the social changes one embodies; and in the literal sense – in manners, speech, social contacts and so forth. More importantly, the notion of cultural style 'breaks with the old dualist concern with traditional and modern orientation' by making it possible to talk about cultural difference without implying that 'modern' is 'Western'. Perceiving the lifestyles of young professionals as signifying practice implies an understanding of their local and cosmopolitan experiences and manifestations as coeval social phenomena (cf. Fabian 1983). Their lives go beyond dualist perceptions of 'modern' and 'traditional'.

The fact that they nonetheless continue to articulate these dualist notions highlights how, in discourse, they need these binary oppositions because any discussion about modernity is based on them. Inspired by Ferguson's 'cultural style', I use lifestyle as a descriptive notion to elaborate on their dress, bodily disposition, consumption patterns – style as self-presentation – as well as an analytic term to point to their lives as signifying practice.

Classifying young professionals

The label 'young professionals' applies to a relatively small group of young adults aged between 20 and 30 years old. Members of this group mainly pursue careers in the private sector, preferably in multinational companies, as well as in local and international nongovernmental organizations. Both the private sector and the NGO sector are well represented because Nairobi functions as the regional centre in East Africa. Their professions range from Information and Communication Technology (ICT) employees, supporting staff, accountants, junior lawyers, journalists, sales executives, bank employees, artists, project coordinators, etc. In the late 1990s, a group of young professionals organized themselves into the Young Professional Platform, which is organized as a network of associates. They meet on a monthly basis to discuss job opportunities and constraints; they invite guest speakers to talk about political or career issues; they organize monthly working days to conduct voluntary work in organizations like an orphanage; and they meet to socialize. The people in this network do not correspond to the young professionals in this study because they are generally older and come from the highest echelons of Nairobi society. The majority of young professionals I spoke to, for example, do not own cars and hope to acquire one when they approach the age of 30 – in 2001 only nine out of forty-nine people in my sample had a car – and travel by public transport. Nevertheless, the fact that they have organized a platform in order to meet like-minded people reflects the emergence of young professionals as new actors in the Nairobi cityscape.

The young adults in this study came from backgrounds ranging from lower to upper middle class, i.e. their parents were employed as civil servants, teachers and nurses, managers, university lecturers and lawyers. It is difficult to speak of social classes in Nairobi. It often seems that 'vertical' links across apparent class boundaries impede the formation of horizontal linkages between those who share the same 'objective' economic situation. Links of kinship, religion, regional affiliation or ethnicity have all tended to be more powerful (Berman and Lonsdale 1992; Ferguson 1999; Geschiere and Gugler 1998) than links of class in Nairobi or throughout

Kenya. Therefore I prefer not to use the notion of class as an analytical concept, but to use it rather as a descriptive notion to account for a social group that has gained opportunities by way of education to distinguish itself from those who have no means of progressing up the socio-economic ladder. That does not mean that there are no class differences; on the contrary, they exist sometimes even within families. Looking at young professionals as a social group, they represent what can be called an emerging middle class that is mainly dependent on salaried positions.

Depending on factors such as the availability of scholarships to enable them to pursue an education, certain individuals or families have been able to improve their socio-economic status. Even within the families of young professionals there are large disparities in career development, creating structures of obligation. For example, Martha's parents managed to get their children to university where they gained a first degree, and from there on the sisters managed to make a career for themselves, while the brothers did not. Martha was able to attend a pilot school in Australia through a scholarship, while her younger brother was trying to make ends meet as a small trader. Her sister was working at an international bank as a junior manager and had married a lecturer at a university. Her elder brother relocated to Meru to work on their family farm because he had spent three years trying unsuccessfully to find a job with his first degree in sociology. Many young professionals have similar situations in their family and when they are able to, they pay for their sisters and brothers to pursue a further education. As a group they often have more in common with each other regarding socio-economic characteristics than they do with their own families.

What makes this group of people distinctive is that they seek careers in the private sectors where they are able to work their way up. They generally have some kind of higher education, whether it is a university degree or a college certificate, as almost all parents invested significantly to provide their children with education. Because of the limited means of the parents and relatives, they have been to national public schools rather than to private schools. There is a strong incentive to work hard in secondary schools because entrance into a university is dependent on the results of the secondary school exams. University loans are accessible to all candidates selected for university entrance, while every year the brightest candidates from Kenya receive scholarships provided by different non-governmental organizations and churches. For those who are not able to get a university qualification, various colleges and private institutions are available. For example, Michael (aged 27) could only afford to attend a few courses in web design at a private college during the ICT boom in the late 1990s. Since then he has worked for several ICT companies and has developed a career by pursuing further courses and 'working hard to prove what you are worth', as he put it. Education continues to play a significant role in the lives of both women and men even when they are employed, as in 2001 twenty-seven out of the forty-nine people in this study were pursuing a degree or course after work.

These young professionals are generally financially independent because of their jobs which are reasonably stable. However, this stability is relative. As they do not generally come from backgrounds with wider networks based on patronage, they are more dependent on the irregularities of the employment market. The ICT sector in particular has proven to be unreliable. Whereas Njeri (aged 26) had made an amazing career out of nothing within the ICT sector, for others it meant being employed for short-term contracts only, interspersed with months of unemployment. In some cases people are even reemployed by the same company. Like other Kenyans, young professionals are vulnerable faced with the irregularities of employers, as there are hardly any regulations and laws to secure the position of employees. In 2001, the majority of people I met were looking for better jobs. The main reason was that they felt they were being underpaid, were working below their qualifications or were subjected to objectionable working conditions such as unpaid overtime. Young professionals are generally very mobile with regard to jobs. Some changed jobs up to five times in 2001 because they were only able to acquire short-term contracts or because of the continuous search for a better position. Some are very good at networking and hoped to find the right job by 'hopping'; unlike some others, these people are not mobile because they are forced to be. For example, Tom (aged 26) left a relatively well-paid job for a short but very well-paid contract with UNICEF and he made sure he was employed again soon afterwards. On the other hand, others like Dawn (aged 27) and Robart (aged 23) could not manage to find a stable job as accountants in the tourism sector and feared for their financial security.

As a result of the highly fluctuating job market, salaries varied widely. The lowest monthly salary earned by one of the people in this study was 23,000 KS (Kenyan shilling, which at the time was equivalent to 230 euro), earned by Dawn who worked at a private hospital. People who have become successful like Dorcas (aged 30) and Ongeri (aged 29) earned a monthly income of 100,000 to 120,000 KS (1000 to 1200 euro). Tom went from earning 35,000 KS (350 euro) at a small nongovernmental organization in early 2001 to earning 65,000 KS (650 euro) a month in a larger nongovernmental organization in early 2002. Although on average the people in this study can be called successful, there is always a fear of 'falling down' because of their dependence on the fluctuations of employment and on foreign subsidies in the case of nongovernmental organizations, or of falling prey to economic changes in the case of industries such as tourism. It is most painful when people actually 'go down', such as happened to Jane (aged 26) who lost her job and could not find another for months. I lost contact with Jane, as she was refusing to answer my calls and e-mails. She was forced to live with her parents and I believe she was ashamed of her downfall and preferred not to meet me as I was supposed to interview her about her lifestyle which, in her eyes, had deteriorated. An eagerness to work hard to make a good career is a necessity. Young professionals take it for granted that they will have to work on Saturday mornings and late at night. For periods of several weeks at a time, Tayiani (aged 28) was forced to work for up to sixty or seventy hours per week as an accountant for a well-known international banking company. She would not complain and instead felt proud to be part of a wider network of professionals. In fact, almost nobody complains about working overtime and they often reveal a sense of pride in going for a drink only late at night after leaving the office.

In conclusion, young professionals as a social group have created a new social niche in Nairobi society, which is made possible by opportunities that are unprecedented in the Kenyan postcolonial era.

Hesitations about ethnicity and issues of belonging

One important characteristic of this group is that, unlike their parents who migrated to Nairobi as young adults, these young professionals were born and raised in Nairobi. Despite a longer history of urbanization in Kenya, this generation stands out from previous residents not born in a rural area because of its scale. The social group of young professionals I describe here is clearly recognizable in the urban landscape due to their numbers and their lifestyle choices. When their parents migrated as young adults to Nairobi for work or education, they wanted their children to have a better start in the competitive school system. As a result of this and as a result of living in a multicultural society where Kiswahili and English are the main languages, the majority of the parents address their children in two languages. A second characteristic of young professionals is, consequently, that while the large majority understand the local mother tongue of their parents, they do not speak it themselves. The only exceptions are people identifying themselves as Gĩkũyũ, who speak the Kikuyu language, although some parents address them in English as well. Because Kikuyu is widely spoken in Nairobi, compared to other local vernaculars which are only spoken in family contexts, many non-Kikuyu also learned to speak it at boarding school and in the public sphere.[13]

However there are exceptions. Dana (aged 29), who identified herself as Gĩkũyũ, was taking Kikuyu language lessons at the language school of the Anglican Church. Among a group of foreign missionaries, development workers and researchers, she stood out as the only local Kenyan. She explained her actions by asking 'How can I be African and not speak an African language?' Dana did not blame her parents for failing to teach her Kikuyu, although she was adamant that her children would be educated to be bilingual. Other young professionals related their inability to speak the local mother tongue or the language of their parents to the fact that their primary and secondary (boarding) schools were multicultural and that Kiswahili and English were the only languages used there. Since attending school occupied the greater part of their time as children and adolescents, they were not encouraged to speak their family vernacular. Moreover, among the youth *Sheng* – the youth or slang language consisting of different ethnic languages, Kiswahili and English (see note 6 in the Introduction) – is widely, and proudly, spoken. They are rather critical of people who speak English with a British or American accent and frequently associate such accents with the Kenyan elite or with a pretentious attitude.

This inability to speak a vernacular can be explained to a large extent by their parents' preoccupation with progress during the first years of independence. The ambitious postcolonial leaders believed that the modernization process would be set in motion through education, through social progress. Parents therefore chose to speak English in their homes, while they continued conversing in their ethnic languages with their relatives. This trend has not been documented or studied. According to Professor Nzioka and Professor Mbatia, from the Sociology Department of the University of Nairobi, this is a continuing trend among parents employed in the wealthier echelons of society, in contrast to parents working in the lower paid sectors, such as shopkeepers and petty traders or those who are unemployed or self-employed.[14] Some parents regret this trend and began to speak a vernacular once more, although they remain a minority. For example, the parents of Maurice (aged 27) deliberately spoke Maragoli to him and his older sisters because the parents were 'Afro-centric'. However, they addressed his younger brother mainly in English and because of that, he cannot converse in Maragoli.

It is most discomforting for young professionals to meet with relatives who do not reside in Nairobi because they cannot easily converse: 'Imagine, me being a so-called Kamba [laughs] and when I meet my cousins we can hardly speak with one another … [serious now]. It's too embarrassing, in fact, my grandparents mock us and it makes me feel bad' (Tom, aged 26). Many recounted that when they were adolescents they were expected to attend the weddings and funerals of their relatives upcoun-try, but once they had left their parents' house they attended such family gatherings less and less to avoid the embarrassment. Another reason for not speaking a vernacular is that fourteen out of the forty-nine young professionals from my sample have parents with different ethnic or na-tional backgrounds who therefore address each other and their children in Kiswahili and English. Among themselves, young professionals speak mainly English and Kiswahili, sometimes mixed with *Sheng*. At their workplaces, English is the official language in speech and writing. Jokes, interestingly, are often told in a mix of Kiswahili and English and some-times stereotypical vernacular phrases are used to poke fun at a particular ethnic group. Young professionals, among others in Nairobi (see Nyairo 2005), testify to Werbner's claim that 'ethnic identities are merely a small fraction of the many identities mobilized in the postcolonial politics of everyday life' (2002: 1).

The absence of vernaculars also has socio-cultural implications for this particular group of urban young professionals. Since the majority of my informants cannot communicate with some of their relatives, they hardly engage socially with their relatives living in the rural areas. The extended families mainly meet for important events such as weddings, funerals, the discussion of matters relating to family capital and sometimes for circum-cision ceremonies or the birth of children. By participating less, or not at all, young professionals drift away from participating in these customary rituals and practices. This is also due to the fact that their lives are focussed on Nairobi and they associate more with their urban relatives. Neverthe-less, as I observed with a few of the older people who were closer to 30, some gradually became more involved with family matters, albeit only with family elders living in Nairobi. This was due to the fact that they were slightly older, that their advancing careers changed their status into that of 'responsible' adults, and that they were able to financially assist family members. Ongeri (aged 29) explained: 'I never cared about these family gatherings [meetings to discuss and assist family members socially and financially], but somehow I feel more like attending them. It's like, I can engage in the discussion now, before I was always preached against.' Hence they become more and more part of the group of wealthier adult relatives and it is likely that they are expected to help their family mem-bers, financially or otherwise.

Many young professionals are rather apprehensive about the lack of participation in customary gatherings or the general weakening of 'tra-ditions' in the urban setting, such as circumcision ceremonies.[15] It is a fundamentally ambiguous trend because on one hand it reveals a process of social change that cannot be reversed and which they are part of, while on the other hand they feel the need to express Africanness. They deplore not being able to speak a vernacular though at times they use it as a means of showing their commitment to overcome 'tribalism', perceived as one of the worst socio-political maladies in postcolonial Kenya. What they term 'tribalism' is in line with scholarly understanding on ethnicity where 'political ethnicity' is distinguishable from 'moral ethnicity'.[16] Thus Kenyans differentiate between being a 'tribalist' and the fact that everyone in Kenya belongs to an ethnic group. A 'tribalist' is a person who strategically manipulates his ethnic origin for political and economic gains, in contrast to a person who identifies ethnicity as culture. The inability to speak ethnic languages has far-reaching implications. Since conversations are culturally embedded, or what Moerman calls 'culturally contexted' (cf. Moerman 1988), young professionals throughout the country are somewhat disconnected from engaging with any ethnic group.

Dawn (aged 27) is an interesting exception among the group of people I spoke with. She joined a Women's Association located in the region where her father originated from, near Kakamega, which provided an opportunity for rural and urban women to cooperate in local initiatives such as providing microfinance for impoverished women, or organizing yearly 'health clinics'. Many young professionals are involved in such initiatives, though these are mainly organized in Nairobi or via their work. Indeed, this group of young professionals refers to itself as trans-ethnic. They actively date persons from different ethnic groups and their social networks, as well as their neighbourhoods, churches and, most importantly, their professional lives, are inter-ethnic. Their friends are often work colleagues, reflecting how the professional context has become an important social environment.

Nevertheless, ethnicity remains a political divider in Kenya and young professionals cannot completely detach themselves from the politics of belonging. Their trans-ethnic position is relative to a certain extent. It is a result of specific characteristics that distinguish their group, notably the fact that many of them do not speak a vernacular. This group of socially mobile, cosmopolitan oriented, young professionals cuts across existing patterns of ethnicity and class. As they cannot completely relate to existing groups and affinities in Kenya, they advocate a trans-ethnic approach to life. However, some of them tend to have more friends from the same ethnic background than others. Moreover, the crisis in 2007 and 2008, when violence swept the country after the Kenyan presidential election in December 2007, revealed how ethnic belonging is a stronger force than they might have anticipated. The Kenyan presidential elections of 2002 and the formation of the National Rainbow Coalition were celebrated by young professionals as the possible end of 'tribalism'; however, when quite a few of them voted for a presidential candidate from an ethnic background unlike their own, the following elections saw a return to former ways of voting. The majority of the people in this study voted along ethnic lines in 2007. When we discussed their safety and the state of the country on the phone, they articulated ethnic sentiments that I had never heard them utter before. Ongeri (aged 30 in 2001) was shocked, terrified and angry. When I phoned him, a large part of his family-in-law had fled from Nakuru and were staying at his house. His sister-in-law had given birth to a daughter two days before and was too weak to travel. She was admitted to hospital in Nairobi when she arrived. Ongeri accused the Kikuyu ethnic group of being responsible for the post-election violence, while those I spoke to who identified with the Kikuyu, such as Pamela, pointed the finger at the Luo ethnic group. (It was not, in fact, simply a matter between Kikiyu and Luo.) I also spoke to Tom on his mobile phone while he was sitting at the counter in the Sports Bar: he told me that 'apparently I have to start hating my neighbour now … I am here with the boys [a close-knit group of four men, from four different ethnic backgrounds] and we swore not to be divided'. It is difficult to assess the meaning of the trans-ethnic stance of young professionals after the post-election violence and since the country went, more or less, back to a normal state of affairs. The situation in Kenya remains volatile because the reasons behind the unrest have not been resolved and there are fears that a spark might set off the violence again.[17] Young professionals are not implicated in the violence, but they are nevertheless affected. Their lives are largely organized along trans-ethnic lines and their ambitions, as described in this study, remain an important unifying element.

Within their families they are less vocal about their trans-ethnic attitudes since older generations tend to be mono-ethnically oriented. Their parents tend not to interfere much in their lives, except for the expectations that elders hold regarding the ethnic background of future spouses. Several recounted how their parents carefully inquired whether their daughter or son also believed it would be more suitable to marry someone from their own ethnic group. Other parents openly told their children not to dare to bring 'home' somebody from another ethnicity, reflecting existing cultural-political rifts between certain ethnic groups in Kenya. In contrast to these familial expectations, the lives of young professionals, their work and a certain section of the media reflect a domain where ethnicity does not exist as a dividing force. Most importantly, it is a world where they met their peers. Several people pointed out to me that they attended – and contributed to – as many *harambees* organized by their mixed group of friends and colleagues than by relatives.[18] It should be noted that some ethnic groups are underrepresented in the professional sphere.[19]

It would be interesting to follow up the study group at some future date and see whether these inter-ethnic dating patterns will be reflected in their marriage patterns. Some claimed that it would be difficult to get permission to marry someone from a particular ethnic group; a few said that although they dated inter-ethnically, they want to marry a person from their own ethnic group; while others believed that their parents would not interfere with their decision if they happened to marry someone from a different ethnic group. The issue is more sensitive for men since they might be financially dependent on their relatives in terms of bride wealth. Depending on whether they have saved enough to meet the demand, they might be more or less inclined to take their relatives' opinions into account. Since young professionals generally delay getting married, it is difficult to predict the outcome of their marriages. Looking at young professionals in their thirties however, a trend of inter-ethnic marriages is discernible. Of the six weddings I know of that were held in 2001/2, four were inter-ethnic and these people were in their early thirties. The men's financial independence, as well as the 'liberal' attitudes of their parents. made a difference in the choice of marriage partner.

Nevertheless, young professionals proudly refer to themselves as transethnic – 'nontribal' – when they discuss the debilitating ethnic rivalries in Kenyan politics. They oppose the Kenyan political system with vehemence. They criticize the political actors as the 'Uhuru generation' who have 'betrayed' Kenya with 'tribalistic' politics that only resulted in 'regressive development' instead of developing the country. In 2001/2 they believed that their generation would make a difference, while after the 2007/8 clash, they were less convinced. Their liberal attitudes seem to be partly related to their more or less unattached lifestyles. The lifestyles described in this study, therefore, are likely to be transitory, depending on the particular age of the young professionals.

Living independently and single

The reality of being unattached, to a lesser or greater degree, from family expectations is only possible because relative financial independence is another important characteristic of young professionals as a social group. This translates into choices such as living on their own in a room or apartment, or with friends or relatives, instead of staying at their parents' house. It is particularly remarkable for women to break away and live on their own because they are generally expected to live with parents or relatives until marriage, unlike men who are considered independent after their circumcision.[20] Many women recounted the struggle of leaving their parental homes to live on their own.

For example, Grace (aged 28) was living with her maternal uncle in an upwardly mobile neighbourhood in Nairobi when her parents decided to return to Kisumu after their retirement. She was 23 years old when she moved out to live in a women's hostel for three months, and then she found an apartment to share with another friend, despite her relatives' objections. Eventually, her aunts organized a 'committee' – a gathering of various female relatives who discussed Grace's 'case'; she had to appear before them to answer their questions and respond to their criticism that she was disrespectful of the care of her relatives. Despite her deferential attitude, she nevertheless refused to give up her apartment: 'I knew that I was being rude, but I had to, I was tired of having my aunt on my shoulders and tired of their endless fights [of the aunt and uncle]. It wasn't fun in that house, I wanted to live my own life, so I just listened to them and bowed my head.' The committee left with the strong recommendation that Grace should return to her aunt's house. She refused to do so and for more than six months she avoided her relatives, including her parents, until everybody seemed to have forgotten about it or at least accepted the situation.

In spite of, or because of, the many social transformations regarding gender roles taking place in Nairobi society, women are expected to be more responsive than men to family authority. The independence of female young professionals is frequently interpreted as a moral breach. For example, Grace was told that her aunts feared she might soil the family name because she might be considered a 'loose' woman. Grace 'understood' their point, but wondered bitterly why her cousin was not called before a committee. Her cousin Mark was quite a famous figure in the Nairobi nightlife scene in 2001. He got a very prestigious job with an international company and during 2001 he was regularly seen in his Mercedes Benz, surrounded by different young women. He became well known because he used to pay for rounds of drinks and because he liked to joke about his manicured hands. Mark was recently married, but his wife never accompanied him. In general, men (in contrast to women) are permitted to show independence and are allowed more leeway in the choices they make. Nevertheless, the financial independence of young professionals makes it possible for both women and men to escape gerontocratic authority.

In general, young professionals delay marriage and choose temporary relationships, which is an important characteristic of the group as a whole. Men are unequivocal about the reasons for delaying marriage: they first have to make a career and achieve a certain standard of living before they can settle down. The following comments by Eric (aged 24) reflect what many men feel: 'Right now, I have nothing to offer [a wife]. As a man you have to take your responsibility [to take care financially] and I am working on that. When I can afford a house and a good life, I will find my woman.' But there is more to it, although they would not mention this in response to my question about why they do not get married. Older men and/or men who are engaged in 'committed' relationships recall a time in their life when commitment-free sexual relationships or multi-partnered relationships were an acceptable phase before they had to get 'serious with life'. There is an unwritten rule that for men the age between 20 and 30 is the time to 'have a life' and to celebrate going out to the full. It is the stage before fully achieving adulthood, whereas adulthood is understood as a phase of giving in to social expectations, of which marriage is the most important. As young professionals, women are also appropriating this norm. Both women and men explain that this is the time for 'fun'. Moreover, many explain that (serial) sexual relations are a necessary life experience. In Chapters IV and V this will be elaborated upon in detail.

One consequence of delaying marriage is that there are significantly lower numbers of parents among young professionals. Almost all the people I spoke to practice some kind of birth control by using condoms, the withdrawal method or the oral contraceptive pill for women. Three women had had an abortion. Two men recounted how they accompanied their girlfriend to the clinic to have an abortion. Of the group in this study, there was one single mother, although she had not severed the ties with the father of her child. One man, with whom the research interview process had to be discontinued because of his transference to Mombasa, got married in a hurry because his girlfriend was pregnant:

Peter, aged 24: 'My friends think I am nuts, that I am giving up my life by getting married now. But you know, Lena is my love, I would have married her anyway, so now she is pregnant, why not now? Of course abortion is not an option.'

Rachel: 'So what about living together then? You can have a child without getting married, no?'

Peter: 'No way… that is impossible, my folks… Our parents insist on marriage, they would disown me if I go and stay [slang for living together].'

Peter later explained that he felt obliged to listen to his father and uncles because he was dependent on them for the bride wealth he would have to offer. In general, men believe that having children will disrupt their lives and that they are not yet ready to take proper care of a family. Women are more ambivalent. Many women recount how 'of course' they eventually want children, just not now: 'Oh yes! I want a chubby baby with nice chubby legs to pamper the whole day, hhhmmm. But I have to wait of course, to find Mister Right and I first need to work … save money …

have a better job … I dunno, I first want my life to get on because having children can backfire on a woman' (Laura, aged 23). Laura voiced how many women feel; they have a mental list of objectives that must be achieved before they settle down and have children. With a few exceptions, most women relate having children to marriage and consider these matters to be interconnected. When women approach the age of 30 and are not in a committed relationship, they become anxious and start to wonder about single motherhood. For women who are over 30 (and therefore not part of this study), the issue of having children becomes more acute the older they get. I know one woman, a managing director of an ICT company, who became a single mother because she 'gave up of [*sic*] finding a man to live with. And what for? I have a maid to take care of the child while I work, I am perfectly happy now.' I know two 'career' women who are over 35 who have decided not to become single mothers and therefore had to accept that they might remain childless or would have to adopt children. According to them, their relatives are disappointed – and some relatives have even tried to pressurize one woman into marriage – but overall their family quietly accepts the situation, albeit with chagrin. Most women recount how their relatives make jokes about the children they expect to see born, sooner or later.

Lastly, religion also plays an important role in a country where almost everybody is a member of a church. As Lonsdale states, the culture of contemporary Kenya is 'soaked in Christianity' (Berman and Lonsdale 1992: 217). The novelist Ngugi, who calls himself an atheist, asserts that 'as a Kenyan I cannot escape from the church. Its influence is all around me' (cited in Berman and Lonsdale 1992: 217). The majority of young professionals call themselves Christians and all of them claim to have respect for the church as an institution. They all attend a service every now and then because of a wedding or funeral, while half of them go to a service regularly, for example once a month. It is common practice to consecrate a marriage by means of a Christian service. All official marriages I know about from the family and friends of my informants have been blessed in a church. This is in contrast with marriages from lower income groups, where it is not uncommon to marry first according to custom, through the payment of the bride wealth. These marriages are often approved by the chief of the area where the husband's relatives reside. Only when the couple has saved enough money will they organize their Christian marriage.[21] This is unlikely to be the practice in middle class Nairobi circles because the wedding has become a site for the display of status and wealth. Moreover, the ritual role of chiefs seems to have been replaced by the church institution. Young professionals attend churches which are frequented by the more successful layers of society.[22] These church communities reflect a common middle class lifestyle. A minority of young professionals call themselves 'saved', which mean they are committed and practicing Christians; for them, religious affiliation is an important means of defining themselves and their sexual practices within accepted norms (as shall be elaborated later on).

Nightlife and dating

In effect, a young professional subculture has developed that displays a vibrant cosmopolitan consumer culture. Their financial ability plays a major role in their ability to spend on clothing and recreation, including going out to the dozens of bars, clubs and restaurants that dot the urban nightscape. Although not all young professionals go out on a weekly basis, the majority do, and the Nairobi nightlife is mainly determined by the shifting popularity of music and places that are considered most hip. Friday and Saturday are 'the nites' to go out dancing and people meet up in small groups and travel to different places on a single night, depending on where the 'fun' is. An enjoyable evening out can include *nyama choma* and *ugali* (roasted meat and pounded maize meal) in an open air residential restaurant, followed by dancing in one of the many stylish clubs such as Carnivore or Klup House, while others like to dine at one of the restaurants and go on to a hip bar or watch a late night film at the cinema. Often people meet after office hours to have a drink at places that are in vogue such as Kengeles, which is in fact only visited by young professionals, or have a snack at Steers, a trendy fast food restaurant.

As a group they have created a 'scene' in clubs, bars or sports centres where they meet their peers. A significant majority work out in the gym to keep in good physical shape, or swim in one of the many pools at the international hotels. The ability to exercise, however, depends on their incomes and is therefore indicative of how far they have been able to develop their careers. They have unlimited access to the Internet via their work and hence communicate with friends and relatives abroad, while staying in tune with global trends by surfing the Internet, reading magazines, listening to music and watching films. Their role models are black US actors such as Denzel Washington, TV personalities such as Oprah Winfrey, or the icon Nelson Mandela. Their liking for music ranges from Congolese *Lingala*, US Rhythm & Blues, local hip hop, gospel, to the South African musician Brenda Fassie. It is, in short, a bustling world of sophistication and lifestyle options with its own signifiers and representations of a contemporary identity. They see themselves as explorers of this new lifestyle in Nairobi.

Leisure, intrinsically related to contemporary consumer societies, is crucial to the lifestyles of young professionals, and enables them to 'have a life' based on the commercialization of amusement. It is also the realm where young adults create a new sexual morality. According to Parker (1991), the desire for sexual experience is based on what he calls an 'ideology of the erotic'. To paraphrase Parker, this system of erotic meanings examines the diverse possibilities for sexual pleasure that have been largely ignored or restricted by dominant ways of conceptualizing sexual life. This means that if in dominant discourse in Nairobi sex is confined to marriage, the possibilities outside marriage – how, when, with whom and how often to have sex – designate a domain of sexual pleasure. As the influence of the family, religious institutions, and the state – that have functioned as the chief regulators of sexual life – weaken, new territory has been opened up for sexual exploration and experimentation. In particular, the nightlife is the new arena to celebrate the newly emerging sexual culture of young urban adults. This subculture is (so to speak) pregnant with eroticism, an eroticism that is intrinsic to how amusement is being globally construed in the media in terms of dress, music and dating. Biaya explains the pull of this leisure by its global character: 'Given the legitimacy with which eroticism is imbued by the centrality of leisure to capital, the circulation of Western eroticism [representations of love and sexuality in the media] has brought a compelling authority to bear on the practices [of] modern African urban subjects' (Biaya 2000: 710).

Eroticism is at the heart of contemporary global lifestyles, linking sexual pleasure and entertainment. This eroticism thrives within the realm of the imaginary, which is played out upon the nightlife scene. 'Going out' entails the promise of 'letting go' by dancing, flirting, meeting people and generally 'having fun', which is frowned upon by society at large. The erotic framework of nightlife focusses on the possibility of transgressing norms, of running the risk of being detected as subversive. As Parker (1991) has highlighted, the notion of transgression is central to the constitution of desire, excitement and ultimately sexual pleasure. The majority of young professionals choose temporary relationships as a means of celebrating 'having a life'. Central to their lifestyles is the practice of dating. This study focusses on these relationships, which are sometimes called 'casual' but are also sometimes perceived as a 'tryout' for a 'committed' relationship. A key element in this study is the ability of young professionals to collectively fashion lifestyles that transform the conventional meanings of sexual conduct. Their biographical narratives include stories that legitimate premarital sexual flings, including ironic stories that dismiss failed romances, or jokes and smirks that mark some behaviour as 'play'. As shall be elaborated later on, to them, sexuality reflects a space to reenact their femininity and masculinity by claiming an entitlement to sexual pleasure as the hip and ambitious.

Young urban professionals and the formation of a contemporary identity

It is this global-erotic subculture – that exists thanks to the commercialization of amusement – and its implicit denial of gerontocratic authority that disturbs society at large. Much of the criticism from older generations focusses on the lifestyles of young professionals, such as the nightlife scene, the style of dress of women, the delay of marriage or perceived 'immoral' sexual behaviour (see Sackey 2003 about a similar discussion on Ghana). The inter-generational conflict is not a matter of tension within their families *per se*, as many young professionals are respected by their relatives for their success. It is expressed in commentaries and critique in the media via, for example, columnists, or via churches and political platforms, and it has a deeper meaning. The more disturbing aspect for their critics is that young professionals embody a moral breach with a past that no longer exists but that is glorified by many Kenyans: they are the visible result of an inescapable transformation that is largely disguised by a discourse of glorifying the past (as we shall see in the next chapter). Young professionals often embody this dilemma themselves, by saying things like 'we cannot live anymore like our grandparents, those days are long gone, but it feels sometimes like betrayal … a betrayal of being African' (Martha, aged 24).

People told me several times that 'we have an identity crisis', which I labelled in the first draft of this chapter as 'an extreme explanation'. After reading the first draft of this chapter, Laura (aged 23) responded likewise:

> You're certainly right about the fact that young professionals are often criticized for being un-African or losing their culture or whatever. It's definitely more of a societal discourse than an interpersonal thing between parents and their own children, but it's there and it's very strong. Also, I think that young upwardly mobile people are very sensitive to it, very self-critical as well, and so the criticism of being un-African becomes bigger in their imagination than it might actually exist in reality… Finally, what people describe as an 'identity crisis' is not at all an extreme expression of what I feel or what many of my friends feel. It's really the most accurate way to describe all this ambiguity and mixed up feelings. It describes the feelings of disconnection, guilt, that we betrayed something, our sense of in-authenticity, the fact that we are confronted daily in Nairobi with the fact that we are NOT the average Kenyan, gives many of us a sense of standing outside history. It makes us unable to truly imagine ourselves as agents of cultural transformation, because we feel like we don't own our culture in the first place. We fear that we are not part of it, but at

the same time we hope that we are not part of it. That's what I understand when he [Robart] talks about an 'identity crisis'. (4 June 2003)

Laura captures the feelings of ambivalence very well: young professionals fear not being part of dominant Kenyan culture, while sometimes they do not want to be part of it. The heart of the matter is that, as 'agents of transformation', their desire to act out a contemporary lifestyle often coincides with certain Western modes, while they also react against this so-called 'westernization' as new imperialism; they are therefore living a reality that is inherently contradictory. Young professionals use the concepts 'African', 'Western' and 'traditional' as reified notions that comprise a discursive field of practices.

These feelings of ambiguity are reflected in the personal experiences of the young professionals, which are in turn the result of the choices they make in their daily lives. Relationships, for example, are affected by tensions created by this halfheartedness. These tensions range from problems in defining practices of romantic love as 'authentic', i.e. not 'westernized' (see Chapter VI); from shifting and contradicting gendered roles within couples; and from having to deal with situations of conflict within the family. Tayiani (aged 28) and Kinyua (aged 30), for example, decided to get married (they are the only couple in this study) after four years of courting. Before announcing their wedding plans to their families, they painstakingly discussed how they wanted to involve their families in their wedding. They finally agreed that they wanted to forego the customary bride wealth requirements. They anticipated their families' disappointment but, despite their wish not to offend their families, decided to make their own plans:

> Tayiani: 'We discussed it carefully and it is both our wish not to pay bride wealth because ... we don't believe in it, it's so ... it is a tradition that has lost its value, well, for us. It has something awkward, to be bought and Kinyua feels the same, he doesn't want to sort of buy me. You know, why has this tradition persisted while others vanished?'
>
> Rachel: 'Well...?'
>
> Tayiani: 'Eh ... well, a lot of money is involved ... many people benefit from it ... you know what I mean'.

Tayiani and Kinyua were very careful not to politicize the issue of bride wealth too much, thereby refusing to explain how much money might be involved in bride wealth or how some families request outrageous payments. With every marriage I attended, jokes abounded about unknown aunts suddenly appearing from 'shacks' – rural areas – claiming to be the bride or groom's best-loved family member. These jokes hint at the greediness of relatives.

The customs associated with bride wealth are often criticized by both women and men. There are many rumours about couples breaking up because of a stalemate in the negotiations between two families or about a couple staying together illegitimately when families could not agree. In the case of Tayiani and Kinyua, they pleaded with their parents to understand their position. Tayiani's mother and father agreed without conflict and defended the couple's decision within the larger family. Kinyua's family was initially offended because they were afraid to be seen as miserly by Tayiani's family. After some negotiations, Kinyua agreed to have a ceremony where his family symbolically presented her family with a goat, to show their welcoming of Tayiani as their daughter. She expressed her own view of this practice as follows: 'I didn't need to give a goat, I wished not to, but I understand their position and for them I agreed to, but it means nothing to me'. During the wedding, the families arranged that a goat would be slaughtered traditionally, and that Tayiani would present Kinyua with the right leg as a sign of her new role as wife, while he would present her with another part. They did as expected, although they had reservations: 'I had to give him this leg to show my subordination to him, that's how it used to be. But anyway, I decided to see it as an African rite.' In effect, she respected the ritual of slicing the goat in a specific manner, which originally reflected the gendered hierarchy within the new extended family, as a gesture to relatives. However, she explicitly claimed that she did not believe in the symbolism which assigns women a submissive role. To her, the ritual reflects a generalized tribute to Africanness. Tradition, then, becomes cultural style; not something they believe in, but a signifying practice that invokes knowledge of form rather than content (Coe 2005; Ferguson 1999).

From the experience of Tayiani and Kinyua, it becomes clear how issues of cultural heritage, generational expectations, lifestyle options and cultural identity bring with them a field of tension and ambivalences, sometimes resulting in feelings of anxiety. This field of tension comprises four interrelated, but sometimes contradictory elements: young professionals perceive themselves as explorers of a contemporary identity; they exhibit half-hearted attitudes towards customary ways of living; they reject 'westernization'; and they advocate Africanness as a mode of identification.

Explorers of a modern identity

Eve, the new glossy magazine which appeared in Kenya in 2001, was advertised as 'the essence of Africa's new woman'. This phrase articulated a feeling shared by many women, like Tayiani: 'I believe we as modern women have the obligation to move on where our mothers could not go further. They were more constrained by tradition, whereas we go beyond parochial ethnic sentiments as is so common in this country. I am African, a modern African woman.' She was a beautiful and slim woman, always well dressed and she carried herself around with dignity, having a slightly reserved attitude. She was a prototypical 'sophisticated' woman and she was conscious of it. Women like her personify, more than men do, the sophisticated personae that are portrayed in the media; 'new' women are more noticeable than men, because they have entered a public domain that used to be the preserve of men.

Sen and Stivens show how the processes behind the creation of a new middle class are thoroughly gendered and they also show how class consciousness takes a gendered form. Writing about affluent women in East and South East Asia, they state that new femininities can be seen 'as central to the very development of the burgeoning societies' (Sen and Stivens 1998: 5). In the Islamic parts of Indonesia, the 'consumer/wife/mother' type of woman is the prototype of middle class success, while in the yuppie subculture of urban Djakarta, the 'consumer/beautiful young woman' type is the icon of middle class status. Various authors show that these 'new' women are created largely within a middle class imaginary reality and explicitly exclude working class and rural women. In Nairobi, a similar trend is to be found among the middle classes. The symbol of the 'new' woman is the beauty queen or mannequin. Beauty pageants are extremely popular and the winners are applauded for making the nation proud and being proper ambassadors for Kenya. Kenyan models who venture out onto the international scene are hailed as Kenyan success stories. They personify the global phenomenon of the Modern Girl (Weinbaum et al. 2008).

Models are generally admired as the embodiment of the latest vogue and illustrations of 'sophistication', but they are not necessarily seen as examples to be followed. Instead, the role models of young professionals are the small elite of very successful professionals like young lawyers, directors, or TV personalities who appear regularly in the print media as success stories. Young professionals who are starting out look up to these people and also consider themselves as belonging to the same group of explorers. According to Michael (aged 27): 'I am only a small worm, now, but what we are, what we represent, is that the sky is the limit!'

Both women and men perceive themselves as explorers of contemporary lifestyles. They distinguish themselves by way of fashionable dress, liberal attitudes and non-conventional relationships. Women typically dress in skirt suits or trouser suits when at work, which is more formal than the trendy, sexy or chic outfits they wear after work and during weekends. Women's hair styling is a major way of distinguishing them as fashionable. Daring women keep their hair very short or braid their hair in lines, which is associated with children or old-fashioned hair styling. Other hairstyles range from using fake hair, 'extensions', to having long hair or long braids. People consciously maintain a well-kept image not only in terms of dress, but also manicured hands (and feet) and a good figure. Many of the women and men in this study participated in sports while at college and the majority worked out at the gym or the swimming pool, some regularly, others every now and then. As well as working on their physiques, men are also fashion conscious. They invariably wear suits at work, while outside the office they take care to wear fashionable shirts, trousers and shoes and carry gadgets such as mobile phones. The best present I could give a man was eau de cologne and on a few occasions I was asked to go shopping with a man to choose a cologne for himself because 'as a woman you can tell a good from a bad one'.

But even more than differentiating themselves by dress, young Kenyan professionals perceive themselves as different from other Nairobians because of their liberal attitudes. Both women and men often explain their choices in relation to their parents' or grandparents' lives and sometimes in relation to people in the rural areas. Kinyua explained it as follows: 'We, our generation, will make a difference I think. Things have changed so much and it all comes together in our generation. I marry Tayiani because of the modern woman she is, I could not marry a woman from upcountry because … our styles are different. I think the future of Kenya as a modern nation depends on us.' When asked why he could not marry a woman from the rural area, he explained that, for one thing, such a woman was more 'traditional' and would not want to pool incomes as Tayiani and he had decided to do. And indeed, for a couple to pool both salaries was considered the most 'modern' thing they could do because it breaks with the customary gendered division in relation to providing for the (nuclear) family. Many women and men place themselves in opposition to the unequal relationship of their parents, mentioning their mother's subordination, their father's extramarital relationships, or a failed marriage that they attribute to their father's dominance. Some men capture the essence of a contemporary relationship by saying 'a modern marriage is a monogamous marriage'. All women refer to the need for equality in a relationship and the need for women to be career women. Though less explicitly discussed, young professionals distinguish themselves by their openness with regard to premarital sexual relations. Since they delay marriage, they feel that it is 'unrealistic' to avoid premarital sex. Moreover, sexual pleasure is an objective of a 'fast' life and essential to their self-perception as a modern person.

Furthermore, the fact that they work in the private sector, which is not tainted with the aura of parochialism as is the government sector, contributes to their sense of being explorers of a fashionable way of living. Often they work with foreigners from different continents. They perceive themselves as part of a global subculture consisting of fashionable dress, the latest music and other crazes promoted by the transnational media such as magazines, TV, films and the Internet. Because of their financial means, they are a small minority who are able to participate in this subculture, and hence they perceive themselves as trend-setters – or 'agents of cultural transformation' as Laura wrote – in Nairobi. They are ambitious to reach certain goals in their careers as well as their personal lives, and they approach life with the arrogance of successful youth. This confident attitude towards life is likely to offend older people, as it negates their role as advisors. For example, Kinyua was initially criticized by his relatives for being 'disrespectful' of custom. But more than that, he had 'dared to question what they considered of importance'. During the negotiations with his family, some uncles carefully expressed doubts about Tayiani's potential to be a good wife, as she was somewhat 'un-African'. The more or less independent position of young professionals is frequently explained as 'disrespectful' because they can, if they want, sidestep their relatives. At these moments, notions of Africanness are often invoked to incorporate them into the larger moral networks of family and ethnicity. However, as Kinyua said: 'Yes, I can see that I am disrespectful in this, but, no way I can fulfil their wishes, it's too traditional'. Young professionals find themselves at the interface of changing notions of belonging and identity, and try to follow their own path.

Young professionals' position towards customary ways of living

Besides the ambiguities of being 'modern', there are the contradictions of being African, as noted above by Laura: 'We fear that we are not part of it [our culture], but at the same time we hope that we are not part of it'. Africanness relates to notions of authenticity, i.e. not 'westernized', and, paradoxically, the people who are seen as most 'authentic' are also those who are sometimes looked down upon. Women and men often position themselves in opposition to rural lifestyles that are seen as 'backward' or 'traditional'. For example, in the discussion about female circumcision, I often heard that it was a 'tradition' that 'persisted' only in rural, 'traditional' areas. This thinking implies a binary opposition of rural as 'tribal', uneducated, unsophisticated and ignorant on one hand, and of urban as educated, sophisticated or 'modern' and knowledgeable about contemporary lifestyles on the other hand. The implicit traditional-modern polarity is misleading here, however, since such oppositions have subtler implications. The polarity is not so much about 'Kamba', 'Meru', or 'Gusii' ethnic cultures versus 'Western' ones, but about the attempt to overcome rural illiteracy, poverty and general inferiority. Since many individuals from the study group are not from very wealthy backgrounds, part of their ambition resulted from a drive 'not to go down and become a poor fellow like the rest of the Kenyans' (Robart, aged 23). 'Ignorance' and 'backward attitudes' are also associated with this meaning of 'tradition'. Women especially refer to these notions when comparing themselves with rural women who are perceived as being backward because of lack of education, but also ignorant about worldly affairs such as careers or contraceptives. When Laura (aged 23) was talking about her rural cousin who got married at the age of 18, she elaborated that 'you can hardly blame these girls, what do they know? They are used to obey men and don't know about condoms, they are ignorant about how to stand up as a woman.' Later she explained that all 'such problems' came down to 'traditions backfiring on women'.

In fact, the notion of tradition is employed in two ways by young professionals. In its first meaning, 'tradition' is used when a custom is considered to be unfavourable or out of date, for example female circumcision or bride wealth. 'Tradition' here acquires a negative meaning. In the media a relatively consensual image of negative 'traditions' is presented, in relation to practices such as female circumcision, or of male circumcision when not performed in hospital, or the marrying of underage girls. One editorial of the main newspaper in Kenya, discussing how several boys bled to death after being circumcised, described the situation as 'a ritual that defies modernity' (Editorial 2001: 6). This comment does not criticize the custom as out of date, since male circumcision *per se* is not considered to be a problematic custom. It is rather the manner in which it is done, 'unhygienic, with blunt objects, in the bush', that is considered backward. The second way in which the notion of tradition is employed is defensively, when something 'modern', 'Western' or 'foreign' is perceived as a threat to Kenyan cultural heritage. For example, 'traditional dances' are considered as customs to be proud of in the context of Western cultural dominance. In contrast to Tayiani and Kinyua, a friend of Grace explained to me how she considered bride wealth to be a 'good tradition', because the ceremonies involved, the symbolic presents and the uniting of two families were 'truly African'. In this sense, 'tradition' acquires a positive meaning, moving beyond ethnic heritage and coming to stand for Africanness. In short, 'tradition' can refer to concrete customs that are associated with (ethnic) cultural heritage, and at the same is used as a rei-fied concept to invoke notions of cultural authenticity in a context that is experienced as hostile to cultural survival. The disparity arising from these two different notions is at the heart of the ambivalent attitudes held by young professionals towards customary ways of living.

In addition to these ambiguities surrounding the meaning of 'tradi-tion', there is another ambiguous aspect related to what is popularly de-fined as 'traditions'. It appears that young professionals have been brought up with a limited definition of traditions. When asked what their customs are, young professionals almost invariably name a specific set of customs – circumcision, traditional dancing, bride wealth – or they present the Masaai ethnic group as performing 'genuinely' traditional dances. 'Tra-ditional dances' are an interesting phenomenon in Kenya. In fact, they are an interesting example of an 'invention of tradition' (Hobsbawm and Ranger 1992). Late President Daniel arap Moi institutionalized 'tradi-tional dances' that were to be performed to welcome him as the president wherever he went. As a tribute to Moi, the state organized an annual dance festival for secondary schools where 'traditional dances' are performed. Since then, 'traditional dances' have been institutionalized to enliven state ceremonies and other official functions. For many young professionals, these dances are one of the more tangible traditions. Cati Coe has anal-ysed how performing and musical arts in Ghanaian schools became a way for the state to represent the nation (2005). Her interpretation, that this kind of (national) cultural heritage functions on the premise that culture can be learned, highlights the degree of alienation that is involved in these situations.

When asked what customs they grew up with, the majority responded that they were not brought up with traditions. Dawn (aged 27) explained how her brother's funeral had been 'colonized' by her relatives much against the will of her parents. Her brother had drowned on a holiday at the coast in the late 1990s, and according to her relatives a death like that should be carefully treated in order to ward off malevolence. Dawn's case is interesting because her 'lack of cultural education', as she named it, was intentional on the side of her parents:

> I had no clue … my parents never told us about these things, they [the relatives] had all kinds of ideas about how the body should be treated and all. My father … he did away with tradition, he says it's useless, he's quite strong on it. I mean, we belong to a clan of the Luhya with the goat as a totem, so we should never eat

goat. My father, to rebel, always eats goat and we have grown up eating goat meat. I never knew this before.

Many others had 'heard' about certain taboos and rites, such as wearing red slippers to ward off evil spirits, but they were never taught to do so themselves. Others, when asked what kind of customs they grew up with, reacted with some embarrassment, like the men who were circumcised in hospital without ceremony. In effect, notions of customary ways of living are more about the rhetoric of 'the old ways', propagating the second notion of 'tradition' described above. It is difficult for the majority of young adults to designate 'traditions' in their own life, as they have a specific notion of what counts as traditional. They do not regard customs such as name giving ceremonies, *harembees*, incorporating aunts' advice in the pre-wedding parties for brides or paying proper respect when greeting their grandparents as traditional or customary.

Despite realizing that social and cultural change is inevitable (see Laura's comments above), young professionals are sensitive about being accused of 'westernizing' as they experience a lack of correspondence with a wider cultural – in the sense of what they perceive as authentic – group. As Martha (aged 24) said: 'It feels sometimes like betrayal of being African'. This sense of betrayal was shared, to some extent, by all those I met. They felt 'in-between' (Atieno, aged 25), or as Robart (aged 23) explained it, 'we have an identity crisis', while Maurice (aged 27) said, 'we want to be modern, we are in fact, but there is always a foul smell about it'. These quotations highlight how much the discourse on cultural identity – trying to find out how to be modern and 'African' – is a minefield. What this 'modern' actually entails is somewhat unclear, while the foul smell refers to what is called 'westernization'.

'Westernization'

Since contemporary consumer culture is seen as Western in origin, the perceived problem – for both the young professionals and the wider Kenyan society – is the uncritical acceptance of material and non-material entities from abroad, as the two following examples show. The first example is an excerpt from an e-mail correspondence with Fredrick, while the second is part of an interview with Pamela (both aged 22 at the time):

[Frederick and I were e-mailing about the difference between the crazes about the World Cup Football in 2002 and the European Cup in 2004]

'Going by several columnists' articles, the loss of authenticity has aggravated the folly of Africa sinking further in the abyss that it finds itself in. The articles of Bindra "if we are not authentic, we are total failures" and Buke "don't watch European football, it's neo-colonialism" hit the point about the malady that dogs our continent. Aping takes the credit for this loss of identity. We cannot simply do things the right way. Our development policies, too, are geared towards benefiting western agendas. Africans suffered immense wrongs of a calculated nature, such as the imposition of foreign languages, the formulation of suppressive (under)development pacts and policies and the portrayal of anything African as backward. We need leaders with insight and originality, not a bunch following blindly the dictates of donors and their pockets. We need to shed off our old colonial mentality of embracing filth we are told is good for us'. (Fredrick aged 22, 28 June 2004)

Pamela: 'You see, the point is that people want to be sophisticated. Okay, it's like, we want to be modern … But then Africans should not take in everything unquestioning[ly], we tend to think that everything is better if it's from the West.'

Rachel: 'In what sense?'

Pamela: 'Well … you know we grew up with taking the West as an example, better schooling, better technology, hospitals … more advanced. And of course these things are good for us, but we tend to look down on our own things because of the West being more advanced. Like … if I see a jeans "made in Kenya" I don't like to buy it, if my friend brings me jeans from London I am happy, never mind they were made in the export processing zone here in industrial area! You get my point?'

Rachel: 'Ok … And why is it a problem for you?'

Pamela: 'Because … it's wrong to downplay our own stuff, to admire Western, because we should be proud being African, we should not wanting Western stuff, like clothes and these gadgets.'

Rachel: 'Gadgets? Like … a mobile phone?'

Pamela: 'Yes, they are wanted because they are Western'.

Rachel: 'But your mobile phone is probably made in China or Taiwan, so what's Western about it?

Pamela [laughs]: '…Ok, no, that's not the point, the point is … that this mobile is a modern thing, therefore Western and … we should be careful for wanting it because it's Western. I mean, you guys dominate all companies and advertisements and therefore are able to decide what is to be sold, we can only hop along, we cannot decide ourselves.'

Fredrick's writings convey the anger I often encountered, while Pamela's words show the more complex nature of 'westernization'. The desire to partake in the consumer culture and to seek new experiences is central to the lifestyle of this emerging middle class. Moreover, items with a specific status are even more desirable, such as the latest models of mobile phones. The most visible way to express a 'sophisticated' lifestyle is through material items such as dress and gadgets and by non-material entities such as music. Frequently, these signs of 'sophistication' originate from outside Kenya and are therefore not value free; that is, they are 'Western' and therefore 'un-African' (see also Burke 1996 on Zimbabwe). Whether something actually originates from the West or not – as with mobile phones – is not the issue; it is the association with the West that causes the friction. The attribution of a lesser status to African things and people is the core issue. However, as Pamela indicates, both 'Africans' and 'non-Africans' engage in this unequal assessment, which is, of course, a painful realization. Africa's and Africans' subordinate role is a recurrent theme which runs through all the life stories.

'The West' remains a source of suspicion, as young professionals read about the slave trade, colonialism and apartheid, and contemporary 'en-slavement' by powerful Western institutions like the World Bank, the International Monetary Fund (IMF) and international corporations. All these are blamed on 'the West'. Moreover, in their role as young professionals they experience 'Western dominance' in a direct manner at work. Some have experience of non-Kenyans, 'you guys', getting promoted more easily than Kenyans; of whites with lesser qualifications getting into similar positions to Kenyans; or of senior officials being recruited from outside Kenya. Even if they do not experience this at first hand, it is often a topic of debate and rumour. Furthermore, Nairobi's range of inhabitants reflects a certain segregation of high class non-Kenyans such as diplomats, the higher ranking employees of the United Nations Headquarters, international corporations and the international nongovernmental organizations, which are well represented in Nairobi. These groups form a small but distinctive white class that, in the experience of many young professionals, exclude even educated and trained Nairobians. All in all, 'Western' dominance is perceived as a structural problem between 'blacks' and 'whites' as they read about the eviction of African immigrants from Europe, hear reports of racism in the United States or discuss the subordinate position of African countries in international politics. They react to what Chakrabarty analysed when looking at how modernity operates by way of exclusions and by the constitution of difference that together generate the Euro-North American sense of a unified subjectivity (Chakrabarty 1992).[23]

Their experience of being treated as second-rate citizens, as Kenyans in Nairobi and as Africans in the larger world, is mixed because of the ambivalence of modernity, and it heightens their sensitivity to racism. During our meetings, when they got to know me better in the research process, some could become very emotional when trying to understand issues like racism. Encouraged by the opportunity to speak out, they would question me on the difference between a black and a white skin or 'why you guys' do so and so. Nyamnjoh and Page (2002) focus on similar sentiments among youth in Cameroon. They describe how representations of whiteness constructed by young black Cameroonians are often contradictory and include both positive and negative judgements. The young Cameroonians are simultaneously drawn to, and exasperated by, a Western vision of modernity. Like the young professionals in Nairobi, they are despairing of the existing local social and political structure and look beyond national contexts for their dreams. But they are equally sceptical about the justice of the global economic context and articulate their doubts in terms of antagonism towards whites and defence of Africanness.

In Nairobi, such frustrations are channelled into the notion of 'westernization', which has become a generic concept to account for a variety of different anxieties regarding social transformation and cultural identity. Young professionals are preoccupied with what they called being 'modern the African way'. What this means, exactly, remains vague; it is more a phrase used to articulate fears of losing some kind of singularity labelled 'African'. In fact, more than searching for something authentic, it is a defensive reaction to Western dominance. In the end, Frederick's frustration originates from the fact that young professionals like him are intricately connected to these power relations in the pursuit of their ambitions and lifestyles. According to Ferguson (1999: 214), it is 'dangerous' to be 'fashionable' because of the disrespect this implies for unfashionable modes. Young professionals want to feel part of Kenya, while they also feel very different from the majority of Kenyans. Their half-hearted attitude reflects a field of tension and anxiety and they often find themselves looking for suitable responses to the ensuing ambiguities. This search centres on balancing 'how not to westernize' and how to take account of their African heritage, while searching for the definition of a contemporary identity. Central to this identity is the use of a reified notion of Africanness.

Africanness

The way in which young professionals identify themselves as 'African' has several layers, and differs depending on whether they view their identity from the perspective of an ethnic group, a Kenyan or an African. The majority identify themselves as Kenyan, a significant number as African and a small number by way of ethnicity. There is a particular pride in being Kenyan and many refer to the vibrant popular culture in Nairobi and its leading function in the region. Feelings of Kenyanness are invoked particularly in relation to national events, such as sports (for example with the international success of Kenyan born athletes), or beauty pageants. Pamela (aged 22) phrased it as follows: 'Kenyan, I am Kenyan in the first place, but that means of course being African'. Others problematized the label Kenyan, like Maurice (aged 27): 'I am African, I belong to Africa, calling myself Kenyan … does not cover it all, Kenyan is a British invention'. According to Nyairo, 'the idea of Kenyanness is its inherent diversity and contradictions' (2005: 10), which is exactly what young professionals embody, though this is not always publicly accepted. Instead, therefore, feelings of Africanness are reinforced in the context of cultural Western dominance and/or in the presence of Westerners. People who identify with an ethnic identity almost always come from mono-ethnic marriages, though not all people whose parents are from the same ethnic group identified themselves with this ethnic group. For example Dana (aged 29), who studied Kikuyu although her parents were Gíkũyũ, did not identify herself as such but as 'African'.

This particular way of identification is not shared with other groups in Nairobi with similar characteristics, such as young professionals who were not born and raised in Nairobi or lower middle class people who were born and raised in Nairobi. The majority of the people from these other groups identify themselves with an ethnic group, as do the majority of Kenyans. I believe that the young professionals in this study differ from the norm for several reasons. First, the inability to speak an ethnic language forces them to identify beyond ethnicity and, second, they form a subgroup as young professionals that is inter-ethnic by definition. Thirdly, they are generally more highly educated and politically conscious and take seriously the role of an intellectual elite engaging in pan-African or Black Power movements, and are generally interested in discussions advocating 'African' authenticity. [24] I did not encounter the assertion for Africanness as much among the elites, and various of the people I spoke to testify to not recognizing these interests in other groups either. Young upwardly mobile people are very sensitive to the issue of cultural heritage because they are very self-critical and because they are far removed from tradition as a lived reality (cf. Coe 2005). Moreover, social mobility cuts across existing normative indexes of ethnicity. Yet, people in this study from Kikuyu, Meru and Embu ethnic backgrounds tend to be less trans-ethnic oriented compared to those from, for example, Luo, Luyha, Kamba and Kisii backgrounds. As mentioned earlier in the chapter, their trans-ethnic attitude is relative and situational.

What several people described as an 'identity crisis' is an explanation of a deep-seated anxiety, which they were not initially eager to share with me. Only much later could we discuss the ambiguities described above, while in the earlier stage of the research the discussion centred on defensive attitudes towards the West, such as those expressed by Fredrick in the e-mail cited above. The themes of 'African' subordination and victimization by the West do not only arise in Nairobi; in fact, they are recurrent themes in a larger discourse shared by Africans across the continent. Mbembe critically discusses the intellectual currents that have resulted in this shared discourse. According to him, these intellectual debates have created a distinctively 'African philosophy' that he considers to be a cult of victimization (2002: 244). Although he confines his analysis to intellectual writings, part of his analysis is helpful in understanding the anxiety of young professionals because, as he rightly states, the resulting ideas have partly been integrated in the 'African collective imaginaire'.

The canonical meanings of the slave trade, colonization and apartheid, and the resulting humiliation, have gained momentum in postcolonial Kenya and have been effectively integrated into the Kenyan collective imagination through the work of intellectuals such as Ngugi wa Thi'ongo, Tom Mboya and Ali Mazrui. The resulting discourse on Africanness has its roots in colonial history. In short, the British colonial administration used the concept of custom and tradition to highlight difference and to eliminate the plurality of custom in its attempt to differentiate Africans from non-Africans. Africans had to be converted to civilization, assimilated from customary society into civil society by way of Christianity and the colonial state. Before and during independence, Kenyatta, the first president, postulated an 'African' philosophy and a criticism of colonialism by advocating 'progress' and 'development'. On closer examination, it appears that the concepts of 'progress' and 'development' were only synonyms for the concept of civilization because, in fact, Kenyatta and the new intellectual elite accepted for the most part the basic categories of Western discourse. These categories are all based on one assumption, namely, the difference between Africans and non-Africans. What happened is that the denial of humanity – or the attribution of inferiority – by colonial discourse forced Kenyan intellectuals into a contradiction of defending the humanity of Africans, as well as claiming that the black race, traditions and customs had a specific character. These responses arose not to defend Africans as belonging to a specific race, but against the prejudice that assigns them an inferior status. However, by fighting the notion of inferiority, Kenyan intellectuals reproduced the very presumptions they were trying to deconstruct (Mbembe 2002: 257).[25]

Kenyan intellectuals still reproduce these assumptions, as this discourse has gained a hegemonic position in explaining current situations. Intellectuals mainly reach young professionals through the media of radio, magazines such as the *New African*, and columns in the daily newspapers. Taking an arbitrary example, Phillip Ochieng, a well-respected columnist and retired professor of political science, has criticized the 'development' industry in Kenya as follows:

> The 'donors' will never admit that our emergencies and development difficulties
> are direct results of seeds of destruction planted by Europe's own 500 years of sus-
> tained plunder of our human and natural resources and markets and destruction of
> our independent work spirit and racial self-confidence. (Ochieng 2001)

These explanations resonate with Fredrick's fulminations.

The canonical meanings of slave trade, colonization and apartheid have
been supplemented by what is called neo-colonialism – or the contemporary political and economical hegemony of the West in Kenya, and Africa,
by means of 'development'. This canon has effectively framed Kenyans'
experience as 'Africans'. During my MA research, I was amazed to discover how well informed secondary schools students were with regard to
an understanding of the history of the African continent in the light of
this canon (Spronk 1999). Their understanding was similar to the concern with racism expressed by young professionals. These responses crop
up against the prejudice that assigns this race an inferior status, so that
defensively advocating Africanness has become common. This sense of
ascribed inferiority was palpable when I talked with young professionals.
While they reproduce the same structures on which these presumptions
about Africanness are based, they also partly deny being 'African'. They
make visible the fact that an Africanness based on a traditional past that is
inherently different from the West is no longer feasible.

In sum, young professionals are entangled in very complex processes
of identification as 'Kenyans', as 'Africans', as 'modern', as 'African' and
as 'modern the African way'. The appeal of older and newer discourses
on Africanness lies in the possibility of 'combining to oppose globalization, to relaunch the metaphysics of difference, to reenchant tradition,
and to revive the utopian vision of an Africanity that is coterminous with
blackness' (Mbembe 2002: 264). In Nairobi, we can observe this complex, variegated process in relation to the eager accommodation with, appropriation of and resistance to labels of 'African' and 'modern'.[26] These
young professionals are situated [on] the interface between the politics
of belonging (Geschiere and Gugler 1998a) and the forces of globalization (Spronk et al. 2005). Their conflicts of loyalty reveal that capitalist
processes create opportunity structures of which young professionals, in
the footsteps of their grandparents and parents, are the successful results,
while at the same time they embody irresolvable ambivalences as the result
of the more unpromising outcomes of capitalist processes.

When Mbembe raises the question of how 'we should conceive the all
purpose signifiers constituted by slavery, colonization and apartheid', he
provides three suggestions, of which two are fundamental to the analysis
of this study. The first is that 'the obsession with uniqueness and differ-

ence must be opposed by a thematic sameness'. He also suggests that 'attention must be given to the contemporary everyday practices through which Africans manage to recognize and maintain with the world an unprecedented familiarity – practices through which they invent something that is their own and that beckons to the world in its generality' (Mbembe 2002: 258). As such, the themes of sexuality, of intimacy and desire, are topics with which people globally identify and which I study in the everyday practices of contemporary lifestyles. Young professionals in Nairobi articulate feelings of cultural estrangement but these should be read in light of the larger processes described above. The older discourses based on canonical meanings continue to exist in contemporary discourses focussing on cultural heritage. The hegemonic discourses of cultural loss and of glorifying the past maintain a static image of the cultural organizations of sexuality, ignoring cultural change that is intrinsic to life and to which the lives of the grandparents, parents and young professionals themselves testify.

Conclusion

The macro-social narrative that runs through this chapter is how changes in sexual relations are linked to Kenya's social transformations. In short, the widespread alienation of African land, the establishment of overcrowded 'native reserves', the entrenchment of patterns of labour migration, and missionary activities that went hand in hand with the larger goal of 'civilizing' 'Africans' resulted in disrupted family lives and shifting conjugal relationships. Such rapid social and economic changes eroded earlier moral systems and social institutions. In short, societal processes starting in the nineteenth century gradually impacted more and more on social organizations of sexuality, such as the institution of marriage. Secondly, when these marriage patterns changed, the practical and symbolic relations between women and men changed too. Eventually, ideas of womanhood and manhood shifted. This process of transformation, in turn, opened up new possibilities and new forms of consciousness. Nevertheless, transformations concerning gender and sexuality have caused an uneasiness about issues of cultural heritage that continues today. At issue here is the fact that socio-cultural institutions like marriage are a key form of social cohesion, for structuring gender roles and for gender identification. If economic or political processes affect these institutions, invariably gender roles shift, which, in turn, affects the relations between women and men, as well as the larger moral system. These shifts imply changes in power relations that do not go undisputed. Moreover, since sexual arrangements are often experienced as being fundamental to society, moral reactions have characterized and accompanied these processes of social change.

One of the effects of social change is the social group of young professionals, born and raised in Nairobi, by parents who aimed to provide their children with an educational background so that they could pursue a career. They have had to work their way up, are relatively independent of family ties and, as they delay marriage, they have created a subculture marked by a 'sophisticated' lifestyle. They perceive themselves as explorers of contemporary lifestyles, which are, however, also at odds with notions of being 'African'. This balance between 'African' and 'modern' causes a deep-seated anxiety. At the same time, their new lifestyles allow for self-expression where love and sex have become central and which young professionals experience as positive. Therefore, love and sexual relationships comprise a field of tension where matters concerning generational conflicts, cultural heritage, Africanness and contemporary or 'modern' lifestyles are played out.

Sexuality was a 'hot' topic in Kenya in 2001 – the period of this study – and continues to be. This is reflected in the plethora of moral discourses that are preoccupied with sexuality. This volatile context partly frames the sexual culture of young professionals because public discourses codify meanings of sex and sexuality. Before focussing on the biographies of young professionals, it is important to describe AIDS as a contextual factor because it plays such a significant role in people's lives. In the next chapter, I will therefore analyse AIDS in the context of life in Kenya.

Notes

1. *A Change of Tongue* by Antjie Krog (2003: 127).
2. On the other hand, if the rural chiefs became upset with the colonial administration, it would be hard for the administration to collect taxes or find workers in the reserves. This system of 'indirect rule' that the British applied to different African colonies depended on the willingness of rural chiefs or leaders to serve as agents of the imperial state (Stichter 1987).
3. Besides these processes, technological improvement and the development of market centres were also affecting the gendered division of labour. For example, foreign made iron utensils and tools that could be bought changed the nature of manual work (Nyaggah 2003).
4. In the literature I found references to adultery but nothing on the specific circumstances. See for example Kanogo 2005.
5. Luise White (1990b) describes how Kikuyu women and men engaged in colonial labour migration, Mau Mau organization and forest life, as well as during their time in colonial detention camps, debated the nature of marriage, gender relations and gender in relation to new ideas of domesticity and larger ideals of nationhood as envisaged in the future after Independence. Her analysis of the inversion of gender roles is important, but since it con-

cerns a relative small group in (post)colonial Kenya, it is difficult to extend these findings. See also Presley 1992.

6. See Thomas (2003) for an interesting overview of the 'female circumcision controversy' and how female circumcision has been a crucial locus of politics for the Kikuyu Central Association (in which Jomo Kenyatta, the first president, played a major role later), as well as in colonial and postcolonial administrations.

7. Christianity's preoccupation with polygamy, which still continues today, has led to effective changes in the institution. That this change has resulted in what is commonly referred to as modern polygamy, i.e. marriage in combination with extra-marital affairs, is of continuing interest to religious authorities.

8. *Uhuru* means freedom.

9. In 1998, data showed that fifty-one per cent of the Kenyan households were headed by females compared to forty-nine per cent headed by men. Other statistics show decreasing levels of polygamy; increasing age of marriage (despite significant differences in age at first marriage among regions); increasing levels of cohabitation in both rural and urban areas; and evidence that fertility rates have been declining over a period of two decades. Furthermore, bride wealth has increased; sexual activity among adolescents has increased; the structures for the support of (extended) family have declined and, instead, others groups – such as church groups, work place groups, clubs and associations – have taken over these roles. Many families where both wife and husband engage in formal employment make use of house-help, nannies and boarding schools (CBS 1996, 2003; Suda 2002).

10. Bessie House-Midamba's study (1990) on class development deals with gender inequality regarding labour rather than with an analysis on class.

11. Stichter's quantitative study focusses on the changes in female-male relations with regard to material appropriation, conjugal power and decision making, and domestic labour, to find out whether more egalitarian relations were coming into being among these emerging middle classes. Her answer is 'no', as the gender roles remained much the same (although the same as what is not clear), with the only change being that women's labour was now a wage relationship. However, she quotes Lewis on West Africa who showed how marriage was still desirable for working women because their control over their own financial resources made it possible for them to maintain leverage and autonomy. It remains unclear why this would not be the case in Kenya. Stichter's analysis is a little too instrumental, and it lacks the opinions of the women themselves. She also compares the Nairobi couples with 'such [couples] as exist in contemporary European and American middle class families' (1987: 178), while feminist critiques have showed how these women lived in non-egalitarian marriages as housewives.

12. It should be noted that Grace interpreted the relationship between her parents as lacking affection in the light of her own understanding of affection. Her opinion might not correspond with the experience of her parents, who may have had a different view of love and affection.

13. Besides the Gĩkũyũ being the major ethnic group in Nairobi, the spread of the Kikuyu language results from the historical proximity of the region where this ethnic group resided to Nairobi.

14. Personal interview with Professor Nzioka on 18 July 2001, and with Professor Mbatia on 5 November 2001.

15. There is probably another reason why they are apprehensive about socializing with their relatives. According to Geschiere (1996, 1997), the context in which young professionals live is considered by relatives to be typical for creating fear of witchcraft, in this case relatives from rural areas and/or from less fortunate positions. The key question is where they would like to be buried, a topic beyond the scope of this research (see Cohen and Odhiambo 1992; Nyairo 2005). Of the few funerals I have heard about from young professionals' colleagues, friends and relatives, the majority took place in Nairobi, except for in the case of a

few people who belonged to ethnic groups originating from western Kenya, such as Luhya, Gusii and Luo ethnic groups, who attach more value to this custom.

16. Berman distinguishes between political tribalism, which concerns manipulation and networking according to ethnic labelling, and moral ethnicity which guides people's perceptions of their group's involvement in broader political, economic and cultural configuration (1998).

17. See, for example, reports by Kenyan journalists on http://allafrica.com.

18. A *harambee* is a fundraising ceremony in the form of a party where the organizers take care of guests in the expectation that the guests will give a contribution. It can be held to raise funds for a wedding, a hospital bill or a communal goal like a church building.

19. Due to historical migration and education patterns, not all ethnic groups are proportionally represented in the social category of young professionals.

20. All ethnic groups except the Luo circumcise men when they are aged between 8 and 14 years. The Luo do not have circumcision ceremonies to mark a boy's entrance into adulthood; instead, during the whole period of adolescence young men are socialized to become responsible and independent men.

21. Kerubo Kamadi, the social worker I used to accompany on her trips to poorer neighbourhoods to place my research in context with the rest of Nairobi society, married in church seventeen years after being customarily married. This is interesting because her husband Francis is a pastor in their (strict) Quaker Church.

22. These churches are, among others, the Nairobi Baptist Church, the Nairobi Chapel (also Protestant), the Holy Family Basilica (Roman Catholic), and Don Bosco Church (Roman Catholic).

23. Hence the need for a history of modernity that will 'provincialize' Europe (Chakrabarty 1992).

24. The majority are sensitive to political discussions in the media, instigated by columnists such as Oyunga Pala, authors such as Ngugi wa Thiong'o or international celebrities such as President Mbeki from South Africa.

25. '… dominant African discourses on the self developed within a racist paradigm. As discourses of inversion, they draw their fundamental categories from myths they claim to oppose and reproduce their dichotomies: the racial difference between black and white; the cultural confrontation between civilised peoples and savages; the religious opposition between Christians and pagans; the very conviction that race exists and is at the foundation of morality and nationality' (Mbembe 2002: 257).

26. They are not the only ones concerned with what they called 'being modern the African way', however. The famous Ghanaian pastor Mensa Otabil, whose *Living Word TV* is broadcast weekly in Kenya, voices the same sentiments: 'For all of us there is a tension between being African and being modern at the same time' (cited in De Witte 2005: 9). According to De Witte, Otabil's vision of modernity is powerful for many because he integrates notions that are commonly thought to be incompatible: 'African' as cultural heritage hence 'tradition', as opposed to 'modern' as western hence 'foreign'. Instead, Otabil postulates an 'African identity as cosmopolitan, he bridges 'the perceptual gap between African and being modern and developed, he offers people a way of feeling connected to and part of the world, of being global citizens without having to lose their sense of "Africanness"' (De Witte 2005: 14). Otabil offered a possible way out for young professionals; however, the majority were not (yet) attracted to becoming 'born again'.

CHAPTER III

SOCIETY IN FLAMES: SEXUALITY IN THE CONTEXT OF AIDS

Kenya has become a society inflamed by sexual desire.

Marjorie Oludhe-Magoye[1]

Phrases like the above quotation, about a society 'overwhelmed by lust', suggesting sexual chaos by invoking images of 'rampant sex', are not uncommon in Nairobi. Such comments exemplify the almost palpable sentiments that have come to characterize the 'AIDS era'. The topic of sexuality is a hot issue that centres on discussions about sexual morality, practice and agency. Although sexuality has always caused explosive reactions, the course that the current debates take originates from specific responses to the AIDS epidemic. The presence and impact of AIDS has worked like a catalyst on the discussions about sexuality by linking HIV and AIDS with sex and death (Farmer 2006; Obbo 1998; Posel 2005).[2] AIDS has forced sexuality to the forefront in public debates, invoking a response that links cultural heritage and ethical principles. These responses are moral by definition, in the way that they imply judgements of events and motivations from a perspective of right versus wrong. The development of discourse on AIDS provides insights into the current moral discussions about sexuality; AIDS forms the context in which young professionals try to find a balance between sexuality as central to self-expression and their cultural identity.

In this chapter I identify the major discourses on AIDS and the way in which they frame representations of sexuality. I focus on the ways in which the combined topic of HIV, AIDS and sexuality is talked about, how it acquires other meanings, which both precede and inhabit the AIDS discourse, and how it relates to dominant institutional frameworks and social classifications.[3] Discourses are the very fabric of the social web. They carry knowledge and truth effects through their capacity to signal what it is permissible to speak of and do at a particular moment and in particular cultural settings. As such, discourses are the means by which people are reified and confirmed as individuals and the means by which people come to 'know' themselves. It is through discourses that beliefs, rituals and truths surrounding gender, sexuality and ethnicity become manifest and dominant. The discourses that I describe here are not neatly identifiable; instead, they overlap, become partly institutionalized or contradict each other at various sites of the public sphere. First, I describe how AIDS is part of the context of life in Nairobi: as a dreaded disease it has acquired meanings that move beyond medical definitions. Secondly, I show how 'Africanist' perspectives link AIDS with social and cultural change and how these views try to show that the neglect of 'African morals' has led to social chaos and general 'immorality'. Thirdly, I focus on the health approach of the government and nongovernmental organizations; and fourthly, on the religious discourse. These latter two constitute the institutionalized discourses that have been major sources of information on AIDS. Distinguishing the various discourses, it becomes clear that they encompass entire bodies of knowledge and different signifying systems, and that they have a primarily interactive nature.

In this chapter I aim to sketch how AIDS is a context of life for young professionals. In general, AIDS did not often figure in the interviews and conversations. They grew up hearing about the dangers of (unsafe) sex and/or condoms and have accepted the presence of HIV/AIDS as factual and something to avoid. AIDS is an integral part of their life, as is their struggle 'not to go down and become a poor fellow like the rest of the Kenyans' (Robart, aged 23), and I will show in what ways it frames their lives. They would comment on the use of condoms when it constrained their sexual encounters, but they took it as a matter of fact.

The understanding of AIDS as a disease of 'immorality' has become a key concept and has gained a dominant position in public debates, demonstrating how AIDS has come to be understood as a sign of the times by many people. Various actors and institutions use the media to voice their perspectives, and the media have also taken it upon themselves to become the main sources of information about AIDS. In the independent media a niche has been created for forums providing information about sexuality that moves beyond conventional approaches. It is exactly this site in the public sphere where the young professionals find their inspiration and sounding board for their ambitions with regard to their love and sexual lives. Lastly, I will describe why and how these media function as identifiers for young professionals and how sexuality has gained a new understanding in the creation of middle class lifestyles. The media also form an indispensable part of the social context of young professionals, alongside AIDS.

AIDS as a context of life

AIDS, like many diseases, is not merely an illness of a diseased body: it also has profound social implications. AIDS is an awful disease, as well as a source of fear (Farmer 2006). These realities are interrelated and have an impact on the meanings of AIDS in various discourses.

AIDS as a phenomenon of fear is built upon the real life tragedies resulting from the disease. The destructive character of the pandemic has affected individual and collective attempts to organize daily life. The loss of loved ones through AIDS is as bitter as any other death, although sometimes the stigma related to it makes the death still more difficult for the bereaved. The families in which both parents have died, and in which relatives (sometimes grandparents) must take care of bereaved children, find themselves experiencing additional social and economic burdens: elderly parents outlive their children and grandchildren; companies and universities demand proof of HIV negative status before they invest in young and talented employees; insurance companies refuse to take HIV positive clients. The highest numbers of infected persons are among the most economically productive age group (made up of individuals between 20 and 45 years of age), suggesting a grim economic future for some families. The strain on both dependants and caretaker relatives increases with the progress of the disease, as it demands long-term intensive care and the increasing use of palliatives. People often say that 'AIDS causes suffering' and when speaking about AIDS, people's body language typically expresses how AIDS is, in many ways, a tragic disease.

Of the young professionals I spoke to, only one woman – Sarah – was HIV positive and she developed AIDS during 2001. About half of the group has had at least one HIV test; the other half had never gone for testing. More men than women have gone voluntarily for an HIV test, while women often elect to have an HIV test as part of a larger medical check up. Apart from Sarah, none of them was affected by AIDS in 2001/2, nor years later when this book came into being. This group used condoms relatively regularly and systematically because, in the words of Peter (aged 24 in 2001): 'Why play with my life? I have too much to lose. I am eager to live my life and it would be stupid to risk it by having unsafe sex.' Similarly, Bernice (aged 25 in 2001) contended that 'AIDS? Oh well, it's there and it's a fact and I need to take care of myself, why risk my life over something stupid like not using a condom?' Sarah actually called it 'stupid' herself: 'I have thrown away my life for something stupid, a moment of carelessness, it's so so stupid'. These young professionals are ambitious and have much to lose by being 'careless', as they called it.

None of the group's nuclear families (parents and siblings) was known to be HIV positive or to have AIDS, or to have died of AIDS, although about half of the group had lost aunts, uncles, cousins and close friends to AIDS.[4] Everybody reported that they knew people who had died of AIDS, whether colleagues, friends, distant relatives or acquaintances. When the young professionals were teenagers they were warned against AIDS through invocations of the evils of sex and the importance of sexual abstinence before marriage. They had all been made aware of AIDS – its physical and moral causes and its physical, emotional and moral consequences. As such, AIDS has become part of life in Nairobi.

Following the recognition of AIDS in Kenya in the second half of the 1980s, health education programmes were put in place, aimed at enhancing public knowledge of the risks of HIV infection. Later on, measures for promoting safer sex practices were established. Information on the nature of HIV and AIDS was disseminated through posters, pamphlets, radio and TV messages and through primary health care services; however, this was done in a relatively *ad hoc* way, because of the reluctance of the government to acknowledge the extent of the problem. Public institutions such as schools, colleges and universities became targets for AIDS education. A little later, the whole population was included by way of work environments, places for social gatherings and the media. At the turn of the century, AIDS had become a common topic in the media. The central message is that HIV is transmitted primarily through (heterosexual) sexual intercourse.

In almost every meeting I have attended in Nairobi, and in nearly every flyer or television programme that I have seen on the subject, the latest numbers of HIV infections and AIDS victims in Kenya was a central point of reference. It is thought that the endless repetition of these alarming numbers will serve to prevent people from engaging in 'risk behaviour', that is, illicit sex, or sex outside the socially approved institution of marriage. The numbers themselves have taken on a life of their own, in their sweeping and frightening statements of death. The monotonous recitals that indicate thousands and even millions of 'HIV cases' or 'death cases' – or, in the common phrase in town, 'Every one out of seven Kenyans has it' – create an uncanny atmosphere marked by implicit or sometimes explicit accusations. Discussions about AIDS became shrouded in demarcations of right and wrong, as in the following statement: 'Long before I understood that AIDS is a disease like cancer, I knew it was bad, something to avoid, but, then I had no clue what to avoid!' (Alex, aged 20). For young professionals, like many other Kenyans, AIDS has become a phenomenon of fear.

According to Nzioka (1996), a professor at the University of Nairobi, the public response to the AIDS pandemic has been moral in essence. Halfway through the 1990s, AIDS provided 'a golden opportunity for moral entrepreneurs to advocate for a return to "traditional normal" sexual behaviour':

> A rift has since emerged between what could plausibly be described as the conservative forces on the one hand, and the liberal modernists on the other. The conservative moralists, led by members of the clergy, and the 'traditionalists' see HIV/AIDS as a consequence of wanton and wild promiscuity, permissiveness, and moral decadence often associated with the adoption of Western liberal moral values. Despite the enormous conceptual difficulties of what could be termed as 'African' in a culturally pluralistic country like Kenya, the moralization of HIV/AIDS has provided the conceptions of what they consider to be an 'African traditional way of life'. .... Generally speaking, the mysteries surrounding HIV/AIDS have opened the flood-gates for the traditionalists to call for the revitalization of 'African' sexual culture; a heightened sense of Puritanism from the clergy who remain opposed to a liberal sexual culture that accommodates the use of condoms; political sloganeering of 'patriotic' politicians who enhance their popularity through anti-Western rhetoric; and a forum for voyeuristic journalism and sensational reporting by newspaper editors. (Nzioka 1996: 566)

From the beginning of the epidemic, AIDS became implicated in different social meanings beyond health matters. These debates operate in the public sphere in an attempt to make sense of AIDS, and by extension, sexuality and cultural heritage in different, and sometimes overlapping, ways (see Posel 2005 on South Africa). Sexuality is a domain over which various groups wield or try to wield authority, by invoking the dangers of AIDS in various ways. AIDS has therefore become a major frame of reference for debating sexuality. It is a catalyst which inflames discussions about sexuality even when AIDS is not the central issue.

The development of the meanings of AIDS cannot be traced to one single discourse. While the biomedical perspective on AIDS gained a hegemonic position from the beginning among health experts, initially it did not reach far among the population because of the *ad hoc* nature and/or delay of prevention campaigns. In the meantime, AIDS became a point of discussion from various perspectives within society as the disease was claiming its victims. AIDS directed the focus at the ages at which people first have sex and the increase in premarital sex, both of which are related to the increase in average age at marriage (National Council for Population & Development 1993). This has led to a continuing preoccupation with the notion that adolescent sex has grown out of bounds. In tandem with the biomedical approach of AIDS, which led to specific representations of AIDS and sexuality, lay perspectives of AIDS gained dominance. Africanist perspectives and ideas about 'immorality' played an important role in the way in which AIDS became common knowledge in Kenya.

Africanist perspectives on AIDS and sexuality

As Nzioka has indicated, the effects that AIDS had on social organizations of life and the realization of the central role of sex in the developing epidemic, has led to extensive reflections about people's morals. These reflections have focussed specifically on the presumed loss of 'African cultural' morals. In the face of social transformation, the notion of cultural loss gained momentum in order to explain the experience of social chaos during the postcolonial era. AIDS came to be seen as an offspring of this chaos.

The Africanist discourse is marked by heated debates that are frequently expressed via the media. The main actors postulating particular sentiments of cultural heritage are older men in power positions in government, in religious institutions and in kinship organizations. Their role as moral guardians is sometimes supported by older women and disempowered men whose social role as elders is – at least in their opinion – not recognized. According to Professor Bahemuka, this closing of ranks indicates that the current discussions and conflicts described in this chapter need to be seen in the context of changing gerontocratic power structures.[5]

The following 'letter to the editor', entitled 'I am disgusted by modern youth', is a typical example of the zealous efforts of 'concerned Kenyans', as they often call themselves, trying to reach others by writing to newspapers, speaking at funerals, *harambees* (see note 18 on page 96), church services or family gatherings:

> In traditional African society, the situation was different [compared to nowadays]. There were values of spiritual uprightness and ethics, which guided society in its sexual behaviour. Sex before marriage was a crime and virginity was a virtue. But today, the traditional way of life governing African societies has been thrown out the window and such values are discarded. What you see now is that young people smoke, drink and have sex. (Ochomo 2001)

This is typical of the sentiments underlying the Africanist discourse that I have often encountered. Sexuality is understood as a natural force that needs to be channelled by rules and moral uprightness. The connection between 'immorality' and AIDS is, first of all, 'bad sex'. There are clues, within the references to sexuality and 'immorality' that open the discussions to a wider historical context. In other words, sex has not always been as 'structurally astray' as it is these days. Here, the letter writer is quite clear about the cause of AIDS – an excess of the 'joy of life' in contemporary society due to a disregard for 'African morals'. The sensitive issue of sexuality-gone-astray has been replaced by the generative concept of 'immorality'. Immorality has a dominant rationale: it explains how sexual behaviour has grown out of bounds and how it has become a banal commodity. The banality of sex is commonly illustrated by differentiating sex for pleasure and sex for procreation. Procreative sex is the sacred meaning of sexuality; it is 'good sex'. Sex for pleasure alone implies anti-social behaviour and, as such, is a root cause of social disintegration. As Dawn (aged 27) explained to me: 'If you keep on having too much bad sex [as a society], then a disease must come out of that'. 'Immorality' is directly related to 'westernization'.

The notion of 'westernization' has become a structuring idiom for many Kenyans to account for the current malaise Kenyans are 'suffering' from. What is called bad sex in contemporary society is seen as having been ushered in by changes in the positioning of sexuality within cultural institutions, like initiation ceremonies or marriage. Before the advent of AIDS, premarital sexual intercourse was not approved of, and this disapproval was endorsed by powerful sanctions. From the time when Kenyan cultures were still authentic until the present, a growing process of immorality is supposed to have taken place gradually together with the breakdown of traditional influence. This glorifying notion of a lost culture that strictly regulated sexual behaviour and sexual patterns has also been analysed by various Kenyan scholars (Ahlberg 1994; Bauni and Jarabi 2000; Chege 1993). Such studies are partly the result of existing discourses, and tend to grant authority to discourses on lost culture.[6] The common discourse states how in the postcolonial period, sexual behaviour has gone astray because of the loss of traditional morals. The corrupting force behind this erosion and negative change is usually taken to be foreign – particularly Western – influence. Africanist discourse is nostalgic by definition, postulating 'African' in opposition to 'Western' and employing a notion of 'westernization' that is amoral because of being 'non-African'. Ochomo (the letter writer) goes on as follows:

> The behaviour of Kenyan youth makes me loathe. As you roam town streets past cinemas, theatres, discos, video halls, churches, schools, universities, and public offices, you cannot avoid seeing the latest hairstyles and clothes. The young people are always smoking and drinking, and I shed tears as I see them dressed in transparent clothes just because the attire is fashionable. If you came to Kenya from another part of the world with a dress which exposed your buttocks and proclaimed it to be latest fashion (Toni Braxton style), in a few days, most of Kenya would be flooded with half-naked youths. (Ochomo 2001)

The casual mention of 'Toni Braxton style' relates to a public discussion when Toni Braxton, a female musician from the United States, won a prestigious music award in 2001. As an Afro-American, she won much praise from the Kenyan public who portray successful Afro-Americans as role models. However, at the presentation ceremony Braxton was clothed in a dress that consisted of two long cloths, draped from the front to the back over her shoulder, leaving the sides of her body uncovered. It was broadcast on TV and pictures were shown in the print media in Kenya, causing an uproar that eventually led to the phrase 'Toni Braxton style' as a symbol of 'westernization'.

The debates in response to the dress of Braxton indicate how volatile sentiments are with regard to cultural heritage, morals and sexuality. It is not uncommon to hear young people speak along these lines because these sentiments articulating a loss of African heritage are shared among all age groups. It is also implied that 'westernization' influences sexual desire in a way that is quite direct. It is repeatedly stated that movies, pornographic material, advertisements, soap operas, dress and music are at the root of corrupting influences.[7] The issue of 'exposure' is often mentioned to indicate the problematic relationship between Western media and commodities and their reception into local systems of meaning. People point to video clips, movies, music or dress for their suggestive qualities, or sometimes for their openly sexual display. According to many, the increasing numbers of such 'nonresidential' items contribute to 'immoral' behaviour. The notions of 'external influence' and of 'the disease of immorality' are seen as directly related: 'external influences' cause people to abandon their 'African morals', leading to 'immoral' behaviour which is thought to result in unwanted pregnancies, AIDS and other diseases. The notion of external influences stands not only for material aspects like movies, dress, music, and so on, but also for different ideas regarding matters of sexuality, divorce, or gender roles. Ochomo loathes his contemporaries who are participating in the globalizing 'joy of life', exemplified by 'fashionable attire' (see also Ferguson 1999: 214).

Because Africanist discourse articulates the loss of cultural singularity that is experienced by many Kenyans, the discourse is shared by many different groups. Images of Africanness are invoked and used by various and diverse factions of society. In the Africanist discourse there is a need to distinguish righteous sex from sinful sex, by focussing mainly on morals implying chastity.[8] This is the point where the religious and the Africanist discourses converge and it is likely that they originate from the same source – the moral panic caused by the presence of AIDS. These discourses articulate the conservative disposition of the main actors in these debates.

In practice, Africanist perspectives regarding 'good' and 'bad' sex exhibit considerable flexibility according to the changing preoccupations in public debates. In 2001, they ranged from debating 'immoral dress', or regarding divorced women as being un-African and thus 'immoral', to the importation of millions of condoms indicating the level of 'immorality' in Kenya. No mention is made of other 'African' customs like female circumcision, polygamy, or the practice of ritual cleansing by having sex.[9] This is also where the Christian and Africanist discourses clash: Christianity condemns these customary practices as sinful. At times, the Christian and Africanist perspectives converge in their conservative comments, but they also articulate existing conflicts within conservative circles. In Africanist discourse, the notion of sexual morals is flexibly used: exactly what these morals are is hardly specified. Instead, 'African' or 'traditional' morals are invoked as self-evident truths.[10] What these truths are is far from clear. Like Ochomo does, invocations of truth are justified by summarizing contemporary bad behaviour. The representation of sexuality in the Africanist discourse remains limited to invocations of chastity based on images of a glorified past and a defiling present. This is in contrast to the Christian, governmental and NGO discourses that have attempted to define certain sexual behaviour more specifically.

Policies of the government and nongovernmental organizations[11]

In an interview I had with Ms Gatua, the director of the Kenya AIDS NGO Consortium in 2001, the phrase 'and then they shelved it' recurred several times. She was speaking about the reluctance of the government regarding the implementation of AIDS prevention programmes for almost two decades.[12] The initial reluctance of the government decreased because of pressure from the international community or donors. The government's need for financial resources forced it to adopt the internationally accepted perspective on how to fight AIDS, and the official policy reflected the biomedical approach to AIDS. Because these programmes were more or less imposed on the government, individual ministers and government officials could still refuse to cooperate or engage in the discussion about AIDS. The government hospitals and clinics had in general been more engaging because they played a central role in the care of HIV and AIDS patients. During the last decade, the adoption by the government and nongovernmental organizations of the generally accepted AIDS paradigm has led to a general consensus in the way in which AIDS is approached and hence how the aims of prevention campaigns are formulated.[13] Sexuality is understood as a self-evident element of human behaviour, which can have negative implications for an individual's health. Public health institutions see it as their responsibility to redirect harmful behaviour.

The policy focus has gone through various stages. Initially the focus was on providing information on modes of transmission and on the need for safe sex, which was later followed by providing more information about the disease itself and about nutrition. In the 1990s, the emphasis on the need to take care of patients became an integrated issue involving the need for the counselling of AIDS victims and creating awareness for the need to accept AIDS victims. As the epidemic unfolded, the problem of AIDS orphans and elderly people who have to take care of their grandchildren was also addressed. Similarly, the dilemma's discordant couples – when one partner is infected and the other is not – face concerning the necessity to engage in safe sex or their reproductive desires, became integrated in the outreach programmes.

The lack of knowledge about HIV and AIDS during the early years invoked many fears. At first, AIDS patients were isolated in hospitals because of uncertainty about transmission. Their corpses were also given a special burial: government officials went to the graveside to ensure that a corpse was buried properly. The first posters to make people aware of the new disease showed images of skeletons, or of a fruit with worms. In the 1990s positive messages became the trend of prevention programmes, such as the portrayal of a happy and caring family in order to encourage people to be 'responsible' and to 'take care' of their families by taking care of themselves, i.e. by using condoms. This change in approach came about because of the realization, as Ms Gatua remarked, that 'fear gives temporary change only. Fear causes fatalistic attitudes. We should not scare people, we should inform them.'

In 1995, the government became more seriously involved in the AIDS prevention programmes. With a loan from the World Bank it started the STI (Sexually Transmitted Infections) programme because of the close relation between STIs and HIV infection. At the same time, churches took the lead with home-based care programmes. From 1995, the media got engaged by providing information and addressing sensitive subjects related to sexuality and gender. In time, government officials followed. According to Ms Gatua, 'the reluctance of leaders is a shameful display, they were afraid it would taint their name to speak about AIDS because of the stigma, they feared losing votes. Government people were dying of AIDS and they still denied it.' The Kenya AIDS NGO Consortium started to organize symposia for civil and religious leaders covering topics such as the need to talk without stigma about AIDS, or about gender issues. Gradually leaders began to address issues like the relation between AIDS and extramarital affairs or wife inheritance, which is more common nowadays. In November 1999, former President Moi declared AIDS a national disaster. Ms Gatua stated that 'Until politicians spoke, people also kept quiet'.[14]

Since the beginning of the epidemic, the core message has been that people should be educated about HIV infection that is caused by sexual intercourse and the risks of unprotected sex. However, the definition of safe sex differs among the various sectors. For non-religious nongovernmental organizations and government clinics, safer sex is viewed as synonymous with condom use, to the great dismay of religious institutions, especially the influential Catholic Church. The government aimed to ensure that condoms are available at affordable prices, or for free. In the early 1990s, public opposition to promoting contraception, led by the clergy, grew. A 'concerned' parent elucidates the complex and delicate nature of this discussion:

> The full evils of contraception, sex without responsibility, will soon befall Kenyans if the project succeeds. Children will be taught how to 'get a kick' with sex. There would be more promiscuity amongst teenagers and teachers; there will be greater drop-out rate from educational institutions; parental authority will wane; there will be less respect for life; more drug addiction; an increase in sexually transmitted diseases and more people contracting AIDS. (quoted in Njau 1993: 2)

It was believed that the availability of condoms would 'promote immorality', which is more or less defined as sex for pleasure. This fierce societal reaction inhibited the government from adopting the promotion of condom use as a formal policy. Instead, advocating condoms as a family planning prophylactic has become the way to circumvent this moral obstacle. The government thus could adopt the abstinence strategy while also providing condoms under the guise of family planning. The hegemonic meanings of 'immorality' and the authority of the religious institutions also force nongovernmental organizations to work within the paradigm of promoting abstinence while discreetly promoting condom use. The ABC approach has become the most common catchphrase. 'ABC' stands for Abstain, Be faithful and use Condoms (or as it is sometimes put, 'condomize'). The messages are meant to be applied sequentially: people should be convinced to abstain, and when married, to be faithful. Only as a last resort is the use of condoms mentioned. In practice, government and nongovernmental organization clinics and dispensaries provide condoms, other contraceptives and HIV tests for a small fee, indicating that the government and international sectors subsidize this health sector despite the many objections.

The resemblance between governmental and nongovernmental organizations' policies is related to the acceptance of the international approach to AIDS. This approach is mainly based on a biomedical understanding of HIV and AIDS, which was initially understood as primarily a health issue. This is not to say that this general perspective denies the relation between, for example, poverty and HIV infection, but it does not include these wider implications in its framework. This approach has had two major implications that have characterized the responses to AIDS in Kenya. One is the way in which categories of 'risk groups' have been defined; the other is how sexuality has become 'medicalized'. Both aspects have had major implications with regard to popular representations of sexuality.

The definition of 'risk groups'

The overrepresentation of prostitutes in the medical discourse on AIDS (see Chapter I) has 'confirmed' certain assumptions about women's social and sexual identity, their risk status and their responsibility in AIDS prevention. In the early 1990s, Nairobi was often cited as one of the cradles of AIDS in East Africa – with recurrent references to its 'reservoir of prostitutes' and hawkers who, together with truck drivers, were depicted as constituting a reservoir of HIV infection – due to the city's central position in the region (see the title of the article by D'Costa 1985). Moreover, the authoritative Western medical paradigm of 'African AIDS' (Patton 1992) crystallized the identities of 'prostitutes in Africa' by defining the female subjects of epidemiological studies primarily through their main risk attribute, namely, multi-partnered sexuality. Both research and interventions identified women as a locus of infection, and therefore the target population for health education and condom distribution in Kenya. This paradigm shaped public and media discourses on AIDS in Kenya because the studies were 'uncritically adopted in the media discourse on AIDS' (Kielmann 1997: 379).[15]

This focus on women stems from the tendency in the AIDS research and programmes to classify social groups both in Kenya (Nyamwaya 1992) and elsewhere (Cáceres 2000). Government agencies and nongovernmental organizations tend to objectify and categorize people in the way in which they conceive of health care projects and facilities.[16] By focussing on certain groups and by employing the concept 'risk group', the complexities of AIDS became more graspable to them. This practice was taken over by the media and other social actors and resulted in the stigmatization of these specific groups. The way in which the issue of AIDS was, and sometimes still is, presented resulted in the creation of sexual hierarchies (Adkins 2001), based on demarcations of proper and improper sex. The result of this process is that the rest of the population, most of whom do not belong to these specific categories, can then distance themselves symbolically from any association with HIV infection through a process of 'othering'. 'Others', like prostitutes and truck drivers, are ascribed certain characteristics in causing AIDS that are not applicable to non-prostitutes and non-truck drivers (Spronk 2000).

Because prostitutes formed a visible and publicly disputed social group, and were easy to distinguish, they became the icon of AIDS. They also became the icon of the meaning of AIDS in Kenya, i.e. a disease born out of wrongdoing. The medical and media interest in this particular group of women coexisted with the existing gender ideology in Kenya. The emphasis on women – and by implication the representation of women's responsibility with regard to AIDS – is part and parcel of the gendered moral discourse which is preoccupied first and foremost with female sexuality. As Nzioka states, 'Kenyan society is largely patriarchal, and dominant sexual beliefs which have informed HIV and AIDS education programmes are based on male chauvinistic ideas. These ideologies of male dominance represent prostitutes as "AIDS-givers" and men as passive victims' (Nzioka 1994: 169). The overall effect is that prostitutes, and by implication all women, received, and still receive, disproportional attention in AIDS prevention programmes, research and the media. Research and intervention efforts geared towards men remained limited for a long period until a change in paradigm initiated by the United Nations was introduced in 2001.

In short, the definitions of 'risk groups' led to a public catchphrase of 'prostitutes and truck drivers' as the main 'source' of HIV infection. This way of representing AIDS has had far-reaching consequences. It led many people to feel that they were not implicated in the epidemic. It led to stigmatization of HIV and AIDS patients and the visual demarcations of what is proper and improper, based on the notion of 'immorality'. As discourses about AIDS echo many other social concerns, the relation between certain groups of women, 'immorality' and AIDS has become common knowledge. For example, one of the first posters distributed by the Ministry of Health and the Red Cross depicts a man following a shapely figure clad in a red mini dress and high heels. Against the backdrop of a city at night, we can see the frontal view of the skeletal figure, which is a mask of death. The caption reads: 'WHAT YOU CAN SEE IS NOT WHAT YOU GET – AIDS KILLS'. Until 2001, such drawings continued to appear in the media.

In a similar vein, for example, the image of a shapely young woman in 'sophisticated' or 'sexy' dress, or at least not old fashioned, makes scapegoats of young professionals because they dress in skirts or trouser suits and shoes with heels. In an interesting twist, they are understood to dress in a non-'African' manner. During my first visit to Nairobi in 1997, my roommate spent a night in police custody after being arrested at six o'clock in the town centre during a 'razzia' [raid] aimed at 'prostitutes and hawkers who spoil the streets'. She called me and when I went there I found a police station filled with female white-collar workers employed at one of the many offices in the centre district. The police excused themselves by claiming that they only took the women who dress 'like prostitutes'. This incident shows how 'sophisticated' or 'modern' female dress has been a bone of contention for years. The following discussions in the media centred on the 'westernizing' style in relation to 'moderate African' style. What this moderate style entails is far from clear. Some debates hinted that 'Western' style is too revealing, as does the letter writer Ochomo cited earlier. However, the women I found in the police station were all dressed in official skirt or trouser suits that were far from revealing or 'sexy'. The fact that they were arrested for looking like 'prostitutes' reflects a preoccupation in public discourse with women's dress (see also Oldfield et al. 2009; Sackey 2003 on South Africa and Ghana).

Medical understandings of AIDS postulated the definition of 'risk groups' and the definition of 'risk groups' resulted in specific understandings of AIDS. These representations limited the debate about HIV infection for a long time. Instead of addressing pressing issues with regard to AIDS, the resulting discourses about AIDS redirected the debates to other social concerns. The biomedical paradigm operated in yet another way in its approach to AIDS; it postulated very particular understandings of sexuality, which we will now look at closely.

The medicalization of sexuality

As discussed in the Introduction, the medicalization of sexuality refers to a process by which non-medical problems become defined and treated as medical problems. Parsons began the analysis of this process with his anthropological description of social control in medical practice (Parsons 1951). Similarly, analyses of the 'medicalization of society' examine how medicine has been implicated in the social control of citizens (Foucault 1990 [1976]), or of women and colonial subjects (Comaroff 1993; Vaughan 1991). The systematic variations – the targeting and monitoring of people through techniques of testing, surveys and health promotion – have become common. The surveillance of sexual behaviour by the state typically occurs in public health care. The 'clinical gaze' (a generally medicalized perspective on the world) transforms this surveillance into control over sexuality by distinguishing healthy from unhealthy behaviour. This process occurs in the population, through public health mechanisms, and (ideally) through self-regulation by a process through which citizens internalize the differentiations between healthy and unhealthy.[17]

The Kenyan government and nongovernmental organization discourse on AIDS uses the clinical gaze to contain societal problems like adolescent pregnancies, STIs and AIDS. The clinical gaze operates through the various programmes, such as primary health care or the STI clinics of the Ministry of Health and of nongovernmental organizations, by defining health and illness. The practice of health promotion relies on a number of basic assumptions. There has to be 'an information giver, a mediator of knowledge, self-positioned experts who have access to the "truth" and see it as their role to mediate the process of truth-giving' (Woodhead 1995: 234). When passed onto the people, it is understood that this medical knowledge saves lives, improves people's lots and enriches experiences. Medical discourse defines the 'problem' – that AIDS results from unsafe sex – and hence defines the 'solution' – safe sex or no sex. As a consequence, people engaging in 'unsafe sex' are judged to be irrational, i.e. improper citizens. The clinical gaze is thus carried further as a way of coercing people to conduct themselves as healthy subjects with healthy lifestyles.

In Kenya this meant that the recognition of AIDS as a disease is subtly embedded in the general understanding of AIDS as the disease of immorality. Despite the long-standing presence and widespread effects of AIDS – resulting in a certain normalization of AIDS – and despite manifold efforts by different groups calling for an understanding of AIDS as an ordinary disease that can befall anyone, AIDS still carries with it these extra meanings. Although nowadays AIDS is perhaps not directly associated in speech with 'immorality', the recurring debates about 'immorality' connect 'socials ills like AIDS' with moral wrongdoing. In a subtle way, AIDS remains related to 'immorality'. In this light, HIV testing acquires a specific meaning. Sarah (aged 25) was the only person from this study who was (known to be) HIV positive, developing AIDS towards the end of the research in 2002. She made a great effort to convince me she had not acquired HIV because of a particular 'immoral' lifestyle; instead, she had been 'unlucky': 'Yes, I have been stupid as to have unprotected sex, but no, that was not my habit. First of all, I was not particularly sexually active, I used condoms, but not consistently and so ... Yaah, only one lapse and your life is gone.'

Reflections on HIV testing in the literature suggest that HIV diagnostic tests may be understood as a technique of surveillance medicine through which the virus is personified (Adkins 2001: 40). HIV diagnostic testing can thus also be understood as a constellation of administrative and discursive techniques whereby the subjects are classified through the securing of a confession as to the 'truth' of their sexuality. It then becomes an assessment of sexual risk behaviour and proper behaviour. The diagnosis is extended beyond the physical examination to the cause of AIDS: the focus is not on the HIV infection through sexual intercourse but also on the kind of sexual intercourse. The meaning of AIDS as a result of illicit sex takes the diagnosis a little further: HIV infection is caused by 'immoral' sex. The medicalization of sex in Kenya thus works partly to legitimate moral definitions of proper and improper sexual behaviour. Where religion used to be the major actor in defining morally acceptable sexual conduct, this task falls now also to medical science.

Another important consequence of the medicalization of sexuality is the depoliticization of societal problems. Rather than a matter of government responsibility, the pursuit of public health has come to be defined as a matter of individual action, where the primary responsibility is located with the individual, who is expected to adopt certain lifestyle choices. Thus, while laying the burden of illness, in this case HIV infection, on the individual, rather than dealing with the social causes of what becomes defined as deviant behaviour, the individual loses autonomy to an institution, such as public health institutions. Within the definition of AIDS as a 'disease of immorality', the blame is placed on the AIDS patient, as HIV infection implies individual sinfulness. The reality that people may have been forced by circumstances to engage in unsafe sex practices is not denied as such, but this broader approach to understanding sexuality does not fit into the medical definition of AIDS.

Summing up, medical responses to AIDS have arisen in three overlapping fields: first in health education and preventative medicine; second in the development of an infrastructure to provide treatment and care for people with HIV and AIDS; and third at the socio-cultural level where dominant meanings about AIDS are established. Medical perceptions of AIDS as a health issue and lay perceptions of AIDS as a disease of 'immorality' have contributed to moral understandings of AIDS and sexuality. The definition of risk groups, the medicalization of sexuality and the patriarchal gender ideologies have limited discussions about sexuality. As a result, sex has become entangled in demarcations of wrong and right, leaving out many other aspects of sexuality.

Christian perceptions of AIDS and sexuality[18]

Religion plays a powerful role in the 'gospel of AIDS', as some young professionals characterized it, since the AIDS prevention programmes established by mainstream Christian institutions have been even more consistently visible than those established by government or by other local and international nongovernmental organizations (Hearn 2002). Many notions regarding AIDS and sexuality, and their interconnection, described above also account for the many religiously inspired AIDS prevention programmes, which resemble the governmental and nongovernmental organization structures in many ways. While AIDS has led to the medicalization of sexuality, the moralization of AIDS and sexuality has gained momentum with it. This means that AIDS and sexuality belong to two domains over which religion maintains a hegemonic position in Kenya, as religion wields authority over the medical and the moral institutions. Sexuality is understood by religion as a natural force with productive and destructive capacities for the individual as well as for the community. As such, sexuality needs to be carefully monitored by Christian principles.

Churches in Kenya contest the authority of the independent state over AIDS (Friedmann 1997). The mainstream churches of Kenya – whether under the umbrella of the National Council of Churches of Kenya (NCCK) or separately (the Church of the Province of Kenya [Anglican], the Roman Catholic Church of Kenya, and the Presbyterian Church of East Africa) – have developed into a political watchdog, whose actions have included criticizing the government in the name of Christian social justice over various political issues, such as ethnic violence and the absence of multiparty elections.[19] Many churches have special advantages in their political battles against the government when addressing AIDS policy. They have funding from sources that lie outside government scrutiny, and organizational networks equalling that of the ruling party. Moreover, they have an almost unassailable position of moral authority that the government can only attack at great risk of a political backlash. Since the mission hospitals of the mainstream churches constitute a significant part of Kenya's health care system, Christianity has a long reach (Friedmann 1997: 382).

In addition, the impact of foreign evangelical mission hospitals should not be underestimated. According to Hearn, US evangelic missions constitute one of the most important non-state agencies in Kenya (Hearn 2002).[20] Their significance lies in their role as implementers of the 'new policy agenda' of the US government's development policy framework that promotes abstinence as the proper safe sex practice. Their highly developed infrastructure and financial abilities make them a prominent actor in the field of Kenya's AIDS prevention programmes (cf. Hearn 2002). In general all churches have responded to AIDS in a similar fashion: promoting marital sex as the only solution for the AIDS pandemic. Religious institutions were probably the main informants about HIV and AIDS during the early days, when governmental AIDS prevention programmes were not as integrated as they are today. The relation of sex to HIV and the resulting moral panic during the late 1980s of the then unfamiliar disease were met by sermons about 'immorality'.[21] The tone for discussion about AIDS was set. Depending on the church denomination, people were warned against the 'effects of immorality', with AIDS called a 'curse from God'. This resulted in the victimization of individual AIDS patients who were sometimes treated as outcasts. Over time, the churches have redirected the content of their AIDS messages, speaking out against stigmatization and calling for compassion, care for patients, and openness. The discussions have been broadened to include topics like gender and sexual politics, the relation between poverty and AIDS, and the political will to fight AIDS. It has become common practice in several churches to demand an AIDS test before a couple can marry, although the mainstream churches only go as far as advising couples to do an AIDS test. Most churches provide counselling when one or both members of the couple are HIV positive. Some churches strongly advise couples to stay together and to have a 'safe' marital life, i.e. to use condoms. Other churches leave the choice open and often people cancel the marriage when one partner is found to be HIV infected.

Many churches provide medical care as well as offering spiritual solace. But AIDS is not just an illness: it is a sexually transmitted disease, and the regulation of sexual behaviour has long been the domain of religion. Prior to the ascendancy of biomedicine, sexuality was the province of religion. It defines sexuality primarily as a moral issue and Christianity in Kenya does so with great authority. Young professionals who say that they are not believers explain that Christian morals are still an important frame of reference: 'Even if you are not saved [being a "true" believer], you believe that religion knows best. We have grown up respecting religion very much' (Martha, aged 24). The indirect social control of religion is a process whereby individuals learn 'how not to' rather than 'how to', from a perspective that sets 'moral' and 'immoral' behaviour against each other. Christian discourse remains an important source of information about AIDS and, to a certain extent, sexuality.

The remoralization of sexuality

From the time I arrived in Kenya in 1997 up to 2004, I have collected letters about AIDS sent to the editors of the main newspapers. The tone has not changed much, but the focus of discontent has differed at times. In fact, every week there has been a constant flow of letters by religiously inspired and 'concerned' Kenyans in the newspapers. Typical examples are:

On behalf of true believers, we are very disturbed about the rising numbers of HIV infections. The issue of condoms contradicts our faith in the true God. For God will be harder on Kenya for giving the devil a chance to carry out his evil work. God hates sin and when people rebel against Him, he fights them through incurable diseases like AIDS and Ebola. (Njeru 1997)

I am a 'True Love Waits' [Christian campaign directed at the youth] believer and I want to call upon my fellow youth Kenyans to CHOOSE FOR ABSTINENCE because God will reward those who are faithful. ABSTINENCE IS OKAY. (Momanjy 1998)

HIV/AIDS is a test for Kenyans. Like drought, floods, famine and earthquakes, it questions our preparedness to turn to God as the only Source of Life. Why should we mislead the youth? Condoms are promoting sexual promiscuity. Chastity is the key, we should value virginity and marriage. (Oguk 2001)

The question of whether God has sent AIDS due to man's immorality is one which only God can answer. My fellow Kenyan, let's avoid blaming one another or God for this terrible epidemic, but rather observe God's law which states that there should be no sex outside marriage. (Kimeli 2001)

The general Christian argument is that 'immorality' has led to AIDS. Immorality became defined as 'sinful sex', which is either premarital sex or extramarital sex. Rightful or good sex is marital sex sanctioned by the Bible and is regarded as a positive and important aspect of the conjugal bond. The cause of immorality, therefore, is the transgression of Christian morals and it is fought by calling for a stronger commitment to Christian teachings, often justified by quotations from the Bible. Many religious discussions about immorality in relation to AIDS focus on the use and implications of condoms. These discussions are inspired by the widespread belief that the availability of condoms will result in more sexual activity. The rising numbers of HIV infections during the 1990s were perceived as justifications of this reasoning, and the following is commonly heard: 'You know, the problem with condoms is that you encourage sexuality. If I give a condom to a youth, don't I tell him that it is okay to have sex? You see, condoms are sinful' (Pastor Mulama of the Don Bosco Church).[22]

The True Love campaign is one of the many organized religious responses to the AIDS pandemic. It is an international Christian movement that made its way from the United States across the African continent to educate young people about sexual abstinence until marriage. Their message is that 'true love waits to be consumed in marriage', and they define sexual relationships as marital and monogamous. It tries not to alienate youth and not condemn their desire for a contemporary identity based on popular music, going out and having 'boyfriend-girlfriend' relationships.

Instead, it hooks into their mind frame, by employing a discourse of love, and advocating abstinence as a responsibility that 'modern' individuals choose because it fits their lifestyle.

The way in which the True Love Campaign addresses the youth by incorporating lifestyle issues is a good example of how religious institutions have reassessed their targets and approaches in the context of the continuing AIDS pandemic. It reflects a larger process of redefining sexual morals. The emphasis on chastity and monogamy is not new, as such; however, the way it is embedded in matters regarding lifestyle indicates the new direction that religious discourse has taken with regard to discussing sexual mores. In the churches the young professionals participate in, for example, an explicit role is carved out for men; as we shall see later on, a 'modern man' is portrayed as a 'monogamous man'. Such phrases point to the need, in this case of young professionals, to redefine gender and behaviour. Instead of only warning against 'immorality' by invoking God's wrath, religious leaders redirect their approach to elucidate exactly what is meant by chastity. Typically, non-married people are told that their body 'is a temple of God' and that sex is a 'marital blessing', i.e. that premarital sex is 'sinful'.

The remoralization of sexuality becomes most clear with regard to the redefinition of the language of sexuality. Sexuality is nowadays discussed in terms of 'faithfulness', 'virginity' and above all 'abstinence'. Phrases like 'immoral sex', 'polygamous sex' and 'teenage sex' are more and more explicitly named in sermons as the antithesis of Christian morals. This is in contrast to the previous idiom where 'marital duty' or 'procreation' would imply sexual intercourse.[23] Religious leaders take it upon themselves, as their moral duty, to distinguish deviant sexual behaviour from proper sexual behaviour: 'These days people get easily confused. There are too many views and people find it difficult to know right from wrong. If many people engage in certain behaviour, others might think it's okay' (Pastor Mbita of the Nairobi Baptist Church).[24] During the same sermon, 'sexual intercourse so as to be blessed with children' was named as the 'only and proper way of intercourse'. Whereas sexuality was usually discussed in more veiled terms, more and more often phrases like 'teenage sexuality', 'homosexuality', 'bestiality' and other 'perversities' are also being used to be as clear as possible in describing proper from improper sex. Moreover, in the many clubs of the churches, organized according to age and marital status, matters of sexuality are deliberately discussed so as not to 'estrange people for whom sex is a challenge being a Christian', according to Pastor Maxwell of the Nairobi Chapel (see also Bochrow 2005 on Ghana).[25] Their point is to define respectable sexuality by clearing out the manifold possibilities of inappropriate sexuality.

A major difference between the Catholic Church and the Protestant Churches is in their attitudes to condom use. The Catholic Church rejects the use of condoms as decided by the Vatican, while other churches have incorporated the promotion of condoms as the 'lesser of two evils'. As far as I have noticed, the use of condoms is not explicitly preached, apart from by a few outspoken leaders, although in services and flyers people are encouraged to 'protect themselves', which has become a euphemism for condom use. Nevertheless, within Protestant circles there are also factions that dislike the idea of condoms. The majority of religious institutions have also appropriated the main slogan of 'protect yourself'. However, they redirect the message away from condom use to safe sex defined as 'only marital sex'. While the Catholic Church is strict in its refusal, the Protestant Churches reveal a highly contradictory position. They preach premarital abstinence and monogamy, while condoms and contraceptives are supplied in their dispensaries and hospitals. The idea that condom use will result in increasing sexual activity is very pervasive and dominates almost all discussions about condom use.

There is a general idea that youth are particularly vulnerable to 'immorality' and most letters to the editor address the issue that the 'youth needs to be protected'. This preoccupation with the vulnerability of young people is based on their (presumed) sexual activity: 'there is plenty of evidence that teenagers need no encouragement to engage in sex. Though there are few sources of reliable information about their sexuality, it is clear that the level of sexual activity is rising' (Onyango 2001). A typical phrase about young people is framed as follows: 'immoral and irresponsible Kenyan youth who indulge in sex only' (Nguguna 2001). Both quotations echo two sentiments. First, they reflect the general belief that young people or adolescents are particularly susceptible to the factors resulting in 'immorality' because of their 'irresponsible' age, so they should be 'shielded' against it. On the other hand, however, it reflects the conclusion that the youth are already 'immoral'. The bottom line of the moral discourses on sex is the fear of improper and inflammable sex, as in unmediated sexual behaviour: sex that upsets the conventional order or sex for pleasure only. The generational conflicts, that are latently present, surface every now and then in the conflicts about choices of lifestyle, church attendance or premarital relationships. The older generation is anxious and labels the current young generation as 'undisciplined', a recurring phrase when discussing young people and especially secondary school students. It is interesting, however, that the immorality discourse is not the preserve of older generations and that young people also participate in it. To Kenyans from all walks of life, 'immorality', or the ultimate cause of AIDS, symbolically, is related to the loss of 'authentic' – 'African' – culture and/or Christian teaching.

Sexuality and contemporary lifestyles

As I have shown, the presence of AIDS as a disease and as a source of fear
has resulted in specific understandings and representations of sexuality. A
discourse has developed which represents AIDS as the disease of immorality, and which gives vent to social concerns about the course of society, cultural heritage and changing power relations. At the same time, an
alternative discourse is developing in the newly constituted public realm
that provides for the desire for knowledge about sexuality beyond a health
perspective. Both discourses frame the context in which young professionals live.

AIDS as the disease of 'immorality'

The dominant representations of AIDS as the disease of 'immorality' loom
as a shadow over people's lives. I often heard people saying that 'AIDS is
a curse from God, because of these immoral days', using the concept of
'curse' as an equivalent to that of chastisement. AIDS is generally perceived
of as a disease born of wrongdoing or transgression. AIDS is understood
as a bad omen, a sign that the social environment is somehow disturbed,
and it is commonly associated with 'sinful', 'bad', or 'immoral' behaviour.
Whether in the form of a direct spell or a more systematic rupture in the
social fabric, AIDS is clearly equated with misconduct. Furthermore, the
relationship between sexuality and HIV generates a condemnation verging
on excitement, especially when discussing matters of sexuality outside the
context of marriage. Talking about sex which is unrelated to the conjugal
bond implies talking about 'irresponsible' and 'careless' sex. Irresponsible
sexual behaviour is 'bad sex' under all conditions, and the causal relationship between being infected with the HIV infection and 'bad sex' is regarded as obvious. Sex by nature is good, since it is considered to be the
source of life. 'Bad sex', on the other hand, signifies deviant behaviour
regarding the socially accepted values: it is by definition antisocial. In general, the discussions about sexuality concentrate on notions of promiscuity,
permissiveness and moral decadence (Spronk 2000).[26]

The unholy trinity of promiscuity, permissiveness and moral decadence
is the major source of inspiration for people using the notion of 'immorality', which flares up from different sections of Kenyan society. People from
all layers of society reproduce the same notion in order to validate the
image of a decaying society in the globalizing world, and many of these
comments about immorality reveal a sense of powerlessness. This sense of
powerlessness is an important key to understanding people's responses to

AIDS in Nairobi, with people citing the postcolonial period as an era of cultural 'confusion' and 'chaos'. In the experience of chaos, sexuality offers, through the concept of immorality, a palpable medium through which to express anxieties and discontent. The statement of the opening epigraph to this chapter – that 'Kenya has become a society inflamed by sexual desire' – should be seen in this context. Prominent actors in the public sphere emphasize the fact that sexuality has gone astray due to corrupting moral practices (which need not necessarily be related to sexual issues; for example, bribing is also 'immoral'), resulting in 'rampant immorality'.

Furthermore, AIDS is a disease of time: it is latent and therefore 'looms' in society. AIDS has an elusive quality that contributes to its uncanny connotations. It has come to stand for the disease of sexual perversity, promiscuity and sexual licence, all of the qualities eschewed by 'proper' citizens. The topic of AIDS is obfuscated by vague and evasive terminology like 'be aware of AIDS' or 'AIDS is there', that lay the whole topic open for suggestive meanings. The leading cause of AIDS – unprotected sex – touches on a fundamental yet secret aspect of community. The power of sex is not discussed, but hinted at. AIDS shocks precisely because it transforms the very source of life into an occasion for fatal danger, and this gives rise to panic, moral crises, and the association of disease with individual moral corruption.

As a disease and as a phenomenon of fear, AIDS has brought the topic of sexuality onto the public agenda through the notion of 'immorality'. AIDS serves to define the affected individual as an 'immoral' other because of the violation of social expectations. The AIDS-related stigma has given rise to its own discourse, a language of human relationships that relates self to other, normal to abnormal, healthy to sick, and strong to weak. It involves all those exclusionary and dichotomous contradictions that allow people to draw safe boundaries around the acceptable, the permissible, and the desirable so as to contain fears and phobias about sickness, death and decay, and sexuality and social chaos. A polluting person is always wrong, as Mary Douglas observed (1966). The inverse is also true: a person judged wrong is regarded as, at least potentially, a source of pollution. The fear of AIDS reveals a fear of the disease itself, but also a fear of even more inflammatory sexual behaviour and the loss of control over youth by elders. As Nelson suggests, often when something is criticized as 'morally wrong' in Kenya, the point is not so much that it is considered 'immoral' per se but that it threatens the gerontocratic and moral authority (1987). For parents and religious and political leaders, the increase in the number of sexually mature young people outside the bounds of marriage is not only contrary to chaste morals, but has also become an issue demanding public regulation. Sex is a permanent, lurking menace and a necessity (in terms of procreation) to the conventional order: the need to control it – as well as the fear of it – underlies the social processes of communication and social reproductions at work in the Kenyan public sphere.

At the same time, an oppositional movement can be discerned. The contemporary discourse on dating practices and sex as pleasure challenges the authority of conventional discourses. The shift in the postcolonial era – from 'arranged marriages' organized by families to 'love marriages' (Spronk 2011) – is epitomized in the media. Such a transformation implies that at the level of representation, sexuality has come to articulate a longing for the sovereignty of the individual above and against the claims of the group. As will be elaborated in Chapter VI, via the discourse on romantic love, sexuality has become central to self-expression, as well as to a fulfilling relationship. When it comes to their personal lives, young professionals seek to forge intimate relations rooted in romantic and progressive ideals. Their aspirations are in line with other young women and men around the world who take up the ideal of companionate marriage as a way to demonstrate their modern individuality (Hirsch and Wardlow 2006).

In the turmoil described above, where the public debates are mainly instigated by actors who are predominantly middle class older men in public functions, a new discourse articulated mainly in the media has provided different ways of comprehending and signifying sexuality. This newly constituted public realm is dominated by young middle class people. A particular niche is being created in the media, in collaboration with the consumer culture, providing alternative understandings of AIDS and sexuality. All media have incorporated AIDS and sexuality as a fact that needs to be constantly addressed.

The public emergence of the intimate

The transformation processes which impact on the social organization of society and give rise to new ways of knowing and being (see Chapter II on the historical processes of subjectivation) are crucial for an understanding of contemporary lives in Kenya. More recent capitalist processes, in tandem with the media, have reconfigured the arena in which constructions of gender are articulated, transforming existing gender roles and providing for alternative modes of relating. The 1990s saw love and sex become an important media topic in Nairobi. The media attention encouraged discussions about sexuality and opened new ways for reflection and discussion. Sexual conduct used to be, and still is, problematized in AIDS discourses, while in the dominant religious discourses sex is discussed only in relation to marriage. In contrast, talk shows on TV and radio have begun to air views on various topics ranging from teenage sexuality to condom use. Soap operas have created opportunities to observe the ins and outs of people's love lives, and popular magazines have provided forums to learn about the blessings and burdens of love and sex. The recent appearance of pornographic magazines (produced both locally and internationally) in street stalls underscored the trend as well.

In contemporary (consumer) societies, the media figure prominently in creating interconnections between people from different classes and cultures, some of whom can now consider alternative ways of being. In Nairobi the media play an important organizing role for young professionals with regard to attitudes, aesthetics and lifestyle. Personal narratives, in the form of confessional stories, have become an important way for them to read and learn about the world. A significant aspect of these accounts is that the narratives concentrate on the intimate lives of people. Plummer calls these narratives 'sexual stories', because they typically focus on the erotic, the gendered and the relational:

> [T]hese personal narratives do not always give a prime focus to the 'sexual' itself, though they are always connected. …. [for example] the personal narratives of AIDS provide stories of illness, politics and grief as much as tales of sex. (Plummer 1995: 15)

These publicized narratives of love, death, sex and happiness, among many topics, are extremely popular in Nairobi. The numerous testimonies of love enduring in the face of opposition – coupled with discussions about trust and cheating – in, for example, the popular *Saturday Magazine* pullout, elicit much debate and reflection. This magazine often provided a starting point for my interviews, because people often referred to what they had read in the latest issue, and said they discussed topics from the latest issue on Mondays in the office.

The popularity of such narratives points at what Pels calls the confessional or testimonial ethic: these 'modern confessions, from Rousseau to Oprah Winfrey, expect a moment of authenticity, of laying bare the facts about oneself' (Pels 2002: 92). Watching or reading about another person's intimate details can operate as a mirror in a place like Nairobi, where relations between women and men are shifting. Various media genres pave the way for personal reflection about expectations and justifications in a relationship. As a result, they offer the possibility for individual Nairobians to develop personal narratives of their own love or sexual lives, as I analyse in the next two chapters. This attention to personal narratives implies a shift away from conventional narratives about relationships as familial unions. The new interpretation of love emphasizes a more personal approach to partner choice, based on increasing values of companionship, egalitarianism, a couple's relative autonomy and the sexual satisfaction of women, rather than just reproduction and ethnic compatibility. These changes in how love and sexual relations are narrated are most significant in the subculture of young professionals as a group (Spronk 2009).

It can be concluded that since the early 1990s, there has been a public emergence of the intimate. The way in which sexuality has been addressed from this point of view is fundamentally different to the dominant ways of conceptualizing sexuality from a health or moral perspective. In the new discourse, AIDS is not denied; instead, it broadens the perspectives on sexuality by incorporating other subjects like love, trust, distrust and passion and includes the effects of the senses like attraction, arousal and satisfaction in the experience of sexuality. Sexuality is understood as a natural element of a person that can bring pleasure, happiness or troubles. The focus is on how to increase the positive elements of sex and circumvent or solve problems. The public emergence of the intimate is embedded in this larger framework of transformations regarding gender and sexuality.

The media provide a range of topics that appeal to urban young professionals. From a commercial perspective, young professionals represent an important market and much advertising is directed towards this particular group. However, for many other Nairobians, young professionals embody a certain ideal, and by way of local magazines and pullouts in newspapers they are able to have a taste of such a lifestyle. Young professionals are the driving force behind a popular, middle class culture. According to Mark Kihenja, a Nairobi based journalist, the media and 'the trendy and hip [people] of Nairobi' are mutually dependent on each other: they follow each other as to what is 'hot'.[27] The counter discourse is symbolized by its modish and progressive style. Writing on Pentecostal public culture in Ghana, Meyer states that the 'emphasis is on style rather than on content or message as such' (Meyer 2002: 70). This is an important observation about popular culture, highlighting the agency of the media in the creation of popular culture and formations of contemporary identities (Nyairo 2005). Young professionals – and other young people for that matter – are conscientious about style, for aesthetic reasons and as a way of distinguishing themselves. At the same time, the media, via its style, have become a major provider of information covering a wide range of issues.

The print media are the site *par excellence* for the dissemination of information about lifestyles, relationships and sexuality. They provide information, advice and reflection about many social concerns young people face. Magazines are very popular and play an important role in the articulation of notions of 'sophistication' or a modern identity. The circulations of international magazines like *Elle*, *Marie-Claire* and *Men's Health* have increased steadily, while more and more locally published magazines have emerged. *Eve*, for example, the first Kenyan woman's glossy, was launched in 2001.[28] The South African edition of *Ebony* has been available for a few years but according to street vendors the sales have significantly increased lately. The increasing presence of glossies has a gendered nature which is biased to women; sales of 'male' glossies covering topics like cars and computers have also increased, although less so.[29] Less gendered, in fact gender balanced, is the popular *Saturday Magazine* of one of the main dailies in 2001, the *Daily Nation*, as well as the popular magazine *Parents* and a variety of Christian magazines. Most magazines use a light-hearted approach to lifestyle matters such as dress, etiquette, career, romance, friendships; they use catchy titles such as 'The condom debate', 'To be or not to be submissive' [about the 'need' for egalitarian relations between lovers], 'Soulmate search', 'Beauty without danger' [about skin lighteners], 'The marriage myth', 'Subtle sophistication' [about social etiquette]).[30]

Magazines such as the popular *Saturday Magazine* play an active role in 'informing Kenyans about all kinds of aspects of life, especially sensitive ones' (Ms Orengo, editor).[31] The *Saturday Magazine* employs a format with recurring topics that emphasize the importance of an up-to-date lifestyle. Every edition shows a female local beauty as the cover model with her name, surname, interests and hobbies. The 'Saturday Regulars' is a column about travel in Kenya or East Africa, while another column called 'Cosy Home' informs readers about 'modern living' and advises on home furnishings. The other regular columns are the 'Lonely Hearts Club' for dating advertisements,[32] 'Eating Out', 'Medical Notes', 'Image Matters', 'Relationships', and letters to the editor. Every edition has several longer articles on various topics ranging from fashion or one of the numerous beauty pageants; gender issues such as women in higher positions; family matters like the sexuality of teenagers; societal aspects like poverty, AIDS or death from diseases, the numerous car accidents, or murder; body maintenance or a feature on gyms in Nairobi; and many articles about relationships and marriages that have broken up, have stalled, remain happy over fifty years or have faced certain difficulties. Moreover, there is also a conscious attempt to discuss sensitive issues like bride wealth, multi-partnered sexual relations, sexual abuse, depression, financial disputes, abortion, alcoholism and all kinds of other problems that couples might face. These items are normally preceded by personal confessions or revelations.[33] The discussions address the topics and events from a 'modern', 'sophisticated', or 'common sense' perspective that are weighed against 'customs', 'old beliefs', or 'unrealistic' perspectives, while never losing sight of the 'African perspective'.

For example, in the 19 January 2002 issue of *Saturday Magazine*, two 'thorny' issues are scrutinized that needed to be discussed 'sensibly' without 'condemning it right away', as that 'would not help any of the women implicated in these situations': the practice of bride wealth and men marrying a second wife. They are described as 'thorny' because they can 'cause major personal distress and unhappiness'. Both topics are introduced by accounts of women who reveal their personal experiences. The topic of polygamy is discussed as a practice which victimizes women, while the practice of bride wealth is more or less taken for granted. However, bride wealth can cause unbearable suffering to a young couple when 'families are asking for too much'. Sometimes people are prevented from marrying and '[I]t is saddening that the world is turning commercial'. Bride wealth is described as an institution or custom that should be seen as in the light of what it was 'meant for': it is 'a parent's blessing [that is] necessary for any marriage, when differences arrive, the couple does not stand alone but will be helped by their relatives to resolve the conflict'. The 'African' perspective is that bride wealth is part of the African heritage; it should be seen as a 'token of appreciation'. However, the contemporary or 'modern' perspective criticizes the practice when families demand outrageous amounts of money. This perspective emphasizes how a young couple should start building their own family life instead of providing for the extended family. Such debates exemplify the type of conflicts many people are facing.

Similarly, in the 26 January 2002 issue of *Saturday Magazine*, the difficulties of 'popping the big question' are discussed: 'It is fairly easy for a new couple to agree on the use of a condom without insisting on knowing each others' HIV status, but what happens when things get serious and the condom has to go? When do you pop the HIV question?' The article starts with how an imaginary couple starts dating: 'For many, until recently, the custom went like this: The couple exchanged addresses. They went on a date. Soon it was romance, passion, sleepless nights and finally – sex!' (page 9). Several couples are interviewed about how they went about this 'complicated' and 'inevitable' issue that 'we all face'. Whereas the couples interviewed in the *Saturday Magazine* article were all HIV negative, in *Parents*, issue 173 of December 2000, couples where one partner was infected were interviewed. These interviews are of a more serious character and both the woman and the man were invited to elaborate on the complications of desiring sex as 'usual', i.e. without a condom, as opposed to 'safe sex'. The need for safe sex is underscored by emphasizing how 'love' means 'taking care of each other, of the children, even after death' and in this case 'love' means 'making love protected'. Such articles meet the demand for information on delicate and complicated issues that people face in reality. Couched as 'lifestyle' articles, they help people and invite ongoing debate about contentious issues.

Like the print media, talk shows on TV and on the radio are platforms where views on various topics can be aired, ranging from teenage love to condom use. The 'Youth Variety Show', for example, is a talk show made for and by teenagers, where they discuss various topics. The format is often one of a debate in which one team supports an issue while the other opposes it. These shows and some radio programmes have become well known for their 'outspoken' perspectives on sexuality. 'Teenage sex' – a primary preoccupation of adolescents – and 'condoms' are a recurring issue in the discussions. Similarly, the soap operas have created a podium for viewing the comings and goings of people's love lives, as for example in the local production *'Heart and Soul'*, the North American *'Beauty and the Beast'* and in some South American soap operas. All in all, the emergence of popular media has created a forum where people can become informed about the blessings and burdens of love and sex.

The media exposure given to love and sex has placed issues of love and sexual relationships prominently into the public sphere. AIDS and sexuality are a recurring theme that is addressed from different points of view, covering issues such as the importance of using condoms when one person in a couple is HIV positive, or when a wife suspects her husband of being unfaithful. It is important to note that the media play a pivotal role in rethinking sensitive issues such as sex, because their discussions about sexuality and AIDS are integrated in a larger framework of social realities and concerns, rather than moral warnings.

Intimacy as part of lifestyle

While most media – such as *True Love*, a popular 30-year-old South African lifestyle magazine – address issues of 'love', incorporating the whole range of sexuality matters, some media are more explicit about matters of sexual practice and experience. The magazine *Parents*, for example, is a 'magazine that cares for you and your family'. The title suggests a broad spectrum of significant topics for the contemporary family, which is indeed what the magazine carries. Every front cover portrays young parents with one child and sometimes two children. The couple portrayed is typically middle or lower middle class, implying an ordinary couple from next door. The articles focus on family matters, religion, finance, work, etc. The focus on relationship issues is primarily on marital issues, like 'How to remain faithful' (June 2001); 'Whose money is it? Shillings and relationships' (October 2001); and 'The cycle of divorce' (May 2001).

However, *Parents* is known particularly, among married and unmarried people, for its weekly column called 'Sex' or 'Sexuality'. It addresses sexual issues such as 'Sex in marriage. The wife's role' (May 2001); 'Sexual fantasy. The games couples play' (September 2001); and 'Vitality and virility. A man's secret to happiness' (June 2001). Sexual practices and principles are dealt with in explicit terms. Sexual positions and the type of gratification that can be expected are described, while the topics of foreplay, fantasy and sexual variation to enhance female pleasure are written about regularly. In one issue, for example, the writer explains how fantasies are 'especially helpful to women who find it difficult to achieve orgasm' (May 2001). In another issue, men's attitudes are scrutinized in the third person: 'He sees a woman as being there to provide him with sexual satisfaction rather than having needs of her own'. In this case, techniques on 'bettering your foreplay' are discussed and explained as 'enriching' for 'him and her' (September 2001). Every week, another aspect of sexual relationships is discussed from a more psychological, physical or emotional point of view. In these discussions, AIDS is mentioned as a reality from which people have to protect themselves by using condoms and being faithful. Contraceptives are portrayed as a useful tool in having a happy sexual life by avoiding HIV and planning the birth of children.

The rationale of *Parents'* editor is reflected in the statement that 'Better sex makes happier couples', and that sex is 'a couple's primary way to show love' (November 2001). *Parents'* message is very clear: sex is 'natural' and positive. The articles only address sexuality within marriage and although they advocate a better understanding of teenage sexuality, they remain within the confines of the conventional discourse that emphasizes marriage as the only site for sex. Nevertheless, while remaining within this conventional boundary, they are rather liberal with their outspoken articles. They hint at the message that sex is a God-given practice, but never explicitly claim to advocate Christian morals.[34] *Parents* has created a unique position. It covers itself in terms of societal values by having married couples among its readers, and it is thereby able to fulfil an important need for information. Many young professionals used to read it as adolescents, or still read it.[35] Men are especially eager to read about women's sexuality, so they can apply the knowledge in their sexual relations. More and more, however, the Internet has become the major source of information about sexual practices and experiences.

A popular *Parents'* column highlights the search for new ways of being and knowing. To have a fulfilling sex life has become a symbol of a truly contemporary person. This does not necessarily imply that it is perceived as a green light to sexual permissiveness. Depending on the person's morals, a sexual life is developed only in marriage for some, while for others it is possible in premarital relationships as well. In contrast to the popular idea that 'sex is a marital duty', which is interpreted among many female young professionals as enforcing the sexual subordination of women, the 'modern' duty is the fulfilment of a mutual orgasm.

The implication of mutual orgasm is that sexuality gains a new interpretation; female sexuality becomes redefined as pleasure and not necessarily as procreation, and male sexuality becomes partly redefined in relation to female pleasure. By connecting sexuality to pleasure, the notion of sexual pleasure is appropriated by individuals in interaction with each other, as we shall see in the following chapters. Public discourse is right in a way; this kind of sexuality is antisocial. In the counter discourse on sexuality, the couple reigns. This is not to say that in the past people did not have sex for pleasure. What has changed is that the meaning of sexuality as the motor of social well-being has been redirected. The importance of mutual satisfaction is now emphasized by the discourse on sexuality as it is espoused by magazines such as *Parents*. Both women and men are advised and encouraged to 'work' on their sex life, as it 'enriches' their personal sexual experiences as well as that of their partner. Personal and mutual sexual happiness becomes an asset of individuals, as well as a symbol for a successful relationship. This resonates with what young professionals are seeking in their intimate relationships: love and sex as a matter of self-expression, as part and parcel of contemporary personhood.

Mutual orgasm as proof of success and/or intimacy in sexual relations has become an indicator among certain young professionals:

These days, we want our part of pleasure. I mean ... We, women, know what to buy in this world and there is no way I could make love with a man and be left unsatisfied. It sometimes happened [that a man did not know how to satisfy a woman properly], men are not yet [as] up to date as women, and then I was so so disappointed. I mean, I don't even consider explaining [to] him what to do with a woman. Imagine! Some don't even realize! (Dana, aged 29)

Ok, as a modern man you have to know how to satisfy a woman, there is no way to ... when you have sex, that only you get satisfied. You have to know what she likes, to postpone her coming, to tease her so that she begs you. Sometimes it's disturbing when you cannot make it, when you cannot satisfy a woman. I once had a girlfriend and she never had an orgasm, it disturbed me to have mine whereas she was left ... nothing. (Ruben, aged 28)

Orgasm becomes an indication of a healthy individual, in two ways. First, experiencing orgasm was often explained to me as the primal urge to feel alive, to achieve the ultimate moment of self-awareness while simultaneously getting lost in the pleasure of orgasm. Second, as sexuality is an important realm for self-actualization as a modern individual, good sex became symbolic of being an up-to-date person. The importance attributed to mutual orgasm, moreover, signified young adults' sense of empowerment. In their definition of sexuality, female sexuality became redefined as pleasure and not necessarily as procreation, and male sexuality became partly redefined in relation to female pleasure. This approach is new, exciting and more engaging for both women and men compared to conventional perspectives on sexuality.

In general, young professionals are searching for new definitions of sex. They want to give a positive meaning to sex in their premarital sexual relationships. Pamela (aged 22, see next chapter) says: 'How can something be wrong when it makes me feel good?' In popular definitions of sexuality, sex is linked to self instead of to reproduction, ethnic compatibility or marriage. What is most notable is that women, in contrast to conventional discourse, also recognize sex as natural, as an embodied element of growing into adulthood. They thus recognize sexual desire as crucial to their identity as women, instead of understanding sexual desire in relation to married motherhood. For men, sexual desire has always been understood as self-evident in conventional discourse; sex is normatively understood as individual achievement. But, as Ruben explains, there is now more to sex for men like him because his sexual potential is also connected to his partner's sexual pleasure. In the new definition of sexuality, then, sexual intimacy becomes a matter of the self as a sexual subject; intimacy becomes an intersubjective experience. Such a sexual relationship, based on the realization of intimacy as fundamental to self-perception, is generally aspired to by young professionals in Nairobi. 'Intimacy', therefore, is the name of the game. It has become a fashionable word in all popular self-help columns in Nairobian magazines advising on the art of good relationships. For young women and men, notions of romantic love and intimacy are increasingly important criteria in selecting a lover or spouse.

Conclusion

This chapter has addressed the way in which AIDS has become part of the context of life for young professionals. Dominant institutional discourses on AIDS (governmental, nongovernmental organization and Christian) have influenced the public representation and understanding of AIDS and sexuality. The convergence of the definition of 'risk groups' arising out of the medicalization of sexuality, the remoralization of sexuality and existing patriarchal gender ideologies have foreclosed discussions about sexuality. This led to an underscoring of popular understandings of AIDS as a disease of 'immorality'. Moreover, it has contributed to the volatile atmosphere that resulted from the moral panic caused by AIDS.

Reflections on AIDS involve reflections at all levels of social and individual being: from being an AIDS victim to a state of being free of HIV and AIDS; from order to disorder; from life to death. AIDS has given rise to new forms of public knowledge. Kenyan society has changed considerably during the colonial and postcolonial periods; even so, sexuality remains strongly associated with social order. Society's age-old preoccupation with the sexuality of its members has gained new and more powerful significance with the advent of AIDS. Africanist discourse postulates that, because of 'external influences', people have diverted from traditional customs and norms, resulting in deviant forms of sexual behaviour that are, in turn, seen as a break with 'African' cultural heritage. 'Bad sex' gradually seems to have replaced good sex, or alternately, the loosening of social control has brought with it much concern about social and moral disorder. 'Immorality' has become the generative concept to explain these processes and changes, as well as the metaphor for deviant sexual behaviour, such behaviour being antisocial in the widest sense of the word. The employment of the notion of 'immorality' links all sections of Kenyan society, because the discontinuities and contradictions of social change have given rise to a sense of existential deprivation and disorientation. Depending on the audience addressed and the social context in which the address takes place, young professionals reproduce the concept of 'immorality' because they share certain feelings of discontent and loss of singularity.

Nevertheless, the dominant moralizing discourses are partly undermined by newer understandings of sexuality as related to pleasure and companionship. This unconventional way of defining sexuality does not openly challenge conventional perspectives but instead subtly creates a niche in the media and in young adults' lifeworlds. Over the last decades, changes in patterns of courtship, the growing importance of Christian wedding ceremonies, and trends towards establishing urban residences with nuclear household organization are all reinforcing an emerging model of marriage that emphasizes the personal relationship between wife and husband. The emergence of practices of romantic love – defined as passionate, personal and erotic – as criteria for selection of a lover, implies the increasing importance of conjugality; and the couple's personal relationship to each other becomes central and is enthusiastically encouraged by the media. The ambition is the development of a mutually fulfilling sexual relationship. The philosophy of *Parents* – that 'better sex makes happier couples' – reflects the development of the new discourse in Nairobi, which is effective because it addresses social realities and personal experiences. This is especially so among young professionals, or more generally, the middle class, where the development of a personal sexual life is seen as a key constituent of contemporary identity. The development of a personal sexual life always involves reflection about oneself, as a woman or man, as a Kenyan, an African, and a modern person. Moreover, as sexuality is also understood as natural, as intrinsically located within the person, the development of a personal sexual life also implies a search for oneself when growing into adulthood. How this process is worked out within individual lives is addressed in the chapters that follow.

Notes

1. *Moral Issues in Kenya. A Personal View* by Marjorie Oludhe-Magoye (1996: 1).
2. Various explanations about the origin of AIDS circulated in Nairobi in 2001/2. It is generally considered a fact that 'immoral' behaviour leads to AIDS, while AIDS itself is understood to originate from various sources not necessarily related to 'immorality'. The tales differ widely, from explanations based on witchcraft, to the corruption of customary ways of life, to international racial relations between African and western peoples and related notions of African predestination. The origin of AIDS is a topic that functions as some sort of watershed for the expression of many contemporary concerns. Here, I focus on a single dimension, namely perceptions related to the concept of 'immorality'.
3. Foucault emphasized that, when writing about discourses on sexuality, it is crucial 'to account for the fact that it is spoken about, to discover who does the speaking, the positions and viewpoints from which they speak, the institutions which prompt people to speak about it and which store and distribute the things that are said. What is at issue, briefly, is the overall "discursive fact", the way sex is "put into discourse"' (Foucault 1990 [1976]: 11). It goes beyond the scope of this study to employ a thorough discourse analysis with regard to AIDS in Kenya, as in who says what, when, how and elaborating on the effects in detail; my aim here is merely to provide a preliminary mapping and contextualization of AIDS discourses.
4. In 2004, Dawn (aged 29 then) suspected that her father had died of AIDS, but no doctor or test had confirmed this.
5. Interview with Professor Bahemuka of the University of Nairobi on July 3, 2001.
6. See also Chapter II on the role of intellectuals in the creation of a specific 'African' universe of suffering created by imperialism and colonialism. It seems difficult for scholars not to glorify the past when discussing historical disruptions.
7. A continuous debate focussed on the Smirnoff alcoholic drinks advertisements on huge billboards all over Nairobi, showing a sexy woman crowded by men. One of my informants complained that 'They depict Smirnoff drinkers as people with immoral principles. What is this about "loose bust"? I now can't order Smirnoff freely. It's just like asking for a loose woman' (Michael, aged 27).
8. Ironically, these chaste morals probably say more about the convergence of Africanist and Christian views than about particular ethnic cultural morals. In the majority of Kenyan ethnic groups, premarital abstinence was not practiced. Furthermore, male circumcision was and is often understood to be a 'green light' to having sexual intercourse; see Chapter V.
9. A salient detail is that the Africanist discourses distance themselves from historical reality in their discussions about 'tradition'. This is in contrast to Kenyatta who, instead of ignoring them, bent traditional discourses to account for certain practices (Kenyatta 1995 [1938]: 130–63).
10. Only a few 'traditionalists' advocated a more profound 'return' to 'African morals' by calling for, among other 'traditions', the reinstitution of female circumcision, ritual oathing, ancestor worship, and polygamy, such as exists in the Mungiki religious movement. They

are, however, not part of the dominant discourse and play an obscure role on the socio-economic margins of society.

11. Among the nongovernmental organizations, there are those that are religious and those that are non-religious. How they differ in their approaches to both sex and AIDS will be discussed in the next section.

12. Officially, the first diagnosed AIDS victim was reported in 1984, which was followed by a silence on the government's side. In 1985, the WHO designed a global AIDS response for governments, which Kenya signed. In 1986 the National AIDS Committee was created, with various subcommittees, and between then and 2000 AIDS prevention programmes operated under the Ministry of Health. In 1987 the Kenya National AIDS Control Programme was created for the more scientific and medical research and services, while the AIDS Programme Secretariat was established to educate the public about HIV and AIDS and to create 'awareness'. After 2000, AIDS became defined as a prime issue and different Ministries became involved, such as the Ministry of Education. Alongside, and in cooperation with, the governmental efforts, the nongovernmental sector has been a major agent in the development of AIDS prevention programmes. At the end of the 1980s, the AIDS problem was picked up by AMREF, Red Cross, and various religious institutions. These nongovernmental organizations started cooperating with the government from 1991 onwards. The problem, however, was that the nongovernmental organizations were limited by the stringent bureaucracy of the government, whose permission they needed to implement the programmes. It became clear that the government was not particularly committed and was merely paying lip service to the WHO proposal which it had signed. In short, lack of funds and lack of commitment have weakened the implementation of campaigns. Out of this frustration, the Kenya AIDS NGO Consortium was created in order to be more effective; it more or less went its own way. At the end of the first decade of the twenty-first century, the management of HIV/AIDS had become a well-oiled concern.

13. It goes beyond the scope of this study to provide a concise overview of the similarities and differences in approach between the Kenyan government and local and international nongovernmental organizations. I am only concerned here with a broad perspective on AIDS and with how the discourse of AIDS developed.

14. The reluctance on the part of government officials results from the puritanical approach adopted by Kenya's political leadership that revolves around personality cults. By refusing to be drawn into public discourse on AIDS and sexuality, the political leaders strove to present an image of respectability. In a country where political leadership wields enormous influence, and where various politicians have died of AIDS, presidential engagement is meaningful. Nongovernmental organizations involved in AIDS prevention programmes, newspaper editors and other agents of civil society therefore fiercely criticized late President Moi's remark about condoms. When the Ministry of Health imported millions of condoms in 2001, Moi had said '[I]f Kenyans could abstain from sex for two years … [these condoms would not be necessary]' (Omari 2001). Politicians also remained quiet, and some still do, because of the strong competition between politicians and religious leaders for influence. 'In the event of a conflict of opinion between political leaders and church leaders, it is the politician who turns out to be the loser' (Nzioka 1994: 568). Nevertheless, certain individuals within the respective ministries have shown themselves to be more committed. The change of regime at the end of 2002 also meant a change in governmental approach. For example, President Kibaki is portrayed in posters facing Kenyans amidst a crowd, calling attention to the fact that AIDS is a 'shared responsibility'.

15. For example D'Costa 1985; Katsivo and Muthami 1991; Moses et al. 1991; Piot et al. 1987; Simonsen et al. 1990.

16. For example, according to Dr Mulindi, senior lecturer at the University of Nairobi and Chairman of the Kenya National AIDS Control programme during the 1990s: '[I]t is imperative that the public is informed and educated about the spread of the AIDS virus. Thus,

our efforts have been geared toward targeted populations within the country. The groups targeted include those at risk, such as youth in and out of school, prostitutes, prisoners, army personnel, long distance truck drivers, including the general population' (Mulindi 1992: 55). Although Dr Mulindi wanted to include 'the general population', the emphasis was clearly on groups that were easy to identify.

17. The process referred to as 'medicalization' has its roots in the latter half of the nineteenth century in Western societies. Medical professionals became interested in behavioural domains that were previously the preserve of religious authorities and moralists: criminality, alcohol and drugs, and sex. The contemporary taxonomy by which sexual behaviour is defined was invented a century earlier, when sexologists created diagnostic categories such as homosexual and heterosexual, hysteria, nymphomania and a host of other manifestations. These labels served to define what was normal and acceptable and what was not, distinguishing 'perversions' from 'acceptable' heterosexual, procreative and monogamous sex. The long tradition of representing illness as a punishment for sin was continued when sexual behaviour was medicalized and transformed into morbidity. In relation to AIDS, both the religious connotations of sin and the medical implications of morbidity come together.

    Foucault makes clear that such medical social control is only evident when there is a spontaneous and deeply rooted convergence between the requirements of political ideology and those of medical technology. He maintains that the medicalization of sexuality that occurred in the eighteenth and nineteenth century was the result of the medicalization of confession, where what had once been considered sin became redefined as pathology (1990 [1976]). Similarly, in Kenya from the 1920s to the 1940s, the 'circumcision' controversy arose because of European missionaries' objections to the Kikuyu practice of female circumcision. They based their objections in part on medical grounds and thus medicalized the 'problem' of female circumcision as an unacceptable practice that should be 'treated'. With regard to AIDS, political ideology and medical technology converge to an even greater extent because AIDS is a social as well as a medical problem.

18. I only deal with the Christian discourses because they have a hegemonic position in Kenya. In particular in Nairobi, Muslims occupy a minor position and, moreover, they hardly engage in public debates but rather focus on their own groups.

19. The Pentecostal Churches were, and continue to be, less involved in the debates about politics. Former President Moi regularly visited Pentecostal Churches and to a large extent ignored mainstream churches.

20. There are 118 American mission agencies in Kenya and they outnumber missionaries in other African countries by almost ten to one. Some of these missions cooperate with the popular Pentecostal Churches.

21. Interview with Professor Nzioka on 18 July 2001; interview with the late Professor Katani Mkangi on 7 October 2001.

22. Interview on 4 August 2001.

23. Interview with Professor Nzioka on 18 July 2001 and with Pastor Maxwell of the Nairobi Baptist Church on 3 November 2001.

24. Sermon on 6 August 2001.

25. Interview on 3 November 2001.

26. I have not been able to trace back the exact origin of the concept of 'immorality' in Kenya. The word has a profound religious connotation, and it was probably initiated by Christians. It is likely that a preacher or pastor originally commented upon 'these immoral times' and, by elaborating upon the evils of 'immorality', a notion came into being to explain the current experience of social chaos.

27. Interview on 3 October 2001.

28. *Eve* is a glossy magazine for upper middle class, professional women aged between 28 and 45 years that appeared for the first time in February 2002. According to its editor Carole Mandi, there was a 'need' for a local glossy. *Eve* makes great efforts to publicize 'African

role models, such as career women, successful mothers, single or married, and dedicated professionals'. *Eve* aims at a group that is 'new, new in the sense that they are women who are not typical dedicated wives in the traditional sense. After society always favoured men, these women choose to fight and have a part of the cake. These women are ahead of what we can expect in the future, we want to be their voice' (interview with Carole Mandi on 30 February 2004).

29. Besides these, there all kinds of erotica and (soft) pornographic magazines sold in the street stalls. They are more expensive and therefore sell in lower numbers. They are very popular though and according to the street vendors, are bought mainly by young men.

30. The *Saturday Magazine*, the weekly pull-out of the newspaper *Daily Nation*, was the only of its kind in 2001/2. Due to its success, many newspapers followed its example. See http://www.nation.co.ke/Features/-/1190/1190/-/7202tz/-/index.html to find its current version.

31. Interview on 20 January 2004.

32. The young professionals who are the focus of this study did not make use of the many personal advertisements that have become very popular, such as the 'lonely hearts club' in the *Saturday Magazine*. From the small survey I made about the people making use of, it can be concluded that these users are generally from lower middle class backgrounds and more often than not from Nairobi.

33. An important contribution is the column by the Amani Centre, a centre for counselling and psychological help. Every week they publish a letter written by an anonymous person, together with the reply. The letters address a variety of issues from childlessness and rape, to psychological illness. During a visit to the centre, I was shown the huge amount of letters they receive every week as well as their archives. According to the director they meet a great demand for counselling and the demand is growing as they become better known. The letters as well as the centre itself are worth further study.

34. Besides *Parents*, there are a few Christian books on sexuality provided by the Family Life Counselling Association of Kenya, a collaborative Christian organization. A book called *The Wonders and Beauty of Sex* (1998) is from a Protestant background but was imported from Ghana. The Christian literature addressing sexuality in such an explicit and positive manner originates from either Ghana or Nigeria.

35. During my MA research among adolescents, many girls and boys read *Parents* kept and shared old issues to read this particular section.

CHAPTER IV

AMBIGUOUS PLEASURES: SEXUAL DESIRE, CAREER, AND FEMININITY

I just can't get you out of my head
Boy your loving is all I think about
I just can't get you out of my head
Boy it's more than I dare to think about

There's a dark secret in me
Don't leave me locked in your heart

Set me free
Feel the need in me
Set me free
Stay forever and ever and ever and ever

La la la
La la la la la
La la la
La la la la la[1]

Professional women between 20 and 30 years old see themselves as explorers of a 'sophisticated' lifestyle in Nairobi. An important aspect of this lifestyle is the appropriation of sexual desire and pleasure as part of a contemporary identity. The understanding of sex as a natural element of a person implies that women are encouraged to see sexual desire as part of their self. However, in the dominant discourse, female sexuality is perceived as non-existent before marriage. Women therefore need to appropriate the notion of sexual pleasure. This chapter elaborates on how they identify themselves as women; how that relates to their sense of self; how sex is defined as an aspect of their feminine identity; and how this intersects with social practice. It deals with women's personal experiences and reflections with regard to sex and sexual relationships. I show how women follow different trajectories or imagined possibilities with regard to their sexuality.

The biographies given here are presented in vignettes. These narratives are then reflected upon against the background of social practice, to show how that practice shapes the women's social, economic and cultural positions and how it intersects with their relationships with men.

I posit that women's understanding of sexuality, in relation to processes of contemporary identity formation as female professionals who consider sexuality as 'natural', is crucial to their sense of self. Similar to women's experiences in Namibia described by Lorway, their knowledge of self is gained through a repeated reflection on the internality of sexual desire. As a result, it is produced through a continual shift in perception between subjectivity and objectivity as a range of ambivalent personal historical events are brought into a coherent narrative structure (2008). As a result, sexual pleasure becomes a desire, a want, an objective that young professional women relate to their notion of modern womanhood, to their contemporary, 'modern', gendered sense of self.

The volatile social context of contemporary Nairobi, as described in the previous chapter, also shapes women's self-perception. It appears that because of the pressures on them, women tend to express a deferential attitude that reflects conformity to the norm, while on the other hand their social positions as career women and their personal aspirations lead them to break with the norm. Some women strategically adopt a deferential attitude towards men, while for others this deference is not simply a strategy; certain conventional notions of femininity have become part of their sense of self. We should be wary of drawing conclusions about gender subordination though, and should recognize the complex and productive aspects of the status quo (Jackson 2007). By analysing how the social context intersects with their personal experiences, I hope to show how the ambiguities that characterize these women's sexuality come to the fore. I analyse how women accommodate the meanings articulated in the previously described dominant discourses, embedded in the social norms, prescriptions, prohibitions and possibilities.

All the professional women in this study were aged between 20 and 30; some were starting a job or commencing a course of study, while others had been working for years or had ventured into more or less settled lives. The chapter is organized by portraits according to the age of the participants. In 2001, Pamela was 22 years old and was studying mass communication at a private university. Martha was 24 years old, had finished her first degree in accountancy and was working and saving money to study abroad. In 2001 she secured a grant and left Kenya to study at a flying school in Australia in order to become a pilot. Njeri was 26 years old in 2001 and was achieving successively better positions in her career. Tayiani was 28 years old and got married in 2001. Dorcas was 30 years old and was the most successful of these women, being a sales manager in a large multinational company.[2]

Female sexuality in Nairobi, Kenya and beyond

The history of Nairobi is intertwined with that of prostitution, revealing a specific narrative in relation to both the evolution and construction of female sexuality in Kenya. The shadow of prostitution is to a certain extent cast over all aspects of African women's sexuality, both under the colonial administration and in contemporary Kenyan society. It is important to understand the extent to which the history of female sexuality has been formulated by local and global social, economic and political processes. Female sexuality has mainly been studied as a societal problem, whereas I wish to study it in relation to processes of identity formation, as experienced in the body and as a pleasurable experience.

Before discussing representations of female sexuality in Kenya, it is important to reflect on the specific history of prostitution in Nairobi. As described in Chapter II, British colonialists sought to make Nairobi, the capital of colonial Kenya, a city of male migrants. Despite this intention, women clustered in the service sector as servants, prostitutes and householders (White 1990a). The migrant labour system prohibited women from moving with their husbands to the city and the 'native' locations in Nairobi became occupied by single men. Over time, however, women also settled in the native settlements of Nairobi having left their homes for reasons such as infertility, widowhood, divorce, being 'runaway daughters', or because of quarrels with their husband or family (Nelson 1987; Robertson 1997; White 1990a). Having little education or training, single women had few lucrative means of subsistence apart from the illegal brewing of maize beer or participation in sexual relationships involving an exchange of domestic services that varied in their durability and the extent of commercialization. The nearly exclusive female monopoly of these activities provided women with some means of gaining bargaining power and property. Some women were able to gain an increasingly advantageous economic position and became active and integrated participants in the local community (Bujra 1975). Women thus played their own role in the colonial history of Nairobi.

In her book *The Comforts of Home. Prostitution in Colonial Nairobi* (1990a), White describes the first group of women in Nairobi to breach normative patterns by taking the opportunity to become financially independent from their relatives. In the absence of formal employment opportunities, these women earned money through prostitution and often became landlords. They went to live in certain quarters in the city, acquired property and became heads of their households. The aunt of Tumi, one of the women in this study, is an example of the type of woman that White describes in her book.[3] Although Tumi did not explicitly mention the origin of her aunt's wealth, she alluded to it with a wink, saying 'you know how a young independent woman could start a life in those days'. Tumi spoke with admiration about her aunt's hardworking attitude and dedication to setting up her own business, how her aunt had brought up a family on her own and how she was able to pay for her children's university education. When I asked Tumi whether she anticipated being like her aunt she replied that she would prefer to have a family that includes a father for the children. However, she indicated that if it proved to be impossible to find a committed husband, she would not hesitate to start a life as a single mother. In Nairobi, single motherhood has a long history. Single mothers have always been, and still are prone to being labelled as 'prostitutes'.

During the early postcolonial period the discourse of 'Africanization' – see Chapter II – emerged in Kenya. The debates about what constituted genuine Africanness tended to create a polarity between rural, traditional, 'African' respectable values, and urban, 'Western', corrupted values. These sentiments became embodied in perceptions of single women in the city, who became figures of public controversy over visible transformations such as the adoption of Western dress and cosmetics and the change in childbearing patterns (Amelsfoort 1976; Bujra 1975; Wipper 1972). The notion of 'prostitute' became a symbol of a wider discourse on 'cultural prostitution', not necessarily linked to sexuality, and its negative impact on women's 'traditional' social status and on Kenyan society in general (Kielmann 1997; Thadani 1979). Nelson (1987) maintains that in the 1980s, women's casual and commercialized sexual relationships were not considered '*immoral*' *per se*, but they tended to be separated from procreation for the patrilineal line. As described in the previous chapter, such moralizing responses tend to arise in periods of social change when conventional gender roles – vital for the reproduction of the patriarchy – start to alter. This generative symbol of the prostitute became a powerful means for criticizing women who deviated from conventional expectations.

In urban Nairobi today, professional women do not operate in insecure and difficult environments, as did the women described by Nelson, but they nevertheless occupy an ambivalent position in relation to conventional knowledge, based on a patriarchal ideology. The arrest of female young professionals in the city centre, described in the previous chapter, reflects how invocations of prostitution can be used to subjugate women. Here, the image of a prostitute becomes associated with any woman rejecting conventional morals, resisting gerontocratic authority and shifting gender boundaries.[4]

The development of a nexus of meanings surrounding prostitution may thus be traced to historical and cultural changes in Kenya. These changes directly altered women's positions in society and indirectly modified perceptions about women and their sexuality. Discourses emphasizing female chastity, female reproduction or female dress code have been part of the social context for generations of women in Nairobi. These discourses generate patriarchal constructions of femininity that have become common sense for many Kenyans. The current generation of women has grown up hearing that women are dangerous when they do not conform to these common sense ideas of femininity. Popular illustrations invoke images of the seductive temptress in fashionable dress, the prostitute roaming the bars of Nairobi, or the heartless career wife. All these representations and common sense constructions of femininity portray women as either pure or impure; they see women as needing to be revered and worshipped but also to be controlled through direct regulation of their sexuality. Within these multiple – and contradictory – images of femininity, the lives of contemporary young professional women are positioned at the interface of both change and continuity.

Apart from the literature on women who prostitute themselves, and earlier studies in the structural-functionalist tradition (see Introduction), it is hard to find a qualitative study on women's sexual lives in Nairobi or Kenya. With the exception of Nelson's study of poorer women in Mathare Valley, an infamous neighbourhood in Nairobi, there is no study dedicated to women's sexual lives and experiences. Shaw's study on female sexuality in Kikuyu society (1995) provides an important critical reflection about representations of female sexuality. Similarly, Leakey (1977) offers an interesting analysis of the relative sexual freedom of women in Kikuyu society, but the discussion does not cover women's experiences. Although there is a small body of literature about female sexuality in Kenya, it tends to discuss female sexuality from particular angles, such as in relation to marriage, circumcision, or reproductive health and motherhood (Spronk 2005a).

The deployment of a supposedly self-evident notion of sexuality that does not include women's sexual experiences has resulted in a specific academic perspective on women's sexuality. In Kenya, women's sexuality is mainly studied as a means of reproduction (among others Ahlberg 1991; Chege 1993; Kaler 2001). In this approach sexuality comes to be defined in relation to reproductive practice and ideology, and female sexuality in relation to motherhood. It goes without saying that reproduction is part of the topic of sexuality, but that sexuality is much more than reproduction alone. The same goes for the topic of prostitution (among others Kielmann

1997; Nelson 1987). Similarly, the studies about female circumcision mainly address the question of why the practice 'persists' among certain ethnic groups (among others Bergsjo 1994; Gwako 1995; Thomas 1996). In this body of literature, the focus is on the institutional and symbolic aspect of female sexuality. Likewise, there is an interesting, though small body of literature on the so-called 'woman-woman marriage' in Kenya, an institution that used to be looked at from a functionalist perspective, which has been analysed more realistically in more recent articles (Chacha 2000; Njambi and O'Brien 2000). These articles, however, do not address ethnographic data about these marriages in order to find out about the women's sexual experiences. A new, unique, collection of women's experiences is provided by a book on female same-sex practices in Africa, which contains a case study from Kenya (Morgan and Wieringa 2005).

Thus, there is a trend to study women's sexual lives not as a topic in its own right, but as a subset of other topics related to sexuality. This trend is discernible for the larger African continent as well. Sexuality research due to AIDS – which has seen a noticeable proliferation – has become the field of study that provides the most information about women's sexuality. As was discussed in Chapter II, we should note that one important characteristic of this kind of research is that it places female sexuality in a negative light. I am not contesting the content of these studies, but I would like to point out how they reflect two dominant perceptions in academic literature about women in Africa. One is that women do not have (or have very little) control over their own sex lives, and the second that a transactional component is part and parcel of women's sexual behaviour. However, taking a closer look, these studies (and the majority of literature on African women's sexuality) only focus on women in particular situations: either on women who prostitute themselves, or on transactional components of a sexual encounter, or on unequal gendered power relations constraining women when negotiating sexual encounters.[5] Most studies do not include groups of women who are not in such relationships in order to compare the differences between the groups (cf. Booth 2004; Pheterson 1990).[6]

Such studies exemplify the generally limited scope of studies in female sexuality, creating the impression that women in Africa engage only in problematic sexual encounters. Collectively the studies tell us that sex as a topic of study is only taken seriously when viewed as a societal problem. It can be concluded that certain perceptions about female sexuality have gained a hegemonic position in the academic literature, at the expense of other aspects of sexuality. This dominant academic perspective on women's sexuality, which implants certain assumptions about women's social identity and sexual lives, has become the reference point from which to speak and write about women's sexuality in African societies. The result is a subtle process of constructing women's sexuality as not just complex, but above all as flawed. Furthermore, taking into account the unequal gendered relationships that many women encounter, the dominant argument can also be turned upside down. Blumstein and Schwartz (1983) have argued that lack of power and dependence on men might lead to women becoming more assertive about sex. They argue that the sexual double standard that portrays men as having greater sexual needs, places women in a logical position to use sexual refusal as a bargaining chip. However interesting as it is, this logic reinforces the socio-economic positions of women in the literature, and it is important to move beyond analyses that portray women as victims.

There is a need to study sex more broadly than simply as a societal problem. People's sexual agency, both women and men's, is related to existing power relations and symbolic constructions of gender that have become common sense. Women are socialized into these understandings of femininity and masculinity and therefore reproduce these constructions themselves. It makes no sense to provide a gender analysis by presenting women as the ultimate victims of patriarchy; the focus should rather be on how exactly they have become entangled in these processes (Cornwall 2007).

A biographical approach to sexuality can show how women (and men) are subjugated by larger structures and how they live their lives as agents acting upon their social environment. It foregrounds women's sense of agency and self-worth, which we need in order to understand women's sexual subjectivity (Wekker 2006). If we conclude that there is a tendency to represent women as victims, it would be tempting to portray them as heroines, or at least as brave women resisting the patriarchal order and other forms of dominant culture in ingenious ways. Indeed, there is a tendency to do so, by using the terms 'empowerment' or 'agency' as synonyms for resistance to relations of domination (Nencel 2005: 133). Abu-Lughod warned against this 'romance of resistance' (1990), while Mahmood states that 'agency' should be understood as 'neither invoking a self-constituting autonomous subject nor subjectivity as a private space of cultivation' (2001: 210). Instead of interpreting young professional women's agency as intentionality or in a positive manner as emancipation, I would rather investigate the 'paradox of subjectivation' (Butler 1997) that highlights women's entanglement in the social relations that govern them, and also forms the conditions for other possibilities for them. Agency, then, is not simply a synonym for resistance to power relations, but a capacity for action that specific relations of subordination create and enable. For example, young professionals are expected to defer to their elders, while their success also grants them esteem and enables them to be respected in return. As a result, they acquire some leeway within the system.

Understanding how people engage in sexual encounters requires not only the mapping of explicit gendered power relations, but also the exploration of people's – both women and men's – intentions, behaviour and justifications. In this chapter, women's sexual biographies are seen as central to understanding their aspirations, their behaviour and their explanations regarding sexuality. Their experiences and their wishes relate to conventional discourses that discourage particular expressions of their sexuality, as well as with those more liberal discourses that encourage them to explore sexuality. As a result, women often express an ambiguous attitude, so as to conform to conventional notions of femininity, while actually undermining these conventions by being or representing the 'modern woman'.

Pamela, Martha, Njeri, Tayiani and Dorcas

In 2002, Kenya's Miss Tourism, Deborah Sanapei Ntimama, was celebrated jokingly as 'Kenya's best export product' or more seriously as 'a woman that makes our nation proud'. As a beautiful, successful and self-confident woman, she was the symbol of contemporary womanhood for many women, the symbol of Kenyan female beauty for many local and non-local women and men. She also epitomized a particular type of woman: urban, very fashion conscious, carrying herself with pride and usually well educated. All the women participating in this study correspond more or less to this image. These women signify what feminist scholars have pointed out: that women are increasingly performing the aesthetics of feminization, which can be understood to be constitutive of increasing reflexivity and detraditionalization of gender. The lives of young professional women are a testimony to social transformations. Despite their being classified as part of a particular subculture and as a particular group of women, it is important to take into account the differences between individual women in this group. By introducing them as individuals through vignettes of their lives, I aim to elaborate on some essentially subjective aspects of sexuality. I have made a small selection from a large group so as to provide space for them to elaborate on personal experience. Despite the large differences between women's attitudes and experiences, there are distinct trends that can be discerned among this group of women. I identified certain stages in the biographies that I found exemplified the whole group of women I spoke with. I discussed these trends when discussing the first draft of the chapter, and the women identified to varying degrees with them. The stages are useful in clarifying women's experiences regarding sexuality: the importance of dating, the game of 'playing hard to get', the insistence on sexual pleasure, the ambiguities associated with being a Christian, and the tribulations of being single when this is not out of choice.

The importance of dating

Pamela (aged 22 in 2001) was an extrovert, and a humorous, sociable person. She was physically short – something about which she liked to joke. Pamela was one of the younger women in this study and she lived with her parents in an average middle class estate in Runda. In 2001, she was waiting for admission to university to study political science or mass communication. Earlier, in 2000, she had benefited from a bilateral exchange programme between Kenya and Japan and she had resided in Kyoto for one year to study at the University of Kyoto. This year affected her close relationship with her family; the physical separation forced her to make decisions without her family's advice as she was used to doing. Back in Nairobi, she tried to maintain her independent position, but was not very successful because she was financially dependent on her parents. She called herself a 'saved' Christian and she used to be active in her church as a youth leader, as a singer in the choir, and as a volunteer helping with the weekly provision of meals for the homeless.

During the time we spent together, she met Emmanuel in church and she fell 'head over heels' in love with him. They dated for about four months, after which they broke up. During our discussions about the break-up, Pamela concluded that her enthusiasm and signs of affection might have overwhelmed him, as she used to send Emmanuel many cards and kiss him in the street in the presence of others. 'Why doesn't he like me kissing him when we meet? Why does that scare them? For crying out loud! If he loves me, why doesn't he like that?' After the usual anger resulting from broken relationships, she was sad rather than angry or bitter, and she was dealing with feelings of rejection.

Pamela and Emmanuel's relationship was marked by deliberations about 'how far' they could go. Since they were both 'saved' they chose not to have sex before marriage and initially they would only 'kiss on the mouth and hold each other', while later they would also 'kiss the French way'. However, after a while they started 'embracing more intensely, like he started to kiss me in my neck and I loved it'. After the first time of kissing the French way, she expressed her doubts as to whether they had not gone 'too far', i.e. whether they had become too physical. She immediately answered this question herself by arguing they were 'true believers' and since they did not have wrong intentions, it could not be labelled wrong. A few weeks after this episode, I met a very distressed Pamela, exclaiming she was 'confused'. She and Emmanuel had met the previous day and had gone to a friend's house so they would not have to meet in a coffee shop as usual. They had listened to music and talked, and had a 'great time'. They had started to embrace, he had kissed her neck, she had undressed his torso and then he undressed her. She kept her bra on and he had touched her breasts and they had fondled each other. She was exalted; it had made her 'feel like a woman!' She said she also felt 'guilty' and wondered whether they had done something wrong. We started a discussion about the definition of sex and she discussed the plight of Christians not permitted to 'indulge in sex'. What confused her was that she reflected positively on this experience saying 'they are always telling me it's wrong, but it doesn't feel wrong. I like it when he touches my breasts, is that wrong?' She continued defining sex by considering the various stages of physical contact. According to Pamela, to kiss was not to have sex, and when undressing, sex would be more 'in the air', but since she had kept her bra on and since they did not taken off their trousers, she could not call that sex. It comforted her that Emmanuel reminded them that they should not continue 'further than kissing' because they were both Christians: 'Now I know he doesn't want me for the sex'.

One week later (a few weeks before they broke up) she was very distressed again. Things were not working out between Emmanuel and her and she was afraid he might break up with her. They had been together the day before we met and she had wanted to repeat the experience they had had the previous week at their friend's house. They had started embracing and she had taken off her shirt like the previous time and, although initially he had responded, Emmanuel later withdrew saying they should not do 'these things' anymore. Pamela reacted with disappointment: 'I don't understand why, is there something wrong with me?' She kept on wondering whether he had not liked her breasts, whether she was not attractive. She experienced his refusal to embrace as a rejection. When I asked whether it could have been his Christian attitude, she continued to won-der whether she was not 'ladylike enough'. Two weeks later Emmanuel put an end to the relationship.

Pamela was an outgoing and joyful person, with a reputation for being humorous: she always had a 'story' to tell. Pamela's narrative illustrates a young woman exploring sexual desire for the first time. Having a boyfriend and becoming, although minimally, physically involved with him, invoked feelings of sexual desire that she related to her womanhood. Having been brought up in a protective Christian environment where girls and boys hardly ever meet without supervision, she was, according to her, 'late to discover the world between men and women'. Unlike Pamela, who said she was a virgin at 22, none of the other women I spoke with (with one exception) was still a virgin. Pamela claimed that as a Christian she valued premarital virginity; however she was not particularly proud of it. It made her feel 'like a child' while she wanted to be seen as a grown woman. She was self-conscious about her transitional status of not being a girl but also not quite qualifying as an adult. As a result of desiring to be identified as a woman, she began to engage in behaviour that she had previously denounced as 'sinful', such as kissing the French way and getting undressed. Three stages characterize Pamela's situation. First, establishing a relationship with Emmanuel provided her with the status of being someone's girlfriend, a sign of being appreciated as a woman. Second, becoming emotionally and, gradually, also physically involved with Emmanuel, she started to 'feel sexy'. This was a positive experience, it made her 'feel like a woman' and, in contrast to what she had been taught to expect, it 'did not feel bad'. She liked the fact that Emmanuel appreciated her body and would comment on her shape. Third, feeling appreciated as a person and as a woman contributed positively to her sense of self. As a result, she felt encouraged to explore sexual desire, something which she had previously avoided.

The fundamental step needed to achieve the status of womanhood for many women is to engage in dating. Although Pamela's parents encouraged her to maintain friends from church, she also befriended other people. Whenever she went out she spent the night at a female friend's house (or at my house). Going out meant being able to align herself with a particular group that she was not yet a part of, yet whose lifestyles she wished to share: her friends were working in the private sector as professionals. In a few years, she would be a young professional herself. Emmanuel was already one, working at an ICT company, and she lamented the fact that she did not yet have enough money of her own to be an equal partner to him. She received pocket money from her parents and sometimes she did odd jobs that provided her with some money. She recounted that at first she was shocked to learn about her new friends' sexual relationships and that she was afraid of having to admit to being a virgin. However, the few friends she told did not react disapprovingly.

When she met Emmanuel and also started going out with his Christian friends, she was at first surprised that they did not consider it to be 'sinful' to go out to bars and clubs or concerts. This encouraged her to continue to engage in the subculture of Nairobi's nightlife. Pamela and her friends did not go out every weekend, more like twice a month on average. Besides taking part in the Nairobi nightlife, they also attended 'Christian' concerts by gospel bands, as well as some of the many functions organized by Christian churches or institutions like the Christian university Day Star. According to representatives of these institutions I spoke to, they feel compelled to organize concerts, beauty pageants and other 'nites', as an alternative to the 'corrupted' nightlife they wished to 'protect' their youth from. As such, Christian institutions have accepted the subculture of young people in which dating is a central fact, although they stress that dating need not include having sex.

The central aim of engaging in the nightlife scene, or going 'bashing', is having a relationship or dating someone. After Pamela and Emmanuel broke up, Pamela remained single for about seven months and it distressed her terribly. She even seemed a little depressed as she was isolating herself by not engaging as much as she used to do with her friends. She felt 'stupid, even ashamed. I know it is actually stupid to feel like this, but I feel like I am missing out ... I just want a boyfriend, I want to be loved'. When she met Nyankami, she was very reserved and she remained apprehensive for months. Slowly, they became more involved and after a few months they were 'very happy, very committed, very in love!' She soon blossomed and became her usual cheerful self. This importance of dating is recognized by the majority of people I spoke with and it played an important role in their lives. Dating was often the topic to start the interviewing process in this research, because it is such a common topic of daily conversation, rumours and personal reflection.

To date means to be recognized as a potential partner: it represents recognition of being a sexually attractive woman or man. It also reflects that people belong to the subculture that is symbolized by 'having a life'; that is, going out, meeting many people, and generally enjoying being young. The importance of dating therefore highlights the importance of expressing a gendered and sexual identity in relation to a contemporary lifestyle. Pamela wanted to be recognized as a woman and therefore she had to adopt certain codes that distinguish women from girls, which include dress, association with a certain lifestyle, 'sophisticated' attitudes and relationships with men. As sexual desire is recognized as a component of growing up that is by definition physical or embodied, becoming sexually active is perceived as part of adulthood. Appreciation from men confirms a positive sense of self, which further encourages women to explore sexual desire as constitutive of their sense of self as 'woman'.

Another aspect many women identified with was the hegemonic influence of Christianity, which reflects, as I explained before, the hegemonic influence of patriarchal ideologies that are often manifested in Christian institutions. Pamela's experience reflects the situation in which the majority of women grow up. Since Pamela's identity formation during puberty was influenced by the norms of her Christian background, her gendered identity evolved around notions about how women's sexuality is framed mainly in relation to the patrilineage. In this perspective, woman's sexuality is defined according to reproductive abilities and sex is part of marital duty (although this does not exclude female pleasure, as we shall see later). Pamela was socialized and had partly internalized normative notions of femininity and womanhood in which premarital virginity is highly valued. She learned that her body is a 'temple for God'. Being in love with Em-

manuel made her push the boundaries of what she had learned to believe
was common sense and morally upright. Although as a 'saved' person she
struggled with her divergence from Christian morals, she felt encouraged
to do so as a 'modern' woman. This is a crucial process recounted by many
women and therefore central to an understanding of women's development with regard to sexuality.

Pamela and Emmanuel broke up before they came to a point where
they might have compromised their views on premarital virginity. (Perhaps Emmanuel even broke up with her because of the fear that they
would 'go too far'.) Many other women in the same position as Pamela
recounted moments of 'giving in', either by 'having sex' without intercourse or by having intercourse. For example, Tumi (aged 24) always
maintained that she never had sex with her boyfriend. When she once
told me she had spent the night at her boyfriend's place I asked how it
was. She explained how they embraced, kissed, got undressed and started
fondling each other. She insisted they did not have intercourse, but had
satisfied each other manually. Later she told me that they had also started
to have oral sex. However, she did not call it oral sex but rather phrased it
like 'we satisfy each other, you know ... he kisses me there [oral sex], I also
help him that way'. She did not call it sex because that would undermine
her insistence that she was a virgin. Both women and men reported 'having sex' without intercourse. According to the men this was only because
women insisted upon it, while women engaging in sex without intercourse tend to be younger women.

Other women recounted that they eventually compromised and had
sexual intercourse. In fact, all women said that the first time they had not
engaged in actual sexual intercourse because they wanted it themselves,
but because they were persuaded to or forced to by their partners. When
I probed a little further, the majority of women explained that they were
not against having sex *per se*, and some were even curious, but that they
would never take the initiative. Other women recounted being half curious, half apprehensive, and having allowed themselves to be taken more
or less by the course of events. Therefore, the fact that women say they
were persuaded or forced to have sex by their boyfriends does not mean
that they actually had sex against their will. That they recounted their first
sexual experience in this way is also a manifestation of the dominant ideology that women are supposed to be passive while men are supposed to
be active in sexual encounters. Of the twenty-four women I spoke with,
six commenced their sexual life more or less against their wishes. Some
women said they had felt pressured to have sex because they were virgins
while their friends were not. Other women felt compelled to 'prove their
love' for their boyfriends by having sex. A few women described situa-

tions where they were more or less forced by their date, who expected to have sex at the end of an evening out.[7] Some women recounted feeling guilty after having sexual intercourse for the first time, and how they were struggling with feelings of wrongdoing. It is important to note that these women were all younger adults, like Pamela.

It is likely, given the experiences of older women, that this concern about having done something wrong diminishes over time, at least with most of them. Women's narrative of exploration orients their self-conceptualization as a 'subject of desire' (Butler 1987) for whom sexual pleasure becomes indexical to their sense of self. The importance of maintaining a proper sexual reputation, however, remains a relevant aspect of women's sense of themselves when engaging in sexual relationships. Nevertheless, women recounted how they had, and continue to have, subtle ways on ensuring that they have sexual intercourse without appearing to be the initiator. How they do this is encapsulated in the phrase 'playing hard to get', as the following story of Martha shows.

'Playing hard to get'

Martha (aged 24 in 2001) was a tall, composed and good-looking woman. She was living on her own in a tiny apartment in lower middle class South B. In the year we met, she was working as an accountant for an international tourist company to save money to continue her studies. She managed to secure a scholarship for one year and left for a pilot school in Sydney, Australia, later that year. She was very passionate about becoming a pilot; it had always been a dream. She anticipated that flying would give her an immense sense of freedom and she dreamt of working for Doctors without Borders in Kenya. Her departure for Sydney was a dream come true. She had never had a 'committed' relationship and would joke about whether she would ever have one because she was not 'an easy lady'.

Both her parents came from the Meru ethnic group. Among some of the Meru, it is customary to circumcise women and several of Martha's cousins are circumcised, as well as her mother and aunts. Her father decided not to circumcise her sisters and her, which made them stand out among their relatives. 'My dad refused to have us circumcised because he was an intelligent and educated man, you know, exposed to the world, and he refused to agree with his sisters and mother to have us circumcised. We stood out.' According to Martha, the fact that they stood out, that some cousins regarded them as 'inferior', made her sisters and her look out for role models other than their own aunts. It also made them 'independent of mind and in our walk in life'. Her mother has always encouraged them to do well in school and Martha and her sisters have become successful professionals.

I have never seen Martha with a boyfriend or a lover. She talked about male friends but always made it clear that they were platonic friends. She was rather sceptical about female-male relationships. First of all, she wondered whether 'a man can be honest for a longer time'. Referring to her unfaithful father, she said: 'It is always the same story; they lie and cheat'. She would say it as a matter of fact, without elaborating too much on the moral implications. Secondly, she stated: 'If I decide to live with a man, I don't expect him to be faithful, they are not, so I will have to learn to live with that: accept it or leave it'. Third, she claimed that playing hard to get was common sense. 'If you want to be respected, you have to play hard to get in order not to be seen as loose. You might not like it, but you are forced to do so to keep a respectable image. And it's good, it is also a way of finding out what kind of man you are dealing with.' Through extensive e-mail correspondence, Martha and I were able to establish an enduring communication about her sexual contacts.[8] After several months in Australia, she wrote to me recalling a discussion we had had before, but this time she was more open. The following are verbatim extracts from letters sent to me between July 2001 and September 2001:

> Remember the time we were discussing my first time in that place near Yaya Centre. Actually about my experience and changes at X [a tourist company], it's still something I am still trying to deal with. You see there is the part of me that is not satisfied of just being a xtian [Christian] and having casual sex becoz biblically sex is for a married couple. So some days [I] am guilty but other days I feel it's a part of life. When we grew up we were expected to go to church etc and be xtian gals [Christian girls]. Ya knu. [You know.] And we were that. But my logic of thinking and how I would bring up my daughter is that I would teach her about church but let her be a free spirit. Becoz I realize that when we got the chance to find out what we didn't know, we went out for it with vengeance. I mean like sometimes we had to block our conscience to do it. And I think that is a part of life and gradually when you have been there, ya then can decide whether to go back to church or to just live your life. There is lots of guilt in me so often coz I feel like I am being two people. I feel that if I am in church I am expected to be what the teachings are and I should be that and if I am not, then I can choose what I want to be. However I always say in my heart that if I met a man and was really in love with him, and deemed a good man, then I could have a sexual r/ship with him and I would be satisfied with it and not guilty coz I will know that is someone I would like to spend the rest of my life with. That way I wouldn't be guilty. Yes, I can relate to the mental idea that if you are normal, you are sexually active. For me it was actually one of the first things that drove me to sex. I began to think that I was not normal, that I was primitive and naïve, that it was a shame to be a virgin at 22. I can honestly say I succumbed to pressure as much as desire to find what is it all about. Ya knu [You know] you walk around feeling like you are not normal coz ya dunno what a woman orgasm is and what do men like in bed etc.

Well, No, I have not had my opinion get stronger after sex with Kilimo [whether she is in love with him]. And it's becoz I have not had any real intimate sex which involves my emotions, body and soul. I have had sex twice since, and I think it's just that my mind is not so into it. It's like I have not really fallen in love with someone yet, maybe when I do then sex will mean something different. But for now, I had sex becoz it was convenient. Don't get me wrong, I wasn't forced to or anything but I particularly don't think it was the ultimate kind of sex I would have had if I was madly in love. I think I did it more out of adventure and wanting to find out what is it like now than anything else. I met Kilimo sometime, then he left town for a job away. So this guy moved back to town and well he lives like 10 minutes from me and we got to spend sometime together. And well one day, ya knu, one thing led to the other, and that's how I ended up having sex with him. After that I called him two days later said I enjoyed sex with him but am not crazy about him and would like us to be just friends, well he agreed though he said he really liked me. Well, we began to spend some time once in a while together and ya know we had sex again later. We have agreed he should get another g/f [girlfriend]. I think trouble is we spent time together and talked and so he began to see who I am, the kind of woman I am and he just getting more and more attracted to me. I don't want to hurt him so I am honest about everything, and yeah am not into anything with him. If he gets another woman that's gud for us coz I will never commit to him, that I know. I don't feel drawn to him. He is a very gud guy, feels like am sleeping with a brother more than a lover. That's a boring way to start a sex life after a long time … I however enjoy sex with him but that's all there is. (23 February 2002)

Martha was a very self-confident woman, eager to make something of her life. For her, 'African womanhood' was an important point of reference in our discussions. Her sense of self was grounded in her confidence of womanhood as being independent, critical and persevering. In her late teens, she used to be more of a 'tomboy' and she avoided attention from men by wearing baggy clothes and being a little rough in her manners. She used to associate femininity with being dependent on men's appreciation: 'African women learn to find confidence in being someone's wife, mother or sisters [hissing between her teeth]. With due respect to my mother, my sister and me cannot live like that. It's not always easy, but we have to search for new ways [of] being woman.' Since her job at the tourist company, she began to appreciate herself in a new light: 'It was as if an undiscovered part of myself was explored. I was valued for my work and it made me a proud woman. I started to dress up and I enjoyed it. I had learned to hide my body and now I learned to be proud of it. I am a beautiful woman and I should enjoy that!'

As Martha stated, she came to believe that 'if you are normal, you are sexually active' and it was 'adventure' that 'drove her' to have sex. Through having sex, she came to 'appreciate her body' in an ultimately positive sense. This appreciation of her female physique made her an even 'stronger' woman because she discovered aspects of her womanhood she had not known before. She also learned to appreciate herself as a professional, which positively reframed her gendered sense of self. As such, she began to approach sexual desire as a subset of her sense of self. In time, she distinguished between 'real intimate sex which involves my emotions, body and soul' and 'convenient [lustful] sex'. This positive approach to sex did not mean she approved of any kind of sexual relationship though, as she had certain moral standards.

To inspire 'respect' was a very important component of Martha's self-esteem. The importance of respect was related to her idea that 'you should carry yourself as a proud African woman'. In her eyes, the opposite of a respected woman was a sluttish woman and she needed to avoid that at all costs. In fact, she gave the impression that she rarely became involved with men; the way in which she talked about herself and the way in which she behaved gave no impression that she met with men at home, in bars or at church. What I observed, however, was the significance of 'playing hard to get'.

Playing hard to get is a social institution in Nairobi's sexual culture; it has become like a skilful art. It is an essential component of the communication between women and men, to their joy and chagrin. It is a cliché about which both women and men complain, though it is also a source of excitement and is fundamental to flirtation. Playing hard to get means a form of communication by which a woman pretends not to be interested in being involved with a man, not even in talking to him; she must appear unapproachable. However, she is able to continue communication in subtle, non-verbal ways. Typically, women express an aloof attitude and the interaction between pushing and pulling is supposed to beguile men. Men are expected not to give up too easily on a woman and to entice them skilfully. In fact, playing hard to get is ritualized flirtation. Men complain that they never know when women are interested and that women complicate matters unnecessarily. But there are two reasons why women like Martha played hard to get.

Martha was careful not to appear too interested in a man or in a sexual encounter because of the danger of being considered an improper woman. For example, she would refuse to return phone calls from men who had approached her because she was careful not to appear too eager, as 'it is tricky to show your interest'. Her fear was that the man in question might consider her as a woman of low morals if she gave in too easily. Moreover, she held women who, according to her, were open about their sexual adventures, in low moral regard; she was careful not to be associated with them. She criticized them for 'selling out their bodies', 'being disrespectful to themselves' or providing men with justification for having 'casual' instead of 'committed' relationships. Her 'proper' sexual reputation was dear to her and she rarely discussed her sexual adventures with friends. Although she was one of the most outspoken women on sexual politics I met, she did not openly express approval of more liberal sexual morals. Playing hard to get was a means of eliciting respect from men by showing she was a respectable woman. It was a means of upholding a respectful sexual reputation.

Furthermore, playing hard to get is a strategy which enables a woman to 'screen' a man. As Martha's account shows, she had little regard for men's sexual intentions. Her father and two elder brothers were womanizers and she had always experienced that as an embarrassment for her mother and sisters-in-law. According to her, men were inclined to be unfaithful because of their interest in sex. Therefore, when meeting an interesting man, it was necessary to find out whether he was interested in sex or whether he was also interested in her personally. It was of importance not to get taken in by one of the womanizers who 'make use of women' to satisfy their 'lust'. Playing hard to get is for many women a strategy of getting to know what a man's intentions are. As Martha argued, if a woman keeps a man waiting he will lose interest if he has no sincere intentions in having a more 'committed' relationship.

Martha was rather extreme in her tactics. When she was interested in a man and thought it was mutual, she would not respond to his first two or three phone calls, and would act 'cool' if they met coincidentally, and delay the first date by telling the man in question to call back another time because she was busy. When she finally agreed to have a date, she would fix the date at least one week ahead. On the date, she would go home early and after the date, the man had to call to check on how she was doing. If he did not, he was dropped because he obviously did not have 'serious' intentions. Martha was not unusual in this, although women have different approaches to keep a man at bay. Some women keep a man waiting for weeks before they agree to a date, others agree to a date within a week but delay sleeping with them. In contrast, Pamela claimed not to be the kind of person who 'plays hard to get' because she became impatient when she fell in love. Although her friends warned her not to move too fast, she responded immediately to Emmanuel when he approached her. The majority of the women in this study adopted delaying tactics.

One reason women give for playing hard to get is that men make a distinction between girlfriends to have sex with and girlfriends who are potential marriage partners. They all cite examples of men who have a girlfriend for some time but, when it comes to marriage, choose somebody else.

Playing hard to get is acted out mainly during the initial stages of dating. Once a couple has become more involved and meets regularly, in other words, once a relationship has been established, playing hard to get no longer plays a role. However, it also has ambiguous connotations. It may be an exciting game to play, but it also leads to men accusing women of being 'spoilt' or 'heartless', and to the stereotyping of Nairobi women as 'difficult' and 'arrogant'. Some women and men say that women, by playing the 'hard to get' game, cause men to be 'players' (womanizers) because men have learned to 'push' and take pride in being able to seduce women. Many people I spoke to also said that it hampered open communication and honesty and created a distance between young lovers that was hard to bridge.

Although she once valued virginity, Martha adopted a more flexible attitude regarding the moral value of premarital virginity once she had decided that sex was 'normal' and 'natural'. Having sex came to override the importance of virginity. By appreciating her sexuality positively, as a cornerstone of her gendered sense of self, she gained more self-confidence in relation to men, but maintained a proper sexual reputation. At the same time, her identity as a professional who was appreciated for her work had heightened her sense of self in relation to her sexuality and being a 'woman' and an 'African'. She thus learned to appropriate sexual desire as a subset to her identity as a contemporary, working woman. Nevertheless, she also felt strongly about moral issues. Although she denounced double standards, she partly reproduced them by insisting on the need for a proper sexual reputation for women. Whereas Pamela and Martha's narratives showed how women appropriated sexual desire as a constituent of their sense of self, although not without ambiguities, for other women such as Njeri sexual pleasure has always been part of their personal composition.

To give and to receive sexual pleasure

Njeri (aged 26 in 2001) was a somewhat abrasive woman. Tall, extrovert and with enquiring eyes, she stood out in a crowd. She had a little house in a small estate on Ngong Road that she called her 'pocket of paradise'. As a sales person, Njeri had changed jobs many times, always looking for greener pastures. The first time I met her in 1997, she started as an assistant in the sales department of a private company and since then she had rocketed via various firms into a position where she could demand an impressive salary. 'I know I can sell like crazy, and I tell them they can fire me if I disappoint them [which did not happen].'

Njeri called herself 'noisy', a common expression used to indicate an expressive person. She grew up with her father after he divorced her mother, 'not because I liked him better, but he had money to pay school fees and my mother was left behind without a single cent'. Her father was a businessman and he would often travel, leaving her brother and her to fend for themselves. 'He was a good man insofar that he took care of us financially, but he was always busy. I learned to be on my own when I was very young, nobody to tell me right from wrong.' Her father did not remarry but had various girlfriends whom he would sometimes bring home. It affected her as 'I knew early in life that morals don't exist. When I got to know about sex, I learned soon enough to do it for my own pleasure because men are only focussed on their own pleasure. So, I became careful of men, not to avoid sex, but [in order] not to be used.' Njeri did not mind talking about her sex life. 'Listen, I have had enough lovers to know what you can get in life. So when I meet a man who is only out for his own pleasure, or if a man does not know how to satisfy a woman, he can leave. I am not willing to accept such behaviour anymore, in the past I used to fake an orgasm in order to get rid of the man as soon as possible, but not anymore.' One time I met Njeri and she said she had 'a story', i.e. something to tell friends. The previous night she had gone out with a 'friend', whom I had not heard of before. They had ended the night at her house and were engaging in foreplay on her bed. However, according to her, his penis was undersized and she had not wanted to continue; she had told him to sleep on the couch. 'I feigned a headache.' It could be a made-up story, but as I have got to know Njeri it is quite possible that she spoke the truth.

I met Njeri when she had been with John for almost two years. However, six months later they broke up. According to Njeri it was because John was a little older and he was afraid she might run away with a younger guy. He would have liked them to settle down but Njeri refused to even start discussing that. They had huge conflicts about John wanting them to meet after office hours, or whenever she was free, while she did not want to commit herself every day. 'He insists on meeting so he knows who I see or not, he wants to control my life', she said. According to John, Njeri 'refused to get real and become serious with her life, she is playing with me and because I know she is a good woman I have not left her yet, but she has to get serious now. She is playing psychological games with me.' After fights, Njeri would make up with him every time by 'being the nice woman he wants me to be, I cook nicely for him, then I give him a massage, then I undress him slowly and nobody can "soothe" [looks meaningfully by raising her eyebrows] him as I can, he is hooked to me and he cannot stand it'. The biggest conflict I was aware of during their time was when John found out that Njeri secretly had had an IUD (Intra Uterine Device) inserted for birth control, while he was under the impression that she was not using anything since they always used condoms. He felt betrayed, as if she did not trust him.[9]

According to Njeri, the relationship between John and her was based on good sex. 'He is just awesome as a lover, I don't know where he got that gift from.' She did not want to talk much about their problems; she would only call me to have a cup of coffee and complain in a rapid flow that I could hardly interrupt. She would always avoid talking about her own role in the relationship with John. Indirectly, she indicated that the problem was that John had different expectations about their relationship and since she 'was not in love' with him, they had better quit. However, she never took that step; it was John who eventually broke up with her. John's suspicion about Njeri's infidelity was well founded, although she refused to discuss it with me and only indirectly indicated she had another lover. The closest we came to discussing it was one time when she took me shopping because she 'badly needed toys'. She meant colourful and/or tasty condoms. 'I really like the cartoon one, I must have the Tweety [yellow bird] one because I like it most.' When I made a joke about the comparison between Tweety's yellow colour and one of John's conspicuous yellow ties, she waved it away with a 'ah, that man has no taste, I won't spend this on him'.

Njeri was one of the few women who did not have to overcome a certain barrier or moral conflict in order to come to terms with her sexual feelings when engaging in sexual intercourse. She could not remember when she had had sex for the first time because it did not 'impress' her. She said laughingly: 'Must have been one of the guys from next door'. Virginity never meant anything to her, but as a teenager she soon discovered that she should not get pregnant. Since then she has always used contraceptives: condoms, the pill or the IUD. When asked how many sexual partners she had had, she answered that according to the norm it must have been too many and that she never kept track of them. Initially, she gave me the impression that she had had 'loads' of lovers. Much later, when we were discussing infidelity, she told me she had been in a serious relationship for three years and she had been faithful all the time. This had been the only man she loved; although he had 'dogged' her (been unfaithful), she still could not forget him. Since then, she had been 'looking for love' and because Kenyan men were 'not endowed' with love, she was 'stranded with sex'. She had become resigned to this situation. Her plan was to earn as much money as possible and, when she was about 30, to have children as a single mother.

Njeri was a woman who wanted to be in control and she realized that this domineering attitude aggravated many men. Her 'noisy' or imperious and outgoing attitude did not reflect conventional notions about the role of women and characteristics of femininity. But she could not care less. Over the years she had learned not to count on anyone, and with her father as an example, she had become suspicious of men's competence as caretakers. Other women would maybe think the same as Njeri, but would nonetheless act deferentially towards men, whereas Njeri refused to compromise. She would play with the fact that she was expected to be more deferential. For example, once in a bar she got our drinks and offered John his drink by coming towards him kneeling down, offering him the beer with two hands and looking downwards, as is customarily expected of women among certain groups. Then she jumped up and started laughing aloud, almost hysterically. Afterwards, she explained that she sometimes felt compelled to rebel against anything that 'irritates' her, such as women's submissive attitudes. In public, she said that John had not given up on her becoming a respectable woman against all odds, and she would make jokes about his naiveté. However, at her work, she behaved professionally and did not offend people.[10] She did not have many female friends because her attitude was an affront to many women.

Her best friends were men, which was partly the cause of John's suspicion. This wider circle of good male friends had been her regular sexual partners; she rarely had one-night stands with strangers because she did not want to sleep with a man she did not know.[11] 'You cannot trust men, you have to know them a little before you share the bed,' she explained. As I observed, she was very generous to these men; they could always borrow money (sometimes huge amounts), or stay the night at her place, and she would 'cover for them up', providing an excuse if they were in trouble, etc. She also expected these men to be generous to her and as proof of their appreciation for her she expected gifts, or to be taken out. Companionship and appreciation were symbolized in this material way. She trusted these men and she regarded them as her brothers. However, when asked whether she loved them, she replied: 'No ... I don't believe in love anymore, you know that. But, okay, I love them as friends, not as lovers.' According to her, one got more involved emotionally with lovers, while with friends one could maintain a favourable and pragmatic distance.

For Njeri, sex was pleasure. During her teenage years she had had 'mechanical sex, you know, the sex as a duty for women and if you're lucky you can enjoy it as well'. She 'discovered' her own body and one lover in particular taught her the 'tricks' of 'real sex'. They would watch porn movies and then try it out themselves:

> I don't think I have not tried out any act, we did it all, and you discover your preferences. I don't like anal sex so much but men just love it. Apparently you guys [whites] like these bondage thing but I never developed a taste for it. I don't need complicated acts, I like it when a man makes an effort and is creative, I want to be spoilt, kissed all over, treated like a queen.

Having sex for Njeri did not mean a 'quickie', that is, when the couple has to rush. She insisted on spending a whole evening or night together, otherwise she was not interested. Therefore, she did not have sex 'often', 'maybe once a week, that's when I'm lucky', but only when John (or another) had time to spend several hours at her place in order to have 'several rounds' of sex. She also wanted to engage in a sexual encounter only at her apartment. She never slept at a man's house, though she occasionally spent the night at John's. Whenever she ended up at a man's house, she preferred to take a taxi back home after having had sex. This rarely happened as she usually managed to organize meeting at her house. Whenever I spontaneously visited her during weekends, there was almost always a 'friend' around. She was also very strict with John that he should call before visiting her, which he – surprisingly – always did.

Having sex made her 'feel like a woman', it 'invigorated' her. Looking at Njeri's life story, it becomes clear that sexual desire has been part of her personal make-up from her adolescent years onwards. After being introduced at an early age (14) to sex, she soon took it into her own hands instead of 'being used' by men. She says she has always enjoyed sex and that she has been lucky to have never ended up in an abusive situation, which she attributed to her careful approach to men. Because sexual desire has been part of her personal make-up, sexual pleasure had become central to her sexual relations with men; sex became the ultimate symbolic interaction of her being a sexual subject. Njeri liked to be desired as a woman and she liked to 'give pleasure' to a man. It was important for her to be a good lover and she cherished the idea that John was bound to her because of their good sex life. Sex was also power: it gave her power over men because she controlled the encounters and because she defined sex as 'giving them pleasure' as a skilled lover. Not many women recounted their sexual experience as 'giving pleasure'. That Njeri was exceptional just shows how the majority of women conceptualize and hence experience sex in relation to the dominant discourses framing women's sexuality as mainly passive.

Sex had always been a positive experience for Njeri, whereas the majority of women recounted having at least some experiences when they felt compelled to have sex. Their accounts of subtle or less subtle force point to the ambiguous situation in which many women find themselves. Sex remains an ambiguous issue for most women and therefore it is unusual to find a woman such as Njeri, who has integrated sex into her personal make-up. Although many women are engaged in the process of appropriating sexual desire, the conventional constructions of female sexuality as passive and chaste weigh down on them. This does not mean that they abstain from sex or do not enjoy sex, but that sex brings with it feelings of anxiety. In Tayiani's case, the transformation from a chaste woman to a sexually active woman is telling in relation to the influence that religion has over women's lives. The point is not that all women are subjugated by religious doctrines, but rather that women like Tayiani serve as far-reaching symbols of 'proper' womanhood.

Chastity and the realization of sexual pleasure

Tayiani (aged 28 in 2001) was a woman with a composed and serious attitude who was 'very beautiful' (several male informants who saw her in my company told me so and asked me to arrange a meeting with her). She is one of the few informants who married during my stay, after dating her lover Kinyua for three years. She came from an upper middle class background – her father was a diplomat and her mother a businesswoman – while Kinyua's parents were low-ranking civil servants in the government administration. During the wedding, the class differences were apparent in the dress of both families, as well as the presents given to Tayiani and Kinyua. Although there we no open hostilities, it seemed that Kinyua's family was not at ease compared with Tayiani's family. Kinyua was a social climber and through his work as a junior manager in an international company he could afford a higher middle class lifestyle compared to that of his relatives. Tayiani's fear, therefore, was that Kinyua's family members might expect to reap some rewards from them and they discussed beforehand that they would support his relatives only selectively, and would never host them for long periods of time. Tayiani wondered whether Kinyua would be able to keep his promise once they were married and whether he would be able to resist familial pressure. They first met in the Nairobi Chapel Church, and they portrayed themselves as staunch Christians. She had a degree in French and was working at a French company as a member of the office staff. She moved from the prestigious Mountain View estate to live with Kinyua in Nairobi West.

Tayiani had a quiet nature and she did not find it easy to speak out about intimate matters. She would always express herself in concealed terms; for instance, she would never say 'having sex' or use the word 'sex' and instead always used the term 'to sleep with'. During her pre-wedding ceremony (a girl's farewell party prior to becoming a wife), the jokes and teasing were more reserved than I observed in other such ceremonies where the wife-to-be would often be mocked hilariously about her sexual capabilities. Tayiani's friends seemed to anticipate her shyness and teased her by providing her with sexy lingerie 'for Kinyua' and joking about the wedding night and whether they would be 'too tired' or whether 'one can never be too tired for that'. Tayiani did not respond and only smiled a little. The evening ended with a game where each one of us could ask 'any question' to Tayiani and she would in turn ask us something. During this game, the atmosphere became more intimate and confidential and after one of us asked

Tayiani whether she feared 'the first time', issues about 'how to take care about your own satisfaction' and 'the difference between vaginal and clitoral orgasm' began to be discussed. Tayiani eased up a little and said she did not know much yet and hoped it would work out well; she trusted that Kinyua would be gentle. She said she was curious to know about a sex life and was looking forward 'to enjoy these things you have always heard of'. She gave us the impression that she had not had sex and the rest responded to her as if she would be having sex for the first time with Kinyua.

Tayiani and Kinyua went on honeymoon for two weeks. First they went for a few days to the Masaai Mara, the famous national park, and then they proceeded to the coast where they enjoyed a beach holiday. They later told me that it had been a wise decision to go on honeymoon immediately so that they could spend time together without any interference by family and friends. When I spoke to Tayiani alone she said that she had been a bit nervous during the first days, afraid of not knowing what to expect and afraid to fail. Rachel: 'Fail what?' Tayiani: 'I dunno ... to fail ... or to disappoint rather, I guess. They always make such a big fuss about making love and so ... you know.'

I asked her whether it had been her first time and she remained silent. She disliked my question. Eventually she said that it had not been her first time having sex with a man. She only told me that her first experience of sex was 'not fun'; she felt 'guilty' about it and therefore it had not been worth it. It was tainted as non-legitimate and contrasted with what she claimed to be respectable. It had caused her much stress to let Kinyua know about this earlier encounter; however, he had reacted in a 'very understanding' way and said that both of them had their histories and they should consider their shared life as a new starting point. She was relieved at his reaction: 'I don't know, we learn to hide somehow for our men and it was so much effort to tell him while I know he is okay. Of course he would not leave me but for some reason you are so scared to admit.' A few months after her marriage she said she was learning a 'new kind of life, new feelings, I have never got to know a man so intimately and although I really have to adjust, I never thought it [sex] could be so great'. She said that during these months 'I have learned a lot about myself, I am too shy for no reason, I am also ashamed for no reason, I am learning that making love is okay, that I can express what I like.' While she had always ignored articles in magazines about sexual matters before, she was actively seeking information these days. 'I am illiterate about myself!' she once said jokingly. After being married she showed a more relaxed, less aloof attitude, and she spoke more easily about intimate matters, although she always refused to speak openly about sex. She said she was 'just happy'.

Tayiani was 'sophisticated' according to the norm of female young professionals, in both appearance and attitude. She perceived herself as a 'modern African woman', thereby elaborating about her lifestyle and professional career. Being 'African' was of importance to her, as many people defined her as a 'point five', i.e. a half cast, because of her fair skin. She often used to insist that she was 'African' by pointing out that her mother originated from the Seychelles and her father from Tanzania. She disliked being called '*mzungu*-like', i.e. like a white person. She liked to be dressed in 'African dress', clothes of West African material and design. In Nairobi this dress is an effective statement. Politicians wear it on meet-the-people tours or when certain international guests are welcomed. One of the men I worked with only wore it during workshops or conferences where he knew there would be an international audience. It has become symbolic of Africanness, as opposed to Kenyanness. Women hardly wear it for daily use, but rather on public occasions like celebrations, going to church or during official gatherings. For Tayiani African dress became a statement, an alternative to being dressed in smart trendy clothes. She claimed that 'we Kenyans have an identity problem, we are not proud of who we are and instead we tend to copy you [whites], but we have to be proud to be black'. For her, 'being modern the African way' was a necessity. She worked as a youth leader in church because the youth are at particular risk of becoming 'westernized'.

Another aspect of Tayiani's contemporary identity related to her Christian faith. Tayiani and Kinyua belonged to a typical middle class church where young professionals and young couples comprised the majority of the congregation. The Nairobi Chapel is a Baptist Church which provides opportunities to meet like-minded people by way of the many clubs, classes and meetings, as well as the Sunday services. The church is actively engaged in providing counselling and advice, especially on issues with which many middle class young adults struggle, such as sexuality, identity and lifestyle. When we were discussing whether they would like to have children, she claimed that their church was 'modern' because married couples are allowed to use contraceptives. She was not ready to have children yet; they needed to settle down first. In fact, many sermons are directed at the choices people have to make about relationships, such as premarital sex, premarital cohabitation, etc. The church approaches all problems and issues from a positive understanding of young adults as 'modern' people. Kinyua once remarked that he had learned to value monogamy as the principle of a contemporary identity: 'A modern man is a monogamous man because he takes responsibility for his family, which are his wife and children'. Tayiani chose a Christian man because she expected to have a better chance at finding a sincere monogamous man, remarking that she would prefer not to marry at all than to be with an unfaithful husband. Being 'saved' or a Christian can thus become a means – or hope – of safeguarding a certain lifestyle and protecting against adultery. Tayiani and Kinyua married with the consent of their church leaders, that is, they had an AIDS test and were found to be HIV negative. They both claimed not to have been worried about it.

As discussed above, Tayiani gave the impression of being a virgin. Although Kinyua had never given her any indication that he particularly valued premarital virginity, Tayiani herself valued it as a symbol of respectability. She would recount how difficult it was to be a 'true Christian' and, in order to avoid the temptation of 'indulging' in non-Christian practices, she chose to have a circle of friends from her church. As a youth leader, she encouraged girls to remain virgins, as it would make them 'proud women'. Tayiani found solace in the church teachings that valued premarital abstinence in the face of social changes whereby female virginity had lost its status. The status of being a respectable Christian strengthened her sense of self in relation to her sexual subjectivity, both before and after her marriage. For Tayiani, marriage was a moral safe haven within which she could explore her sexual feelings. She could now express interest in sharing her new found experience and knowledge, whereas previously she was too shy to do so. The status of being a married woman provided the legitimacy for her to read magazines that give advice about sexual practices.

Tayiani embodied the ideal of middle class married wifehood, which would soon be followed, ideally, by motherhood. Here, Christian morality and other patriarchal ideologies overlap. The normative social biography for a Kenyan woman mandates marriage, sexual activity and childbearing. Bearing and rearing children are considered central to a woman's well being, and sexual activity and consequent reproduction serve to solidify the bond with her spouse, which improves her status. The period of being a newly married woman was a time when Tayiani began to appreciate that their sexual activity and reproductive capacities are an important source of power. Although generally speaking, sex is considered a marital duty for a wife, Tayiani never spoke of it this way but instead formulated it as a self-discovered treasure. Since Kinyua was not a man to reinforce gender roles, he did not insist on conventional female characteristics, such as women having to show sexual neutrality or innocence. According to Tayiani, Kinyua encouraged her to feel free and would tease her by giving her sexy lingerie. Moreover, the Nairobi Chapel encourages couples to work on their sex life; it is portrayed as the key to a good emotional and supportive relationship. In the booklet *The Wonders and Beauty of Sex* (Tabifor 1998), sold in the Religious Bookshop in Nairobi, the religious 'plight' and 'pleasures' for 'the younger generation' are described. Couples are 'enlightened about the mystery of love and sex because they hold the fabric of society, as well as, a blessed marriage'. Couples are encouraged to 'discover the spiritual purpose of sex' and to 'enjoy this delight' (Tabifor: 15, 27, 97). Tayiani found encouragement in such literature to explore her sexual desire. It consolidated her sense of self as a woman and as a sexually active woman.

Although Kinyua was not an authoritarian man, the Christian-inspired gender roles defined him as the head of the household and Tayiani as the deferential wife. Chastity and virtue are extolled as feminine virtues embodying the honour of the family, community and, sometimes, nation. Christian doctrine affected the nature of Tayiani's embodied experience as much as her articulation of it. In church, she behaved slightly deferentially to Kinyua; I observed how she did not leave his side, always stayed slightly behind him, was focussed on his movements rather than on initiating contact with others, and bowed her head slightly downwards and often smiled serenely. This was in contrast to how she was at home and among friends when she expressed a more egalitarian attitude towards him and liked to joke. Her attitude reflected the status of middle class married wifehood and motherhood that is the icon of respectability of the normative order.

Women such as Tayiani are held in high esteem. They uphold certain hierarchies of status and gender roles and they are respected for two reasons: one, for being successful career women and, second, for being 'proper' women. Tayiani represents an ideal according to the norm, while Njeri represents, in a way, the antithesis of Taiyani. Women like Njeri, who visibly do not embody the ideal of married motherhood, are typically portrayed as 'improper' or 'lacking African morals'.[12] Many women, however, challenge the norm in their personal choices because for various reasons they do not aspire to be like Tayiani, in that they do not want to be a 'saved' Christian or do not agree with the practice of premarital abstinence. If Tayiani embodies the ideal of the 'modern' woman through her marital status, many women of her age and social standing do not, because for many women it is difficult to find a marriage partner, as we shall see in Dorcas's case. Moreover, women like Njeri do not want to be like Tayiani.

Boundaries of sexual pleasure

Dorcas (aged 30 in 2001) was a well-dressed, typical 'career' woman with a cheerful personality. She was single in 2001. She was an outspoken person, though not particularly extrovert. She had a certain dignified attitude that reflected both alertness and restraint. Dorcas, the most successful woman in this study, worked as a sales manager in a large multinational. She had made a ca-

reer 'through hard work' because she only had a first degree in accountancy. She 'loved' to work, and if necessary she worked in the evening and on weekends. She had her own apartment in Kilimani, a middle class neighbourhood, which she furnished simply but luxuriously with expensive electrical appliances, furniture and art. She stated that although she would like to spend more time at home, she did not do so because of being alone, and also that it would be too much trouble to invite people over because then she would want to provide dinner. On many evenings she could be found in the more upmarket bars with colleagues and friends who shared the same work rhythm. She once said 'bars are almost my home'. She went to the gym twice a week after office hours and to the swimming pool before office hours. She dressed in skirt suits or trouser suits, wearing high heels and she had an 'Afro hairstyle': she did not use hair extensions [fake hair] or wigs and instead she had either short curls or little braids.

Dorcas had had several 'casual' relationships and one 'committed' relationship, which ended in 1999. She recounted how, gradually, she and her ex-boyfriend grew into a 'strangling' relationship that led to a break-up. After a first 'happy' year, Samwel lost his job and got depressed, as he could not find another similar job. Dorcas would explain his bad moods and irritation as a consequence of his joblessness and would hope for better times. Meanwhile, he moved in with her because he could not afford his own apartment and they started a life as a couple. In the beginning, she enjoyed living together because 'I was ready to become a wife and start a life with someone'. However, conflicts arose. According to Dorcas, Samwel became more and more impossible to live with because 'he wanted to control my life'. He disliked it when Dorcas met her friends in bars and he disapproved when she had to work overtime. 'At first, I would try to suit his anxiety by trying to do as he wished, but he became only more demanding! He started accusing me for being un-African because real African women would not behave like I did. It would be so humiliating to be called un-African that I would try to suit his ideas [by being more at home].' Eventually he became violent and started beating her. 'Do you believe that I let myself be beaten? I mean, it started slowly, a slap, but it got worse, and I tried to understand. For god's sake?! That's our [women's] problem, always understanding and these men don't have to make an effort to understand.' Eventually she left Samwel one evening with the help of her brother; he picked her up from her house to stay for a while at his place. Meanwhile, he communicated with Samwel on Dorcas's behalf and pressurized Samwel to leave Dorcas's house, which he eventually did.

'We all have to accept that my generation of women is not like our mother's generation,' Dorcas told me. She also recounted that she had 'learned' to admit that she had sexual relationships instead of feeling guilty about it and sometimes even denying it. 'You know, we grew up as Christian girls and we would take life as it was. As a working woman I realized things are different, you have to learn to position yourself, sometimes against common sense.' One day I met

Dorcas and a friend at a bar. She had invited her friend over because 'she has to tell you something'. Elizabeth, her friend, felt a little uncomfortable at first, but after Dorcas's encouragement started talking about her marriage. Elizabeth was married with two little children and she was an extremely successful interim manager for some international companies. Recently, her husband had left her because 'he could not cope with her success, he felt insecure', despite having been 'best friends from college onwards'. Dorcas and Elizabeth engaged in a discussion about whether his friends might have influenced him by emphasizing that Elizabeth had become a woman 'with horns', that is, a bossy wife. Eventually, Dorcas exclaimed: 'You see? This is our problem; men's egos are so sensitive to successful women!' Dorcas was terribly frustrated about the fact that she could not maintain a 'committed' relationship whereas she wanted to get married and have children.

Since the relationship with Samwel, she had not been involved in a relationship, except for a few 'hits'. As she stated: 'You know what my problem is? I'm too self-conscious. You know what my other problem is? I only attract married men. Single men don't like me.' She seemed to be more bitter about the difficulty in finding an unattached or single man than about the episode with Samwel: 'They don't like me because I am beautiful, intelligent and I impress with my car instead of only being beautiful.' She commented that men are 'scared to commit' and only want career women as lovers. When she got involved with a man and start dating, there was always a point when the man left: 'The moment I show I would like to become more committed'. Her conclusion that men do not want to commit themselves and are only out for 'fun' was supported by her past relations that did not last long. In 2001, she had a relationship with a married man she 'loved'. The fact that she did not leave him, even though the relationship was not fulfilling, made her very desperate. When I left Nairobi, she had finally decided to break up, remarking: 'I don't believe in love anymore, I don't believe it works. I will remain a single and bitter woman and I hate the idea. I'm sexy, but single.'

Like Tayiani, Dorcas's mannerisms and behaviour, her way of speaking, her likes and dislikes conveyed the image of a 'sophisticated' and confident woman. The differences between them, however, reflect the contradictions faced by many women: all women experience pressures to conform to conventional notions of femininity while they are actually undermining these conventions by virtue of being 'modern woman', partly seen as the opposite of being 'African'. While Tayiani managed to identify with the prevailing stereotype of a contemporary woman in relation to conventional ideas of femininity, for women like Dorcas that was impossible. Despite her bitterness, she still had hopes that she would meet a man who respected her. Her friend Lucy (aged 28), who also participated in the research, proved that it was possible. Lucy had had a steady boy-friend, Nyambane, for three years and their relationship was satisfactory and unproblematic. They were both ambitious with regard to career de-velopment and they supported each other. Nyambane was visibly proud of Lucy, which affected Dorcas: 'That man, he is so ... he truly loves her and that really touches me'.[13]

Dorcas also 'once believed' in virginity 'and all that'. She recounted how her boyfriend persuaded her to have sex during a secondary school holiday. She was 17 years old, and knew little about sex, about her own body or about men. She used to live in a boarding school for girls and they were only told to 'take care of themselves' and not to get pregnant: 'In fact, they scared you about this thing called sex, my mother used to tell me that men are only out to hurt you and that you should always avoid to be alone with a man because of this terrible thing'. When she fell in love with her boyfriend, whom she got to know during the national drama festival, she did not believe 'that thing' could be terrible, or so she said. Although she had decided not to have sex with him, she let herself be per-suaded into having sex and the first time she disliked it. After a few times she began to enjoy it and she made efforts to get to know what sexual acts she liked best. That ex-boyfriend was 'long gone' but, as she said, 'perhaps it's the memory, but I don't think I've ever liked making love as I did then, perhaps it was the innocence of young age'.

Through time, 'sex became like politics. I mean, they promise you the best but instead it's always a struggle to gain something from it. Getting older it becomes a means to get something, you lose the innocent enjoy-ment.' When I asked Dorcas what she meant, she responded by elaborat-ing on the difficulties and contradictions she increasingly experienced as a woman who did not hide the fact that she was sexually active. When she was younger, sex was more of an exchange between equals, between two young people looking for sexual enjoyment. She looked back on that as a time when sex was not 'complicated' and when the man in question and she 'had the same thing in mind', meaning that they had agreed to have a sexual relationship as lovers or as a one-night stand. She had had her 'best time' in college, after having left home and boarding school and hence so-cial control by authorities and relatives. It was a time marked by serial love relationships. When the relationship did not go well, it was not a 'big deal' and the pair would 'depart as friends'. When she got older and became more interested in a 'committed' relationship, it became more difficult for her to find a boyfriend. 'Things got complicated' when she was around 26 years old. She explained the difference between her earlier carefree relationships and the later ones by elaborating how men only wanted 'sex' instead of 'love'. Several women recounted similar experiences, notably that during their college years relations between women and men used to be more egalitarian and easy: 'We used to be more friends with men,' as Lucy (aged 28) once said.

The point is that, with the new status as professionals, when young people had become 'serious' about work and life, the egalitarianism between women and men that they experienced during their college years faded. According to Dorcas, men began 'to have attitudes' and started to behave like her father, an association that she disliked. Her father was directly associated in her mind with her mother's subdued manner. She cited as an example the fact that it is 'impossible' for her to offer a plate of food with two hands while bending a little, in the way her mother did when offering food to her father. After the episode with Samwel, she had become 'wiser' and 'stronger' and she would not 'pretend' anymore. She referred to her relationship with Samwel as a time when she was trying to behave in a more subdued way, to find a compromise. In her words, she was trying to be more of an 'African woman', i.e. being more of a domestic or homely, woman. Many other women, like Dorcas, discussed the tensions they experienced as professional women on one hand, and as girlfriends, wives or mothers on the other. For them, 'African' womanhood stood for caring and being homely, while professional womanhood represented egocentrism and not being family oriented. This concept of African womanhood reflects, of course, the conventional understandings of womanhood that have become common sense. Samwel's behaviour shows a man trying, through emotional blackmail, to force an independent woman back into the normative social mould. Refusing to conform to notions of domestic wifehood, Dorcas felt that the only option left for her was to be the mistress of a man committed to another woman: 'Men either want a *ndogo-ndogo* [mistress] or a wife. For sure, something like a wife with the qualities of a lover doesn't exist here.' According to her, there was no place for women of her calibre.

While Dorcas focussed her bitterness and disappointment on men who have mistresses, she also secretly conducted a number of sexual relationships with married men simultaneously over a period of weeks in late 2001. She justified her behaviour by pointing out she was doing the same thing that men did. She said it was a time of 'great fun'. By engaging in multi-partnered relationships, she thus appropriated the space given to men by society at large through practices of double morality that provide men with more leeway to deviate from the norm. This behaviour corresponds with her appropriation of the professional workplace, a space that formally belonged to men. Only a few women I knew regularly engaged in multi-partnered relationships, and they had to be very secretive about it.[14] Dorcas felt partly empowered by these experiences, but also somewhat 'promiscuous'. She explained herself by talking about the relation between love and sex: 'Real love means real sex and that is what I want, to have sex out of love and not lust'. Whereas no men I spoke with who engaged in multi-partnered behaviour felt promiscuous, all women who did so, except Njeri, struggled with such feelings. These struggles with feelings of promiscuity reveal the ambiguities faced by women. Women were engaged in a process which accommodated sexual pleasure as central to their identity, while it was necessary to preserve their sexual reputation, which was also essential to their self-esteem.

Dorcas's account about her expectations regarding a lover reveals another criterion used to assess the merit of a man: financial means. Many women were careful not to openly claim that they take a man's financial potential into consideration. Instead, this line of thinking emerged indirectly from their remarks and behaviour towards various men during the research. Dorcas, for example, said she had been 'very much' in love with Samwel, as she did not break up with him when he lost his job and became a 'useless' man. Her friend Elizabeth agreed with that and said that 'love can make you blind'. When I asked what they meant, they told me how terrible it would have been for Dorcas if she had spent the rest of her life with a man without a job: 'You cannot respect him and therefore you will eventually lose your love for him'. Looking for a suitable partner therefore means looking for qualities that reflect 'responsibility' and 'ambition to make a life' (to work hard to afford a certain lifestyle). Both women and men have learned that men are the financial providers and a 'good' or 'responsible' man is considered to be a man who can financially take care of others, like his girlfriend or wife and family members. In looking for a supportive boyfriend or husband, women include an evaluation of the man's financial abilities, which is understood as reflecting a serious and hardworking attitude. Men's love and appreciation are thus partly symbolized by their ability to offer financial support. In a society where men are expected to be breadwinners, Samwel was possibly anxious about the fact that he may be regarded as a failure and he might well have perceived himself as a failure. For these reasons, Dorcas never told him the extent of her salary so as not to embarrass him with the fact that she earned more than him.

As with many women of Dorcas's age, the issue of motherhood began to worry her increasingly. In 2000, she had been in a relationship in which her partner, Kimani, had tried to persuade her to have a child with him: 'I thought that was a sign that he truly loved me, ttsssss, men ... While declaring his love to me he fathered a child with another woman. At first I didn't even leave, I believed his lies that the woman had tricked him. Thank God I woke up in time to see what a failure he was. Now ... I want a real man.' Despite her wish to become a mother, she did not consider becoming a single mother. Although she felt she should not delay for too long, because falling pregnant may be more difficult when a woman is older, she said: 'I am not becoming nervous yet, I still have some time'. The majority of women I spoke to wished to have children, but were adamant that they intended to wait until later. Among the reasons they mentioned for this delay were the need to settle down first, meeting the right man, finishing studying in the evening, wanting to enjoy life first. In general, they thought of becoming mothers when they were around 30. Some, like Laura (aged 23), dreamt about the 'sweet little chubby baby' she would love to have, while others were less preoccupied about it. Other than Dana (aged 29), none of the women had children. Of the twenty-four women, three had become pregnant once and had had an abortion. One woman, Millicent (aged 26), became pregnant during the fieldwork. She decided to have an abortion because she was not involved in a 'committed' relationship and because she 'was not ready to be a mother'.

That motherhood did not play a significant role among these women had to do with their age and their aspirations to develop their career first. Women friends of mine, who were in their thirties and single (and not part of this study) had a completely different attitude to having children. Some were outspokenly desperate and although they disliked the idea of becoming a single mother, they nevertheless considered the possibility. Others were preoccupied with finding a suitable marriage partner so that they could settle down and become a mother. Some of these latter women married within the first year of meeting their partner, even though it is common to court for a longer period. A few women I met accepted their fate, that is, they never managed to engage in a satisfying relationship: 'I never met Mr. Right, and I am refusing to marry for the sake of marriage with some kind of dull man. I am sad that I cannot become a mother, but what can I do? My relatives pushed me for years, found me all kinds of partners, imagine …, and it seems they have accepted, haven't heard from them in ages. I guess they gave up on me … It's hard to accept for myself, but what can I do?' (Suzanne, aged 38, a senior manager for an international company). Taking the experiences of these women in their thirties into account, it is likely that younger women will experience similar problems if they do not find a committed relationship.

The trend in which professional women delay becoming mothers is remarkable in a society where motherhood is celebrated as the ultimate symbol of womanhood. That women, despite familial pressures, choose to do so reflects the extent to which their lives echo the effects of social change. It highlights the degree to which sexuality has taken on alternative meanings in relation to their gendered sense of self. It also points out how important the search for a new sexuality has become among young professionals. This search is, however, inherently ambiguous.

Between sexual allure and limited availability

The various stages that female young professionals go through in their sexual relationships with men show that among young professionals there are parallels between the processes of contemporary identity formation, developing a sense of self as a 'modern' woman, and appropriating sexuality as central to self-expression. These women are searching for alternative ways of relating to men through a reconstruction of gender roles; the vignettes quoted depict a continuum in the women's quest for a new sexual morality as the premise for engendering a new society. It is remarkable how fast women incorporate ideas about sexuality and sexual practices as soon as there is some space to do so. In general, women enjoy their lives to the full and approach life in general with the arrogance of youth. 'Having fun' is the foremost goal while they are young enough not to be bothered with social responsibilities. They enjoy being 'sexy', flirting, challenging men with a self-confident attitude and having, or trying to have, a satisfying sex life. They exploit the potentialities of sexual allure as much as they can, encouraged by the new discourse on intimacy as important to a fulfilling life. In short, the notion of sexuality as self-expression for women is being sounded out in Nairobi. They acknowledge sexual desire as natural and thereby appropriate – in the sense of making it their own – the notion of sexual pleasure as integral to their sense of self. Sexual pleasure, then, becomes a desire that is related to their status as career women, but above all to the possibilities generated by being relatively independent from social control, sometimes literally, such as being able to have lovers stay over in their home. However, they build on this aspect of femininity in the context of a prevailing negative discourse on women's sexual desire. As a result, in order to guard their sexual reputation, women often express ambiguity about sexuality towards men. Sex, after all, remains an ambiguous pleasure.

Appropriating sexual pleasure

There is a paradox with regard to female sexuality in Kenya today. Whereas, on one hand, sex is seen as a 'need' or as a 'natural' force and a self-evident aspect of adulthood, on the other hand, there is a lack of discourse on female sexual desire. Dominant discourses in Kenya represent female sexuality only in relation to procreation. Married motherhood is perceived as ultimate womanhood and women who are married and/or mothers achieve the status of respectability. Accordingly, female pleasure is represented as non-existent before marriage, and as passive thereafter. As a result, any talk about women's sexual desires in dominant discourse exists only in terms of the capacity for reproduction, or else as something devouring and lethal, as in the case of 'prostitutes'. Women's sexual reputations are framed around these notions, as women take care not to appear sexually assertive, which translates into a typically aloof attitude that is articulated as playing hard to get. However, as we have seen in the previous chapter, the discourse on sexual intimacy is growing, where sex is described as an embodied sensation. Women take up this discourse, acknowledging female sexual desire which is independent of procreation and hence making sexual desire intrinsic to femininity. Women's narrative of self-awakening points at the process how 'knowledge of the self [is] gained through repeated reflection on the internality of desire' (Lorway 2008: 27). Notions like 'sexual passion', 'feeling sexy', 'having sex with body and soul' or 'making love', employed by women as well as the media, reflect this process. What I would label as the emergence of the intimate points to the new trend in which female sexuality is freely discussed in particular niches in Nairobi.

The biographies of women are structured by the popular story of 'falling in love', a topic which will be elaborated on in Chapter VI. In this discourse sex is linked to love rather than reproduction in the construction of sexuality. Women define love mostly as intimacy, companionship, mutual trust and sexual passion. In such a construction of sexuality, women have to develop a personal sexual narrative which reflects their preferences and justifications in relation to sexual practices and ideas. In the absence of a positive discourse on women's sexual desires, women appropriate notions of sexual desire and pleasure by actively invoking the discourse on love. The way in which they define intimacy as a bodily experience contributes to the way in which sexual desire becomes a matter of the self, of the sexual subject. Sexual pleasure, then, becomes a positive self-identifier for contemporary independent women. Young professional women appropriate sexual pleasure as indexical to their contemporary gendered sense of self. Sex, then, becomes central to identity and sexual intimacy also becomes fundamental to self-expression in relation to others, in this case men. For women it appears to be crucial that they feel appreciated and/ or sexually attractive and that they feel close to somebody whom they appreciate. Men are therefore integral to this process. Eventually, sexual pleasure becomes a symbol of a good sexual relationship.

I can assert from my research that, in general, the younger the women, the more they care about their sexual reputation, and the older the women, the more assertive they are about their sexual pleasure. With age, women's confidence about their sexuality grows. The older women get, the more they learn to deal with conventional expectation, i.e. to be less bothered by it. Nevertheless, all the biographies attest to the tension between sexual allure and the new forms of intimacy postulated by the alternative discourse.

Sexual pleasure and conventional expectations

Although almost all the women interviewed express a critical attitude towards conventional notions of femininity, they have also internalized certain constructions of femininity that are at odds with change. Women embody, to a greater or lesser extent, normative notions of gender. However, they are not simply victims of patriarchal structures but are also partly accountable for reproducing these structures. For example, Dorcas eventually reinforced Samwel's conventional role that underscores gender hierarchies. According to the novelist Calixthe Beyala, a woman like Dorcas fails in her attempt to escape being reified as a domestic and humble 'African' woman. She states that young socially mobile women in Africa refuse to acknowledge their role in perpetuating traditional as well as neo-colonial patriarchal modes of life. Beyala has written several novels in which she gives an accurate rendering of an African woman's frustrations as well as of the woman's own responsibilities for her suffering.[15] I would not go as far as Beyala and state that women do not have a defined objective, or lack self-respect, and instead maintain a false dream of success by focussing on material aspects. The women I described above show that this is not the case, at least for them. Their lives demonstrate the paradox of subjectivation (Butler 1997); they are entangled in power structures that do not simply dominate women, but that also form the conditions for women to act. Women's agency is the capacity for action created and enabled by the interconnection between, on the one hand, specific relations of domination and, on the other hand, their resistance against domination. As a result, they partly reproduce the existing power structures they criticize. The paradox of subjectivation highlights the tension that women experience in their lives.

All the women I spoke with were anxious that once they were married they would have to accommodate normative expectations representing women as caring and homely wives. Their anxieties about marriage were articulated in a frequently expressed concern that husbands would insist on being served food prepared by their wives rather than by a domestic worker. Before she married Kinyua, Tayiani was anxious about whether Kinyua would insist on eating food prepared by herself, as opposed to by the housemaid. (It turned out not to be an issue as Kinyua 'accepted' the food made by their housemaid.) I have never met a woman whose husband insisted that she prepared the food. Nevertheless, this anxiety was expressed to me by many women. It symbolizes the anxieties about male dominance that are persistent in society at large and that women manage to circumvent while they are single and their status depends less on their relationship with men. However, their fear is that marriage – celebrated by society as the symbol of patriarchal order – could mean a reversal of their hard-won social position. This representation of women as wives goes against their personal opinion that doing domestic work undermines their status as career women. Moreover, it undermines their sense of self, which has come to be based on their identities as working women instead of being somebody's wife.

Women expect men to be 'modern', which principally means to them that men should not see themselves as heads of the household. Women wish for more egalitarian relationships, such as those they experienced at college. According to them, however, men are not yet willing to give up their privileged position in the gender hierarchy. It is common for women to complain about 'African men' or 'our African men'. These complaints reveal tensions arising from the conflicting situations that women and men encounter in their relations with each other: conflicts arising from the differences between daily practice as career people, lovers, friends and family on the hand, and gender roles dividing women and men along conventional or patriarchal lines of difference on the other. The complaints also surface when women discuss practices of double morality, especially when men have extra-marital relationships or other multi-partnered relationships. By using the notion 'African men', however, they reify men's behaviour as belonging to a particular African universe. At the same time, they criticize this practice for its patriarchal implications. They are similarly ambivalent, for example, about the trope of the 'African woman' as 'Mother Africa', which they both appreciate and criticize for its normative implications. Communicating ambiguity about Africanness – being a source of pride as well as a source of gender inequality – highlights how transformation in gender roles is entangled in practices of cultural belonging.

Men often complain about the phrase 'typical African men' as stereotyping them, while retaliating by stereotyping women as 'golddiggers'. When women were asked about the notion of 'golddigger', after some probing, the majority said that men are right. They also claimed that women should take more responsibility for their own actions instead of complaining about men. According to them, women are 'manipulative'. Martha even said that women are 'selfish':

It is true what they say [that women are out for money]. When you see a man, you often also look behind him, so to say. A man with money means that he is serious and hardworking and therefore most likely a respectable man, simply said. So, you tend to be sensitive to that. Of course, reality is much more complex, but we have been told by our aunties to check a man's wallet and you tend to internalize these things. I know, I am aware I want another kind of man when I speak of love, but… Therefore, women perpetuate these things in men to be patriarchal.

Women thus also acknowledged their role in reproducing existing notions of gender. They expect men to be providers because it reflects well on a man's success (how money and masculinity relate is elaborated on in the next chapter). They also call for change, and notably that women are ahead of men. Paraphrasing them, to bring about change, men need to help women to get rid of conventions or traditions because both women and men will benefit then. They postulate that conventional norms prevent men from learning from the other half of the nation; i.e. the women who, at this stage in history, seem to be far more advanced than the men in their ability to adapt to new situations. My own view is that women need to help men in engendering new gender constructions because women's ambiguous attitudes confuse men tremendously, as we shall see in the next chapter.

Communicating ambiguity

As products of their society, women embody to a greater or lesser extent normative notions of gender. This embodiment is incorporated into their relationships with men. As women have learned to be reserved in a sexual encounter with a potential partner, playing hard to get becomes an effective tool enabling them to conform to the norms when they are actually interested in the man. Since women and men often meet each other in this game, women do not immediately abandon their reserved attitude, even when it is clear to both partners that having sex is (partly) the goal of the encounter or relationship. Women reported being less inhibited with their partners when they had been engaged for a longer period of time or when they trusted their partners enough to let their guard down. In essence, playing hard to get by young women should be understood as a manifestation of women's ambiguity in relation to men. Ambiguity, meaning any form of communication which is capable of more than one meaning, is thus construed as an 'appropriate mode of communication for a passive female role' (Mitchell and Wellings 2002: 393). Instead of interpreting this behaviour as submissive, it can be labelled more accurately as deferential. These 'wicked women', in the eyes of Kenya's moral guardians, form a group who implicitly and explicitly challenge conventional gender roles and hence normative expectations of respectability (cf. Hodgson and Mc-Curdy 2001). This results in ambiguous situations and causes conflicting emotions that are revealed in their narratives.

Beyala and Butler's enlightening analysis that women are entangled in a paradox of subjectivation is helpful in understanding why women communicate ambiguity towards men. A conclusion that can be drawn from young professional women's narratives is that men occupy an ambiguous position in women's lives as lovers, friends and future husbands, as well as figures of authority and social control. Because of this ambiguous position, women also maintain ambiguous attitudes towards men, typically shaped by a deferential attitude. This deferential attitude bridges the contradictory nature of their experience: on one hand they embody modernity, presenting themselves as 'modern African' women, while on the other hand, modernity implies the negation of true Africanness, making them susceptible to accusations of being 'un-African'. As Ferguson (1999: 214) states, it is 'dangerous' to be 'fashionable because of its disrespect for nonfashionable modes especially for women, upon whom demands of respectability press more harshly'. By displaying a deferential attitude women communicate ambiguity about Africanness, as well as about sexuality.

Embodying transformations

From an economic point of view, the phases in career development (study, first job, promotions) among the majority of young female professionals reveal that their social position becomes strengthened by their professional status. In short, a developing career and an improving financial position are building blocks for self-esteem and the ability to take control over personal decisions. Indeed, many studies emphasize the importance of women's access to and control over economic and social resources (on Kenya, Nelson 1987; Robertson 1997; White 1990a; see also Obbo 1980). Financial independence creates opportunities for operating independently from normative expectations regarding gender roles. Female young professionals' biographies testify to this development; these women seize the opportunities available to them, albeit in different ways. They are able to live a life apart – at least to a certain degree – from familial expectations and other forms of social control. Except for Pamela, who was still dependent on her parents, and Tayiani, who got married, all the women recalled how much living on their own had influenced their lives. To be outside immediate social control implied the possibility of dating men without having to justify their behaviour to an authority. It also opened up possibilities for alternative relationships that differed from the marital norm, such as short-term 'flings' or having sex with male friends, as Njeri and Martha did. As a result of living on their own, women are able to develop their love and sexual lives more or less according to their own personal preferences.

Female young professionals can now occupy a space that was formerly reserved for men, notably the public space of the work floor; through their professions they can also embody characteristics previously defined as male, such as executive power. Their increasing participation in the public arena is an obvious manifestation of the impact of societal transformations on gender roles. The emergence of professional women in the public sphere invariably influences ideas that formerly defined moral authority as male and executive. The older women get, the more openly they criticize the dominant ideology, which inevitably evokes a reaction in which independent women are labelled as being 'not real women'.[16] Their resulting lifestyles become targets for efforts to try and regain social control by different actors in society at large. Their independence, therefore, is situational; in their capacity as professionals they yield authority as experts, while as daughters they may be expected to accept a lesser position in the family hierarchy.

Professional women's lives testify to the fact that societal transformations result in the remodelling of gender roles. The female young professional is not married before 30, and if she is, she is a wife with a professional career, and as such not confined to household affairs with the husband as main provider. The ideology of woman-as-wife, as the only respectable status for women, however, is pervasive. Even when a couple is unmarried, like Dorcas and Samwel, the ideology justifying gender roles in marriage is, and to a certain extent remains, the frame of reference for women and men. In Dorcas's case, when Samwel criticized her by calling her 'un-African' she tried to counter that by becoming more 'homely', i.e. by reproducing and reifying the notion of woman as a caring housewife. Contradictions arise when women like Dorcas, embodying the shift in gender roles, reproduce notions of domesticity on one hand, and the emancipation that results from their lifestyle on the other hand.

It can be concluded that women are changing – internally (by embodying transformations) and externally (by causing shifts in social structures) – the symbolic construction of womanhood that is conventionally linked to notions of motherhood and wifehood, and in which sex is a duty. They express themselves as sexual subjects within a framework of remaining virtuous, resulting in an aloof or 'play hard to get' attitude when engaging with a potential partner. They adopt a strategic and flexibly deferential attitude that reflects conformity to the norm to compensate or balance their lifestyles, which are associated with nonconformity. Such behaviour cannot be explained as being only strategic however; certain conformities have also become part of their personal make-up. Njeri and Tayiani exemplify opposite positions in the continuum in which women operate: Njeri has dissociated herself as far as possible from normative ideology and would sometimes opportunistically employ a deferential attitude, while Tayiani has embodied the normative ideology to a larger extent and developed a sense of self in relation to the normative parameters.

Professional women's independence from social control is a necessary step towards personally directed relationships. The resulting possibility to dissociate from the norm is an important factor in the process of developing sexual desire as essential to women's sense of self. Their lifestyles introduce a new set of sexual ethics – as a consequence of the shift in gender and sexuality – that they come to explore as they grow older. Tayiani's friends often cite Tayiani's husband, Kinyua, as an exceptionally liberal man. Their comments reflect women's experience that gender roles and constructions of sexuality change slowly. Nevertheless, new codes of behaviour between women and men are appearing. Young professionals are initiating an ongoing dialogue between women and men in an attempt to break down the existing poles of tension.

Conclusion

It can be concluded that these women's biographies reflect their personal transformation regarding the development of sexuality as crucial to their self-perception as women. There are parallels between the development of a sense of self as a 'modern' woman and the sense of sexuality as being central to self-expression. Their identity as contemporary women is partly linked to their professional careers, being 'African the modern way' and enjoying sex as a 'healthy' person. The highly sexualized nightlife of Nairobi provides space for women to explore sexual pleasure, encouraged by the emerging discourse on sexual desire as an embodied aspect of sexuality for both women and men. When women feel appreciated and 'sexy' in their interaction with another person, sexual pleasure becomes a matter of their sense of self, in fact, sexual pleasure becomes symbolic of their identity as a contemporary woman. In a context where female sexuality is connected to married motherhood, women appropriate sexual pleasure as constitutive of their gendered sense of self as professional women and they feel encouraged by their situational independence. They include men in this process, as romantic self-expression has become central to contemporary relationships. As a result, women's sexual pleasure becomes indexical of a fulfilling sexual relationship. Nevertheless, the differences between women are great, and these women's experiences move from reluctance and shyness to pragmatism and pleasure.

Professional women's lives are characterized by ambiguity. The women in this study responded to culturally expected prudence, while they also entered into freely chosen sexual relations. In the volatile context of contemporary Nairobi, the shadow of the 'prostitute' or 'immoral' woman looms over women who do not conform to certain expectations. The majority invoked a discourse of ideal femininity in order to normalize their ambiguous situation, while others did not mind being criticized. The ambiguous relationship between, on one hand, reproducing normative perceptions of femininity while, on the other hand, denying such personal notions of the self, results in the communication of ambiguity towards men. Communicating ambiguity reflects the fact that men occupy an ambiguous position in women's lives as lovers, friends and future husbands, as well as figures of authority and social control. In general, these women's actions can be read as both submission and resistance to existing patriarchal norms. In short, young professional women have to negotiate between uncertain boundaries of sexual allure and limited availability.

The differences between women are greater than those between men. This means that women's biographies locate larger changes in gender and sexuality: change entails more promises for women than it does for men, or men stand to lose more as they are the relative benefactors of patriarchal structures. Whereas women need to appropriate sexual pleasure as it becomes central to their self-identification, for men sex is integral to their gendered sense of self, usually from their circumcision and/or puberty onwards. Much of the focus of public and scientific interest and concern remained fixed on the subordinate position of women relative to men, while gender from the male point of view, and changes in gender relations affecting constructions of masculinity, has received far less attention. Men's narratives reflect expected differences from, but also unexpected similarities to, women's biographies. Men's sense of self is also constantly shifting, as the hegemonic discourse on masculinity is far from unambiguous. This is the topic of the next chapter.

Notes

1. Kylie Minogue's *Can't Get You out of my Head* was a popular song in 2001.
2. These women are part of the first group of participants consisting of eleven people who I have interviewed, followed and observed intensively and with whom I have developed such a confidential relationship that I trust what they tell me. Eight women of this group alternated between being single and having 'casual' relationships; one got married; and one had no sexual relationships because of her HIV positive status.

3. Tumi referred to this relative as an aunt, but the woman cannot literally be her father's or mother's sister. It is not uncommon to call distant relatives aunt or uncle.

4. According to Kielmann (1997), the term prostitute is nowadays used to reinforce the boundary between middle class, married, 'saved' women and low-income, single, not 'saved' women. There is, indeed, a tendency to portray middle class Christian mothers as the ideal prototype. However, this applies predominantly to a dominant, ideal image of middle-class married motherhood, while this study shows how in reality middle class women struggle to fit this image.

5. As has been concluded before, there is an over-representation of studies on prostitutes and there is significantly less literature on women who do not prostitute themselves.

6. Pheterson (1990) describes this trend and points out that the medical research on AIDS in Africa has been preoccupied with urban sex workers. One well-known study on AIDS in the early 1990s discussed prostitutes in Nairobi who became world famous for a short time for seeming to be resistant to HIV. The project was a cooperative study between a Kenyan and a Canadian research team, begun in 1983. It is probably the most influential medical research on the relationships between HIV and other STIs.

7. Dawn (aged 27) gave me the impression that she was a virgin because of her pious Christian attitude and her vigilance in not getting involved with men who were 'not serious'. However, after a few months she told me that she was no longer a virgin: she had had a boyfriend for three years, and since they were inseparable – 'he would always pick me up from work, we would meet everyday, he would visit my parents' – she believed that they would get married. At times, he had tried to persuade her to have sex but since she was so adamant about her virginity, he would not push the matter. One day he took her out as usual and drove her to a friend's house, where they appeared to be alone. After a drink he started to 'ask for sex again' and when she refused, he started pulling her pants down and eventually raped her. When he was finished he told her to go and wash and they left the place as if nothing had happened. They continued to see each other as usual, but after a few weeks she fell ill and she went to see a (female) doctor who could not find any disease or the cause of her problems. Although she had not intended to say anything because she was so ashamed of it, she told the doctor. According to the female doctor she was so badly depressed that it had affected her physically. Dawn was advised to seek counselling, which she found in her church. A little while later she broke up with her boyfriend.

8. Since 2001, when Martha left Nairobi, we have communicated by e-mail and telephone. Martha has sent me long letters by e-mail about her adventures and disappointments in Sydney. In 2010, when this book was finished, I had assembled almost eighty printed pages, a unique document that I hope to publish in cooperation with Martha.

9. John actually asked me to mediate in their conflict, which put me in an awkward position. I explained why I thought I was not the appropriate person to do so because although I was a friend to Njeri, I was above all a researcher. I resolved the issue by promising him I would talk to her and try to put forward his point of view. When I did Njeri listened intently but eventually brushed it aside, as she was 'tired of investing in that man'.

10. I first met Njeri at her office in 1998. Over time, I came to know her very differently.

11. Like Njeri, Martha also only slept with men she was familiar with but she had never had a one night stand. As a result, she slept mostly with men whom she considered friends and to whom she felt like a 'sister'. She kept the men she fell in love with at bay and as a result they could not get to know her. When I asked her whether this was perhaps a vicious circle, she said she was aware of it but that she needed to make an effort to sound out a potential lover because she wanted to avoid getting hurt. Her greatest fear was to sleep with a man and fall in love with him only to discover he had 'used' her to have sex. As a result, her demands were high, based on her ideals about 'making love with heart and soul', so that it seemed impossible to find a right partner.

12. Such as in the case of divorced women. In 2001, the issue of divorce flared up when a minister sneered in a parliamentary debate that his female colleague 'is a divorcee anyway', implying her improper status as a defective wife, while conveniently forgetting that more than half of the male ministers apparently do not live with their wives and that the president himself has been divorced for decades (see also Oriang' 2001). Divorce is often criticized in public as 'un-African'. See also page 217 about the public discussion following Ms Wambui Waiyaki's marriage with a younger man.

13. The question is whether Nyambane will continue to support Lucy having a career, especially if she becomes more successful than him. For many men, this is a challenge. When I discussed it with Nyambane, he acknowledged the precariousness of the situation: 'Yaah, that's true, it is not easy when your wife is very successful while you are just doing well. I have thought about it and ... you know, what does it matter if I love her and if she respects me for who I am. I hope I will keep that in mind: the love is important, not status. Of course, it will be difficult if she loses her respect for you, you know, there are two sides in this issue. Men should not be too patriarchal, but women should not expect them to be!' Nyambane laid his finger on the right spot: men fear women's contempt and women sometimes expect men to behave in certain ways that they then criticize.

14. Of the twenty-four women in this study, four engaged regularly in multi-partnered sexual relations, five had done so during their college years, and six sometimes had relationships which overlapped with one another.

15. Calixthe Beyala is a novelist from Cameroon who now lives in France and has published six novels. Three have been translated into English: *Loukoum* (1995); *The Sun Hath Looked upon Me* (1996); *Your Name Shall Be Tanga* (1996).

16. The issue of divorce was and still is an important topic in 2001/2; see note 12. Women lawyers, columnists and other advocates for equal rights began a public discussion in the media where they addressed the practice of divorced women being publicly scorned and humiliated while their ex-husbands are not even mentioned (see Oriang' 2001).

CHAPTER V

AMBIGUOUS PLEASURES: SEX, RICHES, AND MASCULINITY

Girl, you're my angel, you're my darling angel
Closer than my peeps you are to me, baby
Shorty, you're my angel, you're my darling angel
Girl, you're my friend when I'm in need, lady

Uh, uh
Girl, in spite of my behaviour, said I'm your saviour
(You must be sent from up above)
And you appear to me so tender, say girl I surrender
(Thanks for giving me your love)[1]

Professional men between 20 and 30 years old see themselves as innovators of a new lifestyle trend in Nairobi. An important aspect of this lifestyle concerns how they relate to women as equals, whether they are colleagues, lovers or friends. As women move into traditionally male social roles such as professional experts, men are reassessing and sometimes reasserting their masculinity. They are experiencing new obligations and expectations and new ideas of male self-esteem. As will become clear, men's gendered sense of self has to be constantly reaffirmed in the continuous assertion of being masculine enough. Whereas women are engaged in a process of appropriating sexual pleasure, for men sex is a vital component of their gendered sense of self; male sexuality, more so than female sexuality, is seen as a 'natural drive' that makes men masculine. However, men's sense of self is constantly shifting since the hegemonic discourses on masculinity are far from unambiguous. The male gender is constructed around at least two conflicting characterizations of manhood. On one hand, there is the idea that being a man is natural, healthy and innate, while on the other hand a man must stay in control and never let his masculinity falter.

Hegemonic discourses represent men's sexual desire as inescapable, but manhood is also measured by the ability to exercise self-restraint. More- over, hegemonic discourses propound a patriarchal gender order which confers authority on men. As a result, men seem to have an ambivalent at- titude towards sex, which is also reflected in their attitude towards women. Their attitudes are multifaceted because they – at least male young profes- sionals – are responsive to the changing gender order: they want to have more egalitarian relations with women, characterized by companionship, mutual sexual desire and common interests. Men are hence involved in processes characterized by redefinitions of gender in a context of conflict- ing discourses.

Much of the focus of academic, public and scientific interest remains fixed on the subordinate position of women relative to men. Gender dis- cussion from the male point of view and changes in gender relations with regard to masculinity in Africa have received less attention (Lindsay and Miescher 2003; Ouzgane and Morrell 2005). 'Men's lives are thought to take place in the public spheres of production, politics, and work' (White 1990b: 1). Much of the popular discourse and many academic studies on male sexuality in African societies have reduced this topic to one of mono- lithic essentialism, resulting in stereotyped notions of African men. While male dominance is likely to be one of the consequences of patriarchal ideologies, to explain it solely in terms of authoritarianism oversimplifies the processes involved in the constitution of particular individuals' male- ness. Such simplified explanations tend to take at face value some of the representations of masculinity as 'natural' and 'cultural', and hence as self- evident. By focussing on individual men's experiences, the complex rela- tion between existing power relations, symbolic constructions of gender, and sexual agency come more clearly to the fore (Spronk 2005b).

This chapter deals with men's personal experiences and reflections with regard to relationships and sexuality. Individual biographies, presented in vignettes, are then reflected upon against the background of social prac- tice, to show how the social context shapes their social, economic and cultural position and how this intersects with their relationships with women. I analyse how men accommodate meanings, embedded in pos- sibilities, prescriptions and prohibitions in their lives. Moreover, I show how men engage in different strategies with regard to their sexuality. All the professional men who are the focus of this study were aged between 20 and 30. Some were starting a job or commencing their studies, while others had been working for some years and led more or less settled lives. In 2001, Alex was 20 years old and was awaiting university acceptance to study artificial intelligence in the United States. Eric was 24 years old; he had graduated from his first degree in social engineering with academic honours and was looking for a job. Tom was 26 years old, had studied law, and was working as a junior employee for a nongovernmental organization. Maurice was 27 years old; he had abandoned his studies in accountancy and was working as an actor and theatre director. Ongeri was 30, considered to be a successful lawyer, and was working at an international auditing company.

Male sexuality in Nairobi, Kenya and beyond

While the topic of female sexuality in Kenya is underrepresented in the literature, the silence on male sexuality is almost deafening. For a long time, male sexuality was studied only in relation to male initiation and/or circumcision and polygamy. However, such studies focus mainly on the description of the social organization of sexuality, whereas I am concerned with the experiential and sensorial aspects of sexuality. When, during the second half of the twentieth century, demographic studies took the lead in research on sexuality, the focus was mainly on women, and male sexuality was virtually excluded. The realities of AIDS have placed the topic of male sexuality on the research agenda, albeit in a limited way, as I have showed in Chapter I. Although there has been an increase in studies on male gender, unfortunately this is not always translated into the study of sex. In this section I reflect on the notable absence of men's sexuality as a research topic.

White has written, albeit intermittently, about the male clientele of prostitutes and Kikuyu men's private lives during the Mau Mau struggle and detention camps (White 1990a, 1990b). Since the British colonialists sought to make the Kenyan capital a city of male migrants, they introduced official housing compounds for single occupants. Married men had to leave their families in the rural areas and all migrant men were forced to live a bachelor's life. We know little of their sexual lives, except for the references in White's book about the frequency, duration and nature of their visits to women (White 1990a: 56, 84–85, 95–96, 108–109, 200–201). These visits varied from unattached sexual encounters, visits lasting one night and including a bath and/or breakfast, to more enduring relations with women that were reciprocal in kind, for example when men were providing assistance to women in their struggle to remain illegally in Nairobi. From White's book we can deduce that a significant number of men maintained relations with women in Nairobi as well as the wife or wives living in their rural 'homes'. It is likely that during the colonial and early postcolonial period, there were shifting sexual and domestic partners and blurred boundaries between marriages and other types of unions, due to the labour migration patterns (see also Ferguson 1999: 178–84 on the Copperbelt in Zambia). Apart from these few references in White's book, male sexuality in Kenya has mainly been written about only in relation to male initiation, and more recently in relation to AIDS.[2]

A large body of literature exists on male initiation and/or circumcision, from early ethnographic writings onwards (for an overview on boys' circumcision, see Molnos 1973; Wolf 1973). These studies deal mainly with young adolescents, as the majority of men were initiated between 10 and 15 years old. Among these studies is some interesting work on the sexual activity of boys (Blount 1973; Huntingford 1972; Kenyatta 1938). Typically, such accounts offer generalized information such as 'a boy's sex life begins as soon as he has emerged from the seclusion of circumcision' (Huntingford 1972: 789), although without examples or specific accounts. In this type of analysis, male initiation and/or circumcision is typically described as an indispensable aspect of a people's culture, as it used to be an obligatory chapter in a monograph of any ethnic group. In general, this literature on male initiation and/or circumcision typically describes sexual categories and not individual experiences; men's sexual behaviour is presented as self-evident from the moment of initiation. Although not quite based in Kenya but rather on the border of Kenya and Uganda, Heald's interesting, and exceptional, study on gender, violence and ritual takes a different approach; she uses psychology to uncover the subjective aspects of culture, repeatedly stressing the need for phenomenological approaches (1999). More recent studies on male circumcision are conducted within the framework of AIDS research, focussing on the issue of whether male circumcision reduces the occurrence of HIV infection. They do not, however, focus on men's experiences of being circumcised.

Besides the focus on male initiation and/or circumcision, male sexuality is also discussed in relation to the cultural institution of polygamy. Ever since the late nineteenth century, polygamy has been analysed from a cultural and socio-economic perspective, where the focus was mainly on the description and explanation of its social structures (Evans-Pritchard 1950; Forde 1954; Kenyatta 1938; Leakey 1977; Mair 1953). From the 1960s onwards, growing attention was paid to an examination of the transformations of these social structures described from cultural, socio-economic and political perspectives (LeVine and LeVine 1966; Mair 1969; Molnos 1973; Nyamwaya and Parkin 1987; Paulme 1963). None of these studies focusses on sexual behaviour as such, but rather on the general organization of sexuality. They typically describe cultural norms and the statuses, roles and powers conferred on men by patriarchal ideologies in relation to their (future) wives. According to Gutmann, until recently has anthropology studied men as a self-evident category, neglecting men as engendered and engendering subjects (1997). The mentioned studies therefore place sexuality in a social context, elaborating on the division of labour according to gender, reproduction and descent, but they do not engage with men's agency. Besides these studies, male sexuality is mostly studied from a health perspective, qualitatively and quantitatively.

As is true of studies of female sexuality, qualitative studies on male sexual lives in Kenya that are based on individual experiences and sexual conduct are rare. Whereas studies on female reproductive health at least touch upon women's sexuality, this is not the case with studies of men's sexuality. This difference between knowledge about women and men's sexualities in Kenya, and in African societies as a whole, is partly a result of neglecting the role of men in relation to reproduction and health. This was due to the fact that most of the research was feminist inspired, which led to an agenda where women figured more prominently, and also because women take on more biological and social responsibility and experience greater vulnerability. Under the influence of feminism, the theme of masculinity is now seen as inseparable from power; from male dominance and from the structures of society and its serving ideologies (Heald 1999; White 1990b). The limitations of theoretical approaches focussing on women only and the empirical neglect of men have resulted in a gap in knowledge about men's sexuality (Biddlecom and Greene 2000). Biddlecom and Greene show how the objective of a health perspective was, and often still is, to point to ways in which women's contraceptive use could be increased. When AIDS became prevalent, demographic studies took the lead in the research, disseminating presumptions that have dominated the field since (see chapter I), although men are increasingly being included.

Epidemiological surveys of patterns of male sexual behaviour have dominated the field of research on male sexuality in AIDS related research. In the quantitative epidemiological approach, there is an overrepresentation of studies on adolescents. This is the result of the belief that since young teenagers are about to commence a sexual life, they have to be a prime focus of the AIDS campaigns so that they can remain uninfected. Another characteristic of quantitative studies is that they often discuss men's sexuality in relation to condom use. Among these studies, there is a tendency to view male sexuality in relation to 'risk taking behaviour' only (Mfecane 2005; Tadele 2006). Such an approach ignores the relational aspects of male sexuality and the effect is that data about men's behaviour is used without it being placed in its social context. This makes it difficult to understand why certain patterns emerge among particular groups at particular times.

Take for example the work of Caldwell et al., described in Chapter I as prototypical. The authors connect the 'weak conjugal bond' to notions about institutions like polygamy. As mentioned earlier, Caldwell et al.'s work serves as an example of how research on AIDS and male sexuality sometimes relies on presuppositions without outlining its assumptions. The following example illustrates how men's sexuality is approached within the AIDS paradigm. In their article 'Perceived Male Sexual Needs and Male Sexual Behaviour in South-west Nigeria', Caldwell et al. argue as follows:

> Part of a research programme studying methods of combating the AIDS epidemic was a survey and accompanying qualitative research focused on attitudes toward male sexuality and male sexual behaviour outside marriage and the extent and success of female attempts to control it. A survey of 1,749 males and 1,976 females was conducted in urban and rural populations in three states of southwest Nigeria. The majority of the community believes that males are by nature sexually polygamous, although about half the community believes that male sexuality can and should be confined to marriage. These beliefs arise out of the nature of the traditional society and are being changed by new ways of life, education and imported religions. Nevertheless, sufficiently rapid change is unlikely, even if promoted by government, to successfully combat a major AIDS epidemic, and the major strategy should attempt to reduce the rate of transmission, especially in high-risk relationships. (Caldwell et al. 1997)

Some important features of Caldwell et al.'s research can be deducted from this quotation. First, these authors study male sexuality in relation to 'combating the AIDS epidemic', and focus in this context only on 'male sexual behaviour outside marriage and the extent and success of female attempts to control it'. As such, they do not further reflect on whether this is representative of male sexuality in this particular region or not. Second, they relate notions of 'perceived male sexuality' to 'traditional society' and conclude that 'change is unlikely'. As such, they essentialize male sexuality without taking into account the fact that change has taken place over several generations and is still taking place (see Smith 2001). This ahistorical approach indicates that the research outline probably precluded the incorporation of certain data about men's behaviour. Third, their failure to contextualize data renders them vulnerable to accusations of reproducing stereotypes about the promiscuity of black men (Ahlberg 1994; Aina 1990; Heald 1995; Le Blanc et al. 1991). Male sexualities are at risk of being stereotyped precisely because there has been no serious attempt at problematizing the relation between them and patriarchal ideologies.

The point is that this kind of research is based on a survey of perceptions, and is thus based on knowledge acquired through mapping out shared and individual opinions. It seems that researchers take such information as being an accurate depiction of practice and ignore how important it is to 'be aware that this [sexuality] is an area of research where ideology often gets confused with behaviour' (Whitehead 2001: 156). The challenge of sexuality research is to relate perceptions to motivations, emotions and practices, in order to analyse the divergences and interconnections. If perceptions are not carefully considered in terms of how they are embedded in social practice and individual experience, it is questionable to claim authority about sexual behaviour based on surveys that seek information from short interviews. This applies especially to notions of gender, which have a moral value and are perceived as fundamental to the status quo. To take ideas of how men are supposed or said to be at face value not only isolates specific aspects of masculinity and represents these as common and universal, but it also fails to capture the diversity in how men identify themselves as masculine. A valuable analysis on gender which provides a starting point for an analysis of masculinity and self-perceptions is Heald's study on manhood, violence and ritual among the Gisu (1999). She does not carry out a discourse analysis on gender, as is common, but rather she zooms in on vernacular psychology in order to analyse how violence, sexuality and ethnicity intersect in men's self-perceptions. Such an ethnographic approach is also the basis of this study.

In the 1990s, men were discovered as the 'forgotten 50 per cent' in development and health discourse, while studies on men in African societies were taking off. Exceptional books on gender are *Men and Masculinities in Modern Africa* (Lindsay and Miescher 2003) and *African Masculinities: Men in Africa from the Late Nineteenth Century to the Present* (Ouzgane and Morrell 2005). The various articles elaborate on the ways in which African men responded to colonial and postcolonial policies and social transformations that affected, and in some cases profoundly changed, their traditional gender roles. South Africa in particular has pioneered research on male sexuality. For example, the collections of *Changing Men in South Africa* (Morrell 2001) and *Men Behaving Differently: South African Men since 1994* (Reid and Walker 2005) reveal current debates on masculinities in academia, producing in-depth knowledge about the relation between male gender and sexuality.[3] It shows how the attributes generally associated with the often-used category of 'African men' cannot be taken as self-evident. The concept of masculinity also risks becoming flawed because of the danger of reproducing local discourses of a stereotypical masculinity. Instead, the notion of masculinity needs to be studied in the full social context because it is a significant relational category and should be defined in relation to other axes like sex, age, ethnicity, religion, social status etc., all of these identifying different masculinities, or different ways of being masculine.

The lack of research on men's sexuality was a lacuna not only in studies on Africa, but also globally until the 1980s. Gay studies took the lead in exploring this new field of study, and Connell (1987, 1995) was among the leading authors to place the spotlight on the concept of masculinity.[4] The aim was to unveil masculinity, that is, to make it visible in its multiple forms, thus to irrevocably dispel the notion that there is just one kind of masculinity. Connell, inspired by feminist studies, demonstrated how notions of gender are related to power structures not only between women and men, but also between groups of men. She analysed how individual men each enjoy the 'patriarchal dividend', which is 'the advantage men in general gain from the overall subordination of women' (1995: 79) and how being a man confers power. However, not all men share this power equally and not all men exploit it. She developed the concept of hegemonic masculinity, which refers to the process of how an idea of what a 'man' is dominates other ideas, thus creating prescriptions of masculinity that are, partially, binding and which create cultural images of what being a man means. Following Connell's renewed concept (Connell and Messerschmidt 2005) where the agency of women is given greater emphasis and the internal contradictions and possibilities of gender democracy greater recognition, amongst others, I aim to show that some non-hegemonic categories of masculinity have developed in Nairobi outside the realm of patriarchal discourses. Individual men develop their masculine sense of self in relation to dominant images of what a 'man' is, while not necessarily being able or willing to fit the picture.

Looking at the existing literature about male sexuality in African societies, it can be concluded that we do not learn much about men's desires, nor their motivations regarding their sexual behaviour. The topic of adult male sexuality is introduced mainly in relation to AIDS, described within the AIDS paradigm in terms of multi-partnered sexual behaviour, violence and the use of condoms, and sometimes in relation to circumcision. In general, research about men has generated images of African men as domineering, and sometimes as brutal and hence as perpetrators of violence and injustice against women. This widespread image has led to a notion of authoritarian 'African men' that is taken to be self-evident, which leaves little space for individual and group differences. There is an urgent need to expand the research on male sexuality as a topic in its own right.

In this chapter, I present various men's sexual biographies as a way of understanding their aspirations, their behaviours and their explanations regarding sexuality. Their experiences and their wishes intersect with discourses that encourage men's sexuality, while at the same time they regard men's sexuality critically in the context of contemporary lifestyles. The accounts of Alex, Eric, Tom, Maurice and Ongeri show that masculinity is not automatically acquired; individuals constantly need to protect and defend, hence recreate, their sense of masculinity in daily practice. The power they derive from being a man is produced and exercised in various ways, but is also contested via different discourses. It is therefore critical to understand the various social factors in order to understand the construction of masculinity, rather than focussing only on the aspect of dominance.

Alex, Eric, Tom, Maurice and Ongeri

The image of the young professional man as a symbol of the successful 'modern' citizen figures prominently in Nairobi: a hardworking, focussed, fashionably dressed attractive young man with a non-parochial attitude. This image features in advertisements and on covers of magazines and in women's narratives about attractive men. In reality not many young professional men resemble this icon. Nevertheless, all the men participating in this study partially correspond to this image by being urban, having a higher education and being financially able. With the arrogance of youth, they carry themselves with pride as a specific kind of 'modern' man, and they are looked at with awe. The more successful they are, or the better career they have, the more sure they become of themselves. They are classified as a particular group of men within a particular subculture. Nevertheless, it is important to take account of the differences between them as individuals.

By introducing Alex, Eric, Tom, Maurice and Ongeri as individuals through their biographies, presented in vignettes, I aim to elaborate on the essentially subjective aspect of sexuality, while also taking into account larger trends that can be discerned among this group of men. I identified trends that I found were shared by the whole group of men I spoke with. I discussed these trends when discussing the first draft of the chapter, and men identified in various degrees with them. The most important common trends were the importance of circumcision or initiation from boyhood to manhood, and the importance of maintaining manhood by developing a career. Manhood needs to be further maintained by balancing their sexual prowess against their sexual weaknesses. Young professional men draw on different discourses, articulating different notions of masculinity, while at other times their narratives show overlaps between the discourses. These notions vary from perceptions based on the patriarchal gender order, to ideas inspired by Christianity emphasizing piety, education and familial respectability, to views on 'African' masculinity emphasizing sexual prowess, to notions related to contemporary lifestyles. In general, the hegemonic notion of man as the provider leads to ideas of male values such as being 'responsible' – that is, being self-reliant and financially able to take care of others – which in turn reflects a hardworking attitude which confers power on men. Men emphasized elements of all these masculinities in the experience of their gendered self-definition, which were at times contradictory and caused tensions. A healthy man is a sexually active man, but the pleasures of sexuality tend to be ambiguous.

Men's sexual début

Alex (aged 20 in 2001) was a composed guy, with a hint of bravado in his attitude. During the first month of my stay in 2001, I ran into Alex on Kenyatta Avenue in the city centre. We recognized each other from three years earlier when I did my MA research at his boarding school. I remembered him as a polite guy, a little quiet in the group, and shorter than the others. He tried to take up with the popular guys but often went unheard. He often accompanied me from the school to the bus stop, which was a sign of appreciation from his side. When we met this time, we went for a drink and soon he agreed to become the first participant in this study. He was waiting for an acceptance to study artificial intelligence at a university in the United States; meanwhile he was doing a computer course at a college in Nairobi. He comes from a family with two older sisters and two older brothers. His father died when his mother was six months pregnant with him. His mother struggled to send her children to good secondary schools. His brothers and sisters secured scholarships and loans to enter public universities in Kenya. Alex was the only one to go to the US with the financial help of his father's relatives and by means of a harambee *[see Chapter II, note 18]. His mother originates from Tanzania and his father was from the Luo ethnic group in Kenya. He is used to speaking English with his family, mixed with Kiswahili. He did not relate much to his paternal family and he did not get 'cultural education about being Luo', although 'ironically enough I call myself Luo when these issues play up, it's that blood thing: We tend to think in these issues as you belong to your father's line. Mostly, I call myself Kenyan.'*

When he was twelve he became more curious because of his physical changes and he became aware of his own sexual 'potential'. He had sex for the first time when he was 14 and it became 'addictive' for a while. During holidays, he had 'as much sex as possible'. When he was about 17 years old, he got 'bored' with it. These days, he says, he is looking for a different kind of sexual relationship rather than just sexual 'release'. He spoke about using condoms as a matter of course since 'you don't want to throw away your future with having risky sex'. When he was 'addicted' to sex he always carried condoms 'in his pocket' so as 'not to be surprised when there would be an occasion'. Back in The Netherlands I checked the interviews from 1998 and found out that, indeed, Alex was one of the boys who challenged others about not using condoms, calling it 'stupid' behaviour.

I was able to tape most interviews with Alex, as I had done during the previous research and he was not inhibited in any way about speaking freely. The following are excerpts from discussions about his relationship with Millicent, with whom he had been involved for almost three months. He explained that his relationship was 'an advanced stage of friendship, not just boyfriend-girlfriend, but on top of that also good friends'. He contrasted this with his friends' relationships.

Rachel: 'What about your friends' relationships?'

Alex: 'Ok they [the couples] are friends but … there are some things they cannot talk about, or they prefer to talk about it with other people, not with their girlfriend. I believe it is important to talk, unless you are looking for something else [i.e. sex]. We discuss things, we are there for each other. Some of my friends have the same, my brothers don't [laughs].… They mainly look for the sexual aspect of it and then the social status, and something to make them forget problems. They don't discuss personal things with their girlfriend, they don't want the intimacy … they say it would bring them down to speak intimately, it's not being manly. [He is silent for a while] I think intimacy is important, but people survive without it, they want some space.… They don't want to feel controlled by a woman. People don't like opening up about themselves. [He is silent for a while] People have relationships for several reasons, sexual, for the fun, the importance of settling down, the social status. Some speak like there is no love, but maybe they still have to grow up, or they have not a very happy family background.'

Rachel: 'So … you are not afraid to open up?'

Alex: 'No … I don't know why I'm different from my brothers, I don't have this conflict of being "a man" [makes faces emphasizing the word "man"].'

Rachel: 'And did you have sex with Millicent?'

Alex: 'No, we don't … it has not been the right time yet. Because if you do it for the wrong reasons, you will not be able to look at her and still respect her, you will regard her as an object.'

Rachel: 'Would you like to?'

Alex: 'Yes, I would like to [laughs], the right time will come…'

Rachel: 'Did you have sex with other girlfriends?'

Alex: 'Yes I did, then I saw what it did to that relationship, the intimacy broke down, the respect went, because it was for the wrong reasons, curiosity … I didn't look at her in the same way anymore; it was something that you just find yourself doing. We didn't share much, we didn't talk much about other things, it was just for the sex.… According to my friends, they say now [with Millicent] that is not a real relationship, they say that it's not a relationship without sex, that [sex] is what distinguishes it from friendship. That is why if you say you have a girlfriend they think that probably you are doing it, they tend to be apprehensive about it [a relationship without sex]. But … I think you need to build something first instead of relying on sex to build your relationship, get to know each other.'

Five weeks after this interview, and four months into their relationship, Alex and Millicent had sex for the first time. He mentioned it but he did not want to elaborate about it. During our last meeting, before his departure to the United States, we discussed how he would miss her and then he disclosed how having sex with Millicent brought him into a 'higher atmosphere' and how he 'could not have enough of it'. The first time he had been a little nervous because he did not want to 'disappoint' her, but soon they became accustomed to each other. He felt awful having to leave her now. However, they were both 'realistic' enough to know their relationship would probably not last.

Alex recounted how he became 'curious' and eager to know what sex was when he was 12 years old. Sex was a self-evident aspect of growing up as a male adolescent. 'Sex and women' were a common topic in boarding school: 'You looked up to the guys who had had sex and you wanted it too'. During one school holiday, he spent many hours watching TV at a friend's house. There he met a girl from next door and he had sex with her for the first time. He did not want to elaborate on this, as he seemed ashamed about it; he only mentioned that all four of his friends had sex with her during that holiday. He did not like the girl but 'after all' she was 'available'. Later he admitted that he did not like the girl because she did not mind sleeping with the five boys. From then on, Alex became 'addicted' to sex and had 'as much as possible', which was not always easy as he was living in a boarding school. They would sneak out of the compound at night and go to the nearby settlement and try to persuade the 'village girls' to have sex with them, who were 'easy to convince [since] other girls are much tougher'. After a while he lost interest because he 'was doing it for the wrong reasons' and he 'became sort of bored'. He became more interested in 'love'. He recounted how other men, such as his brothers, remained 'stuck in this puberty phase and refuse to grow up'. Alex related his grow-ing into adulthood with becoming more responsible and with a different attitude towards sex. The similarity between Alex and Pamela is that both defined the development of their sexual life in relation to their definitions of adulthood. Pamela wanted to be, or feel herself to be, a 'woman' instead of a 'girl', while Alex felt the need to behave 'responsibly'.

Alex was a little hesitant to discuss the fact that he was not circumcised. In most other groups, when a father is absent, the paternal relatives initi-ate a boy's circumcision. This was not the case for Alex and his brothers, as the Luo ethnic group do not circumcise men. In a country where the ma-jority of men are circumcised and where uncircumcised men are mocked, not having experienced 'the cut' has become a sensitive issue for men like Alex. Since men experience circumcision as the transition from boyhood to manhood, circumcised men like to joke about adult men who have remained 'boys'.[5] In response to the question of what made him a man, Alex answered 'being responsible', the definition of manhood that he was taught by his mother. Responsibility, according to him, was about 'moral conduct' and 'being mentally solid'. He would refer to his older brothers, whom he appreciated very much but who seemed to him 'to have lost focus in life'. He explained how his brothers are 'typical African men' [with a shy laugh], referring to their alleged multi-partnered relationships.[6] He attributed the difference between his brothers and himself to the fact that he was closer to his mother, and hence had learned to have more respect for women. Alex's account exposes the two fundamental yet contradictory characteristics of masculinity, as portrayed in hegemonic discourses on masculinity: taking responsibility and having sex. How these two characteristics differ from person to person varies from one situation to another and how they converge with other axes of social practice is central to an understanding of experiences of masculinities. Unlike the sexual feelings of young women, sexual desire is central to men's sense of manhood from early adolescence and thus having sex almost always contributes positively to their sense of self.

Having sex was a reality for all the men I met, and only one of them was a virgin. Although not all of the sexually active men had had active sexual lives because of religious beliefs, all of them had had sex when they were adolescents, aged 13 to 17.[7] The majority of men recounted similar stories about their sexual début to the one that Alex told. The aspect of peer pressure figured prominently. According to Alex, 'It can have a lot of influence over you when other guys talk about their sexual experiences you look up to them. Yes, I was sensitive to it at first but there was a moment I thought I was being stupid. I am proud to say that I stopped trying to fit in, like I never started smoking, drinking … I know what is good for me, I look around me and see what is good and what [is] not.' Being curious about what makes a man a man was an important incentive in trying out sex. Whether circumcised or not, men recounted the moment of their sexual début as a transition from boyhood into manhood. This is the crucial moment of identifying as a 'man'.

As he grew older, Alex experienced a shift in the discussion about sex with his closest friends. Instead of narrating stories about sexual adventures, he exchanged information about sexual matters with his brothers and friends about, for example, how to satisfy a woman. They watched pornographic videos and read pornographic magazines. One of the friends subscribed to a British magazine. They would watch with a small group of men and comment on the positions and variations on the sexual act. Alex watched for two reasons. First, it was 'exciting' and, secondly, he 'learned' from it. He felt it important to be 'experienced' when meeting a woman and he gained experience by watching pornographic material and by having sex. It was difficult for him to ask a woman what she enjoys when having sex, although he thought it necessary to know because he believed he should not only be focussed on his 'own pleasure'. The issue of sexual experience is of importance to many men, if not all. I often heard that a man must be familiar with having sex if he intends to sleep with a woman. Consequently, many men learn to have sex with women whom they do not consider as long-term partners, as Alex did with the 'village girls' close to his former school. Many men distinguish between 'sex partners to gain experience [on one hand] and sex partners to have fun with and with whom you are more serious [on the other hand]', as Robart (aged 23) once explained.

Lastly, Alex was one of the few men in their early twenties to be explicit about refusing a multi-partnered sex life, instead arguing for the importance of 'love'. Other men who denounced multi-partnered sexual relations were mostly older. Alex believed in neither chastity nor in multi-partnered sexual relations. From his past experiences, he knew that multi-partnered relations did not satisfy him since he got 'bored' eventually. Rather, he was seeking serial monogamous relations based on notions of intimacy. His gendered sense of self navigated between engaging in sex as an unavoidable aspect of being a man to defining sex in relation to intimacy or friendship. With sex as a basis, he related his sense of masculinity to existing notions of responsibility and to being oriented towards the future.

The fact that men's sense of self is strongly related to what men aspire to and are expected to achieve is also clear from Eric's account. Eric's narration further shows the precarious position of young professionals if their career does not progress as envisaged.

Circumcision as constitutive to masculinity

Eric (aged 24 in 2001) was a tall, well dressed and unremarkable man, with a slightly nervous manner. I met him when he had finished his first degree in social engineering with honours and was trying to secure a scholarship to continue with his master's degree. In the meantime he was employed as a salesman, a job that frustrated him so much that he soon left, hoping to find a better job. In the course of the ten months that we worked together he did not manage to secure a scholarship, neither did he find a job as a civil engineer. Terribly disillusioned, he opted for a junior position in an ICT company and channelled his ambitions into working his way up in the company. This meandering and finally deciding not to pursue a masters degree despite his ambitions was a time of intense struggle and fear of failure. He was frequently nervous and restless. He came from a less affluent background than the other men interviewed. This was the driving force to 'study hard and take every opportunity' that came his way. He had three brothers and sisters, of whom he was the only one to pursue a university education, and he characterized his parents as 'typically traditional Kikuyu'. He always insisted on knowing my opinion about certain situations he encountered and wanted me to 'explain women'. He came across as relatively insecure about love and sexual relationships and, without explicitly telling me so, he came to confide his uncertainties by asking my opinion and clarifications about all kinds of issues he did not understand. On 21 November 2001, I wrote in my dairy: 'I realize more and more that Eric just doesn't understand "women", as if it's a category beyond his perceptions'.

Eric could not remember when he started having sex. When in boarding school they sneaked out to the surrounding settlement and 'persuaded' girls to have sex, 'that's how it started'. He also masturbated in school but he did not classify that as sex. He had the 'best time of his life' in college when girls were 'ready available'. They would organize evenings to watch pornographic movies and afterwards they would depart as couples to their rooms. He also recalled the 'craze for the freshers' every new academic year when the first year students were enrolled. Female freshers were easily persuaded to have sex as they were not chaperoned by parents or school authorities and were thus 'happy to break free'. He was ambivalent throughout when discussing his sexual life: on one hand he was content to mention his achievements but on the other hand he was apprehensive about discussing them in-depth. Sex was 'natural' to him – as a man he said 'you have your needs and therefore you go and look for it'. There were moments when he 'needed sexual release': 'Your mind is fixed on it, no it's your body's craving'. In college he had had 'many girlfriends', by which he meant sex partners. Now, he was 'sobering up' as he had to become 'serious' now.

When we met, his girlfriend, Mary, was in the UK for her studies and they had not seen each other for six months; they e-mailed and phoned on a regular basis. They had been together for a year when she left. After a few months Eric said he noticed a change in the tone of her e-mails. When he asked her whether she had been in a sexual relationship she did not respond and he interpreted this as an affirmation. Later, he asked again and she admitted being in a relationship with a Kenyan man. He wanted to know 'how far' she had gone and she answered she was 'confident about herself', by which she meant that she still felt the same for Eric. He decided not to discuss it by telephone. However, he could not accept that she was having a relationship with another man. According to him, when a woman has any sexual relationship it 'goes pretty deep', that is, women get involved emotionally and therefore he considered this to be more than a passing affair. This is in contrast to men, who in his opinion are less emotionally involved and whose infidelity 'means less'. When he asked my opinion about his girlfriend cheating on him, I told him I thought they had nothing to blame each other for, as he had also cheated on her. He agreed in principle but stood by *his point about the difference between women and men. As it appeared later, the crucial issue was that he disliked the idea that Mary had probably discussed their relationship with her new boyfriend. Just as he always 'questions' women with whom he gets involved, he anticipated that Mary's boyfriend might have done the same: 'You question her and you dig out about her previous relations. This means that a woman will criticize the previous relationship because she wants to please you.' He felt humiliated by the idea that Mary might have spoken negatively about him.*

At around this time, his life took an interesting turn. One day, after we had not seen each other for six weeks, he told me he had got 'saved'. This was striking because he once told me how he cornered some preachers in a discussion by overriding them in argumentation. He was proud of it at the time, because he had proved how religion was 'illogical'. Now he stated that he had always 'misunderstood' the meaning of faith until now. During that meeting, he was so overwhelmed by his newfound faith that he could not discuss anything other than the importance of 'Jesus in your life'. Later I asked how he reflected back on his previous sexual behaviour and whether he would still sleep with women: 'Yes, I have slept with my girlfriends, it's a sin. But when you're saved, your sins are forgiven, you actually confess about your past behaviour and you are forgiven and you can start anew. Before I was saved I did sleep with different women and I was not always happy about it, I knew it was bad, and I would feel guilty about it.' He 'believed in abstinence' now. After his conversion we did not have the same discussions as we used to because he now tried to convince me to become 'saved' as well. In time he became less frenetic about his newfound life, but by then it was time for me to leave Kenya.

Many men's gendered sense of self is based on the symbolic importance of circumcision that marks them as men instead of boys.[8] Circumcision not only marks them as men in the eyes of society, it makes them 'feel' like men. According to Eric, being circumcised is 'your footing'; it is central to men's gendered sense of self. Circumcised men define their manhood ritually, and perceive uncircumcised men as morally inferior. In his own crude manner, Eric would say how he 'laughs' at uncircumcised men as he cannot regard them as 'real men'.[9] Like many men, Eric explained its importance by narrating in detail the circumcision ritual itself.

The 'footing' of a man relates to the transition from boy to man, as his uncles and some friends of his father made clear to Eric on that day when he was 11 years old. Before going to hospital, his uncles and some friends of his father met with him at his parental house. They symbolically 'beat' him: 'They pretend to beat you because you insult them with your fore-skin'. They told him what is expected from him as a man, how to talk as a man, how to treat women and how to be a responsible man. He should not cook, he was obliged to start a family, he should behave responsibly and not bring shame to his family. And he should not live in his mother's house anymore. In his grandfather's generation this rule required that the newly circumcised young man should build a new hut in the family homestead. However, this practice is not feasible in Nairobi. In fact, even his father had not done so as he was financially unable to build a house and therefore had to go and live with relatives after his circumcision. Likewise, Eric did not build a house either, 'although they keep on telling the same story'. Since Eric actually lived at boarding school, except for during the few school holidays, it could be claimed that he was not strictly living at home anymore. He had therefore fulfilled the obligation of leaving his mother's house.

Leaving the mother's house is a common rule for different ethnic groups, and Nairobian families seek different solutions, one of which is building a 'cubicle' for their sons after circumcision. This cubicle can be a part of the servants' quarters or a separate room built outside the house. In some families the issue of having to leave one's mother's house no longer has any significance, especially when the circumcision is a mere physical procedure carried out in hospital. In the case of Michael, 27 years old, 'it wasn't much of a big deal': the evening before going to the hospital, his father had a discussion with him about his new status as a 'man' and he was warned to be 'careful as there is AIDS around'. Except for Maurice, who went to his rural relatives' home for his circumcision, the rest of the men had been circumcised in hospital. And unlike Joram, for whom a bull was slaughtered, half of the men recounted their circumcision as a mere formality without any elaborate ceremony or guests, as would have happened in the past; among these men this happened only in the case of Michael. The warning against AIDS had been given as advice to all of the men.

According to Eric, the importance of circumcision is that it 'made' him a man; he experienced it as a turning point in his life. An important result of this rite of passage is the encouragement for men to have sex after circumcision: 'As a man you have to prove to be a man and one way of doing that is having sex and knowing how to have sex with a woman'. He was not told this as such by the older men during the ceremonies, but it was something he 'knew'. Most men perceive circumcision as a 'green light' for having sex and act accordingly. However, for 'saved' or Christian committed boys, it can cause moral conflicts. In my MA research I found that a few boys had experienced similar moral difficulties to Pamela, who was torn between wanting to engage in sex and adhering to her faith by abstaining from sex. One boy confided that he had sex despite being 'saved' and he was praying for this 'sin' to be forgiven. However, he had the feel-

ing that there had been no option since he had been circumcised for more
than a year and still had not had sex with a woman. Not one of my male
informants in this present study, however, recounted such an experience.[10]
A few men mentioned that they thought it 'unrealistic' for religious authorities to emphasize sexual abstinence until marriage. They admitted to
have 'perhaps hesitated', as Robart (aged 23) said, because having sex was
being portrayed 'like you would drop dead at your first ejaculation in a
woman' and that had scared him at first.

When we were discussing Eric's record of relationships with women,
it was important that I did not give any impression that I disapproved of
it. We discussed it in relation to his alleged betrayal of Mary. According
to Eric, it was a 'fact' that women tend to be more emotionally involved
compared to men, which would imply that they have a greater sense of
commitment. According to Eric, when a man is unfaithful by having a
fling it might not mean much, while infidelity in a woman means betrayal.
He truly believed that his behaviour did not affect the relationship as
much as Mary's behaviour did. He was also very annoyed that she kept
the other relationship quiet at first and asked me why women do that.
He complained about how secretive and complicated women are. And
indeed, he had been open with his girlfriend about his affairs because,
according to him, they did not affect their relationship. His attitude towards Mary exposes the practice of double morality in Nairobi. Listening
to Eric, it becomes clear that it was not simply a justification for his own
behaviour but was in fact what he truly believed. However, he could not
bear the thought of her relationship with another man and as a result he
wanted to break up with Mary. He did not know how to go about this, as
she did not want to end the relationship. I suggested that he should tell
her right away that it was over, to which he did not react. When I asked
him whether he was thinking of a 'gentle' way to break up, he said he was.
I had seen several relationships which had been ended in a 'gentle' way
and from what I had observed this meant that the person who initiates the
break avoids speaking directly about it, but instead starts behaving spite-
fully so as to discourage the other in order 'that s/he gets the message'. In
the case of Eric, he tried to avoid a confrontation by 'neglecting' Mary, i.e.
not keeping in touch. He admitted being 'rough' to her in this way. He
later justified his behaviour by narrating how he was not yet able to have
a committed relationship, as he was not settled yet and therefore did not
have much to 'offer'.

Eric focussed his narrative on Mary's behaviour and its implications,
rather than on his reaction. She had offended him and he was dealing with
feelings of rejection. Moreover, Mary was studying abroad, which meant
a ticket to success to many Nairobians, while Eric's career had come to

a standstill even before it had taken off. This discrepancy upset him very much, and in my opinion he projected his feelings of anxiety about it onto Mary's supposed betrayal. His defensive attitude was also triggered by his failure to secure a job. Men's gendered sense of self is largely based on two primary principles: to be able to act responsibly, which mainly implies being financially independent, and to have sex. If Eric had had a job, he would have been able to partially confirm his sense of manhood through being a working professional. Failing to do this, his gendered sense of self became more related to other hegemonic ideas about gender, which ascribe an active sexual role to men. Because sex is so central to men's sense of self, the consequence is that when other characteristics of manhood are not feasible, men like Eric come to rely on dominant perceptions of masculinity, celebrating male sex as inevitable and powerful. Similarly to Eric, Tom also struggled with existing notions of masculinity, trying to find ways in which to define himself as a man. However, unlike Eric, Tom would like to have had a more emotional intimate relationship, something that Eric never mentioned.

Sex as a skill – being a 'good lover'

Tom (aged 26 in 2001) was a witty, attentive and good looking man. At a neighbour's' party, where he was dressed in a smart suit, I got into a conversation with him. After I had introduced myself he reacted: 'Oh, is that you? I have seen your article in The Nation *and I have been thinking of contacting you'.[11] He asked me about the details of the research I was doing and asked whether I might be interested in interviewing him, saying: 'I have a lot to tell you'. Tom had just graduated from university with a first degree in Law and was working at a local nongovernmental organization. He grew up in a comfortable middle class family. While he was still in primary school, his father started behaving 'strange'; he began to beat his children and complained they did not 'respect' him. Over the period of Tom's puberty, his father completely withdrew from social life and claimed not to have any children, or even a family. He suffered from severe depression and only communicated occasionally with his wife. In addition, he sold all the family possessions including the house and the land, and the money disappeared. The small salary earned by Tom's mother, together with some financial support from her relatives, kept the family going, and the children moved to less prestigious schools. Tom emphasized the never-ending support of his mother in his tumultuous life; it was as if he had erased his father from his life. He blamed his father for making his mother's life 'miserable', as he had become 'an embarrassment' to them all. His brother and two sisters did not go to university, and when he started to earn a good salary, he paid his youngest* brother's school fees and occasionally supported his sister, whose husband was try-ing to divorce her and refused to help her out financially. A constant theme in the interviews was his determination, as he put it, 'not to become like my father'. He had set himself high goals in life.

Tom had become very cynical about relationships with women, he 'did not believe in it anymore'. I nevertheless perceived that he was searching for a 'love relationship' because he would endlessly analyse his broken affairs. According to him, until he was 20 he was a 'little dull' and had been 'too busy to spend time on women'. He was involved in various political activities at university. He had a fairly serious relationship for two years, with a slightly older woman, and he was 'not interested' in other women. She became pregnant and decided to have an abortion, against his will. When he heard that she was pregnant he had dreamt about being a father and he was 'heartbroken' when she decided to have an abortion. 'I really really wanted this child, I was not wealthy or what, but I felt I could take care of it like a good father.' She would not have aborted if they had married, but Tom did not want to marry because 'I could take care without these official issues, I wasn't ready to settle down yet'. The relationship turned sour and they broke up. This course of events affected him gravely and he decided to have a vasectomy shortly afterwards: 'Ok … the vasectomy was perhaps a bit of an irrational decision but I just didn't want to be in such a situation again'. Something had 'snapped' inside him, 'it has ruined something in me regarding women. This secretive attitude of them, that behind your back they can even kill your child, it has made me very bitter.' He kept coming back to women's dishonesty. He was very sensitive to anything that could imply untrustworthi-ness; whenever he sensed something negative in his relationship with a woman, he abandoned her immediately.

Since then he had had different affairs and there was a time when he was 'only interested in sex'. During the time we worked together he had different sexual encounters and longer lasting (sexual) affairs of a few months. He would, for example, once or twice have sex with the secretary at his work while also dat-ing another woman he wanted to get 'involved' with. He referred to the first as 'just fun' and to the latter as wanting to 'invest' in her because he wanted 'more'. For the months we worked together I saw him 'very much in love' or 'happy' with a woman, as well as 'frustrated' and 'disappointed' before breaking up with someone. He 'needed' sex and he explained that as men have a higher testosterone level than women, they therefore naturally have more sex: 'A man cannot deny his sexual urges'. However, he grew more and more dissatisfied with casual sexual encounters. Once, on a Sunday morning, he came to our house, obviously distressed. He looked haggard and was in a bad mood. Finally he started to talk. He had taken a girl to his house and when he woke up in the morning he was very disappointed with himself, even disgusted. He had not liked her very much and still he took her home. It had become a habit of his to look for *a woman on lonely evenings and it annoyed him. He felt 'ashamed' of not being able to control his sexual urge; it reflected a 'weak' character. Overall, however, he took pride in sexually satisfying a woman because he made many efforts to 'learn about women's bodies and their orgasms'. He measured the quality of a sexual encounter by his ability to sexually satisfy the woman in question. If a woman got up one minute after the climax to 'do her hair or make a cup of tea, I know she either faked [an orgasm] or I didn't manage to find the right spot'. He liked to satisfy women orally, in particular because for certain women oral sex is something of a taboo. 'I love to see a woman grappling a cushion or the sheet because they are so so hot, trying not to scream out loud.' Having oral sex with a woman meant being unconventional to Tom, as it is generally perceived to be filthy.[12] He considered being a 'good lover' to be an asset of a contemporary man: 'As a modern man you have to know how to please a woman, you cannot be focussed on your pleasure only, like our fathers did … polygamy …'.*

To be thought of as a worthy person was of great concern to him. He interpreted the episode of the abortion as a sign of a lack of confidence in him. He had come to perceive it as a rejection of him as a father and as a committed boyfriend. This sense of rejection was very difficult for him to discuss, although we – eventually – came to discuss anything about sexual practices. Only once did we have a sincere discussion about this, when I was driving to his home, where he was going to prepare dinner for me. The confined space of the car, and the fact that he did not have to look at me, allowed him for once to admit that he feared rejection. We were discussing his feelings for Mercy, a former colleague of his. I knew he liked her, but he had always said they were 'good friends'. Now he told me how deeply in love he was with her. I asked whether anything had ever happened between them, since I had the impression she also liked him. 'Nothing happened, no … Yes, I know she likes me too. It is so silly, so damn stupid, you always want someone to like you and when she sincerely does, it makes me lame, I am afraid she might think I am a total loser and from her mouth I cannot hear it. I prefer her to continue liking me instead of risking that she might dislike me. But I am also not very sure whether she truly likes me, I don't know … And if she doesn't, I will look like a fool if I make a pass at her.' I remarked that he had never before seemed to care if women he approached dismissed him; 'but that is different', he said, it's 'the usual stuff between men and women. But with Mercy, she is different, she is not interested in this game, she is more genuine …. I think I love her.'

Tom was a typical bachelor with a lifestyle that combined hard work with spending his free time in bars and clubs. He earned a relatively good salary but could not afford an affluent lifestyle because he spent quite a large amount each month on supporting his siblings. For example, he saved money by never eating out but only buying drinks, and by living in a small room in a lower middle class area, where he hardly spent any time. He was a popular man and he surrounded himself with women wherever he went. Although women frustrated him, Tom continued to have 'casual' sexual relationships for two reasons, which represented the contradiction in his relationships with them. On one hand he wanted to have a girlfriend who was his 'pal'; he was looking 'for HER in capital letters', someone who fitted his ideal. This ideal was based on his expectations of a 'committed' relationship, which comprised intimacy and mutual involvement. On the other hand, he was at a stage in his life that excluded the possibility of commitment, as he had to make a career first in order to be able to 'offer' a woman anything. Although he was searching for a special partner to love, at the same time he got involved in relationships just to enjoy sex, relationships that were far from loving. According to him, the importance of sex is the power of having sex. In his typical lawyer-like approach of forceful argumentation, he explained that since men have a higher testosterone level than women, they naturally 'need' more sex. Tom resorted to short affairs for sex because they were 'easy'. The terms of the encounter were clear: having 'fun' and sex as part of an enjoyable evening. The relationships he found himself in were therefore of a certain nature: short lived, focussed on sex and without commitment, and resulting inevitably in disappointment because he actually aspired to a different kind of relationship.

Moreover, his inability to engage in the kind of relationship he aspired to was related to three other issues. First, taking his anxiousness about Mercy into consideration, his fear of rejection played a major role. This was first of all related to his experience with his first committed girlfriend, who had had an abortion against his will. He interpreted this as a sign that she did not have confidence in him as a caring and responsible father. When I reminded him that he did not want to marry her in the first place, he ignored my remark. His fear of rejection was also fuelled by his own high expectations of women. Logically, if he had such high expectations of a woman, it was likely that a woman would also have high expectations of him as a man. With Mercy, he was afraid that he may not be able to meet her standards or expectations and therefore he did not dare to find out. The idea of being 'exposed' scared him. In a 'committed' relationship there would be more at stake than the casual encounters he was used to. With Mercy, Tom could not rely on his performance of acting out a certain masculine persona, publicly expected, as a successful young professional man. He would have to be more 'genuine', which implied revealing his individuality.

Second, part of his problem regarding the practicability of his ideal had to do with his difficulty in allowing women to have control over men. What he felt for Mercy automatically put him in a position of emotional dependence. Emotional dependence was something he partly longed for when articulating his desire for a relationship based on love and support, while it simultaneously threatened his feelings of self-reliance, which were so important to him. His masculine sense of self was based on hegemonic notions where masculinity is equated with independence. He experienced the contradiction as if emotional dependence and self-reliance were at odds, hence his fear of 'exposure'.

Another kind of control that relates to this is of a sexual nature. Since men 'cannot deny their sexual needs', they are always somehow dependent on women.[13] This sexual dependence, as it appeared most clearly in the above account when Tom was 'ashamed' of himself, 'weakens' a man when he cannot 'control' himself. While having sex regularly is considered to be a positive aspect of being a man, there is a limit to it. Excessive sex implies that a man is no longer in charge and is therefore being controlled by something that makes him dependent on women. This dependence on sex and hence on women frustrated Tom terribly. These were the moments when he was more responsive to conventional discourses on masculinity; men like Tom and Eric remain sensitive to the idea of men's dominant position. Since men's sexuality in hegemonic discourses associates sexual prowess with power over women, when Tom relied on these understandings of masculinity he minimised the contradictory feelings he was experiencing. At such moments, he justified his multi-partnered sexual life as enabling him to be a man after all.

The importance of independence and self-reliance clashes with notions of relationships as being based on emotional support and involvement; this 'confuses' men like Tom. Different men recounted how modern men easily get 'confused' because they cannot act out the patriarchal ideology within which they grew up and 'be like their father'. The reference to fathers in these discussions was remarkable. Tom had a good reason for wanting to be different from his unpredictable and unreliable father. However, I often heard these men talking about their fathers. They recounted how they disliked seeing their mother being humiliated when their father married another wife, or if they realized their father had a *ndogo ndogo*, a mistress. When sons had a good relationship with their mothers they tended to react strongly against their fathers' behaviour. Moreover, the majority of the men who identified with their mothers advocated an emotionally supportive and equal relationship, contrasting it with their parents' imbalanced relationship, and, as such, criticizing patriarchal norms. Balancing conventional notions of masculinity and alternative ways of relating is a precarious endeavour: in particular the authoritative position ascribed to men is at odds with the more egalitarian way in which younger men relate to women. It highlights the ambiguities that young professional men experience with regard to defining, maintaining and recreating their ways of identifying as a man.

One last, important, characteristic of Tom was his idea of himself as a 'good lover', one who knew how to 'treat' women. Being a good lover had become like an identity badge for him, and he boasted – to male friends, potential girlfriends and me – about being knowledgeable about women's desires. Having sex invariably made him 'feel good' in the first place. When his partner also enjoyed it and when they developed an advanced sex life, that is, not only 'quickies', but also taking time to have sex, it was 'the best'. He called having sex his 'oxygen mask'. For many of these young men, being a proper lover implied sex as a mutual endeavour. They agreed with the young professional women that the notion that many men have of sex as a 'marital duty' is 'backward'. They often refer to the practice of polygamy – which is often publicly named as a 'backward' institution – to stress their point. These discussions are a sign of how notions of masculinities are being redefined.

Love in relation to sexual drive

Maurice (aged 27 in 2001) was a gentle, sociable, humorous man with enquiring eyes. He came from a well-to-do background and he called his parents 'rather Afro-centric'. For example, in reaction to the trend that few children growing up in Nairobi learn an ethnic language, they made an effort to teach their children their vernacular; Maragoli was the only language they addressed their children in. Maurice recalled having had a happy childhood but felt he had disappointed his parents by choosing a career in theatre. His father wanted him to be an accountant and Maurice gave in to the pressure at first and started a degree in accountancy. Then, just before finishing his degree, he dropped out and decided to become a full time actor. He worked at a graphic design company until he managed to get by financially with his job as an actor and drama director. Initially, his parents did not approve, though eventually they accepted his choice and his father is now proud to see his son's name in the newspapers.

When he was ten Maurice reached the age to be circumcised. His paternal relatives gave him the choice to be circumcised in Nairobi or to go 'upcountry' to have the traditional ceremony instead. Upcountry refers to the rural area where Maurice's paternal family originate. His close relatives all lived in Nairobi while distant relatives resided near Kakamega. He and another cousin choose to go upcountry, while the other cousins opted to have a surgical operation in a Nairobi hospital. He identified himself as Luhya. We once discussed the fact that, with me, he often said 'African' when he meant 'Luhya', and he became more aware of the distinction later on.

The year before, he and his girlfriend Nyambura broke up after a four-year relationship. They had been very close and he labelled it a 'good relationship'.

She left him because of their different ambitions in life. Every now and then she had hinted that he should take up his accountancy or advertising job again, but he never paid attention. When she graduated she got a good job that paid well and slowly they grew apart, as she wanted a 'luxurious' lifestyle, which he could not offer her. She left him because of that, but also because she belonged to a different ethnic group. Nyambura was from the Kikuyu ethnic group and her parents had told her not to come back home with 'someone from Western' [the term for west Kenya, often used to refer to the Luo ethnic group]. In the four years they had been together they had not met each other's parents. She eventually told her parents about Maurice and they opposed the relationship. 'I think the pressure became too much. She comes from a wealthy family. Her father had told her he would disown her if she married a Luo – I am Luhya but they don't even know the difference – and I think she started wondering how she would live with me and my meagre salary … she doubted a future together with me, and that also made her decide to break up, the uncertainty and the pressure…. At first, she didn't want to admit it, she would say we had to break up because we wouldn't get anywhere. But it hurt us both, it took me a long time to get over it. I couldn't accept it. She too was suffering, she even left the country, went to TZ [Tanzania], to be away, to get over it all.'

According to Maurice himself he was not 'much of a real man…. I mean, I have had fun enough [sex] but I can also do without it for a while, I don't have this craving for it like some of my friends.' To explain his 'lack of this crave', he told how once a girl, who had admired him for a long time, visited the theatre and approached his friends. His friends organized a meeting and then she explained how madly in love she was with him. He was surprised and asked her whether she knew he had a stable relationship. She knew but would not mind being the second girlfriend. He was taken aback by her courage to come and tell a man how much she liked him; 'that is uncommon for a Kenyan woman'. He asked his friends for advice and they told him to go ahead with it, as it was an 'easy chance'. He did not 'exactly' like her but was 'intrigued' by her courage. 'But I didn't manage, within one week I told Nyambura about this girl and she was mad with anger that my friends had been encouraging me, she felt betrayed. I don't know, I couldn't, I would feel guilty [to have a sexual relation with another woman], she would find out at once because I cannot lie to her. And why would I want it? I was happy with her. According to others I was weak when I explained why I didn't take the chance, even to an extent that I started wondering about my own decision, doubting myself, I didn't want to be seen as weak. That shook me a little, but I still didn't want it.' The girl in question reproached him for being a wimp when he explained that he did not want an affair with her.

Nowadays, he was a 'little lonely' and would look for company with his female friends and occasionally they would end up sleeping together. He was, however, a

little disappointed every time. He compared it to the good sexual relation he had
had with Nyambura because he had loved her. A 'love relationship' was essential
to him: it meant 'being there for each other, taking the other as he or she is, feeling
comfortable, trusting each other...'

All the men I interviewed were circumcised in a hospital in Nairobi, except for Maurice: 'We [Maurice and his cousins] were asked whether we
wanted to be circumcised upcountry and only me and my one cousin
wanted to experience the real thing. Yaah, I am African and I should be
proud of my heritage, this is an important moment for an African boy, to
be circumcised.' He was proud to be exposed to the 'traditional' patriarchal custom in a most direct manner because most 'city boys don't do the
real thing anymore'. His circumcision had been an elaborate ceremony of
seven days, starting with the ringing of the circumcision bells that were
fastened at the initiates' wrists to announce the ceremony. All the elders
from their clan came to talk to them about the importance of the occasion. They were told that they were 'going to be men now' and that they
had to become 'responsible men'. They were told how to treat women by
referring to the old men's life experiences. When a man liked a woman he
'made sure' she got pregnant and then they were forced to marry. As Maurice said: 'That's how they rationalized polygamy in fact; when you like a
woman you should go after her but you would have to marry her. They
would talk a lot about the importance of marriage and the responsibility
of a man. It was boring, I was only 10, marriage means nothing then.'
They also spent one week in a forest, 'which was actually fun, we had to
make our own fires and roast maize and we swam all day in the river'.
When the circumcision wound was healing, their grandfather took care of
them and they were again spoken to. In the end they had to throw a spear
into a young mango tree. A successful attempt symbolized one's proper
masculinity; to miss the tree was a symbol of a weak man. 'God, we didn't
know how to throw a spear and with my first attempt I hit my own back
[laughs out loud], it was a little silly, but the next attempt I managed.'
    Discussing the importance of his circumcision, he admitted that the
ritual and its symbolic value for his new status were most influential:

Maurice: 'About these teachings, my mom also tells me that when I want to show
my wife I love her, I should beat her. She tells me I have to beat my wife in the
early years of our marriage and she will love me. But I don't know ... I wonder
whether a woman will love me for beating her. Would you love me when I beat
you? I don't think so.'
Rachel: 'Well ... does your father beat your mother?'

Maurice: 'No, I have never seen it, perhaps during their early years, but I cannot imagine my father beating my mother, I don't know why she says that. You know, things change, some of these things they told me are not applicable anymore. In fact, I cannot remember well what they have been telling me, it's long ago and all the excitement made me forget what they would say.'

Maurice's account highlights how conventional, patriarchal constructions of masculinity differ from the experience of young professional men. On one hand he was proud to tell me how he had a 'real African' circumcision ceremony, while on the other hand he could not relate to certain customs or notions, like the notion that a husband should beat his wife. The fact that his mother told him to do so, while he appreciates her as a proud woman, made him uneasy. According to him, he owed to his parents his 'African pride' and he looked up to his father as an example of a balanced 'African' man, as he recounted how his father has always supported his mother and the children, did not drink, and there had been no indication of the presence of a *ndogo ndogo*, a mistress, in his father's life. The notion that he should beat his future wife went against his notions of being a good man. Out of respect for his mother, he never asked her why she had told him to beat his future wife. In time, he had decided to forget about 'these traditional issues of men and women. I mean, we are in different times now and we have to find new ways to be together as man and woman.' He remarked how his parents did not live up to this ideal. In Maurice's narrative it becomes clear how Africanness has become a trans-ethnic mode of being, rather than being identified with the traditions of a particular ethnic group.

Maurice's gendered sense of self was constantly being defined in relation to dominant constructions of masculinity. As already stated, he once explicitly remarked that he was not 'much of a real man' by referring to his relative lack of sexual adventurousness. What he meant is that men who engage in multi-partnered sex are popularly acknowledged to be 'real' men. This did not worry Maurice much, unlike Eric or Tom. The difference, it seemed, is that Eric and Tom's sense of self was more embedded in sexual desire as constitutive to being a man. Maurice explained his failure to live up to the ideal of a real man as not having 'this sexual crave', or what is often referred to as men's sexual need. As he recounted above, when a girl showed an interest in him, his friends encouraged him to start an affair. Although he had considered having an affair, he explained he could not start an affair with another girl because of his love for Nyambura: 'We, the men of these days, have to make choices. We cannot live anymore like our fathers, I believe it's not right to be polygamous.'[14] In saying this, he showed that he equated multi-partnered sexual relations with the practice of polygamy. It has become commonplace to associate extra-marital affairs with polygamy.

According to many men, peer pressure was cited as a common reason for engaging in sexual adventures or being unfaithful. They explained that it mostly occurred when going out with a group of friends who then incited each other. Ruben, aged 28, once explained how he had 'dogged' his girlfriend, because he had been persuaded by his friends to spend a night with a woman he liked. He had lied to his girlfriend, saying that he had stayed overnight with his friend because he was too drunk to drive home. She did not suspect anything and it had been quite unproblematic to do it again. His friends covered up for him every time and they had somewhat admired him for the good 'catch' his new mistress was. He recounted how easy it had been and how he was able to 'block his mind', as it was not uncommon for men within his group of friends to have affairs. When discussing the episode he commented: 'I know it's bad ... I think it's because we live in a man's world, we get away with it ... the stupidity of it, the uselessness.' By this, he meant not so much the act of being unfaithful as not 'making a conscious decision but just doing it', the unworthiness of not having been able to exercise self-restraint. Only a few men mentioned peer pressure as explicitly as Ruben, although I often observed that when they spoke to me they expressed slightly different opinions to the ones they expressed to their friends. Keeping up a sexual reputation as a man who 'needs' sex and has no problems finding sexual partners figures as a frame of reference for many men's social encounters. Of the twenty-five men I interviewed, only three of them explicitly countered such notions in public, although a few others did so in private to me but did not articulate it publicly. The fact that these men articulate different attitudes in different situations shows how much those studies that take perceptions of male sexuality as a self-evident concept miss the point. Moreover, the fact that Maurice had no difficulties expressing his relative lack of sex drive shows that, in the context of hegemonic constructions of male sexuality, men live different lives.

Besides peer pressure, the typical family constructions of being a good son also reinforce conventional ideas of masculinity. Maurice's mother might have been a little extreme in her opinion, but it is characteristic that mothers and fathers comment on their sons' performance as men. Parents' desire for successful sons and grandchildren are often accompanied by ideas of proper masculinity needed in order to achieve worthy goals.

Last but not least, women play a decisive role in men's construction of masculinity. The girl who wanted to be Maurice's mistress mocked him for being a wimp when he refused to be unfaithful to Nyambura. Men recounted various examples of how women had expectations of them that reinforced conventional constructions of masculinity. A common complaint was how women expected them to pay when dating and how women challenged them to 'decide on everything like where to go or what to eat' (Maurice). Some men recounted how women expected men to be 'bossy, even rude, like when you have a fight you should not give in too easily' (Robart, aged 23). Tom fulminated about women who expected men to 'chase women despite this talk of emancipation'. Another interesting conflict I witnessed concerned expectations regarding household duties: Mwaluda liked cooking for his girlfriend but she found it hard to let him as she regarded that as humiliating both for a woman and for a man. Maurice also recounted how Nyambura used to say that she loved him for whom he was, a low paid actor, which he doubted. When she left him he interpreted this as meaning that in her mind he was not 'man enough' because of his meagre salary and uncertain career, not man enough to be able to take financial care of her and their future family. From Maurice's account it appears that men have to constantly negotiate their masculinity in order not to be perceived as unmanly or like someone whose masculinity is questionable. Their gendered sense of self is under constant surveillance by their fellow men, friends, colleagues, family, and women. The images of men who 'have arrived' have possibly an even bigger influence, as men such as Ongeri exemplify.

Sex and having 'arrived'

Ongeri (aged 29 in 2001) was an extrovert and somewhat flamboyant man. He was a lawyer at an international auditing company and had a very good salary. He came from an average middle class family with two sisters and one brother. He was living in a spacious apartment with a friend who was a lawyer in a law firm. Halfway through 2001, his family asked him to take care of his younger sister, who was awaiting admission to university, and she came to live with them. This caused quite a change in the nightlife of his roommate and himself, for now Ongeri could not take women home for the night and he had to avoid coming home drunk. He was not happy about it but accepted it as a fact because 'after all she's my little sis'. He was a self-assured man, always gallant and he knew how to carry himself. He spent much time and money in bars and clubs and he would go out for at least three or four nights a week, mostly with his roommate. He planned to get married at 35, when 'he would be ready for it'. For now, work was a priority, as his job was indeed demanding; it was not exceptional for him to work at night and on Saturdays. He did not mind, he was proud to be working for such a renowned company.

He started to have sex in secondary school when 'masturbation was a common first sexual experience for a boy'. Pornography was 'a big thing' when he was in university. The first year he was 'all excited' about it, but later he 'lost interest'. A student with a TV would get films and would charge others to watch. Couples also watched together after they had been together for a while, something he never did because he was afraid a woman would get the 'wrong impression' about him. Also, he used to have a special e-mail account and subscribed to a pornographic site but he also 'lost interest' in that. He called himself a 'good lover' because he 'cared' about the woman's sexual enjoyment. He was proud about his knowledge of female sexual pleasure, or how to 'treat' women, and he enjoyed sex much more when the woman also felt sexually satisfied. He used to be apprehensive about oral sex though later he came to 'appreciate' it and found that women were pleasantly surprised when he satisfied them in this way. According to him, women were more 'conservative' when it comes to 'alternative' sex such as oral sex. His ideal was to have a relationship marked by 'mutual respect and satisfactory sex'.

During one of our meetings he asked me to tape the discussion, as he wanted me to understand his motivations. He explained 'why men naturally need to have sex':

Men feel like having sex whenever they see a good looking woman, they desire women when they see them and they feel like having sex with her. Desire is a physical thing, you feel aroused when you see a woman you like. You feel like having sex with all the beautiful women you see, what you see is what you want. ... Having sex comes as a natural thing, it's part of life and since women are also part of life, they go together. Men naturally need to have sex. Men are naturally polygamous because it is natural to have sex and it is natural to have desire when you see a woman you like. If it were not for the fear of AIDS, the lack of money and constraints put upon us by religion, men would go wild. I mean ... our society is so religious, wherever you are they blare at you about immorality and it obviously impacts on you. They [men] feel sometimes that sex is their right, because they are men and it's natural to have sex and it makes them feel like men. So when they cheat on their girlfriend or woman, it's not that they don't care or don't love her, it is that they feel the need to have sex with this particular woman. What you see is what you want to taste.

At the end of my stay in Nairobi I had known Ongeri for six months. Whereas at first he came alone to our appointments or when meeting with others for a drink, as time went on women often accompanied him. At first he gave the impression of having serial relationships, but I came to understand that he maintained different relationships at the same time. Over a two-week period I coincidentally met him four times with a different woman. With each woman it became clear – through their body language – that they had an intimate relationship, although Ongeri had not at that stage told me about his multi-partnered sex life. During one of our last interviews, we discussed the issue of faithfulness. Without directly asking him I hinted at the various girlfriends he had, apparently at the same time. He explained how he knew 'from experience' that one related differently to different women. By referring to the few women I had met he explained what he meant. He recounted how he felt very comfortable with Atieno and how he enjoyed relaxing with her at home, watching TV and cooking together. However, sometimes it was a bit 'boring' with her, compared to, for example, the time he spent with Lillian with whom he had 'fun'. He went out with Lillian as she was a 'little wild' and therefore 'great fun'. Compared to Atieno and Lillian, Grace was more of an intellectual friend as she shared his political interests and she understood his ambitions. By referring to these three women he explained how 'women have different characteristics … it's unlikely to find all these characteristics in one woman so … you meet someone, she intrigues you for a reason another woman has not intrigued you and you date her'. He was silent for a while, checking my reaction, and asked 'Do you mind?'. Rachel: 'No, you know by now that I'm not interested in making a judgement, I just want to know your opinion'. He looked pensively, replying, 'I guess it's how we men are … or have become…. You know me, you know I'm not a bad man.'

Ongeri was a successful professional whose future had no bounds and he acted as such. He was very popular with women. It was impossible to meet him in a public place for an interview because we would always be interrupted by his women friends. Ongeri was the prototype of a 'sophisticated' man: good looking, well dressed, with a successful career and appreciative of career women. He knew it, and he acted as such.

Ongeri liked to provoke me. He would try to trigger a response by playing the 'male chauvinist card', as he once phrased it. He did so to test whether I would accuse him of being a male chauvinist or whether I was able to see through his game. This was his general attitude towards women initially; being stereotyped as a 'typical African man' annoyed him and therefore he exaggerated it. As he explained: 'I don't want to show how I really am, I am not a chauvinistic pig, but women have to find that out. When women try to find out how you are, you know they are serious about you. You have to be careful for golddiggers.' He assumed that I was used to what he perceived to be feeble Western men, of the type he saw in soap operas like *The Bold and the Beautiful* or US movies. His moods changed from being unpredictable to very serious or even to asking for my involvement in his personal life. For example, we had a breakthrough in our relationship when he needed my opinion on women's sexual pleasures, as he asked me to explain the difference between clitoral and vaginal orgasm. As he usually portrayed himself as knowledgeable in such issues, I could have interpreted this as a lack in his knowledge and skills as a lover.

His attempt to create 'shock and awe' (US President Bush's famous exclamation after the attacks on the Twin Towers on 11 September 2001) was part play and partly serious. His behaviour towards women revealed his conflict; he resisted being taken for granted as macho by exaggerating the image of a 'typical African' man. He did not apologize for behaving in a manner that was frowned upon, such as having several girlfriends, though he wanted me to recognize that he was 'not bad'. This shows how the phrase 'typical African' man is regularly used as a self-evident concept, referring to men as chauvinistic, unfaithful and self-centred. Ongeri thus acted out a persona that was publicly well recognized. Whenever I saw him alone or with girlfriends at home or in a quiet bar, however, he displayed a different attitude. Then he was moderate, attentive and behaved like a gentleman. He treated his girlfriends, invariably, with respect; I never saw him acting in an abrasive manner towards them, nor did he ever complain or speak badly about them. In fact, Ongeri's narrative illustrates how men are caught up in conflicting discourses on masculinity. On one hand, there is the conventional notion of masculinity, encouraging multi-partnered male sexuality. It is linked to perceptions that when a man 'has arrived', that is, when a man has gained a respectable position, it is reflected in the number of women he can maintain, financially and sexually. Ongeri, thus, had gained respect for 'having arrived'. On the other hand, he also regarded himself as a young professional 'modern' man. However, the discourse on contemporary identities critiques multi-partnered sexuality by positioning it as outdated behaviour by, for example, stating that 'a modern man is a monogamous man' (Kinyua, in the previous chapter). A man like Ongeri was sensitive to such a counter discourse, as he considered himself to be 'modern' by definition. Implying that he was reverting to some kind of 'traditional' behaviour was a great offence to him, though it did not make him change his behaviour (yet).

Ongeri was a self-assured man, with the confidence of a person who has worked hard to achieve what he had. He had started off as a student with a government loan because his family could not support his university studies. During his studies he did everything possible to get an apprenticeship in an international company as his strategy was to get noticed, hoping to get a job after his studies. He managed to do this and it proved to him that he was able to pursue his goals. He carried himself somewhat like a winner, and he felt like one. Observing Ongeri, it became clear how being able to entertain others reflects well on an individual, and how it positively contributes to feeling confident. Success, financial ability and confidence are strongly related for men. He recounted how he had waited for the day when he would be able to treat a woman without having to think about the expense. He had always felt that he could never compete with these successful men, and now he was one himself. This long awaited wish and the possibility of finally being 'the man' made him feel 'good' and he enjoyed his social life to the fullest. He found himself in this long anticipated situation of being well to do and he remarked 'why not enjoy the good side of life while I can?' Being able to have multi-partnered relationships meant having a varied sex life and although it had never been his intention *per se*, it suited him well. It 'invigorated' him and he felt like he was experiencing the most sexually potent years of his life. Wherever he entered a bar, he habitually looked over the place and investigated the women.

Ongeri was a typical 'lifist'; someone who 'enjoys life and someone who has the money to enjoy the life of going out every night, dancing, drinking, women, no worries but only fun' (Robart, aged 23). Ongeri recounted how it had not been his goal to have different women but that his situation offered the possibility. Other men justified multi-partnered relationships as a phase in life. The uniting force in these men's lives is the pervasive influence of hegemonic constructions of masculinity that inform them that having sex is constitutive for being a man. Hence, many men have come to experience – 'feel' – and define sex as significant to their sense of self.

Moving between sexual prowess and restrained potency

By focussing on the various experiences of male young professionals with regard to their sexual relationships with women, it appears that there are, as with women, parallel developments between the processes of contemporary identity formation and the way in which sexuality becomes central to self-expression. In contrast to women, however, the issue for men is not to acknowledge sexual desire but to redefine notions of sexual desire. Men's 'need' for sex is paralleled by notions of having to curb their sexual desire as a means of showing male self-restraint. Through debates propounding notions of 'modern men', sexual pleasure becomes redefined in relation to intimacy that, in a different way, also propounds notions of self-restraint. As a result, it leaves the notion that male sexuality is self-evident wavering. Men experience this contradiction in their self-perceptions, and they communicate contradictory understandings of what it means to be a man. Moreover, the continuation of the patriarchal ideology, even while its practical and legitimizing foundations are disintegrating, has also affected young men's sense of masculinity.

Young professional men are searching for alternative ways of relating to women through a reconstruction of gender roles, though they are less politically vocal about it than women are. Women are more active in pursuing the moral space to express sexual desire and have more to gain, whereas men stand to lose a lot. Conventional discourse has always allowed men more leeway compared to women, and the main difference between women and men's biographies is that the discourse on male sexuality partly overlaps with 'Africanist' or 'traditional' discourse. Men's moral space is nowadays being reconsidered as a result of transformational processes regarding gender and sexuality. Men also partly advocate these transformations through the new discourse on love, but doing this requires a redefinition of the privileged position that the male gender is generally ascribed. The search for a new sexuality is exciting, but is also an ambiguous pleasure.

Sexual desire as a physical craving

Dominant discourses in Kenya represent male sexuality in relation to sexual desire and activity. Accordingly, male sexuality is discursively understood as existing and active before marriage. Men's sexual reputations are framed around these notions, and consequently men make sure they do not appear to be lacking sexual desire. Men define their sexual desire as a 'need', an unavoidable physical longing, hence being sexually active is highly regarded and considered 'natural' and a 'man's need' represents a healthy individual. Any physical explanation of this phenomenon is inevitably entangled in the social understanding of what makes a man a man. Having sex contributes positively to feeling masculine, to men's gendered sense of self, and hence to identifying as a man. Male sexuality is defined in notions of achievement, whereas maleness is a subjective experience, experienced through the body. Moreover, sexual prowess represents being an attractive person, being identified as a sexual person and being recognized as enjoying sex. Male sexual pleasure is understood as engaging in sexual intercourse, as experiencing 'sexual release'. Male sexual pleasure is therefore not strictly defined in relation to having sex with another subject, in the sense of sex as a mutual experience, because it reflects more on the individual's accomplishment.

The lack of a positive discourse on men's sexual desires in relation to intimacy has left young professional men in a state of uncertainty. For example, David did not know how to incorporate women's changing attitudes or their expectations. Tom, on the other hand, had a sense of what was expected of him but felt very insecure about it. Depending on the personality of the partner and the type of relationship (casual or committed), engaging in an emotionally intimate relationship clearly causes anxiety among some men. They feel 'exposed' and they fear being considered a wimp or 'unmanly', while at the same time they express the desire for emotional involvement. Other men are less vulnerable to such feelings of anxiety because they tend to be more engaged in love relationships. The majority of men are, in fact, engaged in processes of appropriating sexual desire and pleasure as constitutive to an intimate relationship, which has become related to how they identify themselves as contemporary men. As such, the meanings of sex for men are being supplemented; sex as inter-subjective exchange is now becoming as important as sex as achievement.

All these men defined sexual pleasure as constitutive to their relationships with women, but they reacted in two ways to these transformations. One group of men has come to define sexual pleasure as central to intimacy, to a relationship based on emotional involvement and support. Both Alex and Maurice were focussed on intimacy, mutual trust and companionship in their sexual lives. As such, sexual intimacy involves themselves as sexual subjects in a symbolic interaction with another subject. Framed by a narrative of love, they seek intimacy as a means of self-realization and they justify their behaviour by defining themselves as being contemporary men in contrast to 'traditional' men.

A second group has come to define sexual pleasure as an extension of the hegemonic understanding of potent male sexuality. Sexual prowess then becomes redefined as the ability to satisfy women sexually. It reflects positively on their abilities as men if they can be a 'good lover'. As such, the woman's sexual pleasure is also central to intimacy – though for these men it does not necessarily imply emotional involvement – and companionship. Nevertheless, all men recounted how intimacy was crucial for maintaining a 'committed' relationship. However, many men explained how they could not yet engage in such a relationship because of other demands placed on them, mainly the pressure to develop a career and acquire wealth (see also Smith 2007).

Balancing too much and too little sex

Whereas women were actively seeking emotional attachment, many men described emotional involvement as an ideal they had to postpone because they were not in a position to develop a 'committed' relationship at this stage in their life. Men's successive and/or multi-partnered sexual relationships can partly be explained by this necessity to delay committing themselves to one partner. All the men I spoke with saw multi-partnered relationships as the norm for men, and used this to justify or defend their behaviour. Whether it was Alex explaining how his relationship with Millicent was based on love, or Ongeri justifying his sex life, the issue of multi-partnered sex was the frame of reference. Having several partners has come to represent potent male sexuality and, therefore, men are forced to define themselves in relation to it. The issue of multi-partnered relationships cannot be explained as being intrinsic to Kenyan cultures. The balance between sex, money, responsibility, gaining respect and a sense of masculinity is a precarious one and is central to understanding men's sexual lives. How, then, are these related?

As is highlighted by the biographical accounts from all the men, success, sex and respect are correlated; the pursuit of respect is fundamental to negotiating manhood (this is true in many African societies; see Ouzgane and Morrell 2005). Male students or junior employees constantly referred to the moment when they would be financially able, that is, able to participate as a respected member of society. Being successful, having a commendable job and therefore social standing, is the principal goal for young men. Their worth is measured, by relatives and young women, in terms of how successful they are, and this contributes to their sense of self-worth. The fear of not performing at the expected or hoped-for level was palpable among the men I spoke with. For example, Eric's failed attempt to further his studies meant much more than simply not acquiring a master's degree. It also implied a failure to secure a gateway to better jobs and status in society. Somebody like Tom was very disappointed by his elder brother who appeared to be unable to get a stable job or start his own business. It was an example of how he did '*not* want to end up [his emphasis]'. Talking about relationships or marriage, the majority of men spoke about their plans and future aspirations that needed to be achieved before they could settle down, that is, engage in a 'committed' relationship. To men, it is essential to be successful in their work; this is the only way to be regarded as a 'serious' or 'responsible' person, and is one of the final stages in their adult manhood in order to be recognized as a worthy man. It remains to be seen whether they will or will not gain the respect they wish for, should they fail to succeed in the ways that they envisage for themselves. In Kenyan society, paying respect is part of daily practice in the sense that the enactment of respect is more important than the 'contents' (Van der Geest 2004 on Ghana; see also Heald 1995).

Respect is thus related to success and hence to the availability of money. Therefore, money is also a way of showing success and to show that one has 'arrived'. As I observed, most men like to joke about successful men by questioning their sexual potency or the origins of their success, while they actually admire them. Showing success and prosperity has two effects. One is that successful people are expected to share with others. Furthermore, because financial prowess is symbolic of success it also enhances confidence. Multi-partnered relationships and financial success are seen as going hand in hand. Being able to have several girlfriends implies being financially able. Ironically, women both criticize and expect men's financial means and this is a serious contradiction faced by men. Both success and having sex – since sex is seen as being crucial to the construction of manhood – contribute positively to how men identify themselves as men.

Sex, success and having several girlfriends therefore mutually reinforce each other (Smith 2007). Moreover, the way their self-perception is developed in relation to being a professional man, as an icon of the respectable 'modern' citizen, contributes positively to this process. Sex thus becomes a means and a goal of self-identification. As a result, many men engage in multiple sexual encounters, serially or simultaneously.

However, there is a limit to having copious sex; there is a delicate balance between the necessity of having sex to achieve manhood, being in control of one's appetite, and/or not spilling too much semen which is not in unlimited supply (see also Dover 2005). While Ongeri said it has not been his conscious intention to have many different women, but that his situation offered the possibility, other men said that multi-partnered relationships reflected a phase in life and many explained that their college years were the 'wild years' of their lives. Ruben (aged 26) described it as a game: 'Rat chase we used to call it. We would go to clubs and have a competition on who gets to kiss or take home a girl, or who manages to have more than one girl in one venue without the other girl knowing at all, and maintain this for as long as possible. Sometimes it was pretty ugly when they knew.' The majority recalled a time in their life when sexual relationships without the intention of commitment represented a stage that men go through before they get 'serious with life'.[15] Men give different explanations, varying from a higher testosterone level in men than in women, to justifying it as a necessary life experience before settling down, to presenting it as unavoidable for unmarried people. Or as Maurice put it: 'There is a time to fool around and there is a time to grow up'. This moment of growing up coincides, for many men, with acquiring a stable position or job. The final stage in reaching adult manhood is to gain social standing and hence respect through marriage and fatherhood. For men who consider themselves to be approaching this stage, having multiple sexual partners is considered 'fooling around' and hence not compatible with their desire to gain social status as an adult. Related to this is the feeling that a man should be in control of himself, as lack of self-restraint is seen as evidence of not being man enough yet.

A few men in this study dissociated themselves from friends who continued to engage in multi-partnered sex, claiming that 'a modern man is a monogamous man'. Others engaged somewhat sheepishly in multi-partnered sex. Young adult men are excused for multi-partnered behaviour as it is seen as a passing thing. In fact, men distinguish between multi-partnered relationships and being occasionally unfaithful. Engaging in multi-partnered relationships is precarious as it can be associated with weakness, while being occasionally unfaithful is considered an acceptable possibility when a marriage or committed relationship turns sour or when a couple experiences a time of conflict. One evening in late December 2001 I met Peter (aged 24 and married in 2001) in *Klup House*. He was passionately kissing a young woman, whom I guessed was not his wife. He was visiting Nairobi on a company assignment. After showing visible embarrassment when he first saw me, he came to chat for a while a little later and explained himself as follows:

> Well prof, still studying the natives' amorous lives? [We laughed and joked a little more about 'natives', as well as about 'non-natives going native'. After a while we became more serious and without me asking him, he started talking about his current life.] You know, she [his wife] delivered and the baby takes all her attention, which is fine, I am proud of them both. But … you know … I miss the fun we used to have, I am always indoors these days, taking care of them. So … being here in Nairobi, with these gangsters [his old friends], I felt like letting go, just for once. I don't consider that being unfaithful to her … strictly seen it is of course, but she knows I love her, that I wouldn't really dog her.

Peter expresses an opinion that I heard frequently. In an interesting twist, men manage to preserve the leeway that society has always allowed them, despite their critique of 'dogging', i.e. blatant infidelity and disloyalty towards the partner. Men who give in to temptation see themselves as slightly naughty and irresponsible, but not disrespectful of their women. Having multiple partners is thus a complex and often highly contradictory affair: on one hand it reflects sexual prowess and success, while on the other hand it can be considered a weakness. Some men, like Tom, saw themselves almost as passive bystanders to their own drives so the sex drive became for them a weakness, that is, they felt they should be able to exercise greater self-restraint. A subtle and almost unspoken trend among young professional men furthermore considers multi-partnered relationships as somewhat backward as it is often associated with older men who are still 'polygamists'. Hence some self-conscious men portray themselves in an oppositional way, associating multi-partnered relationships with lack of self-control, backwardness and lack of direction as a contemporary professional man. The emerging masculinities to which men's biographies in this study testify, in fact draw on 'competing images and legacies' (Morrell 2001: 25).

The waning dominant patriarchal ideology

Dominant notions of masculinity are the result of the gender order, which has its roots in the patriarchal ideology that ascribed men a public and dominant role. As I showed in Chapter II, current debates reveal the (fear of) loss of status and power by elders (cf. Lindsay and Miescher

2003) and the attempt by Kenyan men in general to deal with feelings
of emasculation (Silberschmidt 2001). This loss of power just reinforces
patriarchal constructions of masculinity. For example, in 2003 while I was
writing this book, a discussion flared up when Ms Wambui Waiyaki, aged
67, married a man aged 25 years.[16] The marriage incited heated debates
about 'African morals'. Opponents labelled it 'against biblical teaching',
insulting Ms Wambui as the 'shame of African womanhood' and classified
the marriage as 'culturally and biologically improper'. The defenders, such
as the young professional women and men in this study, cited the case
as a 'mirror to a hypocritically sexist society', because only four months
earlier the vice president of the country had married a woman thirty-four
years his junior and nobody commented on that. The general reaction
however, led by church and political leaders, cited Ms Wambui as a bad
example for the younger generations. Such sentiments reveal the experience of loss and anger by a generation whose social foundations are under
attack, couched in sentiments about African heritage. It shows how these
defenders of hegemonic masculinity are vigilant, seeking to guard male
privilege and recreating a gendered discourse for this purpose, reinforcing
conventional gender constructions.

What is changing then? To answer this question we need to recall that
male authority requires a material base, while male responsibility is culturally and normatively constituted (Cornwall 2003). The perception of
the man as the breadwinner has become dominant in Kenyan society; it
is understood as fundamental to the status quo. When asked about their
parents, young professional women and men invariably answered by
elaborating on whether or not their father had been able to assist their
family financially. Society at large requires that men be providers; they
are respected for that and they gain authority from it. Whether it happens sooner or later, becoming financially able is a constituent of a man's
development of a gendered sense of self. However, social change has been
transforming the organization of sexuality and gender for some time. The
increasing participation of women in the labour market has shaken up this
status quo. Even for young professional men, it was difficult to accept
women in senior positions, or even as colleagues. Male roles are becoming
more and more unclear and more contradictory because they have always
been defined in relation to female roles.[17]

Another pillar of the patriarchal order that is changing is men's privileged position with regard to sex. Sex used to be, and conventionally
still is, understood as a 'marital duty'– something that a man could 'demand'. Sex and moral leeway for men have become central to constructions of the male gender. In the phrase 'typical African men', these aspects
come together: it speaks of men who are authoritative, and who engage

in multi-partnered sex 'because of their biological imperatives', which also has become (incorrectly) the explanation of polygamy. The way in which young professional people speak about polygamy, as justification of men's sexual behaviour, and as a cultural explanation, reifies the practice of multi-partnered sexual behaviour as cultural practice. Young professional men see themselves as embodying the transition from their father's generation to the next: 'We, modern men, are in-between. We have polygamous fathers, who are our example, and that affects you somehow. Our sons will look at us and that is why I want to be different. But you know … culture is in our blood somehow' (Joram, aged 23). Joram means that polygamy has often been understood as a cultural practice that distinguishes 'African' men. Hence, 'African male sexuality' – especially in the guise of man-the-patriarch – has been romantically linked to cultural, or perhaps nationalist versions of Africanness, and hence been essentialized as 'natural'.[18] This connection between sex and 'Africanness' is a powerful one for many men. They like to joke about it, and many men initially spoke about 'we, African men' in the interviews. However, gender identities do not emanate from some primordial essence, whose resilience bears testament to perpetual forms of inequality; they are products and manifestations of cultures in motion, as experienced by men themselves.

The fathers of the young professionals in this study are, roughly speaking, the last generation of polygamists in an urban context in the original sense of the term, that is, taking responsibility simultaneously for different wives and households.[19] The overall condemnation of polygamy, together with the rise of the nuclear family, has led to the dissolution of the custom among the younger generations. It has led to what is now called 'modern polygamy', that is, conducting extramarital affairs. Although this practice is publicly condemned, it is also discursively justified as unavoidable. The dividing line between public condemnation inspired by Christianity, and men behaving 'immorally' is, however, subtle. The acceptance of the practice is possible because of the discourse about men's virility justifying men's behaviour. This discourse, with its roots in ideas of primordial Africanness, has discursively replaced the fundamental position that polygamy used to have in the patriarchal order. The idea of male hypersexuality essentializes and reifies the construction and usage of 'African male sexuality'. What can be called the 'culture argument' – when people discuss men's sexuality in terms of it being 'our culture' and thereby referring to the institution of polygamy as the cultural origin – has its roots in the conflation of male virility and polygamy. Young professional men are generally sensitive to this conflation because both the importance of sex and cultural belonging are invoked in this notion.

A new discourse of 'African masculinity' has gained significance among young professional men. This has happened in response to hegemonic white masculinity that continues to exert an influence via media images and through institutions in which white masculinity remains embedded. The majority of the male young professionals, employed by international companies and organizations, typically work for white men. In the night-life of Nairobi, white men also figure prominently as people who have the means to go out and have girlfriends. Some of the male young professionals interviewed felt they had to compete with these white professional men for Kenyan women, so they were visibly proud when I, a white female, accompanied them. On the dance floors of Nairobi clubs, however, black and white men are more equal than they are on the work floor, and in response black men feel free to assert themselves as 'nonwhite' or 'African'. A sense of male hypersexuality has arisen in which 'Africanness' and a contemporary identity are merged. Male sexuality has thus become connected to a sense of African heritage for young professional men.

Much that has been described above as rooted in patriarchal ideologies overlaps with the dominant Christian discourses in Kenya. In Chapter III, I discussed these overlaps, including how patriarchal and Christian discourses have merged into a conventional discourse that has become hegemonic. Emphasizing piety, education and familial respectability, Christian discourses have become a dominant moral frame of reference. However, there are some divergences. Whereas the extended family is of significance from the customary point of view, in general the Christian discourse focusses more and more on the nuclear family. Similarly, while the notion of respect is a central aspect in the construction of hegemonic masculinity in patriarchal discourse, in the Christian discourse the notion of respectability is more central. Respectability and respect are related but different, and are sometimes oppositional. Christian respectability is rooted in moral righteousness and fidelity, while customary respect is also defined as moral righteousness in relation to the institution of polygamy where a husband gains respect according to the number of people in his household. The main overlap concerns gender roles and the construction of femininity and masculinity. This is an area of unanimity where the two discourses meet and reinforce each other in the conventional discourse.

Interestingly, Christianity offers a viable solution for living a contemporary lifestyle (Newell 2005). Christianity, as it is preached in churches like the Nairobi Chapel, Don Bosco and the Nairobi Baptist Church, offers an alternative construction of masculinity. In a morally authoritative manner, the Christian ideology rejects polygamy and sanctions marriage as the only proper place to enjoy sex and gain respect as a father.[20] Infidelity is constantly being referred to as 'immoral' and obstructing a progressive attitude. It is likely that Kinyua (see previous chapter), when he asserts that a 'modern man is a monogamous man', would have taken the phrase from such a sermon. Related to this understanding of progressiveness is the emphasis on the small nuclear family as the icon of contemporary happiness. Women and men are actively called upon to spend time with their children instead of relying on a childminder, which until recently was the typical middle class situation. The role of father, seen as the provider and the anchor of a Christian family, is being redefined as also taking on that of a socially engaged person. Similarly, see Chapter VI on Christian self-help groups; husbandhood is being redefined in terms not only of respect derived from male authority, but also of the respectability due to a morally righteous man. As became clear from Tayiani's account, sex is approached positively in the Nairobi Chapel, as long as it is practised within marriage. Thus, albeit in a redirected form, the importance of sex in a man's construction of his masculine sense of self is maintained in Christian discourse. Patriarchal ideology therefore persists, albeit in different forms and integrated in a discourse on progressive and/or Christian masculinity.

Accommodating change

In the book *Changing Men in South Africa* (2001), Morrell describes three responses of South African men to what he calls the 'transitional context' of South Africa: reactive, accommodating and responsive. Such categories are used as a way of 'mapping the field and making sense of a wider range of responses amongst men to the experience of transition' (Morrell 2001: 6). Although the concept of a 'transitional context' has specific connotations in the national South African situation, we can also speak about transformational processes in Kenya, which began with the grandfathers of the men in this study. Using Morrell's terminology, it can be concluded that young professional men in Kenya are in varying degrees reactive, accommodating and responsive towards the change occurring in the gender order and the resulting changes in constructions of sex.

As a group, young professional men are progressive because they embody social changes that have resulted from and are therefore part of the societal transformation processes described in Chapter III. Embodying change, they challenge dominant notions of masculinity and in doing so, develop new models of how to be 'men'. They also desire a change in gender relationships because, as they see it, they cannot live like their fathers did. The rise of women into professional positions has made it difficult for the conventional gender division of labour in the home to be maintained. In response, young male professionals have become much more participatory in the home, whether when married or living together, and more supportive of their partner's goals (on South Africa, see Morrell 2001: 32). An important aspect of men contributing to women's participation in the labour market is the importance of a double income. During the 'pre-marriage counselling' class I attended in 2001, one session was dedicated to 'finances in marriage', and men were highly supportive of their wives-to-be having a good job. Some indicated that they were proud of their girlfriend's good position, as it reflected positively on her capacities. Moreover, as both women and men remarked, young couples needed two incomes in order to maintain a certain lifestyle. This goal of pursuing a 'sophisticated' lifestyle brings both women and men together. The lifestyles of young professionals in their twenties facilitate change in gender roles, and since men are part of this process, they are considered to be progressive. Of course there are differences among them. Some men actively pursue progressive change, while others find themselves in this changing situation by default, only because their prospective partners are professional women. Nevertheless, the increasing importance of 'love' relationships and the way in which women and men relate more and more on an egalitarian basis as lovers, friends and colleagues contributes to men's responsive attitudes.

Young professional men are also reactive or defensive in certain situations with women. In particular when men fear the contempt of women or when normative expectations prove unavoidable, many men tend to react defensively. In such moments of defensiveness, some men revert to behaviour associated with male authority and dominance. These moments show that feelings of emasculation and the urge to compensate for possible associations with emasculation lurk just below the surface. Men's reputations are based on re-enactments of masculine persona and, hence, need to be constantly guarded against non-masculine features. In short, young professional men tread a careful balance between wanting to be 'different' (more progressive) and reverting to a socialized version of hegemonic masculinity that contradicts their aspirations to be different. This balance is easily upset when a woman expresses contempt for a man; or when a woman has expectations that are based on patriarchal notions; or when a woman is too focussed on the change of gender roles. Therefore, a certain ambivalence towards women remains; men remain on guard so as not to be 'exposed'. Men, in such moments of weakness and fragility, of anxieties and aspirations, while being open to a dialogue with women on one hand, can also revert to emotional blackmail by invoking notions of 'Africanness' in relation to their role as partners.

Overall, young professional men are accommodating. Their initiation into manhood, mostly based on ethnic or 'African' norms and values, invokes the ideal of manhood as responsible, respectful and self-reliant. These notions coincide with notions of a contemporary lifestyle as a professional. Financial independence is a prerequisite for the development of a man and young professional men reside in a material context in which career progression and financial security are now possible, which means they do not have to depend on their relatives. These changes create the possibility of exploring an alternative sense of masculine dignity and autonomy and breaking away from normative expectations as expressed by their relatives and the general public. In doing so, they still draw on normative notions of masculinity, which affirm male dominance, while at the same time alternative constructions of masculinity have also become viable. Young professional men do not want to give up their male power but they are not fighting for the restoration of some pre-existing patriarchal order. I believe that men are gradually beginning to engage in companionate relationships because, together with their partners, they aspire to a new kind of relationship.

Conclusion

What it means to be a man in Nairobi today is not so easily definable and many men experience personal conflict in this regard, in their attempts to embody the patriarchal ideology while at the same time being critical of it. Men's gendered sense of self is based on notions of self-reliance and of being responsible and successful, which command respect from society at large. Sex is central to men's sense of self and forms an important constituent of their identification as masculine, which in turn is related to notions of achievement and success. In the context of contradictory understandings of masculinity, of balancing too much and too little sex, and of women taking up equal positions, men act in order to guard their masculinity. Being partly responsive and partly defensive, men are engaged in a project of redefining masculinities.

The majority of young professional men have managed to develop a masculine sense of self in a context of changing gender constructions. Most of them have managed to withstand pressures which associate manhood with dominance over women, or sexual prowess with having multiple sexual partners, or living by double standards. They do this mainly by drawing on the same patriarchal discourses emphasizing a man's responsibility; as such, their masculine sense of self is rooted in notions of accountability and inducing respect by working hard and developing a career. One area that can serve to reassert masculinity in both the conventional manner and in a new fashion is sex. The power of sex remains indisputable, and a contemporary man is expected to be a skilful sex partner. Further, being a proper lover implies that men's sexualities become related to sex as a mutual endeavour, whereas sex used to be spoken about as a 'marital duty' that men 'take on'. In the search for a new sexuality, pleasure and anxiety meet.

Nevertheless, the 'need' for sex implies the need for women, which implies a certain dependence on women. Such feelings of dependence do not gel with notions of men as self-reliant; they have associations of addiction and weakness. In popular and patriarchal discourses, any hint of dependence is scoffed at by reinforcing notions of masculinity as authoritative. At the same time, the discourse on love is gaining a dominant position in the way people understand dating and sexual relations. The popular notion of 'love' also implies dependence, albeit within a relationship of trust and companionship, which is what the majority of men are seeking. Young professional men, in short, have to negotiate between uncertain boundaries of 'love relationships' and 'being man enough'. The majority of men treated 'love' as a self-evident concept, while women generally made more effort to define it. The lack of literature on men's sexual experiences suggests an absence of discourse on men's desire for non-sexual intimacy and vulnerability, which is not the case in their lived experience. As shall be discussed in the next chapter, the new discourse described in Chapter III involves men, and they keenly partake in romantic love as a form of self-expression.

Notes

1. Shaggy's *Angel Song* was extremely popular throughout 2001.
2. There is a small body of literature on male same sex sexuality on the coast of Kenya. These studies focus on the Swahili Muslims of Mombasa and are therefore not quite applicable to the situation in Nairobi, since Mombasa is a society based on gender segregation in most contexts, unlike non-Muslim societies in Kenya (Amory 1998; Shepherd 1987). There is one biographical account on same sex sexuality in the form of a transcribed sexual life history of a 24-year-old man from the Kikuyu ethnic group (Murray 1998). This is a rather exceptional account of an individual's sexual life. It is, unfortunately, not incorporated in an analysis of sexuality, gender and/or society.
3. It is important to scrutinize this body of literature in more depth, as it is taking a lead in the study of male sexuality in African societies. It has come into being since the 1990s, when '[H]igh levels of poverty allied with rising expectations have proved a tragic mixture for fostering the growth of violent masculinities' (Morrell 2001: 19). Simultaneously, AIDS became another violent reality and prognoses on AIDS soon began to confirm that South Africa had one of the highest numbers of HIV prevalence and AIDS victims. The South African academy responded fast and a remarkable body of studies has appeared. The work on male sexuality, however, exposes a specifically South African (national) account. It is important to realise that the topics of AIDS, sexual violence and local gender issues led to

the steady flow in research on sexuality. For example, the fact of South Africa having the highest rate of rape in the world (Morrell 2001: 20) led to much research on male violence and AIDS. This unusual position has its root in the extremely violent history of the country. Taking into account that violence is somehow normalized in South Africa because of its violent past, these studies cannot be seen as representative for other (southern) African countries. Nevertheless, these books, dealing with the challenges of changes that men face, are seminal for further research in other African societies.

4. For a general discussion about anthropology and the study of male gender, see Gutmann 1997.

5. Recently, men from the Luo ethnic community are being circumcised because of the links between being uncircumcised and higher rates of HIV infection (Abicht et al. 2002). However, I do not know whether or how this relates to changing perceptions of one's masculinity.

6. His two brothers were studying at a public university in 2001.

7. Karuga (aged 25) claimed to be a virgin. However, I am not sure whether this is actually the case. In view of the fact that his narrative conveyed contradictions, such as his accounts of different girlfriends, I think that he might have wanted to confuse me.

8. In general boys are circumcised between the ages of 8 and 14, depending on the ethnic group's customs and whether it is done individually or with a group during a particular season, as is common to certain ethnic groups.

9. Remarkably, I heard such remarks from men of the Kikuyu and Gusii ethnic group, but less from men from other groups. As Eric was from the Kikuyu ethnic group, and taking into account the historical animosities between the Luo and Kikuyu that have taken on an added significance in the postcolonial era, I wonder to what extent the political implication of Eric's remark is more important than the cultural one.

10. Perhaps Emmanuel, Pamela's boyfriend, might have, but I never had the chance to interview him.

11. See Chapter I.

12. The women who worked as prostitutes in Westlands and whom I visited for a while confirmed this by telling me that a significant group of married customers come to them for sexual acts that their wives refuse to do, that is, men who want to be orally satisfied or who want to have anal sex.

13. This reminds us of Godelier's *The Making of Great Men: Male Domination and Power among the New Guinea Baruya* (1986). He describes how, despite the extraordinary power and domination that men in general exert over women, men always remain dependent on women for sex. He explores how men deal with this contradiction in their relations with women, which is similar to Tom's frustrations.

14. This quotation came from a longer discussion on contemporary 'African' identity and traditions: 'We, the men of these days, have to make choices. We cannot live anymore like our fathers, I believe it's not right to be polygamous, like some other retrogressive rituals'. Rachel: 'Like …?'. Maurice: 'Well, there are these rites with funerals, I dunno … like you have to talk to the body, in the case you owe the man some money, you will repay him by paying his wife. I dunno, talking to a corpse sounds like nonsense to me.'

15. Among the twenty-five men who participated in this study, five men never engaged in multi-partnered sex, while nine did so when they were adolescents until their early twenties, and seven did so once in a while. Four men regularly had multi-partnered relationships during the period of research.

16. This exceptional marriage received much media attention, not only because of the unusual age difference where the woman is the senior, but also because she is a national celebrity. Ms Wambui is an icon of the female Mau Mau freedom fighters who took up arms against the colonialist administration. Later, she became known through the famous S.M. Otieno case, when she sued her family-in-law against burying her husband in their rural home, as she

wanted to bury him in Nairobi against customary regulations (see also Cohen and Odhiambo 1992). Although being a female fighter and suing one's family-in-law were not quite
considered proper, people spoke with admiration about her. Her latest marriage, however,
proved to be much more controversial.

17. For married men, the role of husband has become unclear as increasingly men cannot be
granted the status of sole breadwinner.

18. When African male sexuality is romantically linked to cultural or perhaps nationalist versions of Africanness, then changes in male sexuality will necessarily be involved in defining
transformations in contemporary Kenyan society. Such an analysis, however, goes beyond
the remit of this study.

19. The construction of a sexual culture as based on customary practices reveals more about
contemporary times than about the past. According to the various ethnic customs, a man
would only marry several wives if he was financially able to and therefore polygamy was a
moral issue which reflected a hardworking attitude and respectability. An important aspect
of men's larger moral space was the influence of a patriarchal society where men could
marry several wives. Since this cultural institution was surrounded by moral codes regarding
the practicalities, through time a discourse has come into being about men's virility as the
basis for a polygamous marriage (interview with late Professor Katani Mkangi, 7 October
2001). Young professional men justified male hyper-sexuality with explanations about the
positive effects of testosterone on the sexual urge, a more 'scientific' hence viable explanation. A critical challenge in studying male sexualities in an African context is to problematize
the connections between such 'cultural' explanations and men's behaviour.

20. Once a pastor from the Nairobi Chapel called on men in his sermon to make a choice
between becoming 'modern' or remaining 'stuck in traditions', preaching against the phenomenon of *ndogo ndogo* as 'immoral'. In another sermon I once heard that the fathers were
challenged to take their family out for a picnic and actively play 'a ball game' with their
children instead of taking them out to see a movie.

CHAPTER VI

SIGN OF THE TIMES: MEDIA AND THE THERAPEUTIC ETHOS OF ROMANTIC LOVE

On 18 October 2001 I wrote in my diary: 'Sereti and I leave the cinema a little drowsy, as it is when you have been looking at the screen for more than 90 minutes, drugged by the larger than life images and the overwhelming sounds. Sereti sighs and is visibly under the spell of the film. 'Save the last dance' met all her expectations and after this first time she went to watch it another two times. 'It had it all, the love, the struggle, he looked good, the music was like … funky, just right. Oh! I love such a movie; I wish I could watch it all night through. He was great, as you would want a man to be, oh! Rachel, I want to be in love like this.' Sereti calls herself a romantic dreamer and I was amused by her being melted away by the images of love which she sees as the 'supreme winner' in times of hardship'.[1]

On the one hand Sereti, aged 25, had a dreamy character, while on the other hand she could be very strategic and determined in her actions. She had a soft appearance, she was small and she knew how to use her charm to get her way. She worked as a project designer in an international nongovernmental organization in 2001 and lived with her mother and older sister. Her father had died five years before and since then she did not want to leave her mother alone, so she had decided to live with her for the time being. 'My mother is very liberal, I can do what I want and come back home any time, she leaves me to live my own life.' She used to go swimming twice a week 'to keep fit' and she liked to 'have a beer or two' after work. On Fridays and Saturdays she would go out with friends. In 2001 she went on a holiday to Kampala, which was a remarkable thing to do as most Nairobians only take leave to visit their relatives or just to spend some time away from work. In 2002, Sereti went with her sister to Cape Town, and in 2003 she visited Bangkok. In 2001, she started to study for a Master in Business Administration (MBA) in the evenings through the University of Nairobi. This changed her routine, as it meant attending classes four evenings a week and on Saturday mornings. Nevertheless, she was determined and did not mind missing going out.

Sereti often talked about 'real love' and anticipated that she would find it in such a relationship. Sereti showed more interest in my experiences and relationships than any of the other people I spoke to or interviewed. She was very curious about Victor and me, and she loved to visit us and ask Victor all kinds of things as a way to crosscheck what I had told her. In 2001 she was briefly involved with David to whom she 'lost her heart'. With David, she saw her dreams come true: 'David is IT, like he walked out of the movies to find me, Sereti, his princess,' she said to me in an ironical yet pensive way, after it became clear that they were becoming more and more committed. David adored Sereti and after a couple of months they became 'the' couple of their friends' circle: 'They are the example of what so many women want, he is just awesome' (Sereti's friend Esther). Quite suddenly, David broke up with Sereti and years later she says she does not know why. At first in 2001, she said it was an absolute surprise for her, she had not seen it coming. When we spoke again in 2004, she was still preoccupied with what had happened and said 'There were signs I guess, sometimes he could turn moody and he would ask me to leave [him alone], without an explanation'.

After David, she had affairs every now and then but she did not talk extensively about them as they 'mean nothing, what can I say, a woman has her needs si ndio? [isn't it?]'. In 2004 she said she had become 'insecure' about men and she told me about Sam, a man from the United States she had met through her work. He had been kind to her when she had refused to have sex during their first date, which he had respected. After meeting for a few more times they slept together. 'I guess he is sincere but you never know, I mean, it's nice to taste the local dishes eh? [Expression referring to the foreigners who start a relationship with a Kenyan]. But... I liked it.' They had a short affair before he left for the United States and he told her that he would like to see her again. She was filled with doubts: 'An American – of all the men in the world, I need to like an American! But he is gentle and kind,... he tells me sweet things, how beautiful I am.' In April 2004, we had an e-mail correspondence, including the following excerpts:

Hi Rachel,

I need your help. First and foremost, Sam the guy I met is coming in August. I am very excited though I do not know if he'll still want to be romantically attached to me ... but he's coming. I want to go to the coast with him but I don't know where to go that is not swarmed by British and German tourists enjoying Masaai dances. You told me that you guys went somewhere nice the last time you were here, could you please write me details. He wants to travel around Kenya a bit and for now I can only think of [the] coast. Any ideas??? I can't just take him to my grandmother's [where she took me, RS], there's more to Kenya than that, yes? HEEELP!!!

Lots of love, Sereti

One e-mail later:

> I am very excited about this guy's visit and YES I want to be involved with him
> even though if it is not going to be forever, I'm thinking I can't be too fretful about
> the possibility of a relationship, after all I do not have that luxury, so my policy
> is to enjoy myself while it lasts, as long as I don't get pregnant in the process...
> Nuts eh? .... Thanks for the Wasini [Island] idea, I'd love to do that, it will give us
> time to hang out and that's what I want.... What stresses my life is that there is no
> permanence to the whole thing and after two weeks he will be gone and I'll be left
> hanging... But I would have had my fun.

What is the relationship between the films Sereti liked and her personal
life? Why was *Save the Last Dance* such a popular film? How did it affect
the Nairobian public? Or how should we understand complaints by several women and men in this study that they have been 'brainwashed' by
the idea of romantic love? Sereti's narrative depicts a definable thread in
the biographies of young professionals; it directs us to the core tensions
they struggle with regarding the relation between sexuality and cultural
belonging. Focussing on the experiences and practices of romantic love
among young professionals, I will now try and draw out some implications from the previous chapters. The issue of romantic love highlights the
unavoidable ambivalence in relation to their sexual lives, and the resulting
tension between pleasure and anxiety. The romantic practice of sexuality is
a great pleasure enjoyed by young professionals. Yet it is also the ground
where the tricky affair of 'westernization' becomes most intimately linked
with people's personal lives.

In this chapter I will look at the influence of consumer capitalism.
Campbell (1987) has argued how the spirit of modern consumerism is
linked to an eagerness for new experiences, a hedonistic orientation and
infinite desires. The power of consumerism is that it works via the registers
of pleasure and intimacy and in a particular way places love and sexuality
at the centre of consumer desires. The connections between consumer
capitalism, contemporary lifestyles and self-expression – symbolized by
practices of romantic love – are of significance for an understanding of the
ambiguous pleasures of young professionals. As I will show, the introduction of therapeutic ethos – the disposition for reflectivity – into people's
narratives is crucial in this process.

According to Sereti, *Save the Last Dance* was a beautiful love story,
and watching it was a 'moment of bliss' induced by the larger-than-life
images and overpowering sound. The film was advertised as a love affair
crossing borders and this representation of a love story made her fan-
tasize about her own love life. In a society where affection is generally
expressed in somewhat covert ways, viewing images of people showing

explicit affection makes a powerful impression (Spronk 2002). Sereti's fascination is related to a new impetus of the discourse on romantic love that has been employed from early postcolonial times onwards (Mutongi 2000; Thomas 2006), a discourse where love is given a prominent place in the establishment of relationships. Romantic love has come to serve as the ultimate expression of a progressive relationship, in contrast with conventional relationships which were based on 'convenience', that is, compatibility of ethnicity and status as partly decided by the larger family. Moreover, romantic self-expression has become a characteristic of contemporary lifestyle. In this chapter I use romantic love as an analytical tool. What people call love is a complex human emotion interweaving stories, images, metaphors, material goods and folk stories (Luhmann 1982; Padilla et al. 2007). What I label romantic love is how young professionals made sense of their love-related experiences by drawing on collective symbols and practices, which are gaining momentum via the media.

Films, soap operas and music stations on TV, as well as radio, are popular phenomena in Nairobi. For many young professionals it is a must to keep up to date with the latest lyrics and films, while others are eager to discuss certain plots and characters from films and soap operas. The popularity of Hollywood films like *Save the Last Dance* is fascinating since these films are being shown in a completely different societal context to that of the Western public for whom they were made. Does their popularity suggest a blind fascination that could be called 'westernization' – i.e. since Hollywood films do not originate from an 'African' reality they have little meaning in the lives of people from Africa – as both Nairobians and Westerners sometimes suggested to me? In this chapter I intend to explore this complex and continuing problem of cultural imperialism for young professionals who participate in the imagined realities of other cultures as part of their daily lives. I ask how the notion of romantic love is introduced by capitalist processes, imagined via films and soap operas, and reproduced and recreated on the radio and popular magazines. I explore trends in the media and how they create models of romantic love, which people emulate, and how it thus becomes real.

Romantic love and the twin spheres of consumption and mass media

It would require a thorough historical and comparative analysis to validate the idea that 'older' patterns are making way for 'newer' ones. Having described the new avenues that young professionals are engaged in, I believe it is clear enough that they are the latest generation in a continuous process of transformation concerning the reconfiguration of gender and sexuality (see Chapter II). These cultural, social and economic changes have helped to transform the meanings of sexuality, love and gender, as these changes have been progressively incorporated within the emerging mass market and mass media culture in the early twenty-first century. I do not want to present these changes as a break with tradition, because they have involved different generations in a gradual process of transformation. The young professionals' grandparents considered themselves modern when engaging in the labour migration or cash crop economy that enabled them to try out new pathways. The parents of this group of young professionals were also modern in their time, if one thinks about their move from the village to the city and its effect on customary practices. This younger generation in turn sees itself as modern due to the transformations that have taken place as a result of their parents' migration. The shift towards lifestyle choices by contemporary young professionals has coincided with the emergence of the media and its engagement in issues of the intimate. Because of the absence of role models in their interpretation of love and sexuality, young professionals have taken the media as a sounding board.

Ethnographic research on (romantic) love is uncommon; '[in scientific literature] love is treated too ethereally as though separate from the body, [while] sex is often cut off from the spirit' (Gregor 1995: 333). The division between sex and love is what I aim to bridge in this chapter, or what William Jankowiak calls 'the love/sex conundrum' (2008). In previous chapters I explored how sex is related to social, emotional and bodily processes, whereas here, I intend to analyse the manifestations of love. Passionate love in courtship and marriage is not new to Kenya, as many folktales, songs, life histories, and works of narrative fiction attest. Nor is the ideal of romantic love new (Mutongi 2000). Popular music from the early postcolonial period onward has often foregrounded romantic themes; one thinks, for example, of the famous love song 'Malaika' ('angel' in Swahili) (Kidula 2000: 409). During the same period, Hollywood blockbusters, Hindi films, and locally produced popular novels featuring romantic love held strong appeal, and popular magazines included extensive discussions of how to recognize true love and how to ensure that love marriages triumphed over arranged ones (Fugelsang 1994; Odhiambo 2003; Strobel 1979). There also has been, and still is, a rich tradition of students exchanging love letters (Thomas 2006). What is new, however, is the sheer volume of representations and debates about intimacy that place issues of love, relationships and sexuality squarely at the forefront of personal interest and social concerns (see also Chapter III). The media and consumer culture have picked up romantic love as a distinctive characteristic of youth culture in the 1990s, and the ideology of romantic love has rapidly gained a specific meaning for the younger generation, especially for those who are able to afford particular practices associated with romantic love. In fact, representations of romantic love have assumed a global character, yet with distinctive local inflections (cf. Liechty 2003).

Illouz's study on the emergence of the notion of romantic love in the twentieth century as central to the 'construction of a romantic utopia' in US society (1997) puts forward some arguments that are interesting to explore here. Going well beyond a technical definition of capitalism, she looks at how capitalism is characterized by an entire cultural mindset of exchange relationships that have permeated most of US society since early 1900. Since then, consumption and the expression of romantic emotions have progressively merged. By analysing advertisements through various decades in the twentieth century, she shows how romantic love became associated with money, commodities and new technologies of leisure. Commodities have now penetrated the romantic bond so deeply that they become an invisible and unacknowledged force governing romantic encounters. The 'commodification of romance', such as the romantic dinner by candlelight or the diamante ring as the symbol of love, has gained global meanings (cf. Hirsch and Wardlow 2006; Padilla and Hirsch 2008). The crucial point is that capitalism enables the participation of everyone in the economic and symbolic sphere of consumption and romance. According to Illouz, late or advanced capitalism is characterized by a number of features. Especially applicable to young professionals – which marks them as different from other sectors in Kenyan society – are the prominence of the service and information sectors of the economy, the importance placed on lifestyle and the extraordinary growth of the culture and leisure spheres. Further, the rise of the service and information sectors of the economy is accompanied by changes in the occupational structures: young professionals become employed in service sectors, women enter the labour market, and employment comes to mean having the money and the time for holidays and leisure.

Consumerism and the mass media structure the private realm of leisure: '[B]y inscribing the romantic encounter into the consumption of leisure, the practice of "dating" mark[s] the symbolic and practical penetration of romance by the market' (Illouz 1997: 14). Capitalism has thus created a powerfully symbolic space unified by the twin spheres of consumption and mass media using the registers of pleasure and intimacy. Miller (1992), whose study of US soap operas in Trinidad is part of a wider project looking at consumption under capitalism, similarly reveals an active process of societal self-production through which people incorporate material objects and previously unfamiliar ideas into their own social value systems. Capitalism thus enables people to engage in a kind of self-realization through consumption and the mass media. The analyses of Campbell, Illouz and Miller draw attention to how middle classes have the capacity to act on their ambitions for a contemporary identity, which dovetail with my analysis of how sexuality becomes central to self-expression in Nairobi. Despite the collective romantic utopia that seems to be becoming universal, Illouz claims that romance is a matter of class because of its dependence on consumer capitalism. This is the case in Nairobi, as romantic love, mass media and leisure are intricately linked to the economic possibilities available to young professionals and which are exemplified in their subculture by way of dating. This is not to say that people who are less well off do not experience romantic love, but that the practices of romantic love are more class bound. Young professionals' aspirations are in line with other young women and men around the world who take up the ideal of companionate marriage as a way of demonstrating their modern individuality (Hirsch and Wardlow 2006).

The rapid shift among young professionals discussed above from 'arranged marriages' organized as family affairs to 'love marriages', can be seen here. It implies that at the level of representation, romantic love has articulated a longing for and a utopian model of the sovereignty of the individual above and against the claims of the group. In essence, romantic love celebrates moral individualism, as '[R]omantic love has been and continues to be the cornerstone of a powerful utopian vision because it reenacts symbolically rituals of opposition to the social order through inversion of hierarchies and affirms the supremacy of the individual' (Illouz 1997: 10). The threat of the inversion of the social order is of importance in order to understand the criticism levelled at young professionals due to their so-called 'transgressions'. Young adults react against notions of ethnic compatibility and family relations – fundamental to the social organization of community – as the basis for establishing a relationship. Here we come to the core of 'westernization' when it is used to accuse: it points to a deep generational conflict as a result of shifting power relations, a smouldering intergenerational tension which can be seen all over Africa (Comaroff and Comaroff 1999). The irony is that when the guardians of public morals decry the shift from marriage as a family affair to marriage as an individual affair, and call it a betrayal of custom, they invoke a utopian view of customs which does not exist and to which they never adhered themselves (see Chapter III). As Jameson has stated, cultural change is less a matter of content than a restructuring of power relationships (1984).

The other core issue of 'westernization' has less to do with 'the West' than many imagine. Often, the notion of 'westernization' in Nairobi refers to transnational flows of representations of different ways of knowing and being, such as those concerning the notion of romantic love. While young professionals engage with these public representations to reflect on and shape their own relationships, they do not copy Western modes, as the discourse on westernization implies. The media respond to a need for information. Specific media outlets offer forums where questions can be asked and issues of intimacy discussed, thereby enabling new understandings of romantic being and knowing, or what Liechty has called 'new epistemic understandings' of love (2003: 181). The way the media react to people's concerns has, in turn, come to inform individual lives in a reflexive manner. By reading or seeing other people's inner lives, people become engaged in reflecting about their own expectations, desires, experiences and justifications. The manner in which people engage with the media involves a dual process of simultaneous self-distancing (being audience) and self-recognition. By focussing on the media, I intend to show how this dialogue and negotiation are going on all the time between all types of media and young professionals, and how new subjectivities are created in this dual process (Schulz 2007).

In Nairobi, the media reach people via different channels, and here I will discuss cinema, TV, advertisements, radio and magazines according to their popularity and impact. Just as I grew up as a teenager in a cinematic and musical world dominated by US stars and by US media that became part of Dutch popular culture, so it was for Sereti in Nairobi. I 'take for granted a "global" perspective on media' (Ginsburg et al. 2002: 2). Writing about a lower middle class neighbourhood in Nairobi, Frederiksen states that 'global media [have] provided powerful narratives that are used by people in local settings as sounding boards for reflections on how to conduct everyday life and human relations' (2000: 209). These reflections involve complicated identifications that cut across familiar and unfamiliar racial, cultural, and national lines. Discussing Newell's work on Ghanaian popular fiction, Barber states that popular romance narratives in Ghana are 'read as "true": not in the sense of being mimetic representations of reality, but rather true in the sense of being *applicable* to reality' (1997: 357, emphasis in original). It is this applicability to reality that interests me. According to Liechty, the power of film realism – and that of other media – lies in convincing people that representations are possible; it is 'not some representation of "reality" but a representation of plausibility' (2003: 180). My aim is to show the reflective processes in which imaginative (representations of love) and practical (practices of romantic love) manifestations converge with the images and narratives presented in the media.[2]

Representing romantic love: films, television and advertisements

The development of the mass media took off during the 1990s as the result of the introduction of press freedom in 1991. The advent of a multi-party political system in 1992 led the government to liberalize the press laws and, at the same time, to liberalize the economy towards greater privatization and fewer market restrictions. The national broadcaster, the Kenyan Broadcasting Corporation (KBC), used to be the only station in the country and was often criticized for being the mouthpiece of the government. From 1992 there was a new growth of independent radio and TV stations, although the government held a firm grip on the media by refusing permits to many aspiring newspapers, television corporations and radio companies. In time, more and more companies entered the market, and in 2001 there was a variety of TV channels and print media besides the government-controlled media. Furthermore, the widespread adoption of media technologies such as audiotapes, telephone, television, VHS videotapes and later DVDs, mobile phones, satellite television dishes and the Internet have increased communication locally and internationally. Their use and reception have greatly expanded the private, personal and family spheres.

When discussing the supposed influence of Western culture in Nairobi, people often refer to US films. Hollywood films, exported to everywhere in the world, have become an icon of 'Western culture' because of their function in providing a view on 'the West'. Although young professionals are well aware of the differences between the US and Europe, when it comes to the emotionally laden issue of 'westernization', they conveniently regard the two continents as one entity. 'The West' often operates as a frame of reference in their professional work which is linked, often directly, to international corporations that depend on capital and expertise from the West. 'The West' is tangible but also elusive. This makes people curious as to what this West is about, and, more specifically, who these 'Westerners' are. In such a situation, the visualization of 'the West' by way of films plays an important role. US films have become a window on Western society for two reasons. First, the absence of European films explains the hegemonic position of US films.[3] Second, films serve as a source of information about the West and its inhabitants because other sources, such as the press, mainly cover political topics. The media play a decisive role in providing information about the rest of the world, but as far as the topic of love and sexual relationships is concerned, US films and soap operas have become the major source of information.

Many of the people I worked with were very curious about my Western background. They assumed, sometimes quite literally, that what they had watched in the cinema and on TV was typical for Western people, even when they knew it was not 'real'.[4] For example, when discussing romance, Eric asked me how often Victor and I had a candlelight dinner in a restaurant. I replied that we liked to go out for dinner once in a while but that I could not remember whether we had ever had a typical candlelight dinner; he looked at me in disbelief. Likewise, Pamela once asked me how many times Victor gave me red roses and whether he managed to find them in Nairobi. Similarly, Tom was shocked when I suggested an appointment for an interview on Valentine's Day, because he assumed I would be keeping the evening free for Victor to take me out. These examples pertain to the romantic aspects of love, though quite often both women and men also asked me about my relationship with Victor with regard to jealousy, domestic chores, handling conflicts, sex, in-laws, etc. Sometimes they explained that their way of thinking about Victor and me came from what they saw and interpreted from the media. When I told Martha about a fight I had with Victor, she remarked: 'Oh, so you quarrel just like we do? So … Vic is also a typical man, gosh I always thought he looked liked the perfect white man we see in films, being attentive and understanding and all.'

As well as providing a window on the Western world, US films are also a major source of entertainment. Going out to the cinema is a treat. It is the treat dimension of a date and a man will typically take his date to see a film on their first meeting. Women sometimes go to the cinema on a 'girls night out', while men are less inclined to do so with other men and mostly prefer to go for a drink instead. In 2001 there were three major cinemas in Nairobi featuring US blockbusters.[5] Certain films are considered to be a 'must see' and when a film is particularly appreciated, such as *Save the Last Dance*, people go more than once to see it. The majority said they liked 'romantic comedies' better than action and war films, political and drama films, or science fiction or historical films. When asked to judge the films in the cinemas, both women and men ranked the romantic films higher than other genres. By 'romantic films' they mean films with a story line in which a romantic relationship is the focus – the setting or story itself may vary from a more political one (such as the issue of race in *Save the Last Dance*) to comedy (films with actor Eddy Murphy, an Afro-American actor) to real life drama (like the film based on the life of Afro-American musician Tina Turner). The cinemas are new buildings, fashionably styled. They generally have a cosmopolitan air with their red carpets, bars to buy popcorn and Coke, and larger-than-life posters of movie stars.[6]

Locally produced films are virtually non-existent, except for a very occasional film that is not featured in Nairobi cinemas but may appear in African film festivals around the world. Reading about the popularity of Ghanaian and Nigerian films (Haynes 2000; Meyer 2004b), I have often wondered why these are not similarly popular in Nairobi. Most people I spoke with had seen one of the West African productions and they labelled it 'interesting'. Dana (aged 29) called it 'interesting anthropologically, but not quite fun'. Laura (aged 23) said she liked the plots of the Ghanaian and Nigerian films and there was a time when she was 'sort of addicted to them, I borrowed many copies from my Nigerian colleague, but in the end I got bored with them'. A few people remarked that these films ought to be more popular because of their African origin, but they admitted that they still preferred US films. Maurice (aged 27) watched West African films from a 'cultural point of view' and was of the opinion that West Africa should be an example for East Africans because at least the West Africans 'appreciated their own stuff'. However, Maurice was an exception.

According to Pamela (aged 22), Nairobians are 'brainwashed to liking American films because that is what we grew up with. I mean, during school holidays you would watch TV with a vengeance, as if we were starved by the absence of TV in [boarding] school.' Pamela voices the unease experienced by many young professionals; the deep ambiguity between appreciating Western media productions while at the same time feeling the need to reject these for ideological reasons. From their adolescence onwards, young professionals have watched television, which is dominated by Western entertainment programmes because of the lack of finance in Kenya for making local television, although that is changing. The effects of television – in providing a view on the world and representing romantic love – are similar to films, although television plays a different role in people's life because of its daily presence.

Television

When mentioning the influence of films, people often included in their comments the various soap operas shown on TV. Because of their narrative structure and detailed storyline, soap operas probably function even more prominently as a window on Western life. It is likely that as a teenager Pamela had seen more episodes of soap operas than films because of the unavailability of videos in her teenage years. In 2001, US series like *The Bold and the Beautiful, Ally McBeal, The Fresh Prince of Bel Air*, and *As the World Turns*, among others, were all being shown on various channels. In 2000, the first Latin American soap operas were introduced, soon followed by others such as *La Mujer de mi Vida, La Revancha, Esmeralda* and *Deceptions*. US and Latin American soap series were on the whole equally popular. In 2001, the United Nations weekly soap opera *Heart and Soul*, set in Kenya, was introduced. (The United Nations hoped to promote key development and health issues through the story line, and broadcast this series throughout Africa.)

Although strictly speaking the Latin American soap operas are not Western, their appearance is Western in the eyes of Nairobians because they feature wealthy upper middle class lifestyles. Moreover, the actors from the Latin American soap operas are rather 'white' according to Nairobians. Laura remarked that the Latin American actors have Spanish backgrounds, which makes them Western. The emergence of Latin American soap operas in Kenya therefore throws a different light on the complaint of 'westernization', as it implies that US films are in demand and are therefore supplied. The emergence of Latin American soap operas, however, suggests that the dominance of US films and soap operas has also been influenced by supply as opposed to demand. When in 2001 a 'new concept in Kenya' was introduced on the television – a dating game show called *Hairglo* – it was, just like *Big Brother Africa*, very popular and highly appreciated for being an 'African' version.

Although people hardly mentioned soap operas when discussing 'Western influence', the soap operas are significant sources of information in Kenyan people's imagination about 'the West' because of the considerable time people spend watching TV. In most homes the TV is turned on all the time, whether to watch programmes or just to have the TV on in the background. Typically, the TV is also turned on when visitors arrive. During the week, young professionals watch TV to relax from their hectic work and during weekends they socialize with friends on a lazy Sunday at somebody's home watching any TV programme. When going out they pick up friends from home and spend half an hour eating or chatting while watching TV, before venturing out into the Nairobi nightlife. At the end of the month, before salaries are paid and when they might have less money to spend on going out, more people stay at home during the evening. When I visited people at home, I would find them ironing their laundry or sorting out their administration in front of the TV. After an initial period of dating and going out, couples tend to spend more time at home. Watching TV is considered 'fun', 'relaxing' and sometimes 'informative' and 'romantic' in the case of the couples. People prefer soap operas, comedies and romantic films to political talk shows or documentaries, although the majority watch the news every day if possible.

In reaction to the difficulties regarding sex and love, an idealization and romanticization of love occurs, for which encouragement can be found in cinematic media. Many people commented in our conversations on the influence of TV and films in this regard. For example, when I visited Kenya in 2004, Grace (then aged 28) explained her doubts about her relationship with Winston which was gradually evolving into a committed relationship.

Grace: 'I trust Winston completely, he is sincerely honest, that's why I'm thinking of marrying him, but ... he is a little boring sometimes, I wish he was more...'

Rachel: 'More...?'

Grace: 'Well you know, more like ... with my birthday I want to be taken out for dinner and instead he cooked a special dinner for me and gave me a beautiful birthday card... I mean, I don't want to complain but... Oh, I guess I want to be treated like you see on TV and you want to tell your girlfriends next day like "Gosh, you know where Winston took me to, this great restaurant!", I want roses and all, I want something special.'

Rachel: 'You don't think that Winston preparing dinner is special?'

Grace: 'Of course that is special! A Kenyan man cooking for you alone, I at least managed to find one! [laughing]. Yes you're right, I guess I'm brainwashed by TV eh? [looking at me inquiringly].'

Other remarks were in a similar vein, as I heard many times about the 'brainwashing' influence of films and TV. This highlights people's dual relation of simultaneous self-distancing and self-recognition with regard to media.

Yet, many people explained that they took films and soap operas as examples to be followed in real life. Lucy commented on the breaking up of her short relationship: 'I guess we believe what we see on TV is true, about real love, we forget that it's actors speaking, we take it for real.' Or like Alex (aged 20) who narrated with a hint of irony that he intended to get married at 35, buy a house and start a family life 'just like in the films'. During an interview, Tom (aged 26) tried to define 'a man's attitude towards women' as follows:

> We guys, we are not like our fathers, we cannot be. I want companionship with my girlfriend, not the way like my parents but ... I want to share with her, I want us to make decisions together, I want her advice. Just like in that movie I saw the other day, there was this couple who lost a child and then they grew apart because they didn't understand each other's grief. It made me think 'What do I want from a woman? What is my attitude towards her?'

People explained how they liked to watch movies in order to observe others' experiences and the processes of considering choices. According to Robart (aged 23): 'Movie plots are like a test case, you learn from them because they are all about life experiences, and sometimes I recognize a situation'. Many people said they liked the 'plots' of love stories and the subtle exploration of the human psyche. They appreciated that films and soap operas made an effort to construct individuals with vivid interior lives. A few explicitly linked their interest in romantic films to the absence of visible affection between their parents and other adults – a clue to understanding the popularity and influence of these films, as I explain below. These comments suggest that beyond being a window on Western life, films and soap operas serve as a window on the functioning of relationships. If soap operas and films are important media in representing romantic love, another important medium for representing and hence codifying practices of romantic love in a local context is advertising.

Advertising

From the 1990s onwards, advertising shifted its focus from providing information about products to linking products with such intangibles as happiness and warm human relationships as well as fashion, beauty, personality, and the glamorous lifestyles (of some) in Nairobi. By 2001, some of these more elaborate advertisements had appeared in Kenya and people were beginning to discuss which ones they liked best. In response to the demand for mass and luxury goods and the spectacular development of leisure centres, the advertising industry boomed. The new industry provides a symbolic framework for forms of being young, hip and Kenyan through the advertisements, within which new ideals of intense passion are associated with and merged within new practices of consumption. There is more space for local representation in advertising compared to films and soap operas. The advertisements for Tusker beer, for example, are huge and dominant. The slogan in 2001 was 'My beer, my country', and advertisements often showed young professional men accompanied by one or two young elegant women enjoying a beer in a bar. Tusker is promoted as a Kenyan product so that in the Tusker advertisements nationhood, modernity and localness come together: the sense of belonging is created through nationalistic structures of feeling that are commodified and produced for a specific commercial goal. And it works: young professionals, women and men, were proud of 'their' Tusker and appreciated it very much if I joined them in having a Tusker. 'Nothing better than to bless the day with a Tusker', I often heard. There is a variety of local brands of beer and even when people were drinking one of these, they would argue that 'even Germans' liked Tusker better than their German beers.

Advertisements are interesting in the context of the debate about romantic love because they play on existing desires, while simultaneously producing such desires. The streets of Nairobi are decorated with various billboards, from small to huge, advertising a range of wares from soap to stereos. Typically, soap or facial cream advertisements, for example, exhibit a glamorous, young, slim woman whose secret of beauty is that particular soap or cream. A 2001 stereo advertisement exhibited a similar glamorous and bold looking woman in a tiger-print evening dress lying on the equipment. The models on the billboards, on TV, in magazines etc., all convey the same kind of woman: young, slim, beautiful and successful, clearly the image of a 'sophisticated woman'.

As well as the overrepresentation of sophisticated looking women in advertisements, over time images of young professional couples have taken on a larger role. Advertisements focussing on the lifestyle issues of the urban middle classes are increasing, compared to advertisements focussing on the lower middle class family (such as advertisements about rice and cooking oil, which typically show a happy lower middle class family). In the Smirnoff advertisements that became a total craze in early 2000, in which an alcoholic drink was portrayed as hip and cool, the focus was always on a couple. One advertisement shows a fashionable couple in a festive mood on their wedding day, without a hint of the locality being Nairobi, while another one showed a stylish dancing couple, looking like something straight out of a Rhythm and Blues video clip. Significantly, the slogan in the latter advertisement was in Kiswahili slang, in tune with recent trends of rap musicians, who are using *Sheng* (see note 6 in the Introduction) in their lyrics. Several mobile phone advertisements sought to show happy and radiant young couples dressed in smart-casual style. Their radiant joy at being able to reach each other at the touch of a button wherever and whenever was suggested by a halo around their heads that held the two together. From 2000 onwards, the tourist industry discovered the existence of a local market and started advertising safaris and beach holidays for the Kenyan middle class. Every now and then an advertisement appeared showing a happy young couple ready to go on a romantic holiday with, for example, a sunset and some lions in the background.

The huge billboards show what Illouz calls the '(stereo)typification of romantic vignettes' (1997: 43). In Nairobi the (stereo)typifications are fun-loving and romantic couples and happy and self-assured individuals positioned as lovers, surrounded by fashion, red roses, luxury items such as mobile phones, in beautified environments. The beauty-romance link is extended to cover the desire for self-expression. Romance is in turn fostered by the culture of consumption. In both 2001 and 2002, just before 14 February, Valentine's Day, the city of Nairobi was covered in pink colours and red hearts. Valentine's Day had become an amazing public spectacle to show off the prominence of love as the new organizing principle of relationships. One could observe people walking with chocolate boxes, roses and presents wrapped in pink paper hearts. It had become a complete celebration of new modes of loving and dating, with Valentine dinners, delivered bouquets, Valentine radio and TV, and a town dressed in pink. 'Tell your sweetheart how special s/he is!' blared from the radio stations. Some people in this study commented: 'It's totally over the top, it's ridiculous because ... it's too *western* for my taste' (Ongeri, aged 29 [his emphasis]). I believe it is a misconception to judge the celebration of Valentine's Day as histrionic because its dramatic popularity points at an existing desire.[7]

During the last decade, the process of what Illouz calls the 'romantization of commodities and the commodification of romance' (1997: 26) has unfolded at an amazing pace in Nairobi. As a result, practices of romantic love are codified in the public imagination. In the process of codifying romantic practices, the most important aspect is the visualization of romance. Imaginations of romance have found a local expression, often related to a global idiom and codes. Although some people felt uncomfortable with the obsession of Valentine's Day, they were nevertheless attracted to it and participated in it.

The privileging of the image

According to *Saturday Magazine* columnist Catherine Awuor, TV and films are not as influential as is generally thought: 'I don't think it [TV and films] affects us so much, except for ideas of romance like the flowers or when the guy must tell you when he loves you'. Awuor highlights the core issue here. People do not desire to be like the actors; it is more that they feel attracted to the symbols of romantic love. What one sees in Nairobi on the billboards and in the nightlife is the appropriation of symbols that have become a transnational phenomenon. In the newly expanding mass market, the theme of romantic love is being used as an advertising strategy in which the image of the couple has moved to centre stage. Films, advertising, soap operas and video clip images codify romance in visual 'vignettes' of erotic intimacy, luxury and leisure, from Nairobi to Bangkok to Amsterdam. This powerful presence of codified romance in the public sphere is what Illouz calls the 'privileging of the image'. According to her, the repertoire of images, artefacts and stories offered by contemporary global culture is varied but limited (1997: 5). This explains why people tend to comment upon consumerism in Nairobi as 'westernization', while they overlook the fact that they are actually commenting on visual clichés that are part of life in any large city of the world. These clichés have become hegemonic even though they are locally embedded. Originally, these visual clichés had their roots in the West, but the scale of appropriation and the embeddedness in local contexts have transformed them into transnational manifestations of contemporary capitalism.

The media have played an important role by appropriating symbols of romance as part of contemporary lifestyles through the representations of romantic love. The privileging of the image helps in understanding the popularity of the discourse on romantic love in Nairobi. Most importantly, the overt visual depiction of affection has a large impact in a society where affection is generally displayed in more covert ways. For Sereti, the main difference between her parents' marriage and her future marriage is that her parents have 'come to love each other through time', a love which she defines as 'respect for each other' and 'responsibility' towards the family. This is not what she wants – instead she wants a relationship based on love implying companionship, mutual trust, egalitarianism and romantic practices of affection. All but two of the people I spoke with have never seen their parents showing affection (in a romantic way), either physically or verbally. According to Kinyua (aged 30), whose parents 'have a good marriage': 'In our society, you didn't show love, you proved it. So I know my father appreciates my mother and therefore he always makes sure she is comfortable. That is what we see, what they share out of our sight? No idea, we have never seen a touch, an embrace. But they love each other, I'm sure.' Kinyua used the past tense in the first part of the sentence because he referred to an older practice, which he experienced as being in contrast to his own way of loving.

Many people discuss their parents' love for each other as 'appreciation', or 'respect', or 'dedication'. The young professionals themselves also aspire to relationships of appreciation and dedication, although they want this symbolized by romantic practices of affection. Some people explicitly said they never had 'role models' with regard to love: 'What do we know about practising love? Eh? We don't see expressions of love except in the movies, that's why we take them so seriously, because we lack role models when it comes to practising love. My father could not show his love for my mum, he would feel ashamed. Me, I'm not ashamed to show love by kissing in public' (Maurice, aged 27). Pamela, aged 22, said 'What? TV was my brother and sister! When I was young, I absorbed all kissing and embraces; that has affected me in what I want of course. I don't want a traditional man, no way.' The contrast between parents who displayed a more reserved attitude with regard to affection for each other on one hand, and the deliberate visualization of kissing, holding hands and undressing of lovers on the screen on the other hand, has clearly influenced the desires of young people.

According to Sereti, showing affection by being 'romantic' was an important marker of a good relationship, such as saying 'good night' through SMS messages by mobile phone. Moreover, she liked to show her affection by kissing David every time they met, although he did not like to do so in public. He felt a little embarrassed, while she would claim that kissing when greeting was a sign of 'real love' as contrasted to a 'casual relationship'. Sereti found justification for this belief in various films, and showing affection formed part of Sereti's insistence on intimate communication. In *Save the Last Dance*, the emphasis was also on the importance of communication leading to companionship, symbolized by their affectionate kisses. The way in which the young couple in the film managed to stay together despite conflicts, fights and criticism, by being able to focus on their love for each other, was scrutinized by Sereti.

As a result of the increasing presence of the romantic couple in Nairobi's advertisements and other media, the privileging of the image of romance has occurred in the media on a large scale. This privileging takes place by (stereo)typification of romantic vignettes, hence the imagination of romantic love is dominated by these romantic vignettes. The images provided by the media work as a catalyst in engendering romantic ways of being. The images of happiness, love and luxury evoke fantasy, but also inspire everyday practices among young professionals. They provide cognitive maps of romantic behaviour that help young adults orient themselves within the changing mores and situations of today. In effect, the role of images reinforces different ways of being: different ways of being woman, man, lover, friend, hip, sophisticated, worldly and much more. As such, young professionals' lives reflect processes of recreating subjectivation.

The manifestations of romantic love: music

Because TV often functions as a background presence, music channels are extremely popular for continuous viewing while people are at home doing domestic chores. One of the hits of 2001, rapper Shaggy's 'It wasn't me', was often featured on TV; the lyrics are as follows:

> *Honey came in and she caught me red-handed*
> *Creeping with the girl next door*
> *Picture this we were both butt-naked*
> *Love on the bathroom floor.*

The song has a seductive harmonious melody, which contrasts with the content of the words. One day when I popped in at Dana's (aged 29) house to say hello, she was folding up some laundry in the bedroom. When she heard the song on the TV in the living room she screamed 'that song, that's our national anthem!'. She raged on about men's excuses with regard to cheating and their 'weak attitude not to take responsibility and admit when having been unfaithful'. According to others, it was the musical arrangement that made the song so popular: 'It's good to dance to and to create a right mood to seduce somebody on the dance floor' (Michael, aged 27). The tune has an erotically soothing tone and rhythm; it invokes sensuality, while the words are about cheating. For Dana, the contrasting elements of the song echo her own contrasting experiences with the 'father of her child' who always managed to seduce her after another drama of cheating. That is why she screamed out that she considered this particular song the national anthem because, according to her, all Kenyan men cheat and get away with it.

Music channels like MTV and Channel 'O' (a South African channel) are also hugely popular because music plays an important role in contemporary life. Music is in fact one of the identity badges with which to express being hip and up to date. The craze of intense involvement with popular songs is fascinating. Both women and men know the lyrics by heart and whenever the first notes of a popular song strike up at a bar or club, there is a cry of recognition and people stream en masse onto the dance floor. Nairobi's nightlife is characterized by music, and people judge clubs by the music they play. The *Carnivore*, *Klup House*, *Psych*, *Pavement*, *Pizza Garden* and many other places organize different genre evenings like hip hop, soul, rap, rock and Rhythm and Blues 'nites'. The popularity of the clubs changes fast. In one year a club can go from being the hottest 'bash' in town to a place that people avoid because for some reason or another it has lost its glamour. Clubs have to make an effort to maintain a certain image and keep in with the latest craze. The popularity of 'foreign' music, such as that of US musicians, is partly related to the fact that the majority of the MTV clips feature black Rhythm and Blues musicians with whom Nairobian youth can identify. The clothing style, music and choreography of the music clips are similar to those seen on the South African Channel 'O' and other Western productions. The similarity suggests a global culture of certain musical styles – Rhythm and Blues, hip hop and rap – that appeal to young professionals. The rock music that appeals to young white people in the west is not popular in Nairobi and has no status.[8]

During 2001, local musicians drawing on transnational genres were becoming more and more popular. When I returned in 2004 their popularity had increased significantly and several groups were able to produce CDs (see also Nyairo 2005). These bands are part of a transnational music culture. Just like their audiences, they are the trendsetters of Nairobi nightlife: urban, young, fashionable, non-ethnic oriented and self-conscious. Their lyrics deal with contemporary issues like race, politics, generational conflicts and the craving for change, and are marked by critical texts very similar to rap music. Every now and then, Kenyan hip hop songs cause controversy because of their explicit sexual content. These confrontational texts are a novel phenomenon in Kenya, a society where patriarchal authority is seldom challenged publicly. They are often sung in English mixed with Kiswahili or *Sheng* (see note 6, Introduction). This resurgence of local slang is reflected in Smirnoff advertisements, where Kiswahili slang is also used. Nyairo calls these songs 'significant markers of cultural exchange' where various local and global features meet. She presents a very interesting example of a song that relies on a 'traditional' folk song, mixed with the tune of the hit by Marvin Gaye 'Sexual Healing', sung in a mix of different ethnic languages, which reveals the singer as a non-native speaker of the major language (Nyairo 2005). She analyses how this song signals the tension between generations, the diverse cultural backgrounds of the younger generation and their longing for a new sense of belonging.[9] These musicians are very popular in Nairobi and their music is broadcast endlessly on the radio. They symbolize changing lifestyles that are oriented towards cosmopolitanism and highlight the transnationalization of music, dance and sexuality (Mbembe 2008: 110).

Radio is an extremely popular medium (cf. Fardon and Furniss 2000). Even more than watching TV, people listen to the radio at home, before sleeping, in the car or *matatu* [public buses], at the office and in bars. There are various radio stations in Kenya. Some are regionally and ethnically oriented, some are aligned to certain political groupings, while others are commercially oriented and provide entertainment. The young professionals preferred the English-language stations. Radio is the essential medium for the dissemination of music and the popularization of certain lyrics, stars and fashions. The radio presenters are powerful actors in promoting particular styles of music and certain stars or causing the downfall of others. There is fierce competition among radio stations to have up-to-the-minute radio programmes defined by a captivating style and charismatic presenters.

Radio is breaking new ground, perhaps more than other media because it is the medium with the most subversive tendencies. The most controversial media-related topics about the integrity of the press, where even some politicians spoke out against 'such immorality', tended to be discussed on certain radio programmes. The big name in terms of opening up new horizons in 2001 was Caroline Mutoko of Kiss FM. For years she had a reputation for being controversial, as she was known to be fearless in her use of language as well as in her choice of topics. People admired her but also criticized her for being 'too much', according to Ruben (aged 28):

Carol Mutoko is certified Mad. I find [her] kind of gutsyness not the kind that is progressive. In my opinion, she is loud and obnoxious, in other people's opinions, she is crass and fearless. She tackles all kinds of issues, from the mundane to the truly shocking. One minute she wants to know why people lock toilets when they are taking a crap, to the next ... what kind of noises men make when they are making out [read cumming] ... yet on a good day she will interview the British High Commissioner and give him a piece of her mind. She once got into a lot of trouble when she ironically claimed that the Minister of Water had her head full of water, she was taken to court for that. She attacked the same minister too when she and a priest were car-jacked in the middle of nowhere, raising questions as to what their intentions were, parking in the dark. The priest said that he was giving her a document, before she flew off the next day Carol wanted to know if it was a six-inch document?? ... She speaks with a strong British accent and has this buffoon as her sidekick, who acts as a recently come into town up-country layabout in her show. (E-mailed on 15 June 2003)

In 2002, a survey of Kiss FM revealed that Mutoko put off people and she was told to tone down her style.[10] Nevertheless, the point is that people like Mutoko play an important role in opening up the discussion about sexuality in general, thus normalizing discussions about less 'gutsy' topics like condom use or safe sex.[11]

The popular radio programmes have a varied mix of talk shows with visitors, music sessions, information about celebrities, and interaction with listeners via telephone. These are blended with comments on society, politics, sports and stars. They are geared towards entertainment for the youth. One central aspect of this entertainment is relationships between women and men, and radio programmes keep track of (international and local) stars who date each other, marry or divorce, and all kinds of 'facts' about love and 'advice to pepper your relationship' is given. There are many references to love, romance, dating and sometimes sex. For example, when Valentine's Day approaches, all radio programmes are geared towards proclaiming what 'this year's hotspot for a romantic dinner' is, people are interviewed about where they plan to take their 'sweetheart', 'romantic' songs are played to 'get you in the mood for love', and so on.

The reason for the popularity of the radio programmes is to be found in the intimate character of radio. Although it has a public function, radio also has an unrestricted quality because of the lack of visual presentation. It leaves more room for personal interpretation, while the listening it requires suggests a more intimate relationship. Listening to the radio has a more interactive character than watching TV. People take a more distanced attitude with regard to TV and film; they watch and want to be entertained. According to Catherine Awuor, TV is popular because it is readily available. And indeed, Nairobians engage more directly with radio programmes because at the moment of presentation it is still in the making, which allows them to feel part of the process. Many people value radio highly because it has an energetic aura and it is inspirational. They appreciate the distinctive local character of the programmes that focus on local gossip and news in an overdramatic manner which is considered humorous, while at the same time incorporating a global focus blended with music. The exhilarating and enticing role of music is an important element of going out and dating, both important aspects of youth culture.

Practicing romantic love: dating

The imbuing of romantic love with associations of money, commodities and happiness, in combination with the new technologies of leisure, has meant that dating has become the symbolic practice of romance *par excellence* in Nairobi. 'By inscribing the romantic encounter into the consumption of leisure, the practice of "dating" marked the symbolic and practical penetration of romance by the market. This shifted the focus of the romantic encounter from marriage as a permanent and unique union to the fragmented but repeatable pursuit of pleasurable experiences' (Illouz 1997: 14). The experience of the body is unavoidably merged with the representations of romance, which in turn is built up out of the possibilities offered by the wider cultural context – in this case the media. The practices during dating, flirting and going out range from highly eroticized movements inspired by video clips, to particular styles of dress, to using seductive phrases borrowed from films or lyrics, or non-verbal practices such as a telling glance or caress. The media present leisure activities as being equivalent to intimacy and romance, such as the romantic dinner on Valentine's Day or the sensual dance imagined by Smirnoff. The immediate and intense experience of romance is translated into dating, which has become an essential, almost unavoidable practice among young professionals. The symbols and meanings that mark their forms of seduction offer a particular reading, not merely of excitement and desire, but of the significance of sexual life as a whole.

The intense experience of pleasure for its own sake, without being concerned about the views of the wider society, is manifest in the nightlife culture of Nairobi. The media images of romance invoke intense feelings, uninhibited sensuality, instant gratification, spontaneous pleasure and fun in aesthetically contrived settings, far removed from everyday life. Such romance has little room for the values of self-control, effort, and the compromises expected by career and family. The new morality of fun is embodied in the practice of dating. Romantic interactions have become a public form of experience, while at the same time, being erotic,

they presuppose a temporary withdrawal from group and family membership. This temporary withdrawal is manifested in the nightlife of Nairobi.
Without interference from society at large, this is the space where young
professionals can indulge in new ways of behaving. It is a place of rebellion, a sounding board to experience new ways of being. As we have seen
in previous chapters, dating suggests a reinterpretation of the whole range
of sexual meanings. Because of the privileging of the intense experience of
desire, dating practices open up new ways of sexual relating, and expand
the variety and structure of sexual relations. As I concluded in the two previous chapters, women are engaged in a process of appropriating sexual
pleasure as a goal in itself, while men are redefining sexual pleasure so as to
include being skilful in sexually gratifying women. All in all, sexual pleasure has gained a prominent place in the practice of dating and flirting.

In a way, it is a 'free' space where women and men truly meet on an
egalitarian level, precisely because they have created their own moral frame
of reference where, temporarily, the old social constructions are less important. A majority of women remarked how, during their college years,
they related as equals to their male friends and boyfriends (see also Dorcas's account in Chapter IV), but that this soon changed when they left
university. In their college years and later when they were dating, women
experienced a sense of egalitarianism that they associate with the new
path young professional women and men have taken. However, several of
them became terribly disillusioned, when they engaged in longer term or
'committed' relationships. The contested field lies in the dissociation between the equality that they experience when in bed, so to speak, and the
disruption of this intimate world when re-entering the wider social world.
This basic disjunction occurs because the nightlife takes place in a context
where social conventions cannot reach, but once back in society at large,
the conventional gender constructions lurk. This ambivalence is exacerbated by a general suspicion that exists between women and men because
of the prevalent notion among women men cannot be trusted, and the
equally prevalent notion among men that women cannot be trusted.[12]
Nevertheless, despite bad experiences, women and men desire a kind of
egalitarian relationship which they are willing to 'work on'. Print media
play a particular crucial role in this process.

Practices of mediation: magazines

As I have shown earlier (Chapter III), magazines occupy a special position
with regard to the interactive character of media. Besides using romance
as an entertaining component of their content, as films do, they have also

become a major source of practical information regarding the intricacies of relationships. This is not a new phenomenon; from the 1960s, but notably from the 1970s onwards, popular magazines have included information on marriage and relationships, particularly for the elites (Mutongi 2000; see Smith 2001: 132 on different African societies). Nowadays, such information is packed into articles presented as 'real life' events and confessional narratives.

With the liberalization of the media in the 1990s, an explosion in locally produced magazines came about. The oldest and most popular in 2001 was the *Saturday Magazine*, the Saturday pullout of the *Daily Nation*, one of the two largest dailies in Kenya.[13] In 1999 Rhoda Orengo was given the assignment to produce a lifestyle magazine and she has been the editor since then. When I interviewed her, she explained that the *Saturday Magazine* used to have a pullout that was more like an entertainment magazine for the family. According to their market research, women read more than men, so from a commercial perspective they decided to produce a magazine mainly geared towards women aged between 25 and 35 years old, professionals, married and non-married. They anticipated that they would reach men through the women: either that men would read the magazine after their girlfriends or wives had read it, or because the women would discuss what they had read. The goal of the *Saturday Magazine* is to be 'inspirational':

> We intend to be inspirational by on the one hand providing information about all kinds of life situations like relationships, health, and so on. On the other hand we want to break up silences about for example divorce, single motherhood and so on. In fact, women have come to be proactive when it comes to changes in society and we want to reflect that. You can say that society is male-centred and we are female-centred. Also ... we want to play into people's, women's, desires like travelling, a fashionable house, you know things that are not so common in Kenya but that are becoming part of our lives. (Ms Orengo, editor, interview on 20 January 2004)

The main article often focusses on social topics where relationships are central, where different situations and characteristics of relationships are analysed. These articles often take the form of interviews of (celebrity) couples or individuals, concentrating on one issue every week, such as family relations, customary expectations, marriage, love, career, children, parenthood, professional women, etc. According to the editor Rhoda Orengo, relationships are 'of great importance':

> Rhoda Orengo: 'We *have to* [her emphasis] write about relationships between men and women because that is what preoccupies women most. I believe we play an important role because people don't talk about the problems in relationships, but

they are there so we write about it. We make people face their own situations, like
… sometimes people don't realize they are in an abusive relationship and when we
have an article about it we always receive letters about women who say we helped
her to understand her situation.'

Rachel: 'How many letters do you receive on a weekly basis?'

Rhoda Orengo: 'Well … too many, I don't count them anymore, we have one
secretary who stores them, I guess tens every week. Sometimes people come to the
office to ask whether they can talk with an author, we have to send them to Amani
then [a well known counselling centre]. Like the other day a man came to see me
because I wrote an article about women who became extremely religious and he
told me his wife was like that and she was even neglecting their children.' (Ms
Orengo, interview on 20 January 2004)

That people actively respond to articles was also the experience of Catherine Awuor and Oyunga Pala, the two most well known columnists in
Kenya in 2001. Catherine Awuor said she received on average thirty responses by e-mail per week, and sometimes as many as eighty, depending on the topic. Awuor and Pala have written a weekly column for the
Saturday Magazine since it started in 2001. Officially they are assigned to
write about relationships and gender issues, with the occasional exception.
Awuor writes 'informative' columns in a 'humorous' manner, together
with another female author, Wayua Muli, about, for example, lack of affection, couples' fights, depression or the need for cooperation. Her aim is
to 'provoke discussions, write about sensitive problems and generally inform people about that which cannot be said'.[14] In the letters she receives,
people often say they are struggling with the topic she has written about,
and they either ask for advice or describe their personal experience: 'I
think we have taken the role of advisor because the family as it used to be
is not taking that role anymore, like the aunties used to advise you'. I read
a few letters she received and they were what you could call confessional
narratives, quite similar to articles appearing in the *Saturday Magazine*
when a topic is dealt with in the form of a personal narrative. Oyunga Pala
also received ten to sixty letters per week; however, according to him he
received mainly 'hate mail' from women. His columns are of a different
nature. Whereas Awuor writes informatively, with an ironical, critical and
sometimes serious tone, Oyunga Pala's columns are more sarcastic.

The most popular column in the magazine is Pala's 'Man Talk'. My
colleagues and friends used to discuss his articles from the latest edition
of the *Saturday Magazine* every Monday: clearly Pala had become a phenomenon of the early twenty-first century. He wants to be 'like a mirror
but not in an obvious way, I write about things as I see them around me
and thus I want to show the stupidity or the problem with it. But often
I get misunderstood.' His way of working is to write about his 'obser-

vations'. He reproduces stereotypes about women and men because 'I want to show how people actually think like this, so that they realize the ridiculousness of it' – an attitude which enraged some of the women I spoke with. Women in particular take him seriously and believe he is a 'male chauvinist' out to provide men with a legitimating excuse to continue their 'patriarchal ways of living' (Martha, aged 24). I noticed that the people I spoke with quite often misunderstood Pala's sarcasm. Men believed the column was meant to be 'fun' because it is about obvious stereotypes, which they claimed 'are partly true but also make you laugh'. I believe that women reacted so furiously because, although stereotypical, Pala touches on sensitive aspects of contemporary relationships like the importance of money and status.

Awuor's opinion that columnists like her have become advisors seems to have hit the nail on the head. In this respect, *Parents* magazine's weekly column on sexuality (see Chapter III) has become a major source of information for people about sexual issues, from female and male sexuality, to the meaning of sex, and practices of love and affection. More concretely, it deals with topics like sexual pleasure, foreplay, erotic dress and speech, female orgasm, male impotence, female lack of desire, sexual practices and positions, and much more. This column is the most explicit medium on sexual matters that is accessible to Nairobians from all walks of life, as the magazine is for sale on the street and is reasonably priced. The explicit descriptions about sexual practices are remarkable. The magazine is quietly present in a society that generally shuns explicit verbalizations of sex. Whereas references to sex are often critiqued as 'immoral', the matter-of-fact descriptions in *Parents* are condoned. Significantly, this column is targeted at married couples and this way it legitimizes writing about sexual practices.

Several men told me that if there was something they would like to discuss with their girlfriend but did not dare, they dealt with the issue by suggesting that their partner read a particular column from *Parents*. Eric explained how he tried to persuade his girlfriend to be less constrained when having sex:

> Eric: 'Ok... She [Mary] was a little passive; I thought she could not enjoy sex as much because she was passive. So then I decided to get a few copies from *Parents* for her to read. ... I couldn't talk to her about it, so one day I gave her the copies and asked her to read it. Then I left.'
>
> Rachel: 'And... What happened?'
>
> Eric: 'Yaah, she eased up a bit, slowly... I think you were right the other day about women needing to know their own bodies, I think she did not know quite how to enjoy sex and maybe she got to know it, maybe through *Parents*, or maybe she got the hint and talked with her girlfriends.'

Many of the people I spoke with said they read *Parents* as a teenager and gained much knowledge from it. For many women it was an 'eye opener' when they started to explore their sexual desire. *Parents'* message that sex is 'natural' positively connects with young professionals' desire to have a fulfilling sex life. Local magazines further play a major role in creating space for the discussion of emotional and relational problems. Although young Africans have for generations used various forms of media to reflect on their intimate relationships (Behrend 1998; Fugelsang 1994; Larkin 1997), an important shift has occurred with the introduction of a therapeutic ethos.

The therapeutic discourse on relationships

After Sereti and I left the cinema having watched *Save the Last Dance,* we went to have a drink in the cinema bar, a dark red velvet-carpeted, pleasant space. She recounted the story of the film, referring to the film characters and what they had experienced. Gradually, while figuring out why the characters did as they did, she began to speak in the second person 'but suppose he does that to you, one is inclined to react…'. Eventually, she analysed her relationship with David while referring to the film. In her view, she needed to explicitly conceptualize ideas of love and relating because of 'lacking a role model' and because 'our generation want … modern relationships'. She wanted to be 'intimate, not only sexually but also emotionally'. In her relationship with David she tried to bring into practice this ideal of love as a very specific sort of knowing about and 'being close' to another person, 'sharing thoughts' and 'showing feelings'. After watching *Save the Last Dance* Sereti said that David was not as responsive to her as the man in the film had been to the woman. She compared David with the actor and accordingly analysed what their relationship was lacking. In the act of talking about her relationship with David, she construed a personal narrative that was both formative and reflective.

Sereti's account is similar to the experiences of many people I spoke with. Both women and men who went to the cinema expected or hoped their boyfriends or girlfriends would behave towards them in the way people did in the films. Larkin mentions the same type of expectations from men in Kano, in north Nigeria, who had watched Indian films (Larkin 1997: 422). Among young professionals, both women and men commented on their partners by referring to films, and even more to 'real life stories' from magazines. These accounts suggest that narratives from the mass media crisscross individual narratives and generate transformations in constructions of gender and sexuality. This redefinition of gender involves a redefinition of how women and men relate to each other; hence transformation recreates a different, gendered sense of self for women and men. For Sereti and others, media representations of love and sexuality provided them with a sense of what is possible. While Sereti's attempts to learn lessons from the media in her life illustrate the sharp difference between ideals and implementation, she and others continued to look at their own conflicts in the light of how similar conflicts were articulated and resolved in different media. Representations of love and sexuality thus provide models for a new kind of individuated subject that feed into young professionals' search for alternative forms of gender relations. By probing the plausibility of these models, they are engaged in a process of simultaneous self-distancing and self-recognition that is fundamental to the therapeutic ethos and becomes an 'important source of the formation of the self' (Illouz 1997: 198).

According to Illouz, therapeutic discourse is an offshoot of the twin spheres of mass media and consumerism, and as such became an important part of self-formation. The core propositions therapeutic discourse advances is that 'relationships can be divided into "healthy" and "unhealthy"'; intimate relations are 'open to study' and can be 'evaluated by experts'; and people can acquire knowledge about romantic relations 'through work and the application of appropriate strategies and techniques' (Illouz 1997: 198–99). Rather than accepting didactic and moralizing advice from others, the therapeutic ethos insists that the solution to romantic problems lies in self-knowledge and reflexivity. Sociologists have associated the growth of a therapeutic ethos with processes of individualization (Furedi 2002; Lears 1983; Nolan Jr. 1998). An important undercurrent of the therapeutic ethos, Furedi (2002) argues, is the belief that one's emotional well-being is vulnerable to social influences.

While there are strong similarities between the therapeutic ethos of romance described by Illouz, and processes in contemporary Nairobi such as the close alliance between mass media and consumer culture, there are also significant differences. According to Illouz (1997), the therapeutic ethos appeals to middle and upper class US couples because it suggests that they can control intimate relations and fix romantic problems. Moreover, the explanatory function of the therapeutic ethos offers reasons for why things are the way they are. Sociologists have argued that secularization, consumer culture, and the growth of expert knowledge have combined to encourage members of the middle class, in particular, to judge their relations according to quasi-clinical notions of what is 'healthy', in ways that may foster feelings of victimization. According to Furedi (2002: 24), in his critique of a therapeutic ethos, subjects become docile objects of disciplinary knowledge, 'where empowerment means little more than knowledge of voluntary resignation to authority'. By contrast, the attraction of therapeutic discourse for middle class Nairobians lays not only in its explanatory power but also in its potential to provide an alternative relationship epistemology. To wit: by the time therapeutic discourse became widespread in the United States following the Second World War, it was broadly accepted among all social classes that people should choose their own marriage partners. As a result, in that context, therapeutic discourse became a tool that couples could use to fix their relationships rather than to justify their formation or existence. My argument for contemporary Kenya is different; a therapeutic ethos helps young professionals in Nairobi, who are experiencing rapid changes in marriage patterns, to understand and act on their love relations. Therapeutic discourse, with its emphasis on self-understanding and reflexivity, offers young professionals a new way to understand the very foundation of their relationships. They engage a therapeutic ethos to reflect on their personal aspirations and decisions, and to gain skills necessary for enacting lives that they hope will be different from those of their parents.

Although the precise moment of this discourse's entry into the Kenyan public sphere is difficult to discern, it appears to have arrived during the 1990s amid the liberalization of the media. According to Mutongi (2000), the male staff of *Drum* magazine, featured since the 1960s, who authored the magazine's 'Dear Dolly' advice column, offered off-the-cuff advice that aimed to be both didactic and witty. In contrast, today's editors problematize love and sexuality, and rather than offering clear-cut advice and condemning practices such as premarital sex, they encourage self-reflexivity and greater communication within relationships. Whereas previously advice – whether from elders or the media – was directive (Njau 1993; Nzioka 1994), nowadays media experts encourage self-reflection as the most important first step to solving love problems, as Rhoda Orengo's explanation above testifies. The media's foregrounding of personal narratives highlights how middle class Nairobians have shifted away from interpreting marriages as familial unions. By embracing therapeutic discourse, they emphasize the need to choose partners on the basis of companionship, egalitarian relationship, emotional investment and mutual sexual satisfaction rather than familial, ethnic, or reproductive considerations. The question, of course, is to what extent this new perspective will lead to significant changes. This particular group of young professionals was rather ambitious and, perhaps, idealistic. It is quite possible that as they get older they might grow into more normative patterns. Yet, the fact that therapeutic discourse has been adopted in institutional settings, for example in churches as I will discuss below, suggests that its influence might be far reaching and lasting.

In a country where almost everybody belongs to a church or mosque and where, as John Lonsdale states, contemporary culture is 'soaked in Christianity' (Berman and Lonsdale 1992: 217), the adoption of therapeutic discourse by churches is significant. In October 2001, I attended, with my partner, the pre-marriage counselling class of the Nairobi Chapel, a Baptist church with a middle class membership. These classes are organized twice a year for couples intending to get married. Although we had no such intention, after explaining the goal of my study, I was allowed to participate provided that my partner accompanied me. All of the participants appeared to be successful professionals. In general, the women were aged below 30, while the men were near to or above 30. An older couple, around 40 years old, supervised the twelve-session course that concluded with a weekend at a holiday resort near Lake Naivasha. Every session had a theme such as 'what is love?', 'love and sexuality', 'marriage and money', 'managing conflicts', and 'relatives and in-laws'. The goal of the class was to expose them to the unavoidable obstacles in marriage and to prepare them for dealing with those obstacles.

According to Mrs Maxwell, the coordinator, young couples in Nairobi do not have proper role models, as their situation is decidedly different from that of their parents. Most significantly, they have never learned to deal with conflicts between spouses, and according to her, that was the reason why 'many men were unfaithful'.[15] According to Mr Njuguna – the husband of the older couple who led the group – the problem of young couples is that they operate in a 'vacuum' because they are left to themselves: 'There are no aunts and uncles to advise them and even the parents do not address their children anymore. Young couples live in a vacuum because they have not been told how to make their marriages work.'[16] Mrs Maxwell and Mr Njuguna make a very important observation: social change has not only affected gender and sexuality, it has also affected the social bonds responsible for educating people about sexuality (see also Ahlberg 1994; Prazak 2001). The traditional role of certain family members, to educate children about sexuality, has not been replaced, certainly not by parents, as it is difficult for them to speak openly about sexuality to their children (Njau 1993). Many civil society group or institutions attempt to fill this gap, for example churches, women groups, universities as well as the media.

The class sought to present young couples with a middle class way of forging progressive or modern relations and avoiding older or immoral modes of being. To my surprise, the examples given to the class did not specifically focus on their lives as Christians. Rather, the small nuclear family in which fathers play football with their children on Sundays was presented as the icon of contemporary happiness. Similarly, husbands were defined as companions and warned not to take their authority within the household for granted or to make decisions without involving their spouses. The class leaders instructed men to earn their respectability by being responsive and caring fathers and husbands, by being open to emotional and personal engagement with others, and by sharing their own preoccupations and thoughts. Despite the church's Christian theology that considered men to be the heads of households, in the classes, male privilege was not encouraged. Moreover, the ideal of husband as provider proved unrealistic for these couples as wives often earned equal or higher salaries than their husbands. The classes redefined men's household role, from being the authority figure to being responsible for the emotional well-being of their families and being companions to their wives. Christian ideologies and practices thus also portray love-based unions as an essential part of modern personhood (see also Wardlow 2006 on Papua New Guinea).

Class leaders promoted communication as a key concept. The teachers encouraged men in particular to learn to speak their minds and share their preoccupations with their girlfriends. We were given life stories of couples' conflicts to think about and discuss in small groups, and were asked to understand both sides of the conflict. Then we were made to act out a drama, speaking offensively and then non-offensively. The leaders also presented honest communication as a way of avoiding conflicts that were often caused by misunderstandings and ignorance. Moreover, communication was presented as the key to a loving relationship. Participants responded to the class with unequivocal enthusiasm. The women were generally satisfied with the set-up of the classes, stating that it was good preparation and that they had gained much from it. The men generally admitted to having been anxious, but claimed that they had gained an understanding of certain topics or had learned the importance of talking without becoming offensive. One man said he had never realized that 'communication is a skill on its own and extremely necessary in a marriage'. 'You know,' he continued, 'I always thought communicating is talking, but I learned the importance of listening.' Another man explained that he had been a little 'nervous' about starting to discuss financial matters with his wife-to-be, because 'money is so tricky'. Discussing money and relationships in the group made him understand that it was possible to do so without causing tension.[17] Although men were less familiar with these skills, their positive response suggests that they were persuaded by the therapeutic approach, which explained how love is enhanced through communication and how communication is central in making one's relationship work.

The notion of working on one's relationship resonates with older notions of marriage as cooperative – if not egalitarian – partnerships. Odhiambo, drawing on the work of Laura Kipnis, argues that 1970s Kenyan novelists explained adultery by the fact that marriage itself was understood as work: 'as labour for which the spouses need to be compensated either affectively or materially, and in the absence of which marital intimate transgression may occur' (2003: 434). According to Odhiambo, the drama of adultery and the reasons behind it were generally understood as private and personal affairs and were not recognized in the larger public discourses, and that is why they were told in popular fiction. Two decades later, these personal narratives of love and its perils have clearly entered the public domain. More importantly, public discourse promotes a therapeutic ethos that influences the private lives of people such as the young professionals in this study.

The concept of 'making a relationship work' is common in such prewedding counselling classes and in advice columns, and it exemplifies the therapeutic discourse on relationships. Especially in the magazines, the advice columns and informative articles focus on how to 'improve' a relationship, a marriage or a love life (*Saturday Magazine*, 21 March 2001: 4); how to 'avoid mistakes' (*Saturday Magazine*, 8 September 2001: 6); or how to 'learn how to love' (*Saturday Magazine*, 11 June 2001: 5). According to Rhoda Orengo and Carole Mandi (editor of *Eve*), these articles are 'very important' to people, as the many reactions they receive testify:

> You must understand that we are in a kind of transition phase, why do you think more and more women are divorcing? Because they are refusing to live like their mothers … the women of our generation, and men of course, are the explorers of how they want it otherwise. We offer them ideas. (Ms Orengo, interview on 20 January 2004)

Indeed, Sereti was eager to discuss the movies she has seen in a reflective manner because it is a pivotal act in the process of probing the possible avenues of her own relationship. Women articulated this therapeutic narrative more than men did. For men, shifts in relationships and gender implied a more thorough redefinition of masculinity; for women it implied an appropriation of more space to manoeuvre, while for both women and men it implied working towards a more egalitarian relationship. In a way, women had more to gain from it. Since women in general are reasserting themselves in the realm of work, they are rejecting the idea that the institution of marriage is the only way to safeguard their economic standing, and that they must marry to survive. As they become less dependent financially, women are expecting more emotional fulfilment from marriage and are less concerned about the economic security that marriage can provide.

In general, more women than men explicitly invoked the discourse of love. The frames of plausibility offered by various media speak more to professional women's concerns because they experience more directly the constraints of patriarchal ideology. As just mentioned, women look to marriage more to fulfil their emotional needs than to offer economic security. Women used the concept of love more interactively when reflecting on their relationships, as seen in the case of Sereti. She turned the idea of love over in her mind, asked her friends' opinions, came back to David with a few proposals and later evaluated her attempt to 'make her relationship work'. The question of 'what *is* love?', and how it affects the behaviour of partners, is something that women pondered. The majority of men saw love as a self-evident notion. If I asked them why they did such and such, they typically said 'because I love her'. Men found it more difficult than women to answer my questions when I was trying to probe what this meant. Tom (aged 26) desperately called out at one point: 'Oh! You and your difficult questions! I just loved her [the girlfriend with whom he wanted to have a child]! It means that I cared for her, that I supported her, that I respected her ... basically that I wanted our relationship to work.' For men it was, generally speaking, more difficult to translate the effects of a 'love relationship' because men are less inclined to speak about personal issues because of the notion that they are supposed to be self-reliant. As a consequence, men are less engaged in the therapeutic discourse. This is, in fact, a global trend (Whitehead 2001: 156–58).

It is easy to fall for the cliché of 'men want sex while women want a good conversation' because it presumes a simplistic definition of what intimacy is (although the women and men in this study themselves used this cliché). Men indicated that they lack the skills which women have in relation to speaking about intimacy. When talking about love, they mainly referred to confiding in someone, which was understood as intimacy, although not many men used the term 'intimacy'. They said that confiding in a woman is of course contrary to remaining autonomous; hence they feared betrayal, or exposure. This fear inhibited them from speaking confidently with a lover in a non-committed relationship. Since most men were not engaged in committed relationships, they did not often get into situations where there was a chance to speak intimately with their girlfriends.

For a few men, however, it was different. The discourse on love suggests that equal companionship is central to contemporary relationships, and men like Alex (aged 20) and Maurice (aged 27) related to this notion when they said that 'friendship' was most important in their relationships. They distanced themselves from the hegemonic notion of masculinity, and from the social pressures to conform to prevailing notions that men should not appear to be 'soft', or unmanly. Speaking about love and confiding in a woman is typically represented as 'soft'. Alex compared himself with his brothers as they 'were only looking for the sexual aspect of a relationship', while he 'also want[ed] the intimacy'. Maurice called himself 'not much of a real man'. They regarded themselves as different to the norm, which they were in a way, because they made an effort to reflect on the effects of love, as Sereti does above.

This does not mean that other men were not intimate. When Ongeri (aged 29) explained, for example, why he had multiple partners at the same time, he said that he liked being 'homely' with Atieno. He liked to cook for her and watch TV together. The fact that he remained silent about this to his friends because 'they wouldn't understand' and that 'besides, it is only meant for the two of us', implies a closeness and familiarity that indicates intimacy. Likewise, Tom e-mailed me in 2002 about his relationship with Lucy, a relationship he had been 'waiting for all this time'. To indicate the distinctiveness of this relationship he mentioned how he took care of her at night when she had menstrual cramps, by making tea and keeping her warm and comfortable. Men in committed relationships tended to be more inclined to be intimate.

In the public realm, the relation between love, intimacy and sex is presented as self-evident, and the discourse of love is therefore powerful. Men are gradually appropriating love and intimacy, as the biographies of men like Alex and Maurice indicate. However, as Alex put it, this requires that men expose their 'carefully tended egos because we are not used to speak[ing] about ourselves as women do'. No doubt this is because women's growing appropriation of sexual pleasure as central to self-expression corresponds with the therapeutic discourse, which describes it as an important source of the formation of the self. For men, shifts in gender relations imply a more thorough redefinition of masculinity, and men fear being criticized for compromising their masculine identity. Nevertheless, many young professional men are responsive, in various degrees, to therapeutic discourse. An important defining ideal of this group is that they relate to women as equals, whether they are colleagues, lovers, or friends. Young professional women and men are engaged in a joint project because of their distinctive position in society. They see themselves as a Kenyan *avant garde* committed to forging more modern relationships. Most men justify their embrace of greater gender equality by explaining that they are modern men. As a result, both female and male young professionals strive toward more egalitarian relationships. They testify to 'an emerging levelling process of existing differences in the status of women and young men' (Mbembe 2008: 110).

Sign of the times: imaginations and practices of romantic love versus 'westernization', or the perils of modernity

A comparison of northern Nigeria and Nairobi regarding media and the representation of love provides a helpful way to come back to the problematic role of the West. In an article on the popularity of Indian films in Kano, northern Nigeria, Larkin (1997) explained why these films are more popular in the north than in the south of Nigeria. Larkin explains that in the north there is a cultural proximity between Muslim Hausa culture and Hindu culture. It is exactly this proximity that is largely absent in Nairobi. All major cinemas featured the Indian film *Ayaan*, a major production in 2001, and only one person I knew went to see it. However, according to Fugelsang (1994), Indian films are popular in Mombasa, on the Kenyan coast. One similarity between Kano and Mombasa is that both are Muslim societies, and I would not be surprised to find that Larkin's analysis of Kano applies to Mombasa as well. He explains the popularity of Indian films as providing a 'parallel modernity': 'Indian films offer [viewers in Kano] a way of imaginatively engaging with forms of traditions different from their own while at the same time conceiving of a modernity that comes without the political and ideological significance of the West' (1997: 407). In Indian films dress is similar to the Hausa style of dressing, epitomized by long kaftans, while kissing is rare, and nudity is absent. When love songs and sexual relations occur, they are kept within firm boundaries. Furthermore, Indian films place family and kinship at the centre of the narrative tension, based on the strict division of the genders, and these films frequently explore the tension that arises in a society attempting to preserve traditional moral values at a time of profound change. The Hausa audience can identify with these tensions and with other qualities, which are very different in Western film genres. If we turn to the young professional audience in Nairobi, I would expect viewers in Nairobi to appreciate exactly those aspects that Kano viewers dislike in Western films. While, according to Larkin, Hausa and Indian culture share important similarities, this conclusion suggests that Nairobian and Western cultures also have major similarities with which young professional viewers can identity, at least with regard to the above mentioned aspects.

Young professionals are therefore entangled in the volatile public debate so that watching films can no longer be neutral. They are obliged to position themselves in the current debates polarizing 'African' against 'Western' and 'modern', despite the fact that these categories are flawed, as their lives testify. Nevertheless, the sentiments engendered by these debates are so powerful that the viewers in Nairobi feel they cannot escape the imperialistic significance of 'the West' when they watch Western films.

This is exactly the source of frustration for young professionals when they complain about 'westernization': their ambivalence towards 'the West' as a source of pleasure as well as anxiety, and as fundamentally different to their sense of being 'African'. The point is that besides reifying African-ness, they also reify 'the West' as significantly different, i.e. 'non-African' and thus 'non-authentic'. As I explained in the Introduction, their life-styles are not expressions of something 'deeper' – like transitions between distinct social types, distinguishable as traditional and modern – but they are modes of practical action in contemporary urban social life.

Despite the opposition voiced by young professionals towards Western films and other media, through their imaginations of romance they also identify with certain themes of these media. *Save the Last Dance* was adver-tised as a love affair which crossed borders. The contrasts between black (man) and white (woman), lower and middle class, Rhythm and Blues and ballet, and masculine and feminine, resemble conflicts that young professionals can identify with; they parallel the contrasts regarding their cultural anxiety, or moments of distrust in their own relationships. An important point of recognition – or hope – is the message that love is en-during and empowering. The mutual affection between the lovers in the film is an intense bond that is represented as real love; it even resists social obstacles like racial labelling. Love's capacity to overcome social difficul-ties lies in the intensity of romantic love, the theme of the film. The valid-ity of compatibility and affection among lovers is also reflected in the way in which this young couple manages to overcome societal and personal problems, thus reflecting the strength of youth. Such representations of the power of love and youth appeal to young professional Nairobians. When films feature Afro-American actors, like *Save the Last Dance*, people identify with the actors even more.

Despite their reification and rejection of 'the West', young professionals identify with Western dominated media and use it as a sounding board in their lives. Sereti's comparison of the male actor's behaviour with that of David shows that the media provide her with the experience of modernity as a space of imagined possibilities. Abu-Lughod states that 'television drama in Egypt might be understood most directly as a technology for the production of new kinds of selves' (2002: 116) and I believe this is an im-portant point. The media subtly work at personal and interpersonal levels by popularizing a distinctive configuration of narrative, emotion and sub-jectivity. The media advise on psychological well-being and interpersonal relationships through the discourse on love, which presumes a durable emotional tie that can be established with another person on the basis of qualities intrinsic to that tie. As I showed in Chapter IV on women, and in Chapter V on men, when love is essential in the definition of sexuality, sexual intimacy becomes a matter of the self, of the sexual subject, in a symbolic interaction with another. Sexual intimacy and romantic understanding of relationships then become fundamental to self-identification as a contemporary person. The growing cultural hegemony of media images is thus both responding to a particular need for, as well as engendering, new modes of subjectivity and new discourses of personhood.[18]

The popular print and radio media dovetail with social praxis in Nairobi. Foreign films and soap operas offer viewers a way of imaginatively engaging with representations of romantic love, which have connotations of a modernity that comes with the political and ideological significance of the West. This association is the root of concerns, as articulated in the notion of 'westernization', of which the young professionals are often accused and which they also use in a reductive manner when they feel overwhelmed by Western dominance. The controversy over 'westernization' indicates wider concerns about the shape and direction of contemporary Nairobian, or Kenyan, society and culture and not so much about the actual copying of Western modes of being. As I have shown in this chapter, rather than copying, Nairobians make use of media as a sounding board to reflect on their personal lives, exactly because their lives already differ from the stereotypes that conventional perceptions might have. 'These trends suggest that we should be wary of telling any unilineal stories about modernity, melodrama and individualism' (Abu-Lughod 2002: 116).

Conclusion

The wide use and popularity of magazines, films, soap operas, and radio indicates a widespread transformation in perceptions about relationships. All media use different channels, but they mutually reinforce each other in their response to young adults' aspirations and needs. This process affects, implicates and grants agency to young professionals. The interest in the media and among young professionals in love and relationships points to the search for different perspectives on developing one's relationship with oneself. What these mass media in fact reflect is that the younger generations find themselves in ambivalent situations arising from a context where the conventional patterns cannot be upheld. The change points not to a change in relation to love as the basis for relationships, but something more specific: a change in the practices of romantic love. Radio is an important transmitter of trends and plays a role in creating a narrative of romantic love, whereas films and soap operas play an important role in the representation of images of romantic love. Magazines provide the means for incorporation of romantic love on the individual level. Taken together, these media have played a major role in the creation of a discourse on romantic love as one of the main aspects of contemporary relationships in Kenya. Nevertheless, practices of romantic love imply changes in perceptions of love. As Beidelman remarked, 'love, like all strong emotion, is difficult to control, and its course is unpredictable' (1986: 202). In consequence, love and sex can be a potential threat to the social order, as I elaborated on earlier. When young professionals take on new ways of loving, and hence of identifying, society cannot but react. Practices of romantic love, then, become the icon of 'westernization' for older generations and other moral guardians, and others such as Westerners. However, understanding practices of romantic love as westernization misses the point; as the media create models of romantic love, which young professionals use as a sounding board, they become real because these models are not seen as mimetic representations of reality but as applicable to reality.

The personal narrative has become the chosen medium to report on love and to reflect on love. The new interpretation of love emphasizes a more individual approach with regard to partner choice, an emphasis on the need to be compatible with someone. How to recognize this compatibility has become a central concern in Nairobi, reflected by many romantic films and self-help columns. The people I worked with might not have been willing to speak out publicly, but in the confined space of the interview context, they were willing to try out their narratives. They made themselves the subject in their own stories as they recounted their experiences and desires. This view of themselves was reinforced by the context of their lives which positioned them as explorers of new lifestyles, and subjects in transformation processes. This narrative practice informed their sense of self by making use of a reflexive therapeutic discourse articulated in the various media.

We now come back to Sereti, with whom we started this chapter. Young professionals recognize the challenges of achieving such relationships and thus are keen to spot success stories whether reported in the media or by individuals. In 2002, Sereti sent me the following e-mail:

> ... and you see the Kenyan population take in what they read and see. Oyunga [columnist] now is a point of reference in men's opinions, guys take him seriously. This kind of assimilation in magazines and movies just flows in and affects society in one way or the other. I think that one culture cannot remain the same and I think that Kenyans are trying to find a balance. We all want a relationship like that of a movie or soap opera on TV but we know it doesn't work that way. And this is what I really oppose when it comes to what the media is making us [into], we have to find our own way, but that is not easy as you know. By the way?! Do you remember I told you I didn't know a couple that could be my example? I found them, finally, and what I like is that they are not westernized but very African but the man is not

a typical African man, I liked him at once when he handed over the car keys to her to drive when they were leaving church. Real love changes a man eh?!

Sereti's relationship with the American eventually floundered, as they 'did not match'. She was sad, and hoped for a more compatible partner next time. Her hopes were rekindled when she met the couple described above, who became her example, as they were 'modern the African way'. The gesture of him handing over the car keys to his wife indicates how egalitarian their relationship is. It was a symbolic gesture, reflecting their up-to-date status. In Nairobi, romantic love is a sign of the times.

Notes

1. *Save the Last Dance* is about a white teenage girl who ends up living in a back street district of Chicago with her father after the death of her mother. Her parents were divorced and she grew up with her mother in a white middle class environment where she was about to start a career as a ballet dancer. Her father, by contrast, is an exhausted jazz musician living in a small and worn out apartment. The beautiful, delicate blonde stands out in a rough black neighbourhood. She is an outcast at the secondary school until she meets a beautiful black girl who turns out to be a teenage mother abandoned by the boyfriend/father. The friend's brother is 'different' from the other men as he studies hard to 'get out of the projects' [the poor neighbourhood]. He and the white girl become involved in a love affair, which their peers disapprove of because of the racial difference. Eventually hostilities and difficulties affect their relationship to such an extent that they break up, only to discover they cannot live without each other. As a symbolic gesture, the boy comes to watch her delayed entry in the ballet scene, after he had taught her how to dance Rhythm & Blues properly. She performs a new style, in which classical ballet and Rhythm & Blues are fused. Music and dance is the vehicle through which they express their hearts' desire to be together, forever.
2. At the end of the 1990s, the Internet became a booming business in Nairobi. Young professionals make intensive use of the Internet, mainly for personal communication and to acquire information. Chat-groups are very popular and, interestingly, there are many forums discussing issues of cultural heritage and identity at the turn of the century, see for example http://madkenyanwoman.blogspot.com/2005/06/trashin-tradition.html.
3. European films are generally not available, except for the ones shown during the annual European Film Festival staged at the French Cultural Centre.
4. When talking about my Western background, people often remarked 'I heard from so and so who lives in Europe (or United Kingdom or United States) that it's not what you see on TV' and then they asked me to explain 'how it really is'.
5. Indian films are also shown in these cinemas. There are always a few Bollywood films on offer for the relatively small but economically significant group of Indian Kenyans. Non-Indian Kenyans hardly ever watch these films.
6. In fact, Nairobians see more films on TV than in the cinema, as local broadcasting companies KBC, KTN and Nation TV feature older American films on a daily basis. Furthermore, all the young professionals I knew had a video player and regularly watched videos, sometimes legal copies and even more often illegal copies of American films. Copies were shared and lent to many different people and the illegal copy trade is a thriving business.
7. According to Dawn (aged 27), 'you are looked down upon when you don't have a date so ... well, beside feeling sad for not being asked for a date, I was ashamed about it so ... I

bought myself flowers to take to the office as if I had a date, I invented one.' Lucy behaved similarly and invented a story of how a man took her out to a restaurant in order 'not to lose face. It's so so stupid, I know, but I feel like I am not wanted. Not having a boyfriend for so long [six and a half months] makes me doubt myself, especially in the face of others. Everyone has a boyfriend so why not me? I want to look normal.' When asked where the pressure came from, Lucy answered 'It's just around you, not that my friends criticise me, not at all, but it's ... maybe our lifestyles, what we aspire [to]. I cannot watch a movie or listen to the radio or I get the feeling to be a failure.' Lucy's and Dawn's worries highlight the role of the media in creating an influential discourse of romantic love.

8. Interestingly, the clubs frequented by young professionals rarely play *Lingala* music (from Congo), even though young professionals appreciate dancing to it every now and then. When they feel like enjoying a *Lingala* 'nite', they go to different clubs from the ones they normally visit. These latter clubs are typically not 'hip'; they draw a wider variety of customers from different social groups and notably older people (in their forties), and they are also cheaper.

9. Nyairo also discusses the award-winning novel *Discovering Home* by Binyavanga Wainaina (2003). The novel attests to the plurality that informs young professionals' lives and highlights the vitality and determination of this generation. However, with the exception of Maurice, none of the people I spoke with had read the novel. The cultural renaissance that is currently taking place in Nairobi seems, as yet, confined to a small group.

10. Personal communication with one of her colleagues.

11. Liberalization has offered an alternative voice to the people of Kenya. The lack of guidelines and clear media policy has meant there are no restrictions on the content of the independent radio stations' programming or on the content of the press. In 2002 the government decided to try to regain some control. It introduced a new bill that seeks to regulate media practice. However, the Kenyan Union of Journalists, fearing a return to a repressed media, fiercely and successfully opposed this bill. The government defended itself by referring to the need to curtail what is called the 'boulevard press'. From 2000 onwards two new kinds of print media appeared on the street stalls; local porn magazines and a local variant of the gutter press that was often aimed at tainting political and influential individuals. In general people saw these print media as 'beyond morals' and 'filthy'.

12. During the research I was struck by a particular distrust among many women and men. I have heard many times that women and men do not trust each other until trustworthiness can be proven, and even among the few couples I interviewed women and men held such reservations, except for one. The general explanation is that they have seen and experienced so much cheating around them – from their fathers having extra-marital affairs, to their male and female friends secretly cheating on their partners – that unfaithfulness is seen as a bitter reality. A whole discourse on cheating has developed with recurring stereotypes as to why it is impossible to trust a woman or a man; that is, women are out for money and let a man down as soon as they have found a better catch, while men are out for sexual encounters and avoid commitment and responsibility. As a response, a majority tend to expect to be cheated upon sooner or later and become rather defensive and sensitive. A self-fulfilling prophecy has come into being.

The suspicion between women and men when dating highlights how the social and the personal elements of sexuality meet in the inter-subjective moment of a sexual encounter. One can be judged on a personal level, as a good lover or a fascinating person, but also on a social level, as a social persona; a 'hot date' or a 'cool guy'. The status of social persona, however, is ambiguous because it also implies a risk, as hot dates and cool guys might only be interested in 'fun', and then one risks 'being used' or being drawn into a casual encounter. For many people, engaging in a casual encounter is not problematic *per se*, but one should protect one's sexual reputation, i.e. avoid being labelled a 'slut' (women) or a 'player' (men). Both women and men are careful not to get 'hurt' when dating and therefore people find ways of verifying a person's intentions as 'sincere' or not. This probing of potential lovers was a main theme throughout the interviews and they complained that it causes insecurity, resulting in the communication of ambiguous attitudes and a certain degree of suspicion.

13. In 2003, the *East African Standard* introduced a similar pullout on Saturdays, which was clearly inspired by the success of the *Saturday Magazine*.

14. Interview on 19 January 2004.

15. Interview with Mrs Maxwell on 7 November 2001.

16. Interview with Mr Njuguna on 21 October 2001.

17. When I asked the man why he feared conflicts over money, he answered that whenever he had witnessed a fight between his father and mother it was over money. He was afraid that his future wife would also start 'demanding his money', to which she would 'of course be entitled', but which he would also need to support his family, while she would also have her salary. He voiced his concern over how to relate to the role of being the provider, hence financially providing for his wife, while she could have the option of saving her salary and not investing it in the family. Eventually she would have more money to spend on personal expenses, which would make him feel 'awkward' as he would like to provide for her. This is a typical contradiction where gender role expectations clash with changing gender roles as women earn salaries. The solution, he heard during the classes, is that 'modern families' have a shared bank account, into which both the husband and wife put a share of their money, while keeping the rest for personal use. And indeed, many couples who tried to convince me of how seriously they were about intending to get married would say with some pride how they had already opened a shared bank account. It became a symbol of commitment in an up-to-date relationship. It meant that the couple had overcome the complicated issue of having separate or even secret bank accounts, and hence to share household responsibilities. For a man who has been socialized in a context where a man's self reliance and familial responsibility is located in being the provider and not disclosing his financial position, the fact that the Nairobi Chapel encourages young couples to share a bank account involves more than financial matters. When money, respect and one's masculine sense of self are intricately linked, a shared bank account comes to stand for a shift in the construction of masculinity. However, the men in the 'pre-marital counselling classes' were not representative of the men who participated in this study. They were slightly older and, moreover, as committed Christians they were a minority. I did not meet as many Christian men as Christian women aged between 20 and 30 years. According to the women themselves, women are more religious. I would add that the phase in men's life when they are in their twenties, their 'wild years', does not correspond as well with Christian attitudes as when they are getting 'serious' or more settled.

18. A discussion that requires further research on people's relationships is the fact that committed relationships cannot avoid new struggles. According to various authors, the growing instability of heterosexual relationships worldwide has deep roots in socio-economic change, as well as in the increased media emphasis on the 'pure relationship' as the ultimate source of emotional and sexual fulfilment. According to Giddens, 'pressures from women for the transformation of intimacy' clash with men's dominative sexuality and fear of intimate emotion (Giddens 1992). Rubin also identifies deep contradictions in the search for self-fulfilment through another person: 'we are left [by media images] with an extraordinarily heightened set of expectations about the possibilities in human relationships that lives side by side with disillusion that, for many, borders on despair' (Rubin 1991: 160).

CHAPTER VII

CONCLUSION: SEXUALITY AND ITS AMBIGUOUS PLEASURES

You will know who you are when you face pleasure or pressure.[1]

Martha

This study has aimed to bridge central debates in sexuality studies and African studies. It is part of a small but developing field of research on sexuality that seeks to correct the hegemonic trend of simplifying sex in Africa, de-erotizing it to an act devoid of meaning. In the Introduction I set out the challenge: how to understand the ways in which societal factors organize sex and sexuality; and finding out how these processes shape people's self-perceptions and their experiences, even if sex itself is experienced as natural.

As the historical reconfigurations of gender and sexuality coalesce in a particular way in the lifestyles of the young Nairobi professionals, it can be said that they embody emergent new subjectivities. These new modes of being and knowing are often interpreted by others as having developed at the expense of cultural authenticity, and this group of young professionals is characteristically accused of being 'westernized', hence 'un-African'. Sexuality plays a key role here. On one hand, sexuality has become central for young professionals as part of their self-expression as modern subjects. On the other hand, conventional social actors also place matters of sexuality centrally by connecting proper morality with cultural heritage. As a result, young professionals find that they need to balance being African with being modern, which highlights their ambivalent attitude to modernity. Their ambivalence shows in the fact that their sexuality not only entails (the promise of) pleasure but also harbours a potential for anxiety because of the risk of being considered un-African. This study also connects with the literature on postcolonial African subjectivities. In making a plea for a new research epistemology for the study of sexuality in Africa, I have relied on current debates on the transformation of subjectivities in postcolonial societies.

Reflecting on current sexuality research in Africa has helped me to rethink how to study the experience of sexuality. I have had to develop a step-by-step approach linking the personal and the contextual, which I have employed throughout this study. The principle theme revealed by this method has been how sexuality begets pleasure but also causes anxiety in different ways. In this concluding chapter I discuss, from a more theoretical perspective, how discursive analysis and empirical research can help us deal with the challenge of how to connect the personal experiences of sexuality with its social dimensions. The dominant constructionist approach to sexuality has been helpful, but only to some extent. But if we complement it with a phenomenologically inflected approach by using the concept of embodiment and sense of self it becomes possible to understand the experiential aspects of sexuality in relation to postcolonial transformations.

Researching sexuality in Africa

The AIDS epidemic exposed the deficiency of our knowledge about the complexity and variety of sexual behaviour in the African context. As a result, there has been an impressive increase in research activity aimed at responding to this discrepancy. In Chapter I, I reflected on how the vast majority of this research has been conducted from a development or health perspective. It is against this dominant trend in AIDS-related sexuality research that I have developed a new research methodology for studying sexuality in an African context from a social science perspective.

The tendency has been to study sex as a health problem, associated with unwanted pregnancies, HIV infections or sexual abuse. The focus of these studies has been on the specific sexual behaviours that are thought to be most frequently linked to the transmission of HIV. Another unfortunate trend has been the tendency to focus on particular social groups and/or practices and then to take these groups as representative of the whole country, or even the whole continent. A better alternative would be to compare groups or to focus on differences within groups in order to study variation and changes, but this is rarely done. In order to try and understand these research trends, I analysed the work of the group associated with Caldwell (Caldwell et al. 1989a, 1989b, 1991a, 1991b, 1992, 1995, 1997, 2000). They chose, for example, samples of women in a particular region in Nigeria and then generalized about women in Africa. They also portrayed African women as particularly licentious. Their major findings are that African women engage in 'transactional sex' and there is a 'lack of female pleasure'. They arrive at these conclusions without having studied women's personal experiences and they automatically assume that engaging in sex for material gain must preclude any form of pleasure or affection. Their work highlights another rather characteristic tendency of sexuality research – representations of 'African women' as a self-evident category of people who are either victims or prostitutes and, consequently, the assumption that 'African men' are perpetrators of sexual coercion and/ or violence. By studying young professionals' biographical narratives I have shown how such analyses are based on an inadequate research epistemology. Approaching sexuality from a different angle also enabled me to unveil the moral presumptions about 'African sexuality' in such studies. For example, Caldwell's interpretation of the deficient relation between sex, love and riches is refuted by the accounts of Njeri and Ongeri. This misinterpretation calls for more attention in studying how exactly these aspects of sexuality interrelate.

In summary, this study highlights two major flaws in the health-related approaches to studying sexuality. One is that the term sexuality has been used in a self-evident and instrumental manner, rather than being approached with due attention to the full variety and subjectivity of sexual behaviour. Studies that do not take into account the imprecision of the term sexuality start from a flawed position that sees sex simply as an obvious incident or action. In reality it is far more complex than this. The word sex refers to an act, a category, a practice, a gender. Sexuality refers to the quality of 'being sexual', it is a concept depicting the social arena where power relations are played out, and it also refers to sexual desire. These different aspects of sexuality highlight the need to define the term sexuality in terms of sexual practices, desire, identity, etc., in order to clarify what is being studied.

A second, related flaw is that a mainly ahistorical approach has been responsible for grossly simplifying notions of 'culture'. Much research has been impeded by ideas that there is something peculiar about African cultures regarding sexuality. Cultural 'traditions' and 'taboos' are the first things researchers tend to look for in order to account for sexual behaviour, overlooking the more mundane aspects of life such as the influence of poverty on one's psychological well-being or the emotional weight of sex. One such common assumption is that African men engage in multi-partnered sexual relationships because of 'their culture'. An historical analysis of sexuality in Kenya (summarized in Chapter II) offers an alternative explanation: from the colonial period onwards, many married couples were not able to live together due to laws controlling male labour migration. In such situations of separation women and men would have engaged in sexual affairs, likely to be against 'cultural' conventions because adultery was a crime amongst many groups in Kenya. Because sexuality is often presented as embedded in 'age-old traditions', not enough attention is given to such historical and social explanations of particular sexual practices. This study aims to put these types of dominant representations of 'African sexuality' into perspective.

In short, epidemiological studies and/or studies from a health perspective on sexuality have tended to ignore the construction of gendered and sexual identities, the cultural meaning of sexual conduct, and the erotic significance of variant sexual practices in distinct social settings. As this study testifies, there is no way of avoiding the fact that accounts of sex, intimacy and sexuality eventually come down to studying personal sensations. These sensations are comprised of the complex conjunction between physiological arousal, erotic practices and interpretative processes; they are thus situated at the threshold where body and discursive knowledge converge and merge. In other words, culture operates as a frame within which sexual experiences are organized, classified and interpreted. It confers meaning on physiological arousal through labels which contain meanings embedded in norms, prescriptions and prohibitions; for example, it is less accepted for a woman to express sexual arousal than it is for a man. Cultural values also specify how to evaluate the intensity of physiological arousal and provide symbols, artefacts, stories and images in which feelings can be recapitulated and communicated. These communicated feelings are typically the researcher's primary data because we study what people report about sex rather than sex itself. We therefore need to incorporate the cultural context into any analysis of sexual behaviour.

As I indicated in Chapter I, the challenge of sexuality research in Africa is to bring into focus the experiential aspect of sex while continuing to work from a health perspective (which seems inevitable for as long as research remains dependent on development-related finances, which is not the case for sexuality studies in the West). We should not compromise on a solid research epistemology despite pressures to do so, such as the pressure to work towards solutions for so-called risk behaviour which tends to narrow down the research epistemology. This is easier said than done. It is why in this context Obbo called for a certain degree of humility in the current explosion of AIDS-related sexuality studies geared towards formulating answers and solutions (1998). After more than two decades of AIDS research, there is an urgent need to incorporate into the AIDS paradigm that 'the hallmark of sexuality is its complexity: its multiple meanings, sensations and connections' (Vance 1984: 5).

How, then, to study sexuality so as to respect the interface between the social context and personal experience? I have used sexuality as an analytical tool with three foci. First, sex is a vehicle for powerful sensations that are experienced very subjectively. In other words, sex is personal and sex is a medium for expressing a variety of feelings, emotions and needs in a person. In all the biographical narratives I collected, the effects of sexual desire and conduct on the person stood out, from the power of sexual attraction as an uncontrollable force, to the bodily craving for sexual fulfilment. Women and men reflected differently on these experiences depending on their relationships, their view on sex or intimacy, or their anticipation of gendered expectations. In my research group of forty-nine people, the differences between individual people stood out. This is an important observation to make, since large-scale studies, because of their methodology, cannot but generalize and therefore easily negate variety. Generalization itself does not need to be problematic as long as the limitations of this approach are taken into account in the production of knowledge about sexuality.

Second, sex is more often than not an intersubjective exchange between people; it is an intimate exchange, and mutually agreed sexual conduct always implies a degree of confidence or trust. Sex carries a sense of emotional interaction that varies in its nature. The young professionals' experiences show that sex is a means for the expression of different feelings, emotions and needs that are acted upon in relation with another person. People have sex for fun, to fulfil a desire for intimacy, as a physical thrill, to achieve social status, to confirm a gendered sense of self, to exert power, to express love, to humiliate, to conform to expectations, and much more. The emotions and the nature of intimacy can differ. Despite the popular connotations of the term, intimacy does not always imply feelings of monogamous romantic love – 'lovey-dovey' feelings, to use Ongeri's words. Njeri's and Ongeri's narratives in particular show how intimacy can imply friendship or financial care more than particularly codified practices of romantic love (Chapter VI). Perceiving sex as an inter-subjective exchange can be used as a direct call for further research studies to move beyond an essentialist analysis of sex as an obvious act.

Third, because sexuality is also a peculiarly sensitive conductor of social influences, cultural perceptions and political divisions, sexuality is also socially defined. These social aspects inform all the above-mentioned emotions and exchanges. Every one of the biographical narratives I collected testifies to how social meanings frame people's behaviour, their understanding of themselves and their experience. The accounts of, for example, Martha's 'playing hard to get' to Maurice's burden of needing to be seen as 'man enough', show how both people acted in order to preserve their sexual reputation. Sexual ideology and practices are related to notions of health, gender, age, ethnicity or race, religion, social status, familial responsibility, ideas about intimacy, love and affection. Relations of power are typically translated into definitions of sexuality, such as different perceptions regarding chastity defined by gender. The different biographical narratives elaborate how people's sexuality developed in interaction with these social axes. As I explain in Chapter I, conducting sex research is often considered difficult for the wrong reasons.

The pleasures and anxieties of sexuality

The connections between the pleasure and anxiety of sexuality are various. As I worked out the step-by-step approach linking the personal and the contextual, I was able to study sexuality from its diverse angles. In Chapters IV and V, I showed how sexual meanings are individual and often have an emotional basis. Young professional women and men, like others all over the globe, reflected positively about the fact that sex is above all about sensual pleasure or the promise of pleasure. Being sexually active implies being sexually attractive or 'wanted', which contributes positively to women and men's sense of self-worth. The sex act is experienced as a moment of bliss, of physical energies that cannot be negated and sex is recognized as a powerful 'natural' force. Having sex makes people feel 'good', 'happy', 'alive', 'in love', 'sexy', 'loved', 'strong', and much more, or as Martha expressed it: 'Making love connects my body and soul'. Many experienced sex as a vitalizing force, linking its power to its capacity as the source of life, literally and metaphorically. In 2001, Winnie Madikizela-Mandela's phrase 'sex makes the world go round' (which circulated in the Kenyan media) was often used to joke about and to answer my never-ending questions. Sex is often perceived as a 'gut feeling' (referring to excitement, sensuality, release) associated with bodily sensations, and with more complex understandings like 'feeling wo/man' (augmenting a gendered sense of self). These meanings of sex are more centred on the individual, whereas other meanings are relational, seeing sex as connected to love, affection, romance. For Patrick, whose narrative opens the Introduction, sex was a mutual pleasure that augments an emotional bond between lovers.

Personal understandings of sexuality are informed by and intertwined with social factors. For many women, experiencing femaleness through their bodies was a means on feeling empowered. In spite of normative understandings that equate female sexuality with reproduction, they actively appropriated sexual pleasure as an index of their gendered sense of self. However, when pleasure and mutual orgasm become a normative standard in 'modern' relationships, then sex becomes a new kind of obligation, generating insecurity. Several women recounted fear of failing as a competent sexual partner, either because of this new standard or because of the fact that they were never encouraged to perceive themselves as desiring sex for pleasure and therefore felt inhibited to do so. As they got older, most of the women became more sexually assertive, and bolder in taking a position against existing double standards. For all the men, sex was a necessary aspect of being masculine, but for them too the interpretation of sex as an emotional exchange of trust and companionship could lead to uncertainty because it contradicted the idea that male sex is spontaneous. Some men's desire for sex was close to compulsion and for them sex was a means of feeling alive and virile, hence masculine, which is in line with normative ideas of male sexuality. A minority of men resisted this hegemonic notion of manhood by drawing on the discourse on love, in the same way that a minority of women chose to delay sex until marriage. These experiences show that there is a thin line between pleasure and anxiety in sex, and that they are not unconnected or mutually exclusive emotions and experiences.

I believe that there can never be a purely physical, ecstatic or anxiety free sexual encounter. From the young professionals' experiences (which is underlined by other accounts described in the literature), it can be concluded that sex is almost always imbued with some degree of uncertainty, ambiguity or anxiety. Feelings of shame, fear of losing the partner, fear of disappointing, fear about violation of trust, anxiety about failure to enjoy sex or have an orgasm, and fear of arousing suspicion – all these were experienced by both women and men, and only serve to highlight the precarious and complex nature of a sexual encounter. For example, many women endlessly deliberated about whether or not to initiate condom use because they feared arousing the suspicion of their partner about being promiscuous. Other women recounted similar qualms, as well as a fear of violating trust by initiating condom use. Men recounted similar anxieties, though less often. Besides anxieties such as these that were related to social expectations, sex was also used to deal with a range of feelings, such as rejection, insecurity or anger, or to exert power or increase self-worth. For example, Tom dealt with his fear of rejection – related to his experience with his first committed relationship – by having multiple relationships: once he sheepishly said that sex 'boosts my ego'. Njeri, however, would never phrase it in such a way and instead explained how she enjoyed the fact that John was 'hooked to her' because of their 'great sex life'. In Njeri's sexual life the interface of pleasure and anxiety becomes clear in the way in which she enjoyed sex with John to the full, which was important to her, despite the fact that the relationship was troubled with fights, mistrust and frustrations, which did 'not do me well'. It should be pointed out that the pleasurable and anxiety-evoking aspects of sex are not mutually exclusive and that, therefore, such uneasy aspects of sex should not be overproblematized. It highlights the fact that sex is fraught with ambiguity.

In sum, people's explanations about the importance of sex mostly relate to how sex augments a gendered sense of self. If sex is constitutive to people's feelings of being either 'woman' or 'man', then experiencing being feminine and masculine is partly related to normative expectations based on existing gender roles. The structure of gender difference, the subjective positions they prescribe and describe, necessarily limit the ways in which women and men pursue other ways of being. In the dominant patriarchal discourse, sexual reputations have different meanings for women and men in relation to sexual morality. Butler's notion of the 'paradox of subjectivation' (1997) has been helpful in pointing out how women and men both advocate new interpretations of gender – because young professionals unsettle, to different degrees, the patriarchal understanding of sex and gender – as well as reproduce normative understandings of gender.

The hegemonic symbolic construction of women as moral caretakers, guardians of the family, and devoted wives, serves as the norm of femininity even when women deviate from it. As I have shown, women are usually the primary focus of moralizing discourses because the description and management of gender and female sexuality is necessary to the maintenance and reproduction of gender inequality. As products of their society, women have partly internalized these notions. In short, it comes down to women being encouraged to remain chaste and being severely judged when they transgress normative parameters. Women have therefore been compelled to adopt more secretive strategies when having sexual affairs compared to men. They have to constantly negotiate between factors that are associated with deviance on one hand, and aspects that would allow them to be considered respectable on the other. This is typically expressed in the phrase 'playing hard to get', meaning that women should never compromise their sexual reputation by showing an interest in sex too openly. Nevertheless, women appropriated sexual pleasure as part of contemporary personhood, and many enjoyed doing so. In general, the older the women were, the more boldly they pursued sex for pleasure, whether it was via short affairs or by finding out about sex toys or fun condoms. Young professional women, in short, have to negotiate between uncertain boundaries of sexual allure and limited availability.

Men generally had, and still have, more leeway to deviate from the norm. Although men are also encouraged to remain chaste, mainly by the Christian discourse, they are also encouraged to be sexually active, which is endorsed by the patriarchal discourse equating male sexuality with virility and social achievement. Public discourse is highly contradictory when it comes to manhood and morality, and this also impacts on men's sexual behaviour and their relationships with women. Whereas they perceive sex as constitutive to their sense of masculinity, men must also exercise self-restraint and therefore there is a (undefined) limit to sex. A man should not appear to be addicted to sex, because this implies being dependent on women and thus not being self-reliant. On the other hand, a man should not fail in having sex and, above all, in being a good lover. In normative discourse being a skilful lover is not considered crucial to men's sexuality, while in the newly emerging discourse it is. The latter, however, implies that sex is not as spontaneous as it is conventionally understood to be; instead, it needs to be 'worked upon' as sexual skills, like other skills, require knowledge and practice. Many men recounted or hinted at their anxieties about failing to be skilful lovers. The new discourse on sex as central to emotional intimacy challenges conventional constructions of masculinity, and men struggle to balance and incorporate both in their lives as lovers. Nevertheless, the discourse of sex as being natural to men remains hegemonic and most men consider it their right to take pleasure in sex.

Men maintain ambiguous attitudes towards women – and vice versa – because they occupy an ambiguous position in women's lives as lovers, friends and future husbands, as well as figures of authority and social control. As a result, both women and men communicate ambiguity towards their partners and potential partners. It turns out that many sexual affairs are not self-evident anxiety-free encounters. Especially in non-committed relationships, sex is embedded in ambiguity because of social and cultural expectations, as well as the fear of arousing suspicion and violating trust. Further, AIDS poses a realistic threat when people have unprotected sex, which continues to happen although condom use is fairly high. The moralizing discourses on AIDS have further codified sex with a negative meaning in public discourse; as I showed in Chapter III, 'bad' sex is 'immoral' sex, while 'good' sex has come to mean sex that conforms with normative cultural values. These definitions of sex also affect the experience of sex among young adults.

Despite these ambiguities, for young professionals the importance of having sex has its roots in the positive discourse on sex as an expression of a 'fast life'. Going out and having 'fun' is celebrated to the full in Nairobi's nightlife. In the evolving erotic frame of reference of the fast life, sexual pleasure for both women and men becomes fundamental to dating. Sexuality reflects a space for them to re-enact, or 'modernize', femininity and masculinity in the way they claim entitlement to sexual pleasure as the young, the hip and the ambitious. Pamela's eagerness to participate in going out and dating as a means of being recognized as an adult woman shows exactly this. In other words, sexuality assumes a new place in the articulation of contemporary Nairobi personhood, and the concurrence between sexuality, consumerism and romantic love have become central to self-expression. This interpretation of sexuality sets this group of young professionals apart from other groups in Kenyan society to a certain extent. Their interpretation implies a break with normative notions of sexuality and gender, which equate sex with procreation and the maintenance of gender hierarchies. This break makes explicit the fact that gender and sexuality continue to shift (Chapter II), to the detriment of existing gerontocratic power structures.

Middle class lifestyles and self-perceptions

Young professionals see themselves as a vanguard of modern life in Kenya in the twenty-first century. They are part of the emerging urban middle class and they are a particular generation of this class which has been born and raised in Nairobi. Most of them are unable to speak an ethnic language and instead they mainly speak a mix of Kiswahili, English and *Sheng* (see note 6, Introduction). They manage a trans-ethnic circle of friends and colleagues, they are more or less financially independent and they are distinguishable from the larger population by their lifestyle. In other words, young professionals embody the visible results of social transformations. The way they manage their sexual lives more or less autonomously from their extended families is an achievement that positions them as *avant garde* in postcolonial Kenya. Their relative autonomy from their relatives is due to the fact that they are at the 'young adult phase' in their lives; the older the people in this study, the more they attended family gatherings. This raises the question of how they will develop their lives when they settle into marriage and family life (as each one of them intended to). They picture themselves as Kenyans with a cosmopolitan attitude, and they call themselves Africans. Africanness means testifying to an African or black commonality that they are proud of; it is about a kind of sociality which they celebrate by cracking jokes about each other's 'tribes', claiming entitlement to certain ethnic customs as part of a larger African universe, dressing in elaborate west African dress or enjoying *nyama choma* (roasted meat) and a Tusker (local beer brand) before going out. Tumi's reaction, when asked about her cultural background, was: 'My culture? Nairobi I guess. I am so mixed up, my parents being from two different tribes. I used to say that *Sheng* is my mother tongue [laughs].' Nicknaming, greeting practices, the rich popular culture, food preferences, marriage and funeral rituals, flirting practices – these all signify a particular urban Nairobian culture that is their life world.

Since independence, a shift has occurred in Kenya, with urban families becoming more oriented towards the nuclear family. A discernible discourse on lifestyle has given new impetus to the model of a middle class nuclear family with a double income. Significant to this discourse is the importance given to love as the essential condition for a good relationship. Although the majority of young professionals in this study were not married, this discourse is informative to them because of the new pathways they are exploring with regard to how women and men relate. They perceived their future marital relationships as being based on romance and personal choice in contrast to customary marriage, which is thought of as a collective enterprise between two families. I showed how in the written media this new interpretation emphasizes a more personal approach to partner choice, based on values of companionship, egalitarianism, a couple's relative autonomy, and the sexual satisfaction of women, rather than reproduction and ethnic compatibility. Moving away from marriage as a collective engagement implies the emergence of different modes of being: women no longer identify themselves only as daughters, sisters and wives-to-be, while men try to extend their identity beyond that of sons, breadwinners and authoritarians. The discourse on egalitarianism and intimacy developed in response to middle class young adults' aspirations and needs, and it shows how women and men are drawn together in a particular way as lovers (even after they are married) and not necessarily as wife and husband embedded in the network of the extended family that presupposes a different subject position.

In Chapter VI, I showed how the media play a crucial role in responding to the questions and concerns that people struggle with, and hence how the media are a factor in engendering new modes of being and knowing. As many young adults grew up without seeing their parents or other couples showing physical affection, the visualization of the expression of love has an important impact, allowing the discourse on love to gain ground. If the cinema plays a major role in imagining romance, the written media take up where the cinema leaves off. By means of a reflexive therapeutic discourse on relationships, people appropriate conceptions of love and intimacy from these media texts. I have demonstrated how these distinctive affective and narrative forms of romantic love are appropriated by young professionals. An important effect is thus the localization of emotions regarding love and sexuality in the personal domain; the discourse of romantic love, of affection, is the narrative of the individual, the subject of these sentiments. Young professionals find recognition of their distinctiveness of this discourse, which they perceive to be more applicable to them than to their parents' generation. Both women and men repeatedly said that they cannot live like their parents, as for example Maurice indicated when explaining his commitment to his girlfriend Nyambura: 'We, the men of these days, have to make choices. We cannot live anymore like our fathers, I believe it's not right to be polygamous.' His biography, and that of the others, shows how romantic love works to enforce a sense of the importance of the individual subject, the locus and source of all strong feelings, in a symbolic interaction with another person.

The role of the media is reflected in the dating practices of young professionals. I do not mean to suggest that other Kenyans do not date. But young professionals are more involved in consumer capitalism, deeply marked by the twin spheres of consumption and mass media, which structure the private realm of leisure; this includes dating practices. Dating is central to young professionals as a signifying practice that marks their lifestyle. The goal of pursuing a 'sophisticated' lifestyle brings both women and men together; their lifestyle practices become a key indicator of where they belong in Kenyan society. Young professionals are engaged in a continuing process of shifting practices, but since the effects of social change have culminated in this particular social group, their alternative ways are more visible when compared to their parents' generation or to other social groups. This raises the question of whether class is a factor in achieving progressive gender change, which I would answer in the affirmative, although more in-depth research into this issue is needed. The fact that many young professional men are responsive to therapeutic discourse, in various degrees, suggests as much.

However, as I have pointed out throughout this study, beneath the vibrant subculture of young professionals and their spirited attitude to life, many of them experience feelings of anxiety with regard to two fundamental aspects of social life: how they organize and experience their intimate life; and how they identify themselves culturally. The focus of this study has been to understand how these two are interrelated. As young professionals delay marriage and disconnect sexuality from the moral order, they diverge from the gerontocratic moral order. To understand them, it has been important to position them in relation to social continuity and change in Kenyan society. The social organization of sexuality in Kenya has always been in flux and current criticism of young professionals is a reflection of older debates. In Chapters II and III, my analyses showed that sexuality has often been a preoccupation in public debates, because gender and sexuality are generally experienced as fundamental to the social and cultural order. It is not surprising that debates about sexuality always invoke sentiments related to cultural authenticity and heritage.

Earlier, I briefly outlined how in the colonial and postcolonial eras, political and economical processes caused a thorough transformation in Kenyan society. Marriage patterns and related social structures were reorganized by male labour migration, Christianization and urbanization. As a result, the practical and symbolical relations between women and men began to change, hence resulting in shifting constructions of gender, and, eventually, in new self-perceptions or different ways of being and knowing. Traditionally, marriage was a social institution which maintained relations of reciprocity and obligation between ethnic groups in Kenya. But changes in the criteria and the process of partner selection reflect the transformations that have been taking place in the social organization of African societies for generations. I have showed how social transformation has always given rise to feelings of social chaos because changes in communal organization consequently lead to shifting gerontocratic power relations. In Kenya this has resulted in attempts to reverse or halt the course of change by invoking discussions on morality in relation to 'African roots'. The advent of AIDS fuelled the discourse on 'immorality' in the 1990s, as AIDS was seen, and sometimes still is, as the result of the ultimate betrayal of Africanness, as some kind of punishment for not adhering to proper cultural morals. This discourse on immorality neatly conflates concerns about cultural heritage, gerontocratic authority and social organizations of gender and sexuality. It is marked by a glorification of the past, idealizing the customary way of living as the perfect form of society, which is free from disease (AIDS), conflict and poverty. This evocation of a lost world reflects anxieties evoked by the experience of a lost authenticity, or an eroding Africanness, in the face of contemporary changes. In the discourse of idealizing the past, the group of young professionals comes to be seen as the antithesis of this past. In the current debates, 'culture' assumes a different meaning with regard to sexuality; it becomes a political tool rather than a vehicle for some 'deeper' structure of meaning. These discussions about immorality highlight the necessity to not take culture as a self-evident factor of sexuality, and also highlight the root of young professionals' ambivalent attitude towards modernity.

Young professionals navigate between these volatile discussions, and, as we have seen, they get caught in a web of attempts to reify the notions 'African', 'tradition', 'modern' and 'westernization'. Although they consider themselves to be explorers of a 'sophisticated' or 'modern' lifestyle, they resist being seen as 'westernized'. Their difficulty is that while they are very critical of what they call Western cultural imperialism, they are also part of global cosmopolitan processes that are often interpreted as 'westernization'. The contradiction is complete when the same processes that enable them to pursue certain lifestyles are also interpreted as causing the 'erosion of tradition'. Their sense of Africanness is also contradictory. On the one hand it is related to a sentiment of glorifying traditions as truly authentic, while on the other hand, they identify themselves as African because of their trans-ethnic backgrounds and/or lifestyle and progressive attitudes. So their Africanness is far from self-evident, and neither is their 'westernization'; these ill defined or flawed notions highlight the complex position of young professionals. The confusion is compounded by the fact that in public discourse, Africanness is positioned in opposition to modern, and sexuality is placed at the centre of the debates; 'true Africans' are portrayed as upholding conventional morals. This is exactly the nexus of the tension between the pleasure and the anxiety of sexuality for young professionals; as progressive advocators of Africanness, they challenge the gerontocratic hierarchy and its associated morals. That is why women like Dorcas, self-assured and ambitious, wonder 'am I doing right as a modern African woman?' when deliberating on their casual relationships (Chapter IV).

Dorcas's words exemplify how young professionals are wedged in this process as emblems of a postcolonial urban Kenya that is, above all, in flux: 'To be sure, the postcolony is chaotically pluralistic; it has nonetheless an internal coherence. ... It is ... characterized by the distinctive ways identities are multiplied, transformed and put into circulation' (Mbembe 2001: 102). The 'coherence' of (post) colonial Kenya is displayed in the way the continuing reconfiguration of culture, gender and sexuality, since colonialism and into the twenty-first century, join together in the lifestyles of young professionals. By focussing on the nexus of pleasure and desire, I have been able to unearth the intersections between the social and personal aspects of sexuality.

Sex and sophistication – self and embodiment

As I set out in the Introduction, this study analyses how sex feels personal, private and above all natural, and how these feelings always incorporate the rules, definitions, symbols and meanings of the worlds in which they are construed. In my attempts at interpretation I came across various debates that helped me. To bridge the personal experiences and the social context, I was inspired by theorists of subjectivation, who provide the methodology to study how the social context constitutes and informs people's subjectivities. In the debate about postcolonial subjectivities, Werbner calls for a study of the way in which people realize their subjectivities 'existentially, in the subjects' consciousness of their personal or intimate relations' (2002: 2). In order to capture the experiential level of sex and to connect it with the context of young professionals' lives, I complement a Foucauldian analysis with the useful concepts self and embodiment as propounded by Csordas (1990).

In attempting to understand the search by young professionals for a new morality and way of behaving, the work of Foucault has been useful. It is not coincidental that sex was a main focus for him: he studied sexuality as a peculiar dense domain of power relations and social influences

(1990 [1976]). In the spirit of Foucault, I studied sexuality not as a self-evident aspect of my informants' lives, but rather in relation to how the changing discourse on sexuality has been crucial to the development of a modern identity in Nairobi. I have shown how these processes of subjectivation are dual: young professionals as a group are subjected to the effects of social transformation, while at the same time they are constituted as subjects with a reflective mindset.

Young professionals experience the effects of social transformation engendering new modes of being above all as ways of becoming the *avant garde* of Kenyan society. These new modes of being and knowing are connected to particular configurations of being Nairobian, which is built upon an amalgam of different ethnic practices, music and humour; this 'multitude of being' (Nyairo 2005) is expressed in their lifestyles. I have used the notion of lifestyle, inspired by Ferguson's cultural style (1999), as a descriptive notion to elaborate on their dress, bodily disposition and consumption patterns in order to show how their lives go beyond dualist perceptions of 'modern' and 'traditional' as being opposite. It is via their lifestyles that young professionals define their own personalities as persons in contemporary Kenya, and hence where they feel they belong as Kenyan citizens. Their cosmopolitanism does not imply a cultural orientation to the West; instead it indicates the convergence of global and local cultural compliance that they embody. Analysing young professionals' lifestyles as signifying practice shows how their local Kenyan and cosmopolitan orientations are coeval social phenomena (cf. Fabian 1983). Culture, as I have shown, becomes cultural style; not something they believe in, but a signifying practice that invokes knowledge of form rather than content. For example, Tayiani's decision to agree with Kikuyu rituals of bride wealth during her wedding, despite her reservations, was meant as a tribute to Africanness. As she is a non-Kikuyu, moreover, and a child of two different nations, her tribute exemplifies how culture is form rather than content in the cultural melting pot of Nairobi. Young professionals exemplify how cosmopolitanism should be understood as cultural style that neither negates nor favours ethnic, 'traditional' or 'Western' characteristics.

Young professionals are engaged in a continuous process of subjectivation that started, roughly, with their grandparents' generation. On one hand, they are engaged in a dialogical relationship with customary practices and modes of being; they are not detached from these as may be implied in representations of them within certain public discourses in Nairobi. For example, the practice of male circumcision and pre-wedding ceremonies for women testify to this. On the other hand, they are engaged in the process of globalization as cosmopolitan subjects. In emphasizing historical entanglement, this study joins the literature that explores the history of bodily affairs in Africa and changes in postcolonial subjectivities (see Thomas 2003: 19; cf. Werbner 2002). Bayart (2000) calls for an analysis of Africans in relation to the processes involved in the constitution of the self, instead of seeing Africans only as subject to circumstances such as political domination. The point is to understand the 'genesis of new communities of taste, sentiment and other markers of inclusion' (Meyer 2004b: 4) and how they are embedded in larger structures. Young Nairobi professionals are engaged in different processes of subjectivation and identification as professionals, Africans, Kenyans and cosmopolitans, as well as in the role of women, men, lovers and partners.

Elaborating on the lifestyles of specific young professionals has been important in this study to show how modes of being and knowing are engendered. Technologies of the self – such as fashion, social etiquette or progressive attitudes – become a key event of self-identification. In the spirit of Campbell (1987), I have shown how capitalism operates predominantly through the modes of new experiences, a hedonistic orientation and infinite desires as exemplified in Nairobi's nightlife and the dating practices of young professionals. Via the twin spheres of consumption and mass media, sexuality is promoted as a means of identifying oneself as modern. Personal and mutual sexual happiness are represented as progressive qualities, as well as a symbol for a successful relationship. By focussing on people's sexual experiences, and their reflections upon them, I have shown how sexual intimacy becomes a matter of the self, of the sexual subject, in a symbolic interaction with another subject (cf. Jamieson 1998). Sexuality and romantic self-expression have become central to their self-perception as modern subjects.

Such a Foucauldian analysis is helpful for placing sexuality in a broader context; to study sexuality as discursive practice and to show how subjectivity is the outcome of discursive practices. 'Sex acts', as Rubin points out, 'are burdened with an excess of significance' (1984: 285). Ironically, whereas Foucault's interest in sexuality was to elaborate on the rich and conflictual inner world of modern subjects due to changes in the discourse on sexuality, many studies that are inspired by him have a tendency to map out the power relations only. I have shown how the constructionist focus on sexuality as discursive practice tends to neglect the bodily, or experiential and sensorial, element of sex, due to its epistemology that propounds deconstructing gender and sexuality and unveiling power relations. The majority of studies on sexuality in Africa, which in no uncertain terms have put an important issue on the academic agenda, do exactly this. While studying the politics of sexuality is important, it is equally important to take the analysis of sexuality further to incorporate the subjectiveness of sexuality. For example, while it is important to deconstruct how patriarchal society frames many women's gendered lives, this does not address how they *experience* a gendered sense of self. In sum, an over-reliance on unveiling power relations risks overlooking the sensorial and experiential analysis of sexuality and its emotional power.

The question remains how people experience discursive practices. Sex is by and large a sensory experience. My invariable question 'and how does it make you feel?' directed me to how sex makes people feel themselves to be 'woman' or 'man', how sex is experienced as the most spontaneous natural thing, how it qualifies as 'invigorating' or 'release', making someone 'confident', 'sexy' or 'feel good'. These qualities were related to people's identity as young, urban, modern professionals. In order to explore this 'subjectiveness' of sexuality, I have used the notion 'sense of self' studied via and including bodily experiences. Following Csordas (1990; 1994), I employ this notion to point to an inner emotional and embodied life which relates to a person's place in the world. From this standpoint, embodiment is not reducible to representations of the body as an objectification of power or a physical entity or biological organism, nor to the body as an inalienable centre of individual consciousness. The notion of a gendered sense of self has helped me to grasp the experience of sex in relation to people's place in society. It has also directed my focus to how a gendered sense of self affects sexual desire and pleasure, and vice versa. The fact that young professional women appropriate sexual pleasure as central to their feminine sense of self, justifying themselves as modern women, shows clearly how young professionals see themselves in the world.

Using the notion of a sense of self as an analytical tool to elaborate on the process of how people recognize and define their personhood requires a detailed methodology. I propose to study sexuality by the step-by-step approach of researching the personal, intersubjective and social aspects of sex. As these three aspects are closely interrelated they need to be distinguished, but due attention also needs to be paid to the interconnections. Studying people's narrative biographies provides the data to do so because it focusses on the personal experience, while incorporating the person's life in the social context (Wekker 2006). Combining in-depth interviews with participant observation is thus crucial to study how sex is experienced as natural and how it is, simultaneously, socially defined in relation to subject positions such as being wo/man, lover, partner, young professional, 'sophisticated', 'African', modern. Ethnography, rather than epidemiology, provides the methodology that takes into account both the social context by focussing on the processes of subjectivation and personal experience, in order to analyse the intricate interface.

One question which remains is how young professionals see themselves as subjects in Kenyan society that is in 'flux' (cf. Geschiere and Meyer

1999a). In a way, they are conscious of their position and their role in engendering alternative modes of being. And their quest is which course to take in 'being modern the African way' when the context calls for a contrast between locality and non-locality. Caught in discussions about 'westernization', they cannot escape reifying the notions 'African', 'modern' and 'Western', but at the same time they live their life as a matter of course. In fact, feelings of belonging are, and have always been, built upon ambivalence. The debates generated by social transformations are about the very constitution of people as belonging to a cultural group, as women or men, as family members, or as citizens. Foucault suggested that the project of modernity results in sex becoming the 'truth' of the subject's authenticity. Although the parallels with the analysis provided here are striking, there is a difference. The preoccupation of young professionals is Africanness. Contrary to what is often described in the literature on postcolonial subjectivities, for young professionals in Nairobi the heart of the project of modernity is not so much about being modern but a preoccupation with being African. My focus on the tension between pleasure and anxiety has helped me to understand the source of their ambiguous position. By using the notion of the paradox of subjectivation, I have been able to uncover another nexus of pleasure and anxiety – that sex suggests enjoyment but also the fear of becoming 'un-African'. In dominant discourse, female sexuality is understood in relation to reproduction and notions of African womanhood are idealistically associated with motherhood, wifehood and the gerontocratic gender order. When sex is disconnected from reproduction, it threatens women's reputation as 'proper women' and hence their sense of themselves as being respectable African women. The dominant discourse of male sexual behaviour has its roots in ideas of primordial Africanness that connect virility and sex. For men, the new interpretation of sexuality negates perceiving sex as spontaneous, but instead as controllable and partner-oriented; hence sex might jeopardize their masculinity. As the 'African' *avant garde* in Kenya, young professionals find themselves in this paradoxical position. The vantage point of sexuality has enabled me to analyse how sex is central to self-perception, as well as to the moral order, and to discover how these are interconnected with being 'modern the African way' for young professionals in Nairobi.

Note

1. These lines come from one of the poems written by Martha (aged 24 in 2001). It's called 'Being the me that I am':

We may at times find it challenging to be what we want to be
because we want to love and appreciate our people,
we don't want to hurt them
or let them feel disgraced by us.
So at times it becomes difficult for us
to express ourselves genuinely from the heart
and reach for what we want.
But,
it's time we become our own heroes.
Let us reach the heights set for us and go,
expressing our ideas
and taking the risk of being pioneers of new things.
You will know who you are when you face pleasure or pressure.

BIBLIOGRAPHY

Abicht, H., R.C. Bailey, R. Muga and R. Poulussen. 2002. 'The Acceptability of Male Circumcision to Reduce HIV Infection in Nyanza Province, Kenya', *AIDS Care* 14: 27–40.

Abramson, P. 1992. 'Sex, Lies and Ethnography', in G. Herdt and S. Lindenbaum (eds), *The Time of AIDS: Social Analysis, Theory and Method*. Newbury Park: Sage Publications, pp. 101–23.

———, R. Berk and P. Okami. 1995. 'Sexual Activities as Told in Surveys', in P.R. Abramson and S.T. Pinkerton (eds), *Sexual Nature, Sexual Culture*. Chicago: University of Chicago Press, pp. 371–86.

——— and S.T. Pinkerton. 1995. 'Introduction', in P.R. Abramson and S.T. Pinkerton (eds), *Sexual Nature, Sexual Culture*. Chicago: University of Chicago Press, pp. 1–14.

Abu-Lughod, L. 1990. 'The Romance of Resistance: Tracing Transformations through Bedouin Women', *American Ethnologist* 17(1): 41–55.

———. 2002. 'Egyptian Melodrama. Technology of the Modern Subject?', in L. Abu-Lughod, F. Ginsburg and B. Larkin (eds), *Media Worlds. Anthropology on New Terrain*. Berkeley: University of California Press, pp. 115–34.

Achebe, C. 1996 [1958]. *Things Fall Apart*. London: Heinemann.

Adams, V. and S. Pigg. 2005. *Sex in Development. Science, Sexuality and Morality in Global Perspective*. London: Duke University Press.

Adkins, L. 2001. 'Risk Culture, Self-reflexivity and the Making of Sexual Hierarchies', *Body and Society* 7(1): 35–55.

———. 2002. *Revisions: Gender and Sexuality in Late Modernity*. Buckingham: Open University Press.

Ahlberg, B. 1991. *Women, Sexuality and the Changing Social Order. The Impact of Government Policies on Reproductive Behaviour in Kenya*. Amsterdam: Gordon and Breach Publishers.

———. 1994. 'Is There a Distinct African Sexuality? A Critical Response to Caldwell et al.', *Africa* 64(2): 220–42.

Aina, T. 1990. 'The Myth of African Promiscuity', in R. Sabatier (ed.), *Blaming Others. Prejudice, Race and World-wide AIDS*. London: Panos Publications Ltd, pp. 78–81.

Alsop, R., A. Fitzsimons and K. Lennon. 2002. *Theorizing Gender*. Cambridge: Polity Press.

Amelsfoort, V. 1976. *Medical Anthropology in African Newspapers*. Oosterhout: Anthropological Publications.

Amory, D.P. 1998. 'Mashoga, Mabasha, and Magai: "Homosexuality" on the East African Coast', in S. Murray and W. Roscoe (eds), *Boy-Wives and Female Husbands: Studies in African Homosexualities*. New York: St. Martin's Press, pp. 67–87.

Appadurai, A. 1996. *Modernity at Large: Cultural Dimensions of Globalization*. Minneapolis: University of Minnesota Press.

Arnfred, S. (ed.). 2004. *Re-thinking Sexualities in Africa*. Sweden: Almqvist and Wiksell Tryckeri.

Bakhtin, M.M. 1981. *The Dialogic Imagination: Four Essays*. Austin: University of Texas Press.

Barber, K. 1997. 'Preliminary Notes on Audiences in Africa', *Africa* 67(3): 347–62.

Bauni, E.K. and B.O. Jarabi. 2000. 'Family Planning and Sexual Behaviour in the Era of HIV/AIDS: The Case of Nakuru District, Kenya', *Studies in Family Planning* 31(1): 69–80.

Bayart, J.-F. 2000. 'Africa in the World: A History of Extraversion', *African Affairs* 99: 217–67.

Behrend, H. 1998. 'Love à la Hollywood and Bombay in Kenyan Studio Photography', *Paideuma* 44: 139–53.

Beidelman, T.O. 1982. *Colonial Evangelism: A Socio-historical Study of an East African Mission at the Grassroots*. Bloomington: Indiana University Press.

———. 1986. *Moral Imagination among Kaguru Modes of Thought*. Bloomington: Indiana University Press.

Benedict, R. 1934. *Patterns of Culture*. New York: Houghton Mifflin.

Bergsjo, P. 1994. 'African Sexual Rites. Sexual Initiation of Maasai Girls', *Acta Obstet Gynecol Scand* 73(4): 279–97.

Berman, B.J. 1998. 'Ethnicity, Patronage and the African State: The Politics of Uncivil Nationalism', *African Affairs* 97: 305–41.

——— and J. Lonsdale. 1992. *Unhappy Valley: Conflict in Kenya and Africa. Books One and Two*. London: James Currey.

Besnier, N. 1995. 'The Appeal and Pitfalls of Cross-disciplinary Research', in J.A. Russell (ed.), *Everyday Conceptions of Emotion: An Introduction to the Psychology, Anthropology, and Linguistics of Emotion*. Dordrecht: Kluwer, pp. 559–70.

Beyala, C. 1995. *Loukoum: The 'Little Prince' of Belleville*. Translated by M. de Jager. London: Heinemann.

———. 1996. *The Sun Hath Looked upon Me*. Translated by M. de Jager. London: Heinemann.

———. 1996. *Your Name Shall Be Tanga*. Translated by M. de Jager. London: Heinemann.

Biaya, T.K. 2000. '"Crushing the Pistachio": Eroticism in Senegal and the Art of Ousmane Ndiaye Dago', *Public Culture* 12(3): 707–20.

Biddlecom, A. and M. Greene. 2000. 'Absent and Problematic Men: Demographic Accounts of Male Reproductive Roles', *Population and Development Review* 26(1): 81–115.

Birungi, H., C.-C. Undie and P. Aggleton. 2009. 'Recent Research on Sexuality in East Africa', *Culture, Health and Sexuality* 11(8): 747–50.

Blount, B.G. 1973. 'The Luo of South Nyanza, Western Kenya', in A. Molnos (ed.), *Cultural Source Materials for Population Planning in East Africa*, Vol. 3. Nairobi: Institute of African Studies.

Blumstein, P. and P. Schwartz. 1983. *American Couples*. New York: Simon and Shuster.

Bochrow, A. 2005. 'New Ways of Loving for a New Generation?', *First AEGIS (Africa-Europe Group for Interdisciplinary Studies) Conference*. London: SOAS and the ICS.

Bolton, R. 1992. 'Mapping Terra Incognita: Sex Research for Aids Prevention – An Urgent Agenda for the 1990s', in G. Herdt and S. Lindenbaum (eds), *The Time of AIDS: Social Analysis, Theory and Method*. Newbury Park: Sage Publications, pp. 124–58.

Booth, K.M. 2004. *Local Women, Global Science. Fighting AIDS in Kenya*. Bloomington: Indiana University Press.

Bujra, J. 1975. 'Women "Entrepreneurs" of Early Nairobi', *Canadian Journal of African Studies* 32(9): 967–80.

Burke, T. 1996. *Lifebuoy Men, Lux Women. Commodification, Consumption and Cleanliness in Modern Zimbabwe*. Durham: Duke University Press.

Butler, J. 1987. *Subjects of Desire: Hegelian Reflections in Twentieth-Century France*. New York: Columbia University Press.

———. 1990. *Gender Trouble: Feminism and the Subversion of Identity*. New York and London: Routledge.

———. 1993. *Bodies that Matter: On the Discursive Limits of 'Sex'*. New York and London: Routledge.

———. 1997. *The Psychic Life of Power: Theories in Subjection*. Stanford: Stanford University Press.

Cáceres, C.F. 2000. 'Afterword: The Production of Knowledge on Sexuality in the AIDS Era: Some Issues, Opportunities and Challenges', in R. Parker, R.M. Barbosa and P. Aggleton (eds), *Framing the Sexual Subject: The Politics of Gender, Sexuality and Power*. Berkeley: University of California Press, pp. 241–61.

Caldwell, J. 2000. 'Rethinking the African AIDS Epidemic', *Population and Development Review* 26(1): 117–35.

———, P. Caldwell and I.O. Orubupoye. 1992. 'The Family and Sexual Networking in Sub-Saharan Africa: Historical Regional Differences and Present-day Implications', *Populations Studies* 43: 385–410.

———, P. Caldwell and P. Quiggin. 1989a. 'Disaster in an Alternative Civilization. The Social Dimension of AIDS in Sub-Saharan Africa', *Working Papers*. Canberra: Australian National University.

———, P. Caldwell and P. Quiggin. 1989b. 'The Social Context of AIDS in Sub-Saharan Africa', *Population and Development Review* 15(2): 185–234.

———, I.O. Orubuloye and P. Caldwell. 1991a. 'Sexual Networking in the Ekiti District of Nigeria', *Studies in Family Planning* 22(2): 61–73.

———, I.O. Orubuloye and P. Caldwell. 1991b. 'The Destabilisation of the Traditional Yoruba Sexual System', *Population and Development Review* 17(2): 229–62.

———, I.O. Orubuloye and P. Caldwell. 1995. 'The Cultural, Social and Attitudinal Context of Male Sexual Behaviour in Urban South-west Nigeria', *Health Transition Review* 5: 207–22.

———, I.O. Orubuloye and P. Caldwell. 1997. 'Perceived Male Sexual Needs and Male Sexual Behaviour in South-west Nigeria', *Social Science and Medicine* 44(8): 1195–207.

Campbell, C. 1987. *The Romantic Ethic and the Spirit of Modern Consumerism*. Oxford: Basil Blackwell.

Campbell, C. 2003. *Letting Them Die. Why HIV/AIDS Prevention Programmes Fail*. Canada: Heinemann.

Central Bureau of Statistics. 1996. 'Population Dynamics of Kenya. Analytical Report Volume 3', *Kenya Population Census*. Nairobi: Republic of Kenya.

———. 2003. 'Demographic and Health Survey'. Nairobi: Ministry of Health.

Chacha, B.K. 2000. 'Female Husbands? Or Traversing Gender? The Dynamics of Ubusino (Woman-to-Woman Marriage) among the AbaKuria of Kenya', *Biennial Conference of the African Studies Association of the UK*, Trinity College, Cambridge, UK.

Chakrabarty, D. 1992. 'Postcoloniality and the Artifice of History: Who Speaks for 'Indian' Pasts?' *Representations* 37: 1–26.

Chege, J. 1993. 'Politics of Gender and Fertility Regulation in Kenya: A Case Study of the Igembe', PhD thesis, Lancaster University.

Clifford, J. and G.E. Marcus (eds). 1986. *Writing Culture. The Poetics and Politics of Ethnography*. Berkeley: University of California Press.

Coe, C. 2005. *Dilemmas of Culture in African Schools. Nationalism and the Transformation of Knowledge*. Chicago: University of Chicago Press.

Cohen, D.W. and A.E.S. Odhiambo. 1992. *Burying SM: The Politics of Knowledge and the Sociology of Power in Africa*. London: James Currey.

Comaroff, J. 1993. 'The Diseased Heart of Africa: Medicine, Colonialism, and the Black Body', in S. Linderbaum and M. Lock (eds), *Knowledge, Power and Practice: The Anthropology of Medicine and Everyday Life*. Berkeley: University of California Press, pp. 305–29.

——— and J. Comaroff. 1992. *Ethnography and the Historical Imagination*. Boulder: Westview Press.

——— and J. Comaroff. 1999. 'Occult Economies and the Violence of Abstraction: Notes from the South African Postcolony', *American Ethnologist* 26(2): 279–303.

Connell, R.W. 1987. *Gender and Power: Society, the Person and Sexual Politics*. California: California Press.

———. 1995. *Masculinities*. Cambridge: Polity Press.

——— and J.W. Messerschmidt. 2005. 'Hegemonic Masculinity: Rethinking the Concept', *Gender and Society* 19(6): 829–59.

Cornwall, A. 2003. 'To Be A Man Is More Than a Day's Work: Shifting Ideals of Masculinity in Ado-Odo, Southwestern Nigeria', in L.A. Lindsay and S.F. Miescher (eds), *Men and Masculinities in Modern Africa*. Portsmouth: Heinemann Educational Books, pp. 230–48.

———. (ed.). 2005. *Readings in Gender in Africa*. Oxford: James Currey Ltd.

———. 2007. 'Myths to Live By? Female Solidarity and Female Autonomy Reconsidered', *Development and Change* 38(1): 149–68.

Crimp, D. 2002. 'Sex and Sensibility, or Sense and Sexuality', in D. Crimp (ed.), *Melancholia and Moralism: Essays on AIDS and Queer Politics*. Cambridge: MIT Press, pp. 281–302.

Csordas, T.J. 1990. 'Embodiment as a Paradigm for Anthropology', *Ethos* 18: 5–47.

———. 1993. 'Somatic Modes of Attention', *Cultural Anthropology* 8(2): 135–56.

————. 1994. 'Introduction: The Body as Representation and Being-in-the-World', in T.J. Csordas (ed.), *Embodiment and Experience. The Existential Ground of Culture and Self*. Cambridge: Cambridge University Press, pp. 1–26.

D'Costa, L.J. et al. 1985. 'Prostitutes are a Major Reservoir of Sexually Transmitted Diseases in Nairobi, Kenya', *Sexually Transmitted Diseases* 12(3): 64–67.

De Witte, M. 2005. '"Buy the Future". A Charismatic Vision on African Modernity', *First AEGIS (Africa-Europe Group for Interdisciplinary Studies) Conference*. London: SOAS and the ICS.

Douglas, M. 1966. *Purity and Danger*. New York: Praeger Publishers.

Dover, P. 2005. 'Gender and Embodiment: Expectations of Manliness in a Zambian Village', in L. Ouzgane and R. Morrell (eds), *African Masculinities. Men in Africa from the late Nineteenth Century to the Present*. New York: Palgrave MacMillan, pp. 168–82.

Editorial. 2001. 'A Ritual that Defies Modernity', *Daily Nation*, Nairobi, p. 6.

Epprecht, M. 2008. *Heterosexual Africa? The History of an Idea from the Age of Exploration to the Age of Aids*. Athens: Ohio University Press.

Epstein, H. 2008. *The Invisible Cure: Why We Are Losing the Fight Against AIDS in Africa*. New York: Farrar, Strauss and Giroux.

Evans-Pritchard, E.E. 1950. 'Marriage Customs of the Luo of Kenya', *African Urban Studies* 20(2): 132–42.

————. (ed.). 1974. *Man and Woman among the Azande*. London: Faber and Faber.

Fabian, J. 1983. *Time and the Other: How Anthropology Makes Its Object*. New York: Columbia University Press.

Fardon, R. and G. Furniss (eds). 2000. *African Broadcast Cultures. Radio in Transition*. Oxford: James Currey.

Farmer, P. 2006. *AIDS and Accusation: Haiti and the Geography of Blame*. 2nd edition. Berkeley: University of California Press.

Ferguson, J. 1999. *Expectations of Modernity. Myths and Meanings of Urban Life on the Zambia Copperbelt*. Berkeley: University of California Press.

Fernandez, J.W. 1991. 'Introduction: Confluents of Inquiry', in J.W. Fernandez (ed.), *Beyond Metaphor*. Stanford: Stanford University Press.

Forde, D. 1954. *African Worlds: Studies in the Cosmological Ideas and Social Values of African Peoples*. London: Oxford University Press.

Foucault, M. 1990 [1976]. *The History of Sexuality, Volume I. An Introduction*. Translated by Robert Hurley. New York: Vintage Books.

Frederiksen, B. 2000. 'Popular Culture, Gender Relations and the Democratization of Everyday Life in Kenya', *Journal of Southern African Studies* 26(2): 209–22.

Friedmann, G. 1997. 'Church and State in Kenya, 1986-1992: The Churches' Involvement in the "Game of Change"', *African Affairs* 96: 25–52.

Fugelsang, M. 1994. *Veils and Videos: Female Youth Culture on the Kenyan Coast*. Stockholm: Gotab.

Furedi, F. 2002. 'The Silent Ascendancy of Therapeutic Culture in Britain', *Society* 39(3): 16–24.

Geschiere, P. 1995. 'Kinship, Witchcraft and the Moral Economy of Ethnicity: Contrasts from Southern and Western Cameroon', in L.D. Gorgendière, K. King and S. Vaughan (eds), *Ethnicity in Africa: Roots, Meanings and Implications*. Edinburgh: University of Edinburgh Press, pp. 38–52.

————. 1997. *The Modernity of Witchcraft: Politics and the Occult in Postcolonial Africa*. Charlottesville: University Press of Virginia.

————. 1999. 'Globalization and the Power of Indeterminate Meaning: Witchcraft and Spirit Cults in Africa and East Asia', in P. Geschiere and B. Meyer (eds), *Globalization and Identity: Dialectics of Flow and Closure*. Oxford: Blackwell, pp. 211–37.

———— and J. Gugler. 1998. 'Introduction: The Rural-Urban Connection – Changing Issues of Belonging and Identification', *Africa, Special Issue: The Political Primary Patriotism* 68(3): 309–20.

———— and B. Meyer. 1998. 'Globalization and Identity: Dialectics of Flow and Closure', *Development and Change* 29: 601–15.

———— and B. Meyer. (eds). 1999. *Globalization and Identity: Dialectics of Flow and Closure*. Oxford: Blackwell.

————, B. Meyer and P. Pels (eds). 2008. *Readings in Modernity in Africa*. Bloomington: Indiana University Press.

Giddens, A. 1992. *The Transformation of Intimacy: Sexuality, Love and Eroticism*. Cambridge: Polity Press.

Gilman, S.L. 1988. *Disease and Representation: The Construction of Images of Illness from Madness to AIDS*. Ithaca: Cornell University Press.

Ginsburg, F., L. Abu-Lughod and B. Larkin. 2002. *Media Worlds. Anthropology on New Terrain*. Berkeley: University of California Press.

Gluckman, M. 1955. *Custom and Conflict*. Glencoe: Free Press.

Godelier, M. 1986. *The Making of Great Men: Male Domination and Power among the New Guinea Baruya*. Cambridge: Cambridge University Press.

Gouda, F. and J. Clancy-Smith. 1998. 'Introduction', in F. Gouda and J. Clancy-Smith (eds), *Domesticating the Empire. Race, Gender and Family Life in French and Dutch Colonialism*. Charlottesville: University Press of Virginia, pp. 1–22.

Gregor, T. 1995. 'Sexuality and the Experience of Love', in P.R. Abramson and S.D. Pinkerton (eds), *Sexual Nature, Sexual Culture*. Chicago: The University of Chicago Press, pp. 330–53.

Gutmann, M.C. 1997. 'Trafficking in Men: The Anthropology of Masculinity', *Annual Review of Anthropology* 26: 385–409.

Gwako, E. 1995. 'Continuity and Change in the Practice of Cliteoridectomy in Kenya', *East African Medical Journal* 33(2): 333–37.

Hacking, I. 2001. *The Social Construction of What?* London: Harvard University Press.

Hake, A. 1972. *African Metropolis: Nairobi's Self-help City*. London: Sussex University Press.

Haynes, J. (ed.). 2000. *Nigerian Video Films*. Ohio: Ohio University Center for International Studies.

Heald, S. 1995. 'The Power of Sex: Some Reflections on Caldwells' "African Sexuality" Thesis', *Africa* 65(4): 491–506.

————. 1999. *Men and Morality: Sex, Violence and Ritual in Gisu Society*. London: Routledge.

————. 2003. 'An Absence of Anthropology: Critical Reflections on Anthropology and AIDS Policy and Practice in Africa', in G. Ellison, M. Parker and C. Campbell (eds), *Learning from HIV/AIDS: A Biosocial Approach*. Cambridge: Cambridge University Press, pp. 210–37.

Hearn, J. 2002. 'The "Invisible" NGO: US Evangelical Missions in Kenya', *Journal of Religion in Africa* 32(1): 32–60.

Hewett, P.C., B.S. Mensch and A.S. Erulkar. 2003. 'Consistency in the Reporting of Sexual Behaviour among Adolescent Girls in Kenya: A Comparison of Interviewing Methods', *Sexually Transmitted Infections* 80: ii43–ii48.

Hirsch, J.S. and H. Wardlow. 2006. *Modern Loves. The Anthropology of Romantic Courtship and Companionate Marriage*. Ann Arbor: The University of Michigan Press.

Hobsbawm, E. and T. Ranger. 1992. *The Invention of Tradition*. Cambridge: Cambridge University Press.

Hodgson, D.L. and S.A. McCurdy. 2001. *'Wicked' Women and the Reconfiguration of Gender in Africa*. Oxford: James Currey.

Hollos, M. 1991. 'Migration, Education, and the Status of Women in Southern Nigeria', *American Anthropologist* 93(4): 852–70.

House-Midamba, B. 1990. *Class Development and Gender Inequality in Kenya, 1963–1990*. Lewiston: Edwin Mellen Press.

Hunter, M. 2010. *Love in the Time of AIDS. Inequality, Gender, and Rights in South Africa*. Bloomington: Indiana University Press.

Huntingford, G.W.B. 1972. 'Nandi Kinship and Clans (Kenya)', *Anthropos* 67: 771–821.

Huygens, P., E. Kajura, J. Seeley and T. Barton. 1996. 'Rethinking Methods for the Study of Sexual Behaviour', *Social Science and Medicine* 42(2): 221–31.

Illouz, E. 1997. *Consuming the Romantic Utopia. Love and the Cultural Contradictions of Capitalism*. Berkeley: University of California Press.

Jackson, C. 2007. 'Resolving Risk? Marriage and Creative Conjugality', *Development and Change* 38(1): 107–29.

Jameson, F. 1984. 'Postmodernism, or The Cultural Logic of Late Capitalism', *New Left Review* 146: 53–92.

Jamieson, L. 1998. *Intimacy. Personal Relationships in Modern Societies*. Cambridge: Polity Press.

Jankowiak, W.R. (ed.). 2008. *Intimacies. Love + Sex across Cultures*. New York: Columbia University Press.

Jansen, W. 1989. 'Ethnocentrism in the Study of Algerian Women', in A. Angerman, G. Binnema, A. Keunen, V. Poels and J. Zirkzee (eds), *Current Issues in Women's History*. London: Routledge, pp. 280–310.

Janson, M. and R. Spronk. 2005. 'Ambiguous Encounters. Gender in the Context of Modernity in the Gambia and Kenya', in A. van der Kwaak, K. Willemse and R. Spronk (eds), *From Modern Myths to Global Encounters. Belonging and the Dynamics of Change in Africa*. Leiden: CNWS Publishers, pp. 124–38.

Kaler, A. 2001. '"It's Some Kind of Women's Empowerment": The Ambiguity of the Female Condom as a Marker of Female Empowerment', *Social Science and Medicine* 52(5): 783–96.

Kanogo, T. 2005. *African Womanhood in Colonial Kenya. 1900-50*. Oxford: James Currey.

Katsivo, M. and L. Muthami. 1991. 'Social Characteristics and Sexual Behaviour of Women at High Risk of HIV Infection in a Town in Central Province, Kenya', *East African Medical Journal* 68(1): 34–38.

Katz, J. 1976. *Gay American History: Lesbians and Gay Men in the U.S.A.* New York: Crowell.

Kenyatta, J. 1938. *Facing Mount Kenya: The Tribal Life of the Gikuyu*. London: Secker and Warburg.

Kidula, J. 2000. 'Polishing the Lustre of the Stars: Music Professionalism Made Workable in Kenya', *Ethnomusicology* 4(3): 408–28.

Kielmann, K. 1997. '"Prostitution", "Risk", and "Responsibility": Paradigms of AIDS Prevention and Women's Identities in Thika, Kenya', in M. Inhorn and P. Brown (eds), *The Anthropology of Infectious Disease*. Amsterdam: Gordon and Breach Science Publishers, pp. 357–77.

Kimeli, J. 2001. 'Did God Send Aids to Destroy Sinful Man?', *Daily Nation*, Nairobi, p. 6.

Krog, A. 2003. *A Change of Tongue*. Johannesburg: Random House.

Kulick, D. 1997. 'The Gender of Brazilian Transgendered Prostitutes', *American Anthropologist* 99(3): 574–85.

Kweyu, D. 2001. 'A Generation that Shuns Marriage', *Daily Nation*, Nairobi, p. 6.

Lancaster, R.N. and M.D. Leonardo. 1997. *The Gender/Sexuality Reader: Culture, History, Political Economy*. New York: Routledge.

Laqueur, T.W. 1992. 'Sexual Desire and the Market Economy during the Industrial Revolution', in D.C. Stanton (ed.), *Discourses on Sexuality: From Aristotle to Aids*. Ann Arbor: University of Michigan Press, pp. 185–215.

Larkin, B. 1997. 'Indian Films and Nigerian Lovers: Media and the Creation of Parallel Modernities', *Africa* 67(3): 407–39.

Le Blanc, M.-N., D. Meintel and V. Piché. 1991. 'The African Sexual System: Comment on Caldwell et al.', *Population and Development Review* 17(3): 497–515.

Leakey, L.S.B. 1977. *The Southern Kikuyu before 1903. Three Volumes*. London and New York: Academic Press.

Lears, J.T.J. 1983. 'From Salvation to Self-Realization: Advertisement and the Therapeutic Roots of the Consumer Culture, 1880–1930', in R. Wrightman and J.T.J. Lears (eds), *The Culture of Consumption: Critical Essays in American History, 1880-1980*. New York: Pantheon Books, pp. 1–38.

Lévi-Strauss, C. 1969 [1949]. *The Elementary Structures of Kinship*. London: Eyre and Spottiswoode.

LeVine, B.L. and R. LeVine. 1966. *Nyasongo: A Gusii Community in Kenya*. New York: John Wiley.

Liechty, M. 2003. *Suitably Modern. Making Middle-class Culture in a New Consumer Society*. Princeton: Princeton University Press.

Lindsay, L.A. and S.F. Miescher (eds). 2003. *Men and Masculinities in Modern Africa*. Portsmouth: Heinemann.

Lock, M. and J. Farquhar (eds). 2007. *Beyond the Body Proper: Reading the Anthropology of Material Life*. Durham: Duke University Press.

Lonsdale, J. 1986. 'The Depression and the Second World War in the Transformation of Kenya', in D. Killingray and R. Rathbone (eds), *African and the Second World War*. Basingstoke: Macmillan.

Lorway, R. 2008. 'Defiant Desire in Namibia: Female Sexual-Gender Transgression and the Making of Political Being', *American Ethnologist* 35(1): 20–33.

Luhmann, N. 1982. *Love as Passion. The Codification of Intimacy*. Stanford: Stanford University Press.

Luke, N. 2005. 'Confronting the "Sugar Daddy" Stereotype: Age and Economic Asymmetries and Risky Sexual Behaviour in Urban Kenya', *International Family Planning Perspectives* 31(1): 6–14.

———, S. Clark and E. Zulu. 2011. 'The Relationship History Calendar: Improving the Scope and Quality of Data on Youth Sexual Behavior', *Demography* 48(3): 1151–76.

Lurie, M.N. and S. Rosenthal. 2010. 'Concurrent Partnerships as a Driver of the HIV Epidemic in Sub-Saharan Africa? The Evidence is Limited', *AIDS and Behavior* 14(1): 17–24.

Lyons, A.P. and H.D. Lyons. 2004. *Irregular Connections. A History of Anthropology and Sexuality*. Lincoln: University of Nebraska Press.

Mahmood, S. 2001. 'Feminist Theory, Embodiment, and the Docile Agent: Some Reflections on the Egyptian Islamic Revival', *Cultural Anthropology* 16(2): 202–36.

Mair, L.P. 1953. 'African Marriage and Social Change', in A. Philips (ed.), *Survey of African Marriage and Family Life*. Oxford: Oxford University Press.

———. 1969. *African Marriage and Social Change*. London: Frank Cass.

Malinowski, B. 1982 [1929]. *The Sexual Life of Savages in North-western Melanesia. An Ethnographic Account of Courtship, Marriage and Family Life among the Natives of the Trobriand Islands, British New Guinea*. London: Routledge.

Maticka-Tyndale, E. et al. 2005. 'The Sexual Scripts of Kenyan Young People and HIV Prevention', *Culture, Health and Sexuality* 7(1): 27–41.

Mbembe, A. 2001. *On the Postcolony. Studies on the History of Society and Culture*. Berkeley: University of California Press.

———. 2002. 'African Modes of Self-writing', *Public Culture* 14(1): 239–73.

———. 2004. 'Aesthetics of Superfluity', *Public Culture* 16(3): 373–405.

———. 2008. 'The New Africans. Between Nativism and Cosmopolitanism', in P. Geschiere, B. Meyer and P. Pels (eds), *Readings in Modernity*. London: International African Institute, pp. 107–11.

Mead, M. 1950. *Sex and Temperament in Three Primitive Societies*. New York: The New American Library.

Merleau-Ponty, M. 1958. *Phenomenology of Perception*. Translated by Colin Smith. London: Routledge.

Meyer, B. 2002. 'Pentecostalism, Prosperity and Popular Cinema in Ghana', *Culture and Religion* 3(1): 67–87.

———. 2004. '"Praise the Lord": Popular Cinema and Pentecostal Style in Ghana's New Public Sphere', *American Ethnologist* 31(1): 92–110.

Mfecane, S. 2005. 'Sex and Masculinity in South African Townships', *Africa-Europe Group for Interdisciplinary Studies (AEGIS) European Conference of African Studies*, London, UK.

Miller, D. 1992. 'The Young and the Restless in Trinidad. A Case of the Local and the Global in Mass Consumption', in R. Silverstone and E. Hirsch (eds), *Consuming Technology*. London: Routledge, pp. 166–82.

Mitchell, K. and K. Wellings. 2002. 'The Role of Ambiguity in Sexual Encounters between Young People in England', *Culture, Health and Sexuality* 4: 393–408.

Moerman, M. 1988. *Talking Culture: Ethnography and Conversation Analysis*. Philadelphia: University of Pennsylvania Press.

Molnos, A. (ed.). 1973. *Cultural Source Material for Population Planning in East Africa 3: Beliefs and Practices*. Nairobi: East African Publishing House.

Momanjy, O. 1998. 'True Love Waits!', *Daily Nation*, Nairobi, p. 8.

Moody, D. 2001. 'Black, Migrant Mine Labourers and the Vicissitudes of Male Desire', in R. Morrell (ed.), *Changing Men in Southern Africa*. London: Zed Books, pp. 297–315.

Moore, H.L. 1996. *Space, Text and Gender: An Anthropological Study of Marakwet of Kenya*. 2nd edition. New York: Guilford Publishing Inc.

———. 2007. *The Subject of Anthropology*. Cambridge: Polity Press.

Morgan, R. and S. Wieringa. 2005. *Tommy Boys, Lesbian Women and Ancestral Wives. Female Same-sex Practices in Africa*. Johannesburg: Jacana Media Ltd.

Morrell, R. 2001. *Changing South African Men*. London: Zed Books.

Moses, S. et al. 1991. 'Controlling HIV in Africa: Effectiveness and Cost of an Intervention in a High-frequency STD Transmitter Core Group', *AIDS* 5(4): 407–11.

Mudimbe, V.Y. 1994. *The Idea of Africa*. Bloomington: Indiana University Press.

Mulindi, S.A.Z. 1992. 'Strategies for HIV Infection Prevention in a Developing Country: Case Example of Kenya', *Scandinavian Journal of Development Alternatives* 11(1): 53–63.

Murray, S. 1998. '"A Feeling within Me": Kamau, a Twenty-five Year Old Kikuyu', in S. Murray and W. Roscoe (eds), *Boy-Wives and Female Husbands: Studies in African Homosexualities*. New York: St. Martin's Press, pp. 41–62.

Murray, S. and W. Roscoe (eds). 1998. *Boy-Wives and Female Husbands: Studies in African Homosexualities*. New York: St. Martin's Press.

Mutongi, K. 2000. '"Dear Dolly's" Advice: Representations of Youth, Courtship, and Sexualities in Africa, 1960-1980', *International Journal of African Historical Studies* 33(1): 1–23.

———. 2007. *Worries of the Heart. Widows, Family, and Community in Kenya*. Chicago: Chicago University Press.

National Council for Population and Development. 1993. 'Kenya Demographic and Health Survey', *Kenya Population Census*, Nairobi.

Nelson, N. 1987. '"Selling her Kiosk": Kikuyu Notions of Sexuality and Sex for Sale in Mathare Valley, Kenya', in P. Caplan (ed.), *The Cultural Construction of Sexuality*. London: Tavistock, pp. 217–39.

Nencel, L. 2005. 'Heterosexuality', in D.T. Goldberg, A. Kobayashi and P. Essed (eds), *Blackwell Companion to Gender Studies*. Oxford and Maldon: Blackwell, pp. 132–42.

Newell, S. 2005. 'Devotion and Domesticity: The Reconfiguration of Gender in Popular Christian Pamphlets from Ghana and Nigeria', *Journal of Religion in Africa* 35(3): 296–323.

Nguguna. 2001. 'Youth is Indisciplined', *Daily Nation*, Nairobi, p. 6.

Niang, C.I., et al. 2003. '"It's Raining Stones": Stigma, Violence and HIV Vulnerability among Men Who Have Sex with Men in Dakar', *Culture, Health and Sexuality* 5: 499–512.

Njambi, W. and W. O'Brien. 2000. 'Revisiting "Woman-Woman Marriage": Notes on Gikuyu Women', *NWSA Journal* 12(1): 1–23.

Njau, W. 1993. 'The Parental Role in the Provision of Sex Education to Children', *Working Paper*, Nairobi: Centre for the Study of Adolescence.

Njeru, A. 1997. 'Condoms Contradict our Faith in God', *Daily Nation*, Nairobi, p. 6.

Nolan Jr., J.L. 1998. *The Therapeutic State: Justifying Government at Century's End.* New York: New York University Press.

Nyaggah, M. 2003. 'Gender, Family, Race and Social Change', *13th Annual Conference of the Pan African Anthropology Association*, University of Port Elizabeth, South Africa.

Nyairo, J. 2005. '"Modify": *Jua Kali* as a Metaphor for Africa's Urban Ethnicities and Cultures', Mary Kingsley Zochonis Lecture, *First AEGIS (Africa-Europe Group for Interdisciplinary Studies) Conference*. London: SOAS and the ICS.

—— and J. Ogude. 2005. 'Popular Music, Popular Politics: *Unbwogable* and the Idioms of Freedom in Kenyan Popular Music', *African Affairs* 104(415): 225–49.

Nyambedha, E.O. 2008. 'Ethical Dilemmas of Social Science Research on AIDS and Orphanhood in Western Kenya', *Social, Science and Medicine* 67(5): 771–79.

Nyamnjoh, F.B. and B. Page. 2002. 'Whiteman Kontri and the Enduring Allure of Modernity among Cameroonian Youth', *African Affairs* 101: 607–34.

Nyamwaya, D. and D. Parkin (eds). 1987. *Transformations of African Marriages.* Manchester: Manchester University Press.

——. 1992. 'Three Critical Issues in Community Health Development Projects in Kenya', in R.D. Grillo and R.L. Stirrat (eds), *Discourses of Development. Anthropological Perspectives*. Oxford: Berg Publishers, pp. 183–205.

Nyanzi, S., J. Nassimbwa, V. Kayizzi and S. Kabanda. 2008. '"African Sex is Dangerous!" Renegotiating "Ritual Sex" in Contemporary Masaka District', *Africa* 78(4): 518–93.

Nzioka, C. 1994. 'AIDS Policies in Kenya. A Critical Perspective on Prevention', in P. Aggleton, P. Davies and G. Hart (eds), *AIDS: Foundations for the Future.* London: Taylor and Francis Publishers, pp. 159–176.

——. 1996. 'Lay Perceptions of Risk of HIV Infection and the Social Construction of Safer Sex: Some Experiences from Kenya', *AIDS Care* 8(5): 5655–579.

Obbo, C. 1998. 'Social Science Research: Understanding and Action', in C. Becker, J.-P. Dozon, C. Obbo and M. Touré (eds), *Vivre et Penser le Sida en Afrique / Experiencing and Understanding Aids in Africa*. Dakar, Paris: Codesria, Karthala, pp. 67–79.

Ochomo, K.L. 2001. 'How to Prevent Spread of AIDS', *Daily Nation*, Nairobi, p. 8.

Ochieng, P. 2001. 'Depency Syndrome', *Daily Nation*, Nairobi, p. 9.

Odahike, P.O. 1981. *Demographic Perspectives in Zambia: Rural-Urban Growth and Social Change*. Manchester: Manchester University Press.

Odhiambo, T. 2003. 'Troubled Love and Marriage as Work in Kenyan Popular Fiction', *Social Identities* 9(3): 423–36.

Ogola, G. 2006. 'The Idiom of Age in a Popular Kenyan Newspaper Serial', *Africa* 76(4): 569–89.

Oguk, S.G. 2001. 'HIV/Aids is a Test for Kenyans', *Daily Nation*, Nairobi, p. 6.

Ojwang, S.B.O. and A.B.N. Maggwa. 1991. 'Adolescent Sexuality in Kenya', *East African Medical Journal*: 74–80.

Oldfield, S., E. Salo and A. Schlyter. 2009. 'Editorial: Body Politics and the Gendered Crafting of Citizenship', *Feminist Africa* 13: 1–11.

Oludhe-Magoye, M. 1996. *Moral Issues in Kenya. A Personal View*. Nairobi: Uzima Press.

Omari, E. 2001. 'Moi: Why I'm Embarrassed over Condoms', *Daily Nation*, Nairobi, p. 4.

Onyango. 2001. 'Condoms are Not the Solution', *Daily Nation*, Nairobi, p. 6.

Oosterhuis, H. 2001. *Stepchildren of Nature. Krafft-Ebing, Psychiatry and the Making of Sexual Identity*. Chicago: University of Chicago Press.

Oriang', L. 2001. 'Trust Mama to Bring Senses Back to Politics', *Daily Nation*, Nairobi, p. 8.

Ouzgane, L. and R. Morrell. 2005. *African Masculinities. Men in Africa from the Late Nineteenth Century to the Present*. New York: Palgrave Macmillan.

Oyěwùmí, O. 1997. *The Invention of Women. Making an African Sense of Western Gender Discourses*. Minneapolis: University of Minnesota Press.

Packard, R.M. and P. Epstein. 1991. 'Epidemiologists, Social Scientists, and the Structure of Medical Research on AIDS in Africa', *Social Science and Medicine* 33(7): 771–83.

Padilla, M.B. and J.S. Hirsch. 2008. *Love and Globalization: Transformations of Intimacy in the Contemporary World*. Nashville: Vanderbilt University Press.

Paglia, C. 1991. *Sexual Personae: Art and Decadence from Nefertiti to Emily Dickinson*. New York: Vintage Book.

Parker, R. 1991. *Bodies, Pleasures and Passions: Sexual Culture in Contemporary Brazil*. Boston: Beacon Press.

———. 2001. 'Sexuality, Culture, and Power in HIV/AIDS Research', *Annual Review of Anthropology* (30): 163–79.

Parsons, T. 1951. *The Social System*. Glencoe: Free Press.

Patton, C. 1992. 'From Nation to Family: Containing African AIDS', in A. Parker, M. Russo, D. Summer and P. Yeager (eds), *Nationalisms and Sexualities*. New York: Routledge, pp. 218–34.

Paulme, D. 1963. *Women of Tropical Africa*. Berkeley: University of California Press.

Pels, P. 2002. 'The Confessional Ethic and the Spirits of the Screen. Reflections on the Modern Fear of Alienation', *Etnofoor* 15(1/2): 91–120.

——— and O. Salemink. 1999. *Colonial Subjects: Essays on the Practical History of Anthropology*. Ann Arbor: University of Michigan Press.

Pheterson, G. 1990. 'The Category "Prostitute" in Scientific Inquiry', *Journal of Sex Research* 27(3): 397–407.

Piot, P. et al. 1987. 'Retrospective Seroepidemiology of AIDS Virus Infection in Nairobi Populations', *Journal of Infectious Diseases* 155(6): 1108–12.

Plummer, K. 1995. *Telling Sexual Stories. Power, Change and Social Worlds*. London: Routledge.

Posel, D. 2005. 'Sex, Death and the Fate of the Nation: Reflections on the Politicization of Sexuality in Post-Apartheid South Africa', *Africa* 75(2): 125–53.

Prazak, M. 2001. 'Talking about Sex: Contemporary Construction of Sexuality in Rural Kenya', *Africa Today* 48(3): 82–98.

Presley, C. 1992. *Kikuyu Women, the Mau Mau Rebellion and Social Change in Kenya*. Boulder: Westview Press.

Reid, G. 2003. '"It's Just a Fashion!". Linking Homosexuality and "Modernity" in South Africa', *Etnofoor* 16(2): 7–23.

————— and L. Walker. 2005. *Men Behaving Differently. South African Men since 1994.* Cape Town: Double Storey Books.

Robertson, C. 1997. *Trouble Showed the Way. Women, Men and Trade in the Nairobi Area, 1890-1990.* Bloomington: Indiana University Press.

Ross, E. and R. Rapp. 1997. 'Sex and Society. A Research Note from Social History and Anthropology', in R.N. Lancaster and M.D. Leonardo (eds), *The Gender/ Sexuality Reader: Culture, History, Political Economy.* London: Routledge, pp. 153–68.

Rubin, G. 1984. 'Thinking Sex: Notes for a Radical Theory of the Politics of Sexuality', in C. Vance (ed.), *Pleasure and Danger: Exploring Female Sexuality.* London: Routledge, pp. 267–319.

————— 1991. 'The Catacombs: A Temple of the Butthole', in M. Thompson (ed.), *Leatherfolk. Radical Sex, People, Politics, and Practice.* Boston: Alyson Publications.

Sabatier, R. 1988. *Blaming Others: Prejudice, Race and Worldwide AIDS.* London: Panos Institute.

Sackey, B.S. 2003. '"Apuskeleke". Youth Fashion Craze, Immorality or Female Harassment?', *Etnofoor* 16(2): 57–70.

Sahlins, M.D. 1985. *Islands of History.* Chicago: University of Chicago Press.

Salo, E. and P.L. Gqola. 2006. 'Subaltern Sexualities', *Feminist Africa* 6: 1–12.

Sawers, L. and E. Stillwaggon. 2010. 'Concurrent Sexual Partnerships do not Explain the HIV Epidemics in Africa: A Systematic Review of the Evidence', *Journal of the International AIDS Society* 13(34): 1–23.

Scheper-Hughes, N. 1992. *Death without Weeping. The Violence of Everyday Life in Brazil.* Berkeley: University of California Press.

Schoepf, B.G. 1991. 'Ethical, Methodological and Political Issues of AIDS Research in Central Africa', *Social Science and Medicine* 33(7): 749–63.

Schulz, D. 2007. 'Drama, Desire, and Debate: Mass-Mediated Subjectivities in Urban Mali', *Visual Anthropology* 20(1): 19–39.

Seidel, G. 1993. 'The Competing Discourses of HIV/AIDS in Sub-Saharan Africa: Discourses of Rights and Empowerment vs Discourses of Control and Exclusion', *Social Science and Medicine* 36(3): 175–94.

Sen, K. and M. Stivens. 1998. *Gender and Power in Affluent Asia.* London: Routledge.

Shaw, C.M. 1995. *Colonial Inscriptions. Race, Sex and Class in Kenya.* Minneapolis: University of Minnesota Press.

Shepherd, G. 1987. 'Rank, Gender and Homosexuality: Mombasa as a Key to Understanding Sexual Options', in P. Caplan (ed.), *The Cultural Construction of Sexuality.* London: Tavistock Publications.

Shilling, C. 2003. *The Body and Social Theory.* 2nd edition. London: Sage Publications.

Silberschmidt, M. 2001. 'Disempowerment of Men in Rural and Urban East Africa: Implications for Male Identity and Sexual Behaviour', *World Development* 29(4): 657–71.

Simone, A. 2001. 'On the Worlding of African Cities', *African Studies Review* 44(2): 15–41.

—————. (ed.). 2005. *Urban Africa: Changing Contours of Survival in the City.* Dakar / London: CODESRIA / Zed Press.

Simonsen, J.N. et al. 1990. 'HIV Infection among Lower Socio-economic Strata Prostitutes in Nairobi', *AIDS* 4(2): 139–44.

Smith, D.J. 2001. 'Romance, Parenthood and Gender in a Modern African Society', *Ethnology* 40(2): 129–51.

———. 2007. 'Modern Marriage, Men's Extramarital Sex, and HIV Risk in Southeastern Nigeria', *American Journal of Public Health* 97(6): 997–1005.

Spronk, R. 1999. 'AIDS, a Disease of Modernity. Adolescent Narratives about AIDS in Middle Class Nairobi'. Department of Sociology and Anthropological, University of Amsterdam.

———. 2000. 'The Disease of "Immorality". Narrating AIDS as "Sign of the Times" in Middle-Class Nairobi', *Etnofoor* 13: 67–87.

———. 2002. 'Looking at Love. Hollywood Romance and Shifting Notions of Gender and Relating in Nairobi', *Etnofoor* 15(1–2): 229–40.

———. 2005a. 'Female Sexuality in Nairobi: Flawed or Favoured?', *Culture, Health and Sexuality* 7(3): 267–79.

———. 2005b. '"There is a Time to Fool Around and There is a Time to Grow Up". Balancing Sex, Relationships and Notions of Masculinity in Nairobi', in D. Gibson and A. Hardon (eds), *Rethinking Masculinities, Violence and AIDS*. Amsterdam: Het Spinhuis Publishers, pp. 44–74.

———. 2007. 'Beyond Pain, Towards Pleasure in the Study of Sexuality in Africa', *Sexuality in Africa Magazine* 4(3): 6–14.

———. 2009. 'Media and the Therapeutic Ethos of Romantic Love in Middle-Class Nairobi', in J. Cole and L.M. Thomas (eds), *Love in Africa*. Chicago: University of Chicago Press.

———. 2011. '"Intimacy is the Name of the Game": Media and the Praxis of Sexual Knowledge in Nairobi', *Anthropologica* 53: 1–15.

———, A. Van der Kwaak and K. Willemse. (eds). 2005. *From Modern Myths to Global Encounters. Belonging and the Dynamics of Change in Africa*. Leiden: CNWS Publications.

Steeves, H.L. 1997. *Gender Violence and the Press: The St. Kizito Story*. Athens: Ohio University Press.

Stichter, S. 1987. 'Women and the Family: The Impact of Capitalist Development in Kenya', in M. Schatzberg (ed.), *The Political Economy of Kenya*. New York: Praeger, pp. 137–60.

Stillwaggon, E. 2003. 'Racial Metaphors: Interpreting Sex and AIDS in Africa', *Development and Change* 34(5): 809–32.

Stoler, R. 1979. *Sexual Excitement. Dynamics of Erotic Life*. London: Marerfield Library.

Strobel, M. 1979. *Muslim Women in Mombasa, 1890-1975*. New Haven: Yale University Press.

Suda, C. 2002. 'Women Basic Education, Community Health and Sustainable Development', in J.M. Bahemuka (ed.), *Family and Child Welfare. A Monograph of Papers*. Nairobi: University of Nairobi and UNESCO, pp. 82–99.

Sudarkasa, N. 2005. 'The "Status of Women" in Indigenous African Societies', in A. Cornwall (ed.), *Readings in Gender in Africa*. Oxford: James Currey Ltd, pp. 25–31.

Tabifor, H.R. 1998. *The Wonders and Beauty of Sex. Discover the Correlation between Sex and Love, Destiny, Virginity, Marriage, Inheritance, Abortion and Health*. Nairobi: Alpha and Omega Centre.

Tadele, G. 2006. *Bleak Prospects: Young Men, Sexuality and HIV/AIDS in an Ethiopian Town*. Leiden: African Studies Centre.

Thadani, V. 1979. 'Women in Nairobi: The Paradox of Urban "Progress"', *African Urban Studies* 15(3): 67–83.

Thomas, L.M. 1996. '"Ngaitana (I will circumcise myself)": The Gender and Generational Politics of the 1956 Ban on Clitoridectomy in Meru, Kenya', *Gender and History* 8(3): 338–63.

———. 2003. *Politics of the Womb. Women, Reproduction and the State in Kenya*. Berkeley: University of California Press.

———. 2006. 'Schoolgirl Pregnancies, Letter-writing and "Modern" Persons in Late Colonial East Africa', in K. Barber (ed.), *Africa's Hidden Histories. Everyday Literacy and Making the Self*. Bloomington: Indiana University Press, pp. 180–207.

Thornton, R.J. 2008. *Unimagined Community. Sex, Networks, and AIDS in Uganda and Africa*. Berkeley: University of California Press.

Tuzin, D. 1995. 'Discourse, Intercourse and the Excluded Middle: Anthropology and the Problem of Sexual Experience', in P.R. Abrahamson and S.D. Pinkerton (eds), *Sexual Nature, Sexual Culture*. Chicago: University of Chicago Press, pp. 257–76.

Undie, C.-C. and K. Benaya. 2006. 'The State of Knowledge on Sexuality in Sub-Saharan Africa: A Synthesis of Literature', *JENDA: Journal of Culture and African Women Studies* 8. http://www.jendajournal.com.

Van de Port, M. 2005. 'Registers of Incontestability. The Quest for Authenticity in Academia and Beyond', *Etnofoor* XVII(1/2): 7–22.

Van der Geest, S. 2004. 'Grandparents and Grandchildren in Kwahu, Ghana: The Performance of Respect', *Africa* 74(1): 47–61.

Van Eerdewijk, A. 2001. 'How Sexual and Reproductive Rights can Divide and Unite', *The European Journal of Women's Studies* 8(4): 421–39.

Vance, C.S. 1984. 'Pleasure and Danger: Toward a Politics of Sexuality', in C.S. Vance (ed.), *Pleasure and Danger. Exploring Female Sexuality*. London: Pandora, pp. 1–27.

———. 1991. 'Anthropology Rediscovers Sexuality: A Theoretical Comment', *Social Science and Medicine* 33(8): 875–84.

Vaughan, M. 1991. *Curing their Ills: Colonial Power and African Illness*. Cambridge: Polity Press.

Vincent, L. and C. McEwen. 2006. 'Labouring to Love: Romantic Love and Power in the Construction of Middle-class Femininity', *Indian Journal of Gender Studies* 13(1): 37–61.

Wainaina, B. 2003. *Discovering Home (Winner of the 2002 Caines Prize for African Writing)*. Nairobi: Wainaina, Binyavanga.

Wardlow, H. 2006. 'All's Fair When Love is War: Romantic Passion and Companionate Marriage among the Huli of Papua New Guinea', in J.S. Hirsch and H. Wardlow (eds), *Modern Loves. The Anthropology of Romantic Courtship and Companionate Marriage*. Ann Arbor: The University of Michigan Press, pp. 51–77.

Watney, S. 1990. 'Missionary Positions: AIDS, Africans and Race', in R. Ferguson and M. Gever (eds), *'Out There'. Marginalisation and Contemporary Cultures*. New York: MIT Press, pp. 89–103.

Weeks, J. 1977. *Coming Out: Homosexual Politics in Britain from the Nineteenth Century to the Present*. London: Quartet Books.

———. 2003. *Sexualities*. 2nd edition. London: Routledge.

Weinbaum, A.E., L.M. Thomas, P. Ramamurthy, U.G. Poiger, M. Yue Dong and T.E. Barlow (eds). 2008. *The Modern Girl around the World: Consumption, Modernity, and Globalization*. Durham: Duke University Press Books.

Wekker, G. 2006. *The Politics of Passion*. New York: Columbia University Press.

Werbner, R. 2002. *Postcolonial Subjectivities in Africa*. London: Zed Books.

White, L. 1990a. *The Comforts of Home. Prostitution in Colonial Nairobi*. Chicago: The University of Chicago Press.

———. 1990b. 'Seperating the Men from the Boys: Constructions of Gender, Sexuality, and Terrorism in Central Kenya, 1939-1959', *International Journal of African Historical Studies* 23(1): 1–25.

Whitehead, S. 2001. *Men and Masculinities. Key Themes and New Directions*. Cambridge: Polity Press.

Willemse, K. 2007. *'One Foot in Heaven'. Narratives on Gender and Islam in Darfur, West Sudan*. Leiden: Brill Academic Publishers.

Wipper, A. 1972. 'African Women, Fashion, and Scapegoating', *Canadian Journal of African Studies* 6(2): 329–49.

Wolf, J.D. 1973. 'Circumcision and Initiation in Western Kenya and Eastern Uganda', *Anthropos* 78: 369–410.

Woodhead, D. 1995. '"Surveillant Gays": HIV, Space and the Constitution of Identities', in D. Bell and G. Valentine (eds), *Mapping Desire: Geographies of Sexualities*. London: Routledge, pp. 231–44.

Zigon, J. 2009. 'Phenomenological Anthropology and Morality: A Reply to Robbins', *Ethnos* 74(2): 286–88.

INDEX